# Your Career Planner

ELEVENTH EDITION

Cheryl Bonner

Susan Musich

**Kendall Hunt**
publishing company

Action icon used throughout text: sarahdesign/Shutterstock.com
Pause icon used throughout text: Dvoishnik/Shutterstock.com
Tips icon used throughout text: sarahdesign/Shutterstock.com

Cover image © Shutterstock, Inc.

**Kendall Hunt**
publishing company

www.kendallhunt.com
*Send all inquiries to:*
4050 Westmark Drive
Dubuque, IA 52004-1840

Copyright © 1980, 1982, 1984, 1988, 1992, 1995, 1999, 2002, 2005, 2009, 2017 by Kendall Hunt
Publishing Company

ISBN 978-1-5249-2318-1

Published in the United States of America

# Brief Contents

# Contents

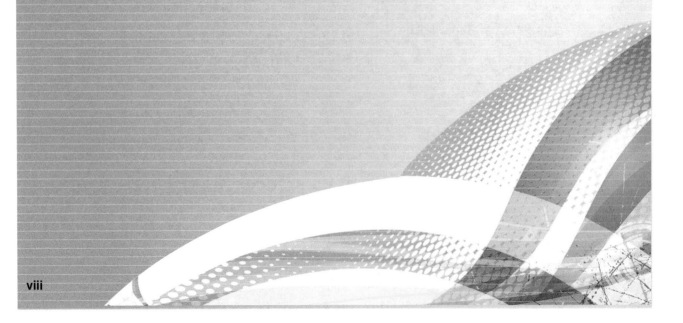

# Preface

## Career Planning—There Is an APP for That!

It seems that there is an APP for everything. Our APPS help us locate the nearest coffee shop, do our banking, listen to music, know the weather, and follow our favorite sports teams just to name a few. Perhaps you have a favorite APP—that one APP that you cannot live without.

When it comes to discovering a career direction, learning about ourselves, exploring occupational choices, connecting with established professionals, or undertaking a job search, an APP would be helpful.

APPS are tools. APPS are self-contained programs. APPS are user friendly.

This book was created with APPS in mind. While it is not a quick electronic tool, it is nonetheless a tool for you to use. It is designed to provide you with information and give you ways to put it to use.

You may be using this book as a part of a class, a workshop, or for your own personal discovery.

There is not currently an APP that will identify and fully access all of your career data and tell you exactly what you need to do with your life and how to get there. But, by taking a close look at the individual sections, you can develop your own understanding and implement a plan that work for you.

Software concept: cloud of program icons isolated on white background

Scanrail1/Shutterstock.com

## Key To The Book And Its Apps

This book has sections we have called APPS. Each APP has a different purpose. As you can see on the table of contents, the APPS relate to the important parts of the career discovery and implementation process. Special APPS will help you if you are an international student or have U.S. Military experience.

*Aha!* **Moments:** Record key points and discoveries that are critical to the development of a realistic career plan in this APP. Throughout this book, there will be the times when you learn something about yourself, work, careers, or the entire process of discovery—record these in this APP.

**APP ACTIONS:** This APP contains assessments, activities, experiences, and assignments you can use to help you learn information about yourself, careers, the job market, and apply these to your career plan. These are referenced throughout the sections of the book. When you see the APP ACTION icon, you will be directed to the APP ACTIONS section for details.

**PRESS PAUSE:** Because this is about your self-discovery, you will frequently be invited to pause what you are doing, taking time to stop and think and respond. Pressing pause is exactly what you do when watching a movie or listening to music or playing a game. It is stopping and doing something else for a few minutes then going back to the original activity. While tempting to skip and come back to later, the PRESS PAUSE activities are designed to get you to react to the content at that moment based on recently presented information. They are designed to help you think about and react to the content.

**TIPS:** Throughout the book, you will see the TIP icon. These are nuggets of information which elaborate on a point or provide insights for further research.

We are delighted that you have decided to use this book as a part of your journey! Perhaps one of you will actually develop an APP that will assist in this process or even pull together all of this information and point a person in a direction.

---

### www.YourCareerPlanner.com

In the meantime, we invite you to participate in this interactive experience. It is not a movie to watch or a ride to be enjoyed. You are an active participant because like the title of book, this is YOUR CAREER PLANNER.

# Acknowledgments

This book is built on the foundation of decades of work and research. We send our thanks to John Kelly and Nancy Pat Weaver for their work on the very first edition of the book. We send a very special thank you to our collaborator of many years, David Borchard. Over the years, we have worked to build on the work begun decades ago. While we have missed his partnership in the writing of this edition, you will still find his inspiration throughout the pages that follow.

The first edition was written in the days when there were very few printed books on career planning for college students. We appreciate the vision of the early authors. They nurtured the idea from a small spark to a warm fire that still burns today. Their contributions to the field of career development have inspired many career practitioners. More importantly, their work has changed the lives of countless college students seeking direction and pathways to the future.

We also thank our students and clients. They have shared their career journeys with us – entrusting us with their unique stories. We have adapted our thinking and our tactics as we have interacted with generations of career changers and job seekers. Their journeys have inspired our writing.

Finally, we thank our families. You were so patient and loving. The "one more minute" that was never just one and the many times real life occurred in the background as we tried to find new and fresh ways to help college students and other adults plan their careers.

And because "life happened" even while we wrote this book, so we understand why dreams get deferred and plans get derailed. To those who will read this book and navigate the applications and reflections, we encourage you to be persistent! There may not be an APP to make it easy, but the career story you will write (and the career plans you will make) as you progress through this book and the days after will be well worth the effort.

Enjoy your journey!

## Cheryl Clark Bonner

Cheryl Clark Bonner, M.Ed., is a career program director and a counselor. She has over 30 years of experience working in various higher education settings including private and public universities and community colleges. She is currently the Director of Alumni Career Services at Penn State University where she provides services to meet the career/life management needs of alumni and facilitates networking opportunities for alumni and students. She is a founding member of the Alumni Career Service Network (ACSN), the

professional development organization for this relatively new field. As a part of this organization, she has the opportunity to be a part of a team of experts who support the professional development of providers of career services to college alumni including the development of conferences, webinars and other training opportunities. Originally trained to be a special education teaching through her undergraduate degree, she continues to use her passion for education by creating learning opportunities for students and adults on the many aspects of life long career development. She is a frequent speaker at conferences and training events on the topics of career, life management, mission and calling. She has developed career and work related courses that have been taught in both the traditional classroom setting and through distance learning.

Cheryl is an ENFP who enjoys being involved in many things and projects. Realizing that life cannot be satisfied just the worker role, she is an adult education facilitator at her church, an amateur photographer and a learner of new things. During her free time, she can he found with husband Bill working on their home and garden, strolling along the nearest beach, or exploring a new town.

## Susan Musich

Susan Musich, M.Ed., is a globally-recognized international career expert. She is the founder and executive director of the award-winning Passport Career program designed to help professionals, from student through to post doc, effectively and strategically manage career transitions. Susan has worked for more than 20 years as a global career advisor, consultant, trainer, manager

and faculty and has individually coached more than 10,000 culturally diverse individuals—from undergraduates through PhDs/postdocs and from entry-level professionals through executives—all who have relocated to over 140 countries.

Susan has coordinated global research and studies and published over 400 articles on global career transitions. Susan led multiple studies and an extensive research project with 50 researchers focusing on effective cross-border career strategies. She has written or co-authored 13 career and job search books.

Susan insights and knowledge have come from her extensive experience working for The World Bank, the U.S. State Department, the U.S. Peace Corps, The George Washington University's Global

MBA Program, Accenture, Save the Children, Readers Digest Publishers, and other global organizations and universities. During her 10 years leading the global career services and global mobility at The World Bank, Susan provided support simultaneously to the International Finance Corporation (IFC), International Monetary Fund (IMF), InterAmerican Development Bank (IADB), Pan-American Health Organization (PAHO) and the Organization for American States (OAS). She was the liaison to 16 UN agencies coordinating a global career program to support tens of thousands of relocating staff and their professional partners seeking employment in their destination country.

Susan is a frequent speaker on international careers and global mobility topics and has delivered more than 150 presentations and training activities in over 35 countries. Susan has a bachelor's degree in Communications and Journalism from Northern Arizona University and a master's degree in Education Development from George Mason University. She studied abroad in Mexico and has lived and worked in Australia, Costa Rica and the Philippines. She resides in the Washington, DC area.

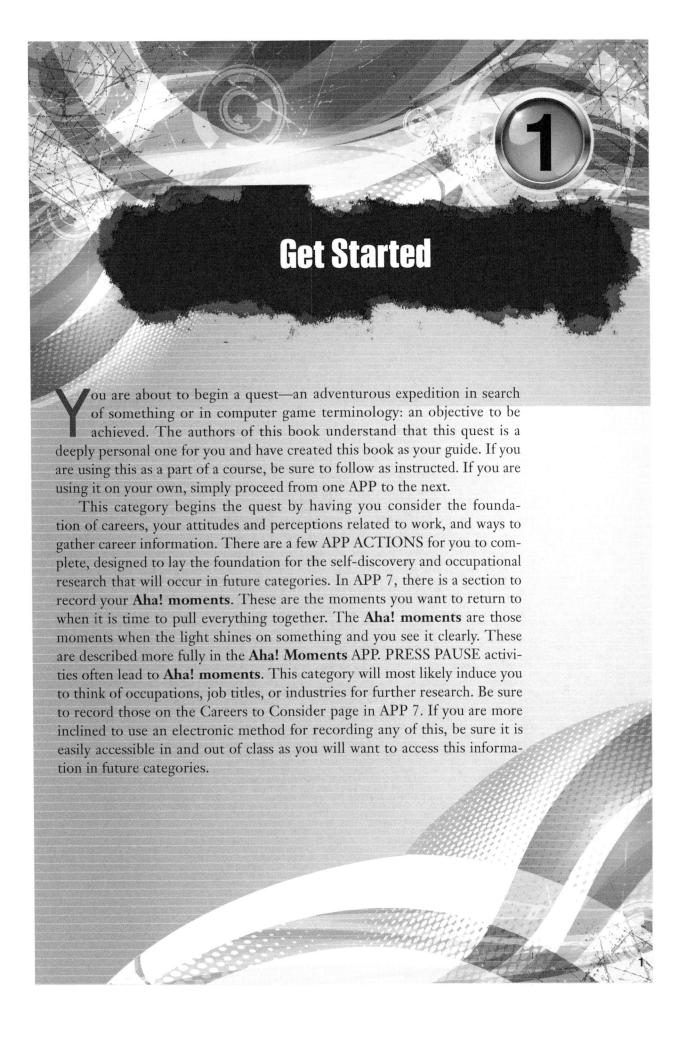

# Get Started

You are about to begin a quest—an adventurous expedition in search of something or in computer game terminology: an objective to be achieved. The authors of this book understand that this quest is a deeply personal one for you and have created this book as your guide. If you are using this as a part of a course, be sure to follow as instructed. If you are using it on your own, simply proceed from one APP to the next.

This category begins the quest by having you consider the foundation of careers, your attitudes and perceptions related to work, and ways to gather career information. There are a few APP ACTIONS for you to complete, designed to lay the foundation for the self-discovery and occupational research that will occur in future categories. In APP 7, there is a section to record your **Aha! moments**. These are the moments you want to return to when it is time to pull everything together. The **Aha! moments** are those moments when the light shines on something and you see it clearly. These are described more fully in the **Aha! Moments** APP. PRESS PAUSE activities often lead to **Aha! moments**. This category will most likely induce you to think of occupations, job titles, or industries for further research. Be sure to record those on the Careers to Consider page in APP 7. If you are more inclined to use an electronic method for recording any of this, be sure it is easily accessible in and out of class as you will want to access this information in future categories.

## APP 1.3    APP ACTIONS

Your Career/Life Roles
Your Career/Life Decisions of the Past
Career Predictions
Your Life and Work

## APP 1.1 Managing Your Career in Today's World

**Do you know people who:**

*There used to be a long-term pact between employee and employer in exchange for lifelong loyalty; this pace has been replaced by a performance-based, short-term contract that's perpetually up for renewal by both sides.*

—Reid Hoffman and Ben Casnocha, The Start-up of You

- Make career choices on the basis of their best talents and top interests?
- Align their career aspirations with the economic realities of the marketplace?
- Draw upon the best available resources for help in making career decisions?
- Manage their careers on the basic principles of good marketing practice?

If so, you know people who know themselves and are sufficiently knowledgeable about the realities of marketplace economics to enjoy career success and sustain employability in rapidly changing times.

### A Brief History Lesson

Career management has become a far more complicated process in the twenty-first century than at any previous time in history. In your grandparents' era, most people were employed in large corporations and probably spent their entire work lives with a single organization performing similar types of job functions the whole time. Career choice in those days was a matter of deciding what company to work for if you were "blue-collar" inclined or what profession to pursue if you had "white-collar" origins or aspirations. Getting ahead in those days meant promotion, and career development meant climbing a "career ladder." Back then, people were primarily concerned about job security, which meant staying employed with your organization until you could retire with a company pension supplemented by Social Security. But that was then, and that's history.

Significant numbers of working adults still do work in large organizations today but recent trends show greater numbers of people working in smaller businesses or working for themselves. But whether employed in a large or small organization managing your career in today's knowledge-based economy is decidedly different than in the industrial-based economy of yesteryear. In our twenty-first century world, there are few corporate ladders to climb, few people will spend an entire career within a single organization, and the old idea of job security is a fading concept. Change is a constant dynamic in today's work-place, and that requires being far more flexible, creative, and self-reliant than your grandparents ever dreamed of being. Career choice and career management in our twenty-first-century world is a new ballgame, and we all need to learn how to play it well. The change in employment patterns requires a shift in career-related mind-sets. In today's knowledge- and technology-based economy, we need to replace a preoccupation on job security with a focus on market-savvy employability.

"The world of work has changed. That's obvious. What isn't so clear is how that change will affect our employment. If the gold watch and career ladder are gone, what kind of relationship will we have with our employers?" writes career expert, Peter Weddle. In his blog, he suggests that the new metaphor is like that of your "high school sweetheart." Like that first love, "You'll meet a great employer, fall in love with the organization and the work it offers and you'll commit yourself to both, until the bloom—for whatever reason—wears off the rose. That may take two or three or even four years, but when it does—and it almost always will—you'll store away the (good) memories and move on to your next romance, full of curiosity and optimism about the future."[1] As you begin your quest, the changing nature of employment complicates the decision. You will most likely not be a farmer or factory worker or sales person because you came from a long line of farmers, factory workers, or sales people. You will also probably not begin work at a very entry-level job in an organization and rise to the top floor corner office. The very nature of how and where we work is changing.

However, focusing on not just occupational titles or organizations, but on your own unique qualities, you will discover career paths that can sustain major shifts in the structure of employment.

## Gathering Career Information— Johari Window

As you undertake your own self-discovery, you will realize that there is information others always knew about you but you never knew. Like when a relative says, "I always knew you were good at creating fictional characters. When you were a little kid, you would make up these complex stories filled with interesting people and animals. You would go on and on with your story telling, sharing more and more about these talking animals and colorful people." You might have forgotten all about that but once reminded it is information you can use for your career development.

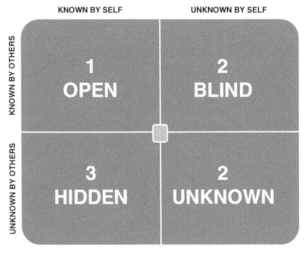

|  | KNOWN BY SELF | UNKNOWN BY SELF |
|---|---|---|
| KNOWN BY OTHERS | **1** **OPEN** | **2** **BLIND** |
| UNKNOWN BY OTHERS | **3** **HIDDEN** | **2** **UNKNOWN** |

Joseph Luft and Harry Ingram developed the Johari window.[2] While initially developed as a communication tool to increase understanding between two individuals, it is also a helpful illustration of the self-discovery process.

As you can see, there is information that you know and you have not yet shared with others and it is not easily discovered by spending time with you. There are lots of reasons why information is not shared. Many times, it simply doesn't seem important. Other times, it is a private dream that would run the

risk of being criticized or discounted if shared. Other times, it is something that may be viewed as negative so it stays hidden.

Then, there is information that you have that others also have. Perhaps, it is your ability to do math, or listen to others, or care for animals.

The information that is known to others about you but you don't know can be disconcerting. It is like when someone points out that you had green gunk stuck between your front teeth. You wonder how long it has been there and didn't you didn't know. Who else noticed it? Why didn't THEY tell you? When it comes to career discovery, an important part of information gathering is asking trusted friends and relatives for their input. This is not to release you from the decision, but to give you insights you may not have known previously. Like gunk in your teeth, sometimes this information will reveal negative things that need to be managed or discarded. Or, it can shed light on a new path to explore.

Finally, there is the information that is yet to be discovered. There are reasons why this information is still unknown. You may be good at sky-diving or gardening or connecting to international travelers, but you have never been put in a situation where this has been tested. You may have information about yourself that is connected in your brain to another experience. It is not until you begin to think about it in the context of career planning that it comes to light.

Self-awareness is a critical component of career decision-making. This information about who you are will help you make informed decisions as opposed to jumping from one thing to the next.

As you progress through this book, you will be developing a greater understanding of yourself. You will be able to articulate concepts that are important to you and see how they apply to careers. In some cases, you will be learning a new vocabulary that closely aligns with how work is defined. If you always knew that you wanted a career that would provide enough money for you to live and not have to worry about the job disappearing or being easily let go, in career language that would be a value called security.

In the upcoming sections, you will have the opportunity to think about your strengths and the ever-changing economy. By the end of this book, you will have greatly reduced the unknown to self square and increased the known to self square.

PAUSE

What is one thing that you know about yourself that relates to career?

Is this known to others? Why or why not?

## Playing to Your Strengths

How does anybody chose their profession and manage a career in today's world full of so many choices and in a state of constant change? Career counselors and personal coaches are often asked what are the best professions to pursue or what's the best course for advancing in one's career. The answer is, it depends. It depends less on organization-based job security and more upon who you are and your unique talents and interests and what role you want work to play in your life. Understanding what occupational and professional opportunities are available in the workplace of today and tomorrow is important. The key to personal success in work and life, however, is based in knowing yourself and in what arena you are best equipped to provide business-relevant value.

Whether beginning or changing a career, we all need to become effective marketers. In this regard, it's important to understand the difference between advertising and marketing. Advertising is about promotion. It involves trying to convince someone to buy what you are selling. Advertising is what you do when you "pump-up" your resume with highfaluting language in an attempt to make yourself look profoundly desirable. Marketing, on the other hand, involves assessing the needs of the marketplace and determining how to meet a real need with a viable product or service. While an exaggerated resume is a tactic used by some aspiring job seekers to get hired, staying employed depends on being able to perform well what you promote. A sure way to fail is to successfully advertise something you can't successfully deliver. Marketing, conversely, involves truthfully representing the "real thing" in the "right way" to the "right place."

In effective marketing, you need to know your product and the market. In career management, the product is what you bring to market through your personal strengths, which we refer to here as *motivated strengths*. The "right place" is an employment niche that fits your particular brand of personal

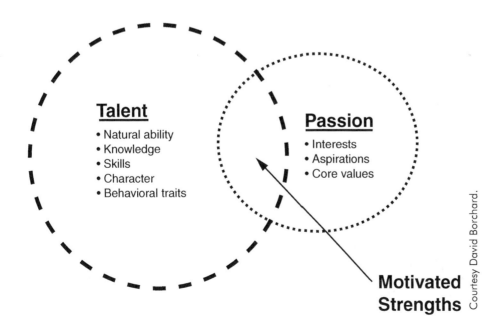

**Talent**
- Natural ability
- Knowledge
- Skills
- Character
- Behavioral traits

**Passion**
- Interests
- Aspirations
- Core values

**Motivated Strengths**

Courtesy David Borchard.

attributes and aspirations. State in the Motivated Strengths diagram conceptualizes the way in which talent unites with passion to produce "motivated strengths." In this perspective, talent is a combination of your natural abilities, the knowledge you have acquired, the skills you have developed, and the positive aspects of your personality. Natural ability refers to your unique gifts of potential. Some of us come into the world gifted musically, some athletically, some analytically, some linguistically, some creatively, and others with a broad array of capabilities rather than any standout, specific talent. Your natural abilities serve as the basis for what you can and can't excel in mentally, physically, and personality-wise.

Because a talent represents a potential, it remains a latent ability, a dormant possibility, unless it's developed. What you are capable of today is a matter of which of your abilities you have developed into what you know (knowledge), what you have learned to do well (skill), your personality attributes (character), and how you have learned to manage yourself in the world (behavior).

A personal strength, however, goes well beyond your talent to include your passion, or what motivates you. Passion includes your deep-seated personal interests, which are those things that energize you. Values are what you care about most deeply. To develop a talent into strength requires motivation, and that's where passion comes into the picture. You might, for example, be as gifted scientifically as Marie Currie or creatively as Frank Lloyd Wright but lack the motivation to develop and apply those particular talents. It is possible, of course, to have a passion to do something for which you lack a sufficient degree of god-given talent to succeed. Someone might, for example, aspire to be an astrophysicist but lack the requisite innate ability to master quantum physics or to think outside of the box, and outside of the known universe for that matter.

The key in successful career management is to find and define the place where your talents connect with your passion. Without the passion connection, you are like a car without a battery. Having a passion minus the right kind of talent is like a battery minus the vehicle. To be a high performer and to sustain that over time you need both the engine (talent) and the battery (energizing power source).

Gerisima/Shutterstock.com

## A Quirk of Nature

There are challenges to this process of defining your motivated strengths, one of which has to do with a peculiarity of nature. In the maturation process, a young person's talents develop well before his or her uniquely personal interests crystallize. By the age of 12 or 13, you can pretty much tell what a youth is going to be good at and where his or her talents lie. You can distinguish the gregarious extroverts from the quiet contemplatives. You can see who can shoot a basket through a hoop at 20 feet and who can make you laugh. You can see who is good at numbers and who is skilled at drawing. You can also see those who possess natural leadership traits, those who can follow, the lone wolves, and the crowd pleasers. What you can't see in a youthful adolescent, however, is who might *enjoy* high finance, who will *aspire* to elective office, and who will develop a *passion* for designing the architectural structures of our twenty-first-century lifestyle.

Deep-seated interests and autonomously inspired personal aspirations evolve with maturity and are unlikely to fully crystallize until into one's 20s. It takes life experience and maturity to develop your unique nature and to appreciate the gifts of your distinctive intellectual and creative endowments. There are, of course, exceptions to this. Mozart knew at a young age that he was a composer, Picasso painted Picador at the age of eight years, Tiger Woods was playing golf at the age of two, Michelangelo was no doubt drawing little masterpieces before achieving adolescence, Michael Jackson was performing at the age of five, and General George Patton may have been playing strategically with toy soldiers when barely out of diapers. For most of us, however, maturation develops like good wine, and great wines take time along with nurturing "aging" conditions. Individuals tend to grow their interests in their own time, and some of us just require longer to ferment into the full-bodied vintage self.

The consequence of this quirk in nature is that many individuals often make career choices before their interests fully mature. Because talents gel before interests, many young people are encouraged to do what they are good at before they really come to know for themselves where their work-related passions might reside. That's why Stewart, a past client of ours, became a physician only to realize at the age of 48 that he would much preferred to have been a poet, a philosopher, or a professor of humanities. Regina, another of our past clients, became an accountant at her father's urgings because she was "good with numbers," only to realize in her 30s that she was energized far more in creative endeavor than in analytical activity. Learning about yourself is a lifelong journey, and finding your way in life and career is an ongoing exploration. Some of us acquire accurate self-knowledge early in life and make choices that are consistent with the strengths we inherit and develop. Some of us think we know who we are and what we want before time and experience matures us. Some of us don't have a clue as to who we are and what we want and go forth into the world utterly confused and uncertain. No matter where you fall on the spectrum of self-knowledge and astute decision-making, keep in mind that each of us possesses unique strengths and that there are far greater rewards in playing to your strengths than cruising through life on someone else's plan for you or overlooking your personal strengths in pursuit of fame, fortune, or soulless materialism.

Gustavo Frazao/Shutterstock.com

Realizing and defining your motivated strengths is challenging, but the satisfaction of doing so and creating a self-realizing vision for your future is well worth the investment. It's an endeavor that pays dividends through ongoing adventures in self-discovery and the sense of fulfillment that comes through applying your unique endowments and interests in a good marketplace fit. Believing that you are using and developing the best you have to offer in work worth doing is psychic pay that's hard to top.

List a few things you were good at as a child.

How was this reinforced or supported?

Did you ever dream of using these skills "when you grew up" and if so, how?

## Finding Your Direction in The Work World

Successful career management today is similar in a number of ways to managing a business. Profitable businesses are clear about the unique value of their product line and the market niche in which their product or service has special appeal. What's the likelihood of an enterprise staying in business trying to sell cheap wine in an upscale neighborhood or a car dealership attempting to sell BMWs in a pick-up-driving community? Like a successful business venture, you need to have a product line and gear it to a market where there is a need for what you offer and are motivated to deliver. For a business, a product line is what it's known for, which is a combination of the brand and the product line. When you hear the name of a company, what comes to mind? Certainly, it's the products but what you associate with is also the brand. When you think of certain companies, you might think of words such as innovation, breakthrough technology, upscale glitzy products, creative

Rawpixel.com/Shutterstock.com

kentoh/Shutterstock.com

advertising, and trending. All successful companies pay a great deal of attention to establishing and maintaining their product line and brand identity.

As individuals we also get "branded." Some of us become known for our creativity, some for outgoing personalities, some for humor, and others for being clumsy, flighty, or unmanageable. As an individual, your brand is the reputation you acquire, and the product line you want to establish your brand around is your motivated strengths. Our premise in this book is that an effective personal product line consists of well-conceived and smartly articulated motivated strengths, and your "brand" is up to you to create and safeguard.

## Career Management is a Marketing Challenge

To capitalize on your strengths, you first need to recognize and define what they are and be able to articulate them with accuracy, clarity, and appeal. In that regard, imagine, if you will, that all-time basketball great Michael Jordan had no concept of his particular kind of athletic abilities, and instead of focusing on basketball pursued a career in something like accounting, information technology, or perhaps art. In fact, Michael might have done fine in some other line of work. But, it's unlikely that he would have been exceptional in another occupational pursuit. In fact, he did give professional baseball a try, only to discover he was not good enough to make it to the majors. In a similar manner, think of a musician you admire. We have many examples of award-winning music singer/songwriters who are clearly exceptional performers. But, most probably, these talented musicians would have been merely good at public relations, mediocre at selling insurance, or even a failure at information technology.

It's our belief, founded in years of counseling experience, that not only famous people and standout stars like Jordan possess genius. We think that just about everyone is capable of genius of a kind. It is just that, to become the genius of your genetic potentials and particular motivations, you need to know the specific nature of your unique qualities of genius and where and how to apply them to achieve fullest manifestation. Something else to remember is that most geniuses do not operate in the realm of fame and visibility. They are more likely to be happily applying their strengths in less visible ways, doing well in a cause they care about. Unfortunately, all too many of us never discover our unique strengths and go through life with our gifts undiscovered and unfulfilled. To prevent that from happening to you, it will be important to become an effective marketer of your unique kind of genius. Please be aware of the difference between bragging and effective marketing. Bragging is an ego-based behavior that turns others off when people talk about themselves with excessive pride. Marketing, on the other hand, involves accurate and authentic communications to acquaint (or educate) an intended audience about a product or service of real benefit to them.

You can't, we repeat, market anything you're unable to accurately translate into words. Putting words to your motivated strengths can be highly challenging, however, as it involves attempting to objectify a subjective domain. Putting words to your motivated strengths requires defining your inner world of passion and potential, which is a bit like trying to describe a concept such as love, spirituality, or appetite to someone with no experience of such things. No one else can see into the realm of your inner potentials, your aspirations, or the sources of your inner motivations. As of this point in time, even the most powerful of computers can't detect these inner qualities. Only you can accomplish this task. It's for that reason that a good portion of this book is devoted to facilitating your self-understanding and to help you define, put words to, market, and apply your motivated strengths.

SK Design/Shutterstock.com

## Career Management and Personal Product Lines

In reference to The Motivated Strength diagram on page, we want to emphasize the concept that motivated strengths occur where talent connects to passion. It illustrates that there is seldom a perfect overlap between an individual's talent and his or her passion. There are a number of reasons for this, one of which we have alluded to earlier, that talent manifests before passion. Another reason for the lack of a perfect match between Talent and Passion has to do with the fact that rarely do we get to do in life, in our educational development, or in our work only that which strikes our fancy. Even when you engage in a favorite activity, whether it be work or hobby, you probably have to draw upon things you can do well but don't particularly enjoy. Pat, for example, is an artist who loves to paint in watercolor and has a real gift for it. But to do her work and sell her art, which is important if you want to make a living through art, she has to do many things she doesn't particularly enjoy, such as keeping track of inventory, ordering supplies and equipment, managing her studio space and her sales outlets, advertising her art, negotiating sales prices, keeping track of art expenses and profits, paying taxes and attending to dozens of other chores. She can do all of these things and do them well. It's just that these chores come with the territory. If she were unable to do these things well, she would be in real trouble. Either she would have to hire someone to do what she doesn't enjoy or languish as an artist, neither of which is a viable option.

The career management point here is that to enjoy and be successful in work, and hobbies too for that matter, choose first and foremost what connects most deeply with your personal interests. Just make sure also that it fits with your talent. Choosing for passion without consideration for talent is a mistake equal in magnitude to a choice that applies your talent but fails to connect with passion. A career choice for passion minus talent leads to frustration, disillusionment, and failure. A choice for talent minus passion dooms one to a low-energy existence, which means you can do it but you're just not motivated to do it. Trying to sustain a successful career minus either of the two ingredients essential for career success and life satisfaction could be every bit as challenging as canoeing upriver, against a strong current, with a spoon for a paddle.

Key to successful marketing is to know the product line and the market niche for your particular brand of motivated strengths. In general, a product line is comprised of three motivated strengths. Three seems to be a magic number when it comes to marketing your personal priorities. Anything less than three motivated strengths generally is insufficient for a brand-defining product line. Promoting more than three motivated strengths waters down a product line and renders your offering bland. This is, of course, a general rule of thumb as opposed to a career management dictum. Someone heading

Rawpixel.com/Shutterstock.com.

## Product Line Examples for Selected Professions

| Profession | Motivated Strength 1 | Motivated Strength 2 | Motivated Strength 3 |
|---|---|---|---|
| General manager | Project management, team leading, coaching, motivating | Business acumen, discerning critical priorities, setting goals and planning | Problem-solving, judgment, decision-making, assuming responsibility |
| Economist | Analytical research, abstract reasoning | Conceptualizing, plausibly synthesizing facts | Communicating complex information |
| IT manager | Keen understanding of information technology | System thinking and innovative problem-solving | Business insight combined with resource allocation |
| Elementary education teacher | Creativity in delivering instruction | Resourceful classroom management | Communicating with influence and impact |
| Public relations director | Leading creative opinion—influencing projects | Writing influentially for a wide variety of audiences | Conceiving and delivering motivational presentations |
| Military officer—junior to mid-level rank | Inspiring, motivating, leading through example | Exercising authority, disciplining | Decision-making, problem-solving, resourcefulness |
| Counseling psychologist | Nonjudgmental, active listening; connecting empathically | Facilitating self-knowledge-enhancing interactions | Intuiting possible causes and curative possibilities |
| Architect | Creative design and conceptual problem-solving | Structural engineering | Assessing client needs and devising creative options |
| Criminal investigator | Deductive and inductive reasoning | Conducting fact-finding interviews | Assertive investigative persistence |
| Trial lawyer | Extracting relevant insights from all sources of data | Creating sound rationale from logic and legal precedent | Quick thinking and communicating persuasively |
| Race car driver | Competitive spirit, performing best under pressure | Agility and split-second timing | Astute mechanical intelligence |

in a general management track may need to specify a more expansive product line while another heading in a career direction such as cartooning or musical theatrics, where narrow and deep expertise is required, may need greater emphasis on one or two priorities.

For additional information on the strengths associated with various types of professions and occupations, see the Department of Labor's *Occupational Outlook Handbook* available at: www.bls.gov/oco/home .htm or the O*NET at www.onetonline.org/

## Finding Your Marketplace Niche

The figure below shows the relationship between the marketplace and an individual's product line. This figure also represents the consequences of four types of career choice. The first of these, the "Unsuited Fit," represents the worst possible choice an individual could make, as it is ill suited both to one's talent and passion. Such a choice might be a bit like a world-class artist such as Pablo Picasso opting for a career in accounting, or television talk-show host Oprah Winfrey pursuing a career in data management. The consequence of such a career choice is obvious: failure on all fronts.

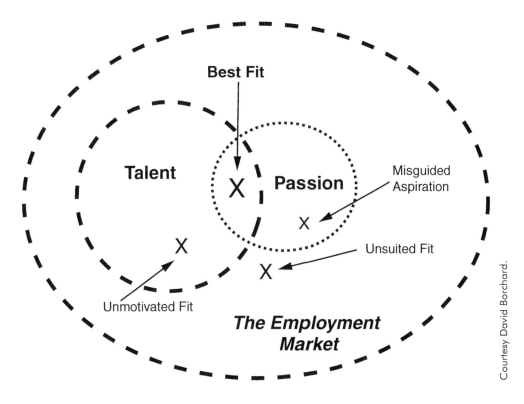

Courtesy David Borchard.

The second choice, "Unmotivated Fit," is one in which an individual's talents are well suited to the market needs, but ill fit for the individual's passion. Can you see the long-range consequences of this kind of choice? How do you stay motivated when you can't generate much interest in your work, no matter how good you might be at doing it? Unfortunately, the workplace tends to be full of those who have made just this kind of choice. How would you like to be the manager of a team of talented individuals who had little interest in their work? In situations where sustained high performance is essential to business success, management has to constantly seek ways to motivate employees lacking enthusiasm for their work. That's why so many organizations are constantly seeking inducements such as promotions, performance-based salary increase, cash bonus awards, and employee recognition awards to spur performance in individuals lacking strong interest their work. These kinds of inducements tend to work, but they are short-term fixes.

It is extremely difficult to sustain high motivation for long when you are doing something that fails to connect with your core interests. You can perform with enthusiasm when you have your sights set on an achievement goal, such as promotion, performance-based bonus, or special reward of some kind. But, lacking strong motivation for the work, you soon lose enthusiasm once the goal has been achieved. Think also of the consequence to motivation associated with someone who works hard in single-minded objective for a promotion but doesn't achieve it. In such a situation, management has a dual problem: a disillusioned employee performing low-interest work.

A question you might rightfully ask is why would anyone choose and/ or pursue a career that wasn't a good fit for their motivated strengths? A choice to chase high income and/or prestige might result in a sense of gratification. But, unless such efforts are congruent with one's self-realization needs, the glow of achievement will be short-lived and achieved at a cost to self-fulfillment. You are going to be most successful and enjoy your work more when you make choices that connect your talent with your passion in a way that meshes with the needs of the marketplace, a choice in the figure above represented by "Best Fit."

In a "Best Fit" situation, you are going to be self-motivated and remain so for as long as you sustain the connection between motivated strengths and marketplace niche. You are also likely to be happier in life, more fulfilled as an individual, and very likely a healthier person. How would you like to work on a team in which everyone on it was in a "Best Fit" situation? Imagine what it might feel like going to work on Mondays in such a team. Visualize what it would be like managing a team of high performers engaged in a "Best Fit" situation. In this regard, it seems that employers could achieve greater benefits through helping their human resources transition into "Best Fit" situations than by looking for ways to induce high performance from employees in "Unmotivated Fit" situations. The problem is that achieving this objective can be exceedingly difficult. Furthermore, individuals are better situated to market themselves into "Best Fits" than leaving it to the employer to do it for them. This brings us back to why becoming an excellent marketer of your motivated strengths is important if you want to experience the benefits of self-realization and personal fulfillment in your career.

There is one other career choice aspiration warranting mention, which we refer to as "Misguided Aspiration." This is a case of someone thinking they would love to do something for which they lack the necessary talent, personality, or even physical stature. A colleague of ours, somewhat jocularly, cites an example of this in his own case by revealing that he aspires to be a jockey. He adds, however, that achieving such a desire is highly unlikely as he is 55 years old, 6' 3" in height, and weighs in at about 250 pounds. He then suggests that should ever they start racing elephants in a senior citizens league, he'll be among the first to saddle up. In a somewhat more serious vein, someone might hope to become a rock star, but if lacking musical talent and showmanship, this would be a pipe dream.

It's not just a poor fit of natural ability or learning capabilities that can lead to "Misguided Aspiration." Personality is also important to factor into one's career choice. A highly extroverted personality, for example, is unlikely to enjoy work involving intensive individual and solitary effort. An introvert, however, might find such conditions to be a perfect fit. Highly creative and abstract thinkers are certain to become bored in activities engaging them in work of a conventional and concrete nature. Making poor choices in matching personality to work has unhappy consequences. We know of someone, for example, who was hired for a public relations position because she was extremely adept in putting on a great front in a job interview. It turns out, however, that while she could interact rather well with the media, she could not get along with her staff or work colleagues. Almost every business interaction with these individuals evolved into a huge fracas. She became such an annoyance, in fact, it became necessary to fire her and replace her with someone having the temperament to get along with both the media and work colleagues.

A final point worth mentioning here is that you might well be able to grow into a "Best Fit" situation if you possess the right kind of potential and personality but lack only the knowledge and skill necessary to excel. This is especially true when starting a career or a new job, when you are unlikely initially to have the knowledge and skill necessary for high-level performance. That usually takes some seasoning. The important point here is that while you cannot change your ability potentials or the nature of your personality endowments, you can acquire new knowledge and skill. Angela's story, which follows, is a case in point.

## Case Study   Angela

Angela, a bright 23-year-old civil engineer, sought career counseling because she was unhappy in her work. She was in her first job out of college, a civil engineering position with a state highway administration. Through assessment work with her counselor, Angela discovered she had strong creative interests that were not being fulfilled in her highly analytical and technical position. Appreciating her creative inclinations, her counselor asked on what basis she had elected to major in civil engineering. Her answer was that because she had been good in math and science in school, her teachers had encouraged her to go into civil engineering, where such talents could "shine." The rationale she bought into was that old barriers previously hindering women from entering traditionally male professions were disappearing, and that there would always be a strong need for civil engineers. Beyond that, she was seduced by the fact that you can make good money as a civil engineer. That seemed like pretty sound logic, at least on the surface.

It is difficult to sustain performance over time if you can't muster up motivating interest in your work. Angela, recognizing this fact, was determined to make some enhancements in her career. As a first step in this process, and with help from her counselors, Angela identified her motivated strengths to be creative design, spatial problem-solving, and facilitating communications interactions. This was her product line, the core strengths around which she hoped recreate her career direction and establish a new "brand" identity. With that, she developed a functional resume showcasing various ways in which she had used these strengths to create business-relevant results. This type of resume, highlighting your product-line strengths, is often used when you are starting out in a career or wanting to make a career-enhancing shift in your work. For Angela, developing her marketing document proved useful in that it:

- showed convincingly how she had used her motivated strengths to produce business-relevant results;
- served as the basis for generating ideas concerning what other areas of the organization might have a need for her unique brand of strengths;
- represented her very differently than she had been previously identified. Now, instead of being viewed at as a junior civil engineer, she was able to present herself as a creative designer, a special problem-solver, and communicator who could articulately convey ideas and facilitate difficult conversations;
- served as a powerful resource for focusing her discussions with individuals she identified as knowledgeable resources for exploring new work possibilities;
- was a referral document for individuals with whom she had conducted information interviews to forward on to other sources who might be interested in her strengths.

With her new marketing document in hand, Angela began meeting with individuals she identified as working within areas of the organization that might be a fit for her motivated strengths. She developed a list of questions to guide her meetings and make the best use of their time together. Angela found these visits to be exceedingly rewarding and was gratified to see the interest with which people responded to her initiatives. It turned out that her approach to career management was unique in an organization where people had traditionally been tracked on the basis of their title and job classification—being a civil engineer was a brand that stuck with you throughout your career. Now, however, Angela was approaching her career in a uniquely different way. She was seeking a niche for her brand of strengths rather than following a traditional, job-title-determined path.

Too55/Shutterstock.com

The outcomes of Angela's efforts were highly successful; she found an excellent fit for her "product line." She was able to obtain a developmental work assignment (a temporary try-out assignment) with the landscape architecture group. That group, it turned out, was delighted to have a young person join their team, with her unique assets along with her effervescent energy. Her youthful creativity and knack for spatial design fit well with the mission of this group. Of particular interest was her ability to establish rapport with and handle difficult communications challenges. Highway landscaping often has a significant impact on communities, and residents of areas to be affected by new design have been known to express their concerns rather vociferously. To address community concerns in such areas, the highway administration conducts forums to provide citizens an opportunity to discuss and have input into final plans. With her communications abilities, which include a knack for facilitating discussions fraught with disagreement, highway management saw Angela's potential and was happy to give her a try with a developmental assignment.

When we last heard from her, Angela was thrilled about her new situation and had begun taking courses in landscape architecture at a nearby university. In addition to the coursework, Angela needed to acquire experience in learning "tricks of the trade" relative to the unique function of highway landscape. She was willing to learn new skills that were directly in line with her interests and so well suited to her talents. An additional feature of her new work assignment was that she brought a youthful vitality to a group staffed mostly by older men, many of whom would be retiring in the near future. She was on a team, therefore, that she could learn from and carry forth the knowledge and experience of these individuals when they moved on. That also meant future career possibilities for her on a rather small team that had previously provided few employment options, an all-around win-win situation.

PAUSE

Based on Angela's story, list a few observations regarding career selection.

In what ways are you able to apply Angela's story to your own?

## Implications From Angela's Story

Angela's initial "Unmotivated Fit" situation prior to moving on to a better fit is not unusual. Too many individuals make career choices based on insufficient "self" information. Through our years of combined career counseling experience, we have seen how poor choices often lead to job dissatisfaction, performance problems, and lack of personal fulfillment. Following are three examples selected from clients whom we have counseled.

John worked hard to get a degree in economics, and that led to what seemed like a good job in research at a prestigious institution. Within a year, however, he found that while he could perform this type of analytical work, it was not something he enjoyed. He had come to realize that what did engage him was interacting creatively with people in a helping capacity.

In similar vein, after obtaining a bachelor's degree in business administration, Hannah accepted a position involving primary emphasis on coordinating a complex variety of administrative activities. Though she was good at these types of tasks, she found the work tedious. To extract herself from this predicament Hannah decided to obtain an MBA degree. She was moved to make this decision on the assumption that advance education would somehow resolve her dilemma, even though she had no idea of how this might help.

Then there was Sam, who, after 20-some years of selling technology products, was completely burned out and seeking rejuvenation. After so many years devoted primarily to "making a living" with little thought about what would make him happy, he was now desperate to find something that would regenerate his lagging spirits and provide a greater sense of purpose.

With the help of career counseling, these three individuals are now in the process of making career shifts better suited to their interest-based strengths.

John is applying to graduate schools in psychology. His goal is to obtain the professional credentials that will enable him to pursue a passion for helping individuals in the developing world in need of therapy to resolve mental barriers standing in their way to a better life.

Hannah realized that obtaining an MBA degree was unlikely to somehow magically transform her disenchantment with organizational management. Instead she elected to apply to graduate programs in early childhood education to pursue a passion for working with kids.

Sam is exploring ways and means to draw upon his technology background to bring learning solutions to education through the use of advance technology. He is particularly drawn to the applications of learning technology in poor urban areas.

In the case of Angela, she might well have plunged on ahead in a career direction suited to her talents but not to anything she could experience with passion. Had she continued on the path of her degree and job title, she might well have ended up as yet another of those individuals who come to work, put in their time, but live for the weekends and holidays. Her work colleagues were entrenched in the mind-set that work is what you must to do to have the means for doing what you really want to do outside of work. One of the

DGLimages/Shutterstock.com

problems with this kind of thinking is that if your work drains your energy, you don't have much vitality left over for life outside of the job. Fortunately for Angela, she was willing to go against the tide of convention to look for ways in which to make her work more satisfying. As a result of her efforts, she is now engaged in work she loves and is operating at a higher energy level both on the job and in her life. The organization also received a benefit from the new direction in her career, in that it now has an energized high performer on the job rather than just another individual functioning at less than full potential.

A secondary benefit of Angela's rejuvenation experience is that she became a role model for others who had been languishing in their jobs. A number of others, observing how much happier she was as a result of her self-directed change, elected to follow her example to see if they too could rejuvenate their lagging spirits by improving their situation at work. Some have made satisfying changes, some not, and others are in progress. Those who have made successful turnarounds more often than not benefited from the support of others including career counselors, supportive managers, wise mentors, and helpful friends.

Making wise career choices is difficult to do on your own. Angela is clear that she would not be where she is without the help and support of someone with the knowledge and resources to help. The lesson for anyone wanting to make a fulfilling career choice or to change their career is clear—take full advantage of available resources such as college counseling centers, community resources, life and career coaches, organizational human resource services, and scores of smart and helpful people.

## Finding Your Career Niche

The dictionary defines *niche* as "a position or activity that particularly suits somebody's talents and personality or that somebody can make his or her own." Once you have defined your product line, in terms of motivated strengths, the marketing challenge becomes finding a suitable marketplace fit. Seeking a good fit necessitates both research and creativity. There is no magic here to reveal the one right thing for you. In fact, there probably is no single right thing for you. More likely there are a number of options that might fit well with your strengths and, of course, there are countless numbers of poor choices you could make.

Marketing lessons from industry are directly applicable to successful career management. You don't want to invest your time, money, and efforts in preparing for a marketplace need in decline or one that is glutted or to advertise what you can't deliver. One of our mentors, authors, and counselors Dr. Borchard, became acquainted with an important lesson from marketplace reality the hard way. The first of these occurred years ago when he elected to major in geology because he found the subject matter fascinating. What he failed to realize, however, was that while the study of geology in college is a social activity, jobs in geology are decidedly not. It wasn't until he graduated with a bachelor's degree that he realized what work options were available in geology and he knew for sure these were of no interest. In retrospect, he learned how important it is to acquaint yourself with the likely consequences of your choices. Had he taken the time to investigate the field of geology, he would have realized that geology was not a good fit for someone who enjoyed working with people, had creative self-expressive needs, and was far more fascinated with matters of the mind, emotion, and behavior than in rocks, minerals, and the physical structures of the earth.

At one point, he took advantage of career counseling that focused first and foremost on the inner world, on self-knowledge. From that experience, he came to understand and appreciate what qualities he could bring to a career. Through his counseling experience, he clarified his motivated strengths to creative conceptual design, client-centered empathetic interaction, and designing and delivering educational processes. He also learned that he was a right-brain, intuitive, feeling-oriented, and introverted thinker, all of which were completely new and fascinating career-relevant insights—his own **Aha! moments**. From this knowledge he could see why neither geology nor a few of his previous jobs were good fits for his strengths and attributes of personality. With this newly acquired self-awareness, and support for doing a more thorough exploration of relevant possibilities, he eventually settled on counseling psychology as his career direction. That was nearly 30 years ago, and to this day, Dr. Borchard is eternally thankful for taking advantage of available resources to make a well-considered, satisfying, fulfilling career-direction choice.

Now in the senior stage of life, Dr. Borchard's career mission is to convey the insights he has acquired, the knowledge developed, and the lessons learned from his life and work experiences to those open to and interested in making well-considered life and work choices. Dr. Borchard was an original author of this textbook. His continued support of the authors of this book conveys his hopes that you count yourself in this category and are ready to engage in the challenging and fascinating process of self-discovery and life/work decision-making upon which this book concentrates.

In the book What the Dog Saw: And Other Adventures, Malcolm Gladwell[3] shares this about his own career path. In his book, he writes:

*Growing up, I never wanted to be a writer. I wanted to be a lawyer, and then in my last year of college, I decided I wanted to be in advertising. I applied to eighteen advertising agencies in the city of Toronto and received eighteen rejection letters, which I taped in a row on my wall. I thought about graduate school, but my grades weren't quite good enough, I applied for a fellowship to go somewhere exotic for a year and was rejected. Writing was the thing I ended up doing by default, for the simple reason that it took me forever to realize that writing could be a job. Jobs were things that were serious and daunting. Writing was fun.*

*After college, I worked for six months at a little magazine in Indiana called the American Spectator. I moved to Washington, DC, and freelanced for a few years, and eventually caught on with the Washington Post—and from there came to The New Yorker. Along the way, writing has never ceased to be fun . . . . . . !*

Gladwell never thought of a career in writing. Perhaps there are careers that you never thought about. During the time you spend in this course, you will have the opportunity to think about skills you like to use and careers you can pursue.

Make a list of some of the things you enjoy doing.

Quickly think of careers that use these skills.

Throughout this book, you will have many opportunities to think about how your own unique make up connects to careers. Hopefully, you will be like Gladwell and find a way to make a career based on your skills and interests. And hopefully, unlike Gladwell, you will be able to do it before you have 18 or more rejection letters.

**Tierra identifies her motivated strengths to be:**

- Complex analytic research
- Computer and quantitative skills
- Problem-solving through precise data analysis

**Which of the following career choices represent "best fit" for Tierra? Rate each choice on a scale of 1 to 10 for how good of a fit, with "10" being an excellent choice and "1" being extremely poor.**

- Graphic design _____
- Aeronautical engineering _____
- Architecture _____
- Journalism _____
- Economics _____
- Environmental engineering _____
- Accounting _____
- Pharmacology _____
- Biology _____
- Hospitality industry _____

**Without knowing anything about Tierra, other than these three statements, why did you select these ratings?**

**Raj identifies his motivated strengths to be:**

- Creative self-expression
- Developing and managing group agendas
- Inspiring enthusiastic interaction with audiences of all ages and backgrounds

**Which of the following career choices represent "best fit" for Raj? Rate each choice on a scale of 1 to 10 for how good of a fit, with "10" being an excellent choice and "1" being extremely poor.**

- Computer science _____
- Criminology _____
- Elementary education _____
- Psychology _____
- World history _____
- Business administration _____
- Law _____
- Medicine _____
- Environmental science _____
- Public relations _____

1. Without knowing anything about Raj, other than these three statements, why did you select these ratings?

2. What implications does this have for your own career discovery?

## Careers in Demand

The demand for certain types of work is dependent upon economic conditions and the current and developing needs of the marketplace. Attempting to ascertain what types of career-related special knowledge and skills may be required in coming years necessitates attempting to forecast factors likely to impact future work. We can't know, of course, what will drive people's fancies in future years, (e.g., hula hoops in the 1950s, the "Beatle Craze" in the 1960s) nor what science and technology may bring our way (e.g., TVs in the 1950s, laptops in the 1990s, cell phones currently), but we can assess what conditions are likely to affect employment needs of the future. We know, for example, that a high-technology-based economy needs highly educated workers possessing strong computer competencies. That in turn drives employment needs for areas such as research in science and technology, marketing and sales of technology, information technology support, educators at all levels, technology policy workers at all levels of government, and so on.

While we will spend more time on this topic in future sections, take time now to begin your thinking on this important aspect of career decision-making. Rate how significant you believe the following factors are likely to be in shaping the nature of work in future years.

**Use a rating scale of 1 to 10 in making your choices, with "1" indicating little if any impact and "10" indicating a powerful impact.**

- Aging baby-boomers _____
- Advances in science and technology _____
- Terrorism on an international scale _____
- Climate change _____
- Growing energy needs _____
- The global economy _____
- The needs of the developing world _____
- Educational needs of adults _____
- Illegal immigration _____
- Clean water availability _____
- Crime and crime prevention _____
- Aesthetic needs of an affluent population _____
- Governance needs at the local and national level _____
- Waste management for an expanding population _____
- Religion and spirituality _____

**How we access entertainment** _____

- International tensions, geopolitics _____
- Health management _____
- Social responsibility displayed by individuals and corporations _____
- Social networks _____
- Agile work places (work from anywhere) _____
- Shortages of certain skills _____

Identify at least five additional trends or factors impacting the marketplace now, or over the next decade, that you believe are likely to have a significant impact on work in future years.

We are frequently tempted to make career choices based on predicted high growth fields, industries promising high incomes, or trendy careers. Thinking about work-influencing factors, take a minute to make a note of any of the factors and/or trends that might be of particular interest to you and your career aspirations, being sure to make your choices on what clearly inspires your interests. This brief reaction may result in a few careers to consider or **Aha! moments**; so be sure to record them in the **APP 7: About Me**.

## Internal and External Factors

Before we move to the next section, it is important for us to remind you that you will be dealing with many factors as you look at your career. We often group them into two categories called "internal factors" and "external factors."

**Internal factors**—This area looks at the things that you have control over and the things that are core to you. It is about your personality, the things which are important to you, your passions, how you like to make decisions, and how you like to learn.

**External factors**—This is often about things you cannot control such as the economy, the decisions made by others, and the weather!

It is important to note that external factors have an impact on your career. But the greater impact comes from how you react to these factors—it is about how you respond to the external world. For example, you have no control over the weather. If you wake up and it is raining, you can decide to stay inside to completely avoid the rain, go outside and jump in the puddles, or walk cautiously around the puddles while carrying an umbrella to keep from getting wet.

Throughout this book, you will spend significant time understanding the factors that make you YOU! Self-reflection is an important and valuable process. There will also be time to look at the external factors and take these into consideration as you make career choices. Successful people do not avoid the external factors nor do they wish and wish and wish they could change them and get stuck doing nothing. Successful people take the time to manage external factors and often take advantage of them to make good choices.

Name any company and you will most likely find that there was a problem a founder wanted to solve and the timing was right to make that idea happen. Think about how many companies today got their start:  Zappos began because the founder couldn't find shoes at a mall. There was no major online retailer specializing in shoes. The personal need met a need in the marketplace (http://www.zappos.com/d/about-zappos). Marriott began as a place to get a cold root beer during a muggy summer in DC. The story is told that founder J. Willard Marriott was living in DC and found few places to get a cold drink (http://www.marriott.com/about/culture-and-values /history.mi); and Under Armour began because the founder was tired of sweaty cotton T-shirts during football practice. He realized after extensive research that there were athletic benefits to synthetic fabrics (http://www. uabiz.com/company/history.cfm).

For these and other companies, the "time was right" to launch an idea. The external factors that created a need helped to make the company a success. As you read the stories behind the success of all companies, you will also read about the internal factors that contributed to the success. You will read about the internal characteristics of vision, drive, planning, research, team development, and persistence.

The successes of the companies referenced above are based on many factors.  Follow the links or look at the stories of other companies. What were the internal and external factors that allowed the founder to create a successful company? (Hint: For Zappos, think about where he was living and what year it was.)

Spend time over the next few days thinking about the problems in the world that bug you! Do you have any ideas that could solve them?

What external factors would have to exist in order for your idea to be a success?

What internal factors would you need to see your idea come to reality?

## Summary

There are some things we get to choose and some we don't. You don't get to choose your natural talents and traits of personality: you do, however, get to choose if and how you develop your talents. Though you don't have the option of selecting what engages your interests, you can exercise management control over how fully you will pursue your interests in life and work.

Here are key points we hope you will take away from this chapter:

■ Understand that career development is a marketing challenge, and become an effective marketer of your unique blend of talents and interests.

■ You don't have to pursue your career solely in what you are good at. It's knowing which of your best talents connect to unique personal interests and core values, where the potential for fulfillment and sustainable energy resides.

■ Career management in today's world is an ongoing process rather than a one-time event.

■ You need to know both how you are developing as a person and where the market for your special "brand" of strengths resides.

■ In marketing, you have to make your product visibly desirable to the intended market. In career management, it's important to make your motivated strengths evident to your target market.

■ You are going to enjoy your work and your life and be more successful when your motivated strengths are engaged in work that is congruent with your personal attributes.

## Endnotes

### APP 1.1

1. Reference http://www.weddles.com/workstrong.

2. https://www.mindtools.com/CommSkll/JohariWindow.htm.

3. Malcolm Gladwell, *What the dog saw: and other adventures.* (New York: Back Bay, 2010).

## APP 1.2 Developing Your Career Vision

### Do you know people who:

- Unwittingly avoid or consciously refuse to make decisions?

- Make small decisions easily, but panic about making decisions that will impact their future?

- Have gotten into their career more by accident than by planning and preparation?

- Hang onto jobs they hate for security rather than risking seeking their real passion?

If so, you know people who have settled for less freedom and a lesser quality of life because they didn't know how to make decisions or because they were unwilling to make difficult choices.

kurhan/Shutterstock.com

### How Would You Enhance Your Life If You Became a Big-Time Lottery Winner?

*How do you go from where you are to where you want to be? I think you have to have an enthusiasm for life. You have to have a dream, a goal and you have to be willing to work for it.*

—Jim Valvano

- Buy a dude ranch in Montana?
- Start your own furniture-making shop?
- Study psychology in Zurich?
- Create your own bed and breakfast lodge?
- Create an Outward Bound course for disadvantaged kids?
- Study foreign languages and explore the world's cultures?
- Become a Zen master?
- Become a computer guru and live on a mountaintop?
- Study acting and go for the big time?

## Work, Life, And The Lottery

Have you noticed how many people dream of winning the lottery, assuming that doing so would instantly and automatically improve the quality of their lives? What would you do if you won the lottery? Let's say that you won enough money to support yourself (and your family, if that's in your picture) in grand style for the rest of your life.

iQoncept/Shutterstock.com

Would you, as a wealthy person, include work in your future? If so, you just might be one of those few who have discovered a rather well-kept secret, but we're getting ahead of ourselves here! (You will have to read on to discover what that is.) If you're sure that you would never work if you didn't have to—why is that? Could it be that you view work as a drudge, an unpleasant activity made necessary perhaps because of original sin, a family or cultural work ethic, or just the basic need to keep bread on the table? Do you see work as a necessary evil that keeps you from what you would rather be doing?

It probably comes as no surprise that most people report that they would quit their jobs without a moment's hesitation should they hit the lottery big time.

Why would anyone freely elect to work, for that matter? There's only one reason, say most people—"to make a buck!" Actually, there are some very good reasons for working, even if you don't have to. Psychological research suggests there are at least five basic motivations for working:[1]

1. income
2. having something to do with our time and energy
3. a way to achieve identity and status
4. a way of having personal and professional relationships
5. a source of meaning in life.

Regardless of the motivations for work, most people still think their lives would be better if they didn't have to work. But consider this group of retirees. They all retired relatively young, in good health, and were financially secure with lots of disposable income. After a few years of travel, visiting, and leisure activities, they began to get restless. One by one, they got part-time jobs, began volunteering, and took up new hobbies. Conversations with them revealed that they missed the sense of structure, the camaraderie, and the sense of purpose and identity that work had given them. The one thing they did have that many of us lack was the

faithie/Shutterstock.com

choice regarding what to do with their time. Pretend that you were able to "retire" at your current age or that you won the lottery. How would you spend your time?

Imagining what you might do if you won the lottery is actually a productive way to expand your thinking on how to have a more interesting life. Common responses to that question are things like travel, pay off bills, permanently inhabit the beach, do absolutely nothing, and buy a new car/house/wardrobe. If traveling is your answer, think about this: Where would you go? What does traveling really mean to you? How long would you want to do it? And, what would you do when the "bloom" eventually wears off traveling? Or, if your vision involves paying off bills, rushing off to the shopping malls, or simply doing nothing—consider how those things would enhance the total quality of your life.

Money, in itself, doesn't automatically produce a meaningful life (nor does a life of ease). While we're not advocating poverty here, we are aware that people whose lives have been full and interesting used their time, talents, and energies for work they cared passionately about. This may be what British playwright George Bernard Shaw (1856–1950) had in mind in reporting that he wanted to be totally used up when he died. He wanted to have no unused talents nor unfulfilled life/work desires left in reserve on his last day here. Perhaps Shaw, who needed almost 100 years of vigorous living to achieve his stated desire, was advocating for a fundamental principle of life vitality. Most of us really want to be engaged in things that are interesting and worthwhile!

When you have a vision for the life you really want, ask yourself, "Is there any way I might possibly achieve that without the aid of a big lottery win?" Many of us use money, or the lack of it, as an excuse to avoid going after what we truly want in life. In truth, you already have something more powerful than money. You have natural endowments, including your mind, your creativity, and life energy (maybe even your good looks). Our world could greatly benefit from the cumulative effect of a lot more people pursuing what they care deeply about. Why not be one of them? The next time you're inclined to buy a lottery ticket in hopes of becoming rich, consider instead meditating upon a vision of what a fully engaged and challenging life might be. Note how a career can influence your life in the following table.

### A Few Things Your Career Will Dictate or Influence

- Esteem and self-worth
- Talents used and developed
- Interests that are expressed and energized
- Financial resources
- The nature of organizations with which you will associate
- Where you will live
- Kinds of people with whom you will associate
- Time, energy, and resources for:
  Leisure
  Family
  Personal growth
  Professional growth
- Kinds and levels of responsibilities you will have

- Lifestyle
- Health and vitality
- Longevity
- Activities you will perform
- Type of knowledge you will acquire

- What you will be learning
- Employment contract
- Your friends and associates
- The contributions you make

## Defining Career

There are many ways to be engaged in things that are interesting and worthwhile. Paid work is just one of them. We spend a lot of time at work. Ideally, work shouldn't be a means to an end. We shouldn't just work so we have the money to live outside of work. Work, when it engages our unique combination of talents, interests, personality, and values, contributes to meaning and fulfillment. In fact, we believe that it is such an important aspect of our existence that this entire book is written to help you find the type of work that is the best fit for you. However, paid work is just one of the many life roles that we play that make up career.

Donald Super, a person who studied career development in America in the last half of the twentieth century, proposed the idea that a career is really made up of many different life roles.[2] People who are happy in their careers are those who are able to integrate those roles together. Super proposes that we play the following roles: child, student, worker, homemaker, spouse/partner, parent, citizen, and leisurite:

### Child

Beginning at birth, this role is played until the death of our parents. Throughout childhood, we play this role for a majority of our time. As we reach adulthood, we may play this role less or more depending upon our family structure. Many people find themselves playing this role more as their parents' age and they need assistance with health care and financial decisions.

### Student

Most Americans play this role through formal education from 1st until the 12th grade. The setting for the student role could include public, private, and even home schooling. After completing the formal training, the role is played on and off as individuals pursue advanced degrees, engage in noncredit courses related to work or other life areas or interests, or any other way in which we are involved in learning.

### Worker

This refers to the paid work role. It could be a part-time job such as delivering papers or the full-time job of newspaper reporter. This is the role that we will concentrate on throughout this book.

Rawpixel.com/Shutterstock.com

Constantin Stanciu/Shutterstock.com

M. Stasy/Shutterstock.com

### Homemaker

At some point, most people will be responsible for a home, be it a house with the white picket fence, a downtown penthouse, or a college apartment that is shared with three roommates. In the beginning when a person establishes a residence separate from one's parents, this role addresses the various responsibilities of home operation, including decorating, bill paying, food preparation, and maintenance.

### Spouse/Partner

This role centers on the building and maintaining of a satisfying long-term relationship with another person. Some people never play this role, others play it until death, while others play it intermittently.

### Parent

Like some of the other roles, not everyone will choose to play this role. This role involves the activities of raising children. It is a role that is played with the most effort during the child's early years. It begins to taper off as the child becomes more and more independent.

### Citizen

Many people give back to their communities in some way. This role addresses the ways in which we participate in our communities. Some people are involved on school boards or other volunteer political offices; others belong to civic groups or seek involvement in local educational or religious communities.

### Leisurite

Leisure time seems to be rare in today's society, but how we spend our leisure time can provide balance to the other life roles we play. A person who spends a lot of time with other people in the worker role may elect to spend leisure time alone in activities such as running or hiking. Leisure time also allows for the pursuit of other things that may not be found in the other roles, such as physical activity for a person with a sedentary job or gardening for a person who enjoys physical and aesthetic activities but has no way of integrating them into other life roles.

Super noted that we play these roles throughout our lifetimes. At some points, we may be playing all eight roles. The concept of life-role theory can be exciting. It tells us that career does not just have to be relegated to the 9-to-5 workday, but that career, like the strands of a rope, is the integration of all the roles we play.

When we talk about career, we mean all of it. Not just the paid worker role but the volunteer experiences, families, free-time activities, and more. Like the pieces of a puzzle, when they all fit together, they work to make a complete picture. Most people do not play all of the roles at once, and some do not even play all of the roles during their lifetimes. You may choose not to enter into a serious long-term relationship with another person, or you may choose not to have or adopt children. You may decide that you don't want to spend time in the citizen role. Some people choose not to work for pay so they are able to spend their time taking care of children and a house and participating in volunteer activities. Those people who are happy in the combination of life roles they have selected, according to Super, are those who have found a satisfying career.

This concept is incredibly freeing. People suddenly don't have to get all of their interests, abilities, values, and other needs met in one single occupation. Translated, this means the pressure is off to make one choice that is going to be the perfect decision for the rest of your life. Let's consider the following example. Jane was considering two occupations but was torn because one paid a lot of money (a value) while the other allowed a greater contribution to society (another value). Since these two values seemed to carry equal weight, there didn't seem to be a best answer other than to explore other occupations. When Jane considered the options based on the life-role theory, she decided to pursue the occupation that paid more money as her worker role, but began to volunteer in the community youth center as her citizen role. Jane found a job she really liked and was able to meet the one missing value through her volunteer activities.

What about you? Do you feel pressure to select the one right career that is going to be the be-all and end-all? Do you believe that you have the freedom to express yourself and find satisfaction in a variety of different roles? Our life roles allow us to explore career choices as well. A volunteer opportunity at a local vegetable co-op might pave the way for a career in horticulture. Saturdays at a homeless shelter might open the possibility of a career in psychology, social work, or even politics as you seek to find ways to alleviate poverty, not just help support those in this situation. How are you using your various life roles to explore careers and discover your passions?

## A Personal Guide

But how do you discover what a deeply fulfilling life and career would consist of? How can you know what your unique interests and best potentials really are? How do you find a meaningful career? Clearly, these are perplexing questions for everyone. But don't give up; there is hope. A willingness

ACTION

Complete **Your Career/Life Roles** in App 1.3

to seriously address questions such as these is an important step in getting answers. Remember that career in terms of paid work may not be singularly satisfying. Use this book to guide you in your quest for greater self-understanding so that you can make a career choice that is best for you, but be aware that some of the deeper questions of life and meaning and purpose may not be found in getting a better job. Other books are available on these topics of spirituality, love, and personal acceptance. Dick Bolles writes that most of us move from "I need to find a job that I like" to "I need to find my purpose in life." He offers that these are deeper questions of the heart that are unique to each of us and probably won't be answered through a book such as this.

As we consider our lives, we are often quick to run to our families or friends to find the answers. We forget that we may actually be able to find the answers within ourselves. We come to this life equipped with a wise inner guide. Unfortunately, far too few of us ever consult with or pay attention to our own inner counsel. We're just too busy and preoccupied with the sights, sounds, and activities of the outer world. Devoting quiet time for self-reflection directed to important life and career questions can lead to "discernment." Discernment comes from the Latin word *discernere*, which means "to separate, to distinguish, to determine, to sort out."[3] Intuition is a human capacity, a form of intelligence accessible only in the vast reaches of our quiet minds. Accessing it involves asking the hard and specific questions of ourselves, tuning out the loud music and other outer-worldly distractions vying for our attention, and tuning into the quiet consultation of our inner guidance system.

## Lifelong Career Decision-Making

Many people think of career choice as a simple act governed by the single-minded logic of getting a good job. If you're a college student or a re-careering adult, your career-selection logic might be to complete an academic program that leads to a top-paying job, regardless of what the job might be. Such a motivation involves this potentially dangerous assumption: When I get a job with a high salary, my life will fall into place.

There is far more to life than a high-salaried job. We have seen too many people whose single-minded focus on a high-paying job has brought them to the sobering realization that their jobs have come to control their lives. That might be OK if you love your job, but what if you don't? What if you find it doesn't utilize and develop your talents and/or engage your interests? What if it conflicts with your core values?

Aysezgicmeli/Shutterstock.com

What if you become a fast-track manager and then one day are stunned to realize that your kids are being brought up by their nanny because you've been too engaged in work? For reasons such as these, we urge you, regardless of your life stage, to give the process of creating your future serious attention.

Career/life decision-making is an ongoing and lifelong process because we're going to be faced with important life and work choices for as long as we're around. In a way, our lives are like books of many chapters. Your book of life has some past chapters and many more, we hope, in the future. Your career and life book probably has some overall general direction (a storyline) to it with major and minor themes emerging and fading. We write our books one chapter at a time. Here we are concerned about your future chapters, especially the next one.

Career and life decision-making involves work in two realms—the inner universe of self and the outer world of possibilities. Exploring the inner realm involves assessment and self-discovery, particularly in identifying and defining those interests, values, and skills you identify as important to your future. The outer universe of work requires that you learn about possibilities and options available and suited to your unique talents and attributes—now and in the future.

As you become involved in this process of writing the next career chapter of your life, you may feel restricted by any number of circumstances and conditions that appear to be limiting your options. If so, please bear this in mind: The work world is huge, multidimensional, and ever changing. We'll have more to say about overcoming your barriers later on, but for now keep this simple truth in mind: There are always more opportunities than any single individual, on his or her own, can possibly be aware of. So, whether or not you are currently more motivated by material success than inner values, here is your best strategy: Find a career direction that you could really enjoy and that would capitalize on your top strengths and personal assets.

## Jobs and Careers

The term *career* is often misunderstood. Often you hear the terms *career* and *job* used interchangeably. We think of *job* as employment. It's what somebody is paying you to do. Jobs have traditionally been viewed as long-term positions for which we were hired, given titles, and provided an annual salary along with some associated benefits. Traditionally, jobs came with job descriptions. These defined what kinds of tasks and responsibilities you did and did not do (That's my job! That's not my job!). If we are to believe futurist thinkers such as William Bridges, author of *Job Shift*,[4] and Jeremy Rifkin, author of *The End of Work*,[5] jobs are disappearing! The concept of job came in with, and now may be going out with, the industrial era. We may need, therefore, to begin thinking of employment in a very different way. William Bridges advocates thinking of ourselves as contracting agents with expertise suited to particular kinds of work for hire.[6]

A *career* implies that you have prepared for and are building expertise and experience in a particular field, trade, or business endeavor. *Career* defines the general nature of work that you see yourself prepared (or preparing yourself) to perform. *Career* serves as a frame of reference for the kinds of work you will seek, qualify for, and accept. It is also the context in which you will continue to develop new skills and insights. Ben Affleck's career is acting; he's had a number of jobs making specific movies. An airline mechanic may master her trade (career) through a combination of training and supervised work experiences and obtain employment (jobs) with various airlines throughout her career.

## Career And Self-Concept

From our earliest days, we get personality programming and career-image shaping messages from our families, cultures, and social environments. As we develop, we acquire an image of ourselves, a self-concept. Most of us are not even consciously aware that we possess one, but it's there, and it is very likely to be reflected in our behaviors and actions. The important point here is that we unconsciously seek jobs and pursue careers to match our inner self-image. For example, people who acquire self-images that are neat, well-organized, and good with numbers may seek careers as accountants or actuaries (these are the folks possessing statistical skills who do things like compute insurance rates and analyze how likely we are to have an accident if we own a small red sports car with a great big engine). Those who develop an intellectual's self-concept may pursue professions featuring rigorous mental concentration such as law, physics, or literary scholarship. Those who acquire a nurturer's self-view may track themselves toward career roles as social worker, nurse, or vocational rehabilitation therapist.

Unwitting career selection works well for some, but not for all. The problem is that our self-concept may evolve from an inaccurate understanding of our true nature. Some of us acquire self-limiting and handicapping concepts in the form of lack of self-confidence. From an early age, self-concepts begin developing in response to what we hear our parents and elders say about us, such as "Isn't she just the perfect little mother," or "He's just like his father" (when Father is a lawyer, or stone mason), or "He's going to be a super athlete," or "She's a mental wizard." When others make observations, either negative or positive, they influence the shaping of our youthful self-image.

A poor self-concept undermines your career development as well as your life satisfaction. Fortunately, we can change our self-concept over time and through conscious attention. By taking a more deliberate and systematic approach to determining your skills, personal traits, preferences, needs, and

Sunny studio/Shutterstock.com

values, you can bring your self-image into line with your true abilities and desires. You can also greatly enhance your self-confidence by knowing what you are particularly good at and what you can achieve with your talents and abilities. The payoff for generating an accurate self-concept can be tremendously gratifying. This kind of self-knowledge can guide you through appropriate employment and career changes, make you more resilient in dealing with life's challenges, and guide you in finding a sense of security within yourself, even in difficult times.

The observations of others can provide a wealth of information when taken in the right context. When people blindly follow the ideas that others have for their lives without taking into account any potential cultural, personal, or other biases, they run the risk of following careers that are not well suited for them. However, the opinions of others can give you clues about your personality, temperament, strengths, and talents that you may not naturally realize. Take a minute to reflect on the feedback you have been given from those you respect. Think of observations or suggestions that they have made and write them in the space below. For example, reflect on things your family has noticed about you. Perhaps they think that you are a great cook, good with little kids, skilled with technology, a talented speaker, a loyal friend… all of these will provide you with insights into potential careers. Bosses, teachers, and friends also have given you feedback. Before you move on, take a minute to quickly jot down these observations.

**Family:**

_____

_____

_____

**Teachers:**

_____

_____

_____

**Supervisors:**

_____

_____

_____

**Friends:**

_____

_____

_____

**Others:**

_____

_____

_____

## Positive Mental Imaging

Negative thinking undermines decision-making ability. Could you conceive of anyone performing successfully as a decision maker if his view of the world allowed him to see only mediocre and/or uninviting options? People able to see a future filled with interesting opportunities willingly invest in effective decision-making.

As you begin this decision-making process, we offer you a challenge. See if you can entertain a viewpoint that the future presents you with limitless possibility and that your opportunities now are greater than at any time in history. Try out the assumption that the future will present you with continual opportunities for such things as:

- discovering just how excellent you are capable of becoming;
- growing and developing in ways you've barely dared to dream about;
- making satisfying contributions;
- creating and operating your own business;
- working from your high-tech cottage on a mountaintop;
- becoming a cyberspace citizen of the world.

It may be worth noting here that there are many kinds of work that you would dislike and/or not perform very successfully. There are also many types of work that you would fully enjoy and in which you could thrive. The kind of work that fits us depends upon our uniqueness. We have different fingerprints and different interests. We are also uniquely talented. Fortunately, there are many different kinds of work available now, and there will be even more in the future.

## Career Decision-Making

In spite of the critically important role that career plays in life, most people slip into careers and their associated lifestyles with very little forethought or preparation. In fact, most of us spend more time selecting new clothes or a new car than we do in deciding upon our careers. Based on years of experience in assisting career seekers and job hunters, career planning specialist Richard Bolles concludes that most people choose their occupation absentmindedly, and make career decisions in haphazard fashion—without awareness that there are real alternatives from which to choose.[7]

Making a decision is required whenever we are faced with more than one alternative or confronted with unsettling circumstances. Whether we rationally or intuitively settle these questions or reach our conclusions consciously or unconsciously, we have made our decision. Many of us are afraid of decision-making. Actually, we're probably afraid of making a wrong choice or even one that's less than perfect. For these reasons, too many of us look for others to tell us what to do, while others of us master procrastination, and some of us even put off coming to a decision indefinitely.

Unfortunately, avoiding decisions does not result in eliminating risks or unwanted outcomes. At best, not making a decision results in keeping things the way they are, and at worst, we miss a window of opportunity to avoid an unpleasant result or set the stage for a good outcome. This is true even with everyday decisions. For example, if you stay at home on a Saturday evening because you can't decide

Rawpixel.com/Shutterstock.com

whether to go to the movies, see a play, go bowling, or visit a friend, the result is the same as deciding to stay at home. Incidentally, staying at home by choice feels much better than staying at home out of default because you couldn't make up your mind.

In a more serious vein, what are the consequences to people in jobs they hate (or an academic program that does not suit them) when they do nothing to change? The result of indecision is predictable. They are, in effect, deciding to stay with an unsatisfactory situation. By not deciding, you forfeit the opportunity of achieving a better outcome.[8] In a sense, you give up your control of the situation. Your performance, self-confidence, and attitude could suffer as a result.

## Steps to Career-Planning Success

Separating career/life planning into smaller steps makes the choice process less daunting. In this book, we use six steps. Each step of the way, you will be gaining knowledge to help you make decisions about your next life chapter and insight for goal setting.

**Step 1.** Identifying skills is accomplished by examining talents and competencies. App 2.1 shows how your skills are revealed through everyday activities you have performed well at home, in school, and in voluntary and paid jobs. You will also determine which of your strengths will best enable your career success.

**Step 2.** Clarifying personal preferences is accomplished by discovering your natural traits and interests to see which careers best match your style. App 2.2 helps you to do this by exploring your thinking style—the way you prefer to access information and use your mental gifts. App 2.4 explores your personality-related interest patterns. App 3.1 helps clarify your true needs and values—your "deep-core" motivators.

**Step 3.** Finding interesting options draws upon the self-knowledge acquired in the earlier steps to identify careers of potential interest. At this point, you will be compiling a master list of your better options. App Section 4.0 will show you how to discover and explore your occupational alternatives.

**Step 4.** Making a choice helps narrow down your alternatives and identify your best career selection. App 3.2 helps you evaluate these career alternatives in terms of your skills, preferences, and occupational outlook. *You may want to revisit this chapter several times in the years ahead as you are faced with critical new life and career choices.*

**Step 5.** Setting goals and making plans involve developing the specific goals and plans needed to translate your career decision into action steps. App 3.2 will also show how to design meaningful goals and plans for a career that will fit into the life you want to have.

**Step 6.** Implementing your career helps you turn goals and plans into reality. App 4.0 shows how to overcome barriers that can disrupt your best-laid plans. App 5.0 shows you how to develop an effective strategy for obtaining work related to your career goals.

After you have completed the steps (and even along the way), it is important that you review your decision. For the most part, this will occur after you have completed this book. As you go along, you will probably take small steps toward your career. Perhaps you decide to become a veterinarian. You start on the road to this career by taking a science class, you get a part-time job at a veterinarian's office so you can be exposed to the occupation, and you volunteer at the SPCA. After a few months, it is important to think about things. Use your discernment and listen to your inner voice. Honestly, look at your new experiences and the information you have gathered about yourself. This will help you know if you want to continue on or if you need to adjust your goals based on your new knowledge of work and of yourself. If you decide that this wasn't the best choice after all, then go back through the six steps and determine a better choice. Most people are afraid of making the wrong decision, so they either pick something and force themselves to live with the result (like it or not), or they don't pick anything and stay in their current situation. By reviewing the choices as we go, we allow ourselves the freedom to make slight adjustments or even major changes before too much time has been invested in the decision. The original veterinarian decision can be adjusted to a veterinary technician if we realize that we could be just as satisfied in this similar occupation with less time and money invested. Reviewing our decisions along the way helps us to have more control of the outcomes.

## Case Study   Noel

"I just don't know what colors to use for my holiday decorating," mused a recent client. Noel had come to the office for a follow-up career counseling session. Her counselor was not sure how this impacted her career goals, but they had an hour to spend together, so the conversation was allowed to play out. As she continued, Noel shared that she wanted to make her room look inviting and reflective of how she was—not a remake of a store. It was important for her to bring others into her space—and that her space reflects her taste and her moods. She laughed as she shared her quest for her "true holiday self"— from taking color quizzes (she is violet), to style quizzes (modern and traditional mix), to looking in magazines and online. Since she rejected using violet as her holiday color theme and had no idea what modern holiday style meant, she was stuck.

Some would have laughed at her dilemma and told her to just do what she always did and get on with it. But a keen listener would have realized that making others feel comfortable in her space was not only important, but also she was willing to invite others into her world. Not restricted to holiday decorating but all year long, she wanted to work and live in a place where she could be comfortable sharing herself with others while making them feel welcome and nurtured. It was important for her space to reflect her growing sense of herself. On the basis of this understanding, it was not a case to be dismissed but something to help her figure out. By figuring out this, it could give her insights into her career journey.

Is there an app for this? As of yet, there is no app that allows a person to put in a list of wants and out pops the solution to holiday decorating. But there are ways that you gather clues that can be used. Since she had already done some exploration, she was ready to make some decisions about the information she had gathered. With some help, she decided that the best way for her to narrow down her choices was to evaluate the information she had gathered and would be gathering.

She decided to do that by becoming aware of her thoughts and emotions regarding a possibility.

Armed with this, she went online and to the mall to see some of her ideas in real space. She noted her negative reactions to color and design—too traditional, too nontraditional, too religious, too bright, and too dark. She also noted the aspects that got her to take a second and third look—sparkling, natural, earthy, and common with a twist of the unexpected.

She returned for her next meeting armed with pictures and plans to give her room a feel of the mountains she remembered as a kid after a light snow fall but had a homemade feel. She happily shared of her plans to use pinecones and sparkling lights, browns and blues as colors, and a candle that reminded her of the mountain air.

How do you think Noel could apply her steps of making decorating decisions to her career decision-making? (Think about why holiday decorating was important to her and her process.)

What ideas do you get about your own personality or career process from her story?

PAUSE

## Change and Transitions

Difficult times are unavoidable. Nancy Schlossberg is a researcher and professor who studied adults in transition. She discovered that the people who were able to maintain a positive attitude regarding the transition and were able to gain control over the transition were those who came out the healthiest. She defines a transition as an event or nonevent that alters our lives.[9] Transitions can be things like going to college, changing jobs, getting a promotion, or moving to a new city. They can be negative things like the loss of a parent or a job. We can't avoid transitions no matter how much we'd like to. But the secret to dealing with the natural transitions in life is how much control we have over them. If we decide to take a job in a new city because it is a good professional opportunity, we have a lot of control over the transition. If, however, our company moves to a new city and we can either go or lose our jobs, then we may feel that we don't have a lot of control over the transition.

An unwelcome job dissolution announcement can be to a career what an unexpected terminal medical diagnosis is to a life—a devastating shock. But both kinds of notices can also serve as wake-up calls. In either case, denial tends to be the first predictable reaction, followed by anger and grief. A growing body of literature on this subject suggests that those who are able to move through these emotional stages and accept death's inevitability are able to let go of their attachments to the past and then move through life's final transition—often in an apparent state of bliss. In a similar manner, the death and dying of a lifestyle or career can awaken us to the inevitability of life-affirming change and transition.

While impending physical death signals an ending to the reality that we have known in this dimension, career death can actually awaken us to intriguing new possibilities and a rebirth experience in the here and now. Many who have gone through major career transitions report that their job loss was actually a blessing in disguise, as is suggested by this quote from one of our career-changing clients: "It forced me to reassess myself and discover new interests that have led me to work I like much better."

When you think about your career, how much control do you believe you have over the factors that will impact your career decisions? If you are in school or are thinking of going back to school, who will determine what your major will be? Do you believe that it is your choice, or are there family members or employers who are insisting that you select a specific career path? The more you own the decision and keep control over it, the better you will be able to select a path that is best for you.

We can't always avoid unexpected shocks such as losing a job, but we can be better prepared for change by viewing career decision-making as a continuing, lifelong process rather than as an occasional event. We can do this by integrating the two separate but intimately related universes: the evolving inner world of self and the rapidly changing outer world. The career development model in the below figure shows a relationship between the separate worlds. These two worlds have a simultaneous impact on our lives.

The figure below suggests that a variety of dynamic forces are always acting upon us as we pursue our careers. These forces are generated from both the outer and the inner worlds. A major change in either realm upsets a preexisting equilibrium and initiates an inner drive to regain a personal comfort zone. This process works much as thermostats that regulate room

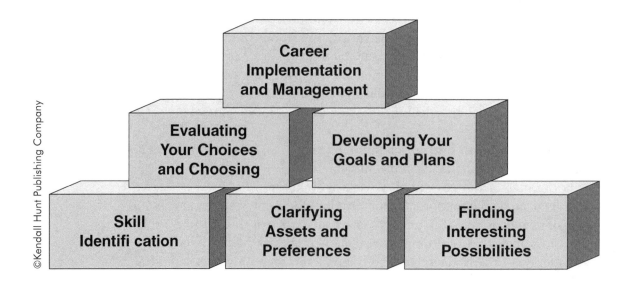

©Kendall Hunt Publishing Company

temperature. We all possess a thermostatic-like regulating mechanism that operates to keep our systems at a self-determined, albeit unconscious, comfort zone. When anything upsets this idiosyncratic setting, our system reacts by attempting to return things to normal.

With a job loss, emotional trauma is experienced not only from the actual loss of salary and benefits, but even more so from the perceived loss of status and sense of self-worth related to intangible factors such as job status, title, position, or organizational association. The reaction to such a traumatic event can rob us of hope and leave us not only frightened and reeling, but unsure of who we are or the meaning of our life and work. Concentrating our problem solving and decision-making solely on getting another job won't necessarily reestablish homeostasis, that is, return us to our old personal comfort zone. In terms of the career process model, such effort would make no more sense than merely repairing the body of a car damaged in a head-on collision without attending to the engine. When the world dramatically changes around us, we need to change ourselves in appropriate ways. An important aspect of this change must address the human engine—the self (see table below.)

A major change within the inner realm of the self (physical, psychological, and spiritual) can also upset the psyche's equilibrium and produce career ramifications. Dramatic and unforeseen changes, such as the loss of a dearly loved one or a traumatic deterioration in one's own health, are sure to disrupt an established sense of personal order. But there are other

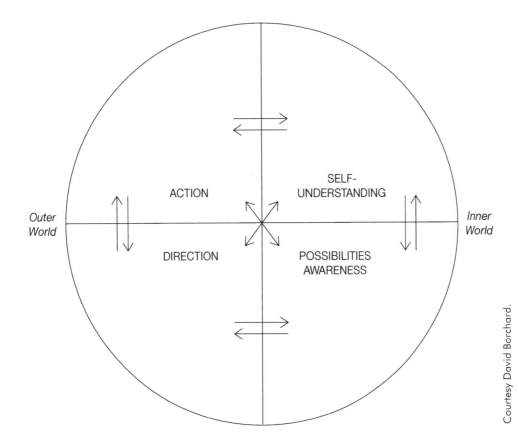

Courtesy David Borchard.

and less apparent dynamics that generate perplexities for the inner world—confrontations with one's aging, emotional burnout, personal meaning crises, personal values shifts, spiritual awakening, and existential angst, for example. Even those just beginning their careers struggle with understanding themselves, becoming independent from parents, and establishing themselves as adults.

**Ten Keys to Career Opportunity and Employability in the Current Marketplace**

1. Know yourself—your marketable talents, motivations, and assets.
2. Define yourself in value-added terms.
3. Have marketplace awareness—know where your assets and energies can contribute.
4. Be future intelligent.
5. Clarify your career field and become a visible performer.
6. Actively participate in a professional association.
7. Develop and maintain an active network in your field.
8. Have a professional development plan—invest in your future employability.
9. Become a career change and transition master.
10. Take responsibility for your career future through your daily decision-making.

The model shows that our attention continually moves from a focus in one quadrant to another as we respond to the dynamics of inner and outer forces. There is no sequential order to this process; we just might jump from any quadrant to another at any time. Expanding personal insight may lead us to ACTION, and some actions may force unpredictable SELF-UNDERSTANDING or create interesting new DIRECTIONS. New POSSIBILITIES may occur to us at any time—even in the shower, driving to work, or over a beer with a friend. It should be noted that we begin this cycle in our early formative years, with the evolution of our self-concept, and that there is no end to this process.

A career/life decision is one that has had a significant effect on your career and your life. In the spaces provided, list several of the most significant career/life choices you have made so far in your life. Examples include: early childhood memories (changing training wheels on bike, joining a youth choir, etc.), first work experience, summer job, selection of high school courses, decision to attend college, first job, job change, getting married, having children, leaving home, moving, joining the service.

Take time to think about this more in the APP ACTION that follows.

Complete **Your Career/Life Decisions** of the Past in App 1.3

 **Paula**

At the midpoint of what seemed to have been a secure career track, Paula's position as an accountant with a Washington, D.C., commercial real estate firm abruptly ended with a job-termination notice. Like thousands of others in the finance industry, Paula was the victim of a tidal wave of mergers, consolidations, and "right-sizings." Even though she had been successful as an accountant, she had never fully enjoyed this kind of work. However, since she was unsure what else might be better and because she was fully supporting herself with a nice salary and benefits, she had stayed with the job, giving little consideration to her future. But then, in her 40s, the job termination convinced her that the time had come for a major career change. She concluded that since seeking job security would be a blind alley anyway, she might as well invest the time and energy to discover what she really wanted to do.

Before receiving her job termination, Paula had been preoccupied with the outer-world dynamics of her career. Now, shocked by the unexpected job loss, she was forced into reassessing what to do next. In terms of the career development cycle, she was catapulted from the ACTION quadrant into the SELF-UNDERSTANDING quadrant. She could not go back to what she had; those kinds of positions were melting like old snow in warm spring showers. But after long tenure in one industry, she felt unprepared to deal with her major predicament—what did she want and what was available?

Paula decided to engage the services of both a professional therapist and a career counselor to obtain deeper self-awareness and to help clarify her personal interests and career possibilities. Her self-inquiry focused around questions such as: Who am I now? What do I truly value? What are my core personal assets? What do I really want? What new possibilities are available or could I create?

With new insights into these kinds of questions, she moved on to the POSSIBILITIES AWARENESS quadrant of the model. She began developing a lengthy list of options that would capitalize on her top talents and engage her strongest interests. We often encourage clients in this phase to develop 40 or more possibilities

without being too concerned about their practicalities. The most important thing here is to tap creative ideas, particularly those that connect with personal potentials and passions. The emphasis is on quantity rather than quality. The rationale for this is that you can't get to real quality without first generating powerful ideas. Such ideas tend to originate intuitively and creatively rather than deductively and analytically. Analysis is called for later in the decision-making process when the wheat (brilliant ideas) must be separated from the chaff (unworkable ideas).

Paula was able to choose a new career direction after exploring those she believed to be her best bets. Self-assessment helped uncover a creative bent (new awareness after concentrating on her analytical skills for so many years) in the form of love for art and aesthetic appreciation of old buildings. Through information interviews with people in the arts, architecture, and related fields, she discovered the historic preservation field and learned which colleges offer degrees in that specialty. She went on to obtain a bachelor of science degree at one of these colleges, doing so well that she opted then to continue on for a master's. When last heard from, she was preparing to work with an architectural firm in the business of restoring and regenerating deteriorated downtown centers of historical communities.

Paula recognized that this transition would probably not be her last. Yet in spite of the temporary nature of today's career situation, she has a sense of security that comes from preparation for the reality of the changing world in which she lives. She has a much clearer knowledge of who she is, what she wants in her life and career, and how to market her strengths. Although she doesn't know how long her current employment situation will last, she feels confident in her ability to market herself, get jobs, and create income-generating work as a consultant. She no longer intends to find job security with a Fortune 500 corporation but is much more content to work in smaller organizations where she can make a difference and have some fun in the process.

## Critical Issues and New Realities

Change in today's workplace is of such magnitude that the reality we once knew is undergoing radical alteration. Futurists refer to change of such magnitude as a *paradigm shift*. Paradigm shifts bring both negative and positive outcomes. The bad news is that little remains of our once relatively stable and predictable occupational world. The good news is that the new era has opened up unprecedented opportunities for just about everyone willing to take advantage of them. Doing so, however, necessitates creative decision-making and assertive transition management.

The current thinking is that average American workers will change careers eight to ten times during their work lives. This is up from the five to eight figures that had been used in the 1990s. Why the change? What is happening in the work-force that is causing this?

The Bureau of Labor Statistics tracks changes in the workforce through the use of experts who study industry, demographics, consumerism, and economics. Through the collection of data, they seek to make sense of the trends related to labor and then to make predictions about the future. The wise career changer will use these data in making career decisions. As previously stated, the way we work no longer comes in predictable patterns. Americans no longer work in an arena where they begin at the bottom and work their way up the corporate ladder. The pyramid picture of work is fading and the way to the top is often from outside, not from the bottom. Lateral career moves are typical. Many people actually leave one company and return at a higher level a few years later. Employers want to know: "What can you do for me?"

### Promoting Ourselves in the Marketplace

How do we prepare ourselves for a viable career? Futurists, such as career transition expert William Bridges, advocate that we begin thinking about ourselves careerwise as a personal business in which we offer specific products to those customers needing what we have to offer. Our product is the skills, knowledge, and personal assets that we possess.

No matter which work mode we choose to pursue in our work and career, we must undertake a number of career management tasks in order to maintain our employability. We need to stop thinking about ourselves and presenting ourselves by job labels. We should be able to clearly and comfortably define ourselves via our marketable attributes—our expertise, personal assets, knowledge, and viable experiences. We should also be able to define ourselves in terms of the value that we can add to potential employers. Value added can best be translated from our past achievements that demonstrate our transferable skills and point to our future potentials and capabilities.

We'll want to master the skill of presenting ourselves via the service we can offer and/or the knowledge and skills we have acquired and can demonstrate. It is important that we market ourselves on the basis of specific contributions we have made and demonstrate how these have translated into important and definable results, such as how we generated revenue, brought in new customers or retained old ones, enhanced quality of service, motivated people to work together more effectively, trained employees to use new technology, creatively solved significant problems, or produced new opportunities. Many have called this our *skills portfolio*. It will be critical that we show what we can do, not just where we obtained our degrees and where we have worked.

The set of skills you bring to the table is more important now than ever before. People are hired because of their ability to meet a current need. Whether this is a skill to be performed, an area of knowledge to be applied, or prior industry experience, people are hired to get the job done. Because of an emphasis on skills, it is easier to transfer from one career to another. Repackaging the skills learned in one occupation and moving them to another allows for career mobility. By staying current on industry trends, the savvy person is able to make timely moves. There are times when industry change is not predictable, but more often than not the signs are there long before the layoff notices come. It is almost impossible to find any career that has long-term stability. However, with an understanding of transferable skills and market trends, it is often possible to be prepared to make career moves ahead of market downturns.

**Marketplace Conditions**

With all of the information that is available, how does a career planner make a choice? It is important to note that there will always be some factors that are known and some that are unknown. The successful integration of your own personal career profile coupled with an intelligent gathering of information about work will yield a good career choice. In future sections, you will have the opportunity to integrate your self-awareness with your knowledge of the workplace.

There are a few ways to ingrate marketplace conditions into a career decision. The easy way is to simply listen to the advice from a teacher or older friend or relative without doing any research. The flip side is to do a lot of research without taking into consideration the wisdom of others in an industry or field. We will spend more on the second side a bit later.

Consider this scene from the 1967 classic movie, The Graduate, as we are told that the future is in plastics. In the beginning of the movie, Benjamin is at his house, attending a party his parents have thrown to honor his college graduation. A family friend offers seemingly sage advice.

| **Mr. McGuire:** | I want to say one word to you. Just one word. |
| **Benjamin:** | Yes, sir. |
| **Mr. McGuire:** | Are you listening? |
| **Benjamin:** | Yes, I am. |
| **Mr. McGuire:** | Plastics. |
| **Benjamin:** | Exactly how do you mean? |
| **Mr. McGuire:** | There's a great future in plastics. Think about it. Will you think about it? |

It is a classic scene and over 50 years later still resonates with us. Why? Because we have all been there. Advice for the future provided to someone at the beginning of their career from a seemingly wise elder.

Today, plastics could be replaced by healthcare or computers or big data. Students are encouraged to pursue the perceived growth industry of the moment.

Like a tip to buy a certain stock, it is often shared as a well-intended (if not wise) ticket to wealth and success.

But this brings up two very important points: 1. Success is an individual definition. For example, some families value the security of a paycheck over satisfaction regarding how the money is earned. This is often a dilemma for many students. How to balance the values of their families against their own career interests. What if he showed little to no aptitude for the plastic industry? What if Benjamin hated business management or production and really wanted a career helping people.  One thing he could do is not ignore the "future is in plastics" advice completely but consider how to apply his real skills and passions for helping people and work in the Human Resources department of a firm in the plastics industry.

Secondly, you have to have some interest or skill to make it work in any occupation. Using good data and advice as factors to find growing industries should not be ignored. However, if you have no passion (at best), or no aptitude (at worst), for a given field, then even if the industry consistently does not have enough talent to meet the need, you may simply not be employable. If you do manage to get a job, you may wind up miserable or even quickly fired.

As you research careers, remember that the easy way initially is to randomly select an occupation that is in high demand and ignore all of the other factors.

The workplace is continually changing. The need for labor is a direct result of the needs for goods and services. Remember the economic concept of supply and demand? The workplace corollary is: if consumers demand a certain product or service, this will drive up the need for workers related to the product. We can predict certain needs for products and services. For

Pressmaster/Shutterstock.com

example, the fact that baby-boomers are now retired or quickly approaching this stage indicates that there is  an increased need for all things related to aging, including healthcare, assisted living, and some areas of leisure.

At the same time, certain factors are impossible to predict. Interest in fad diets in the United States influences our choice of foods and thereby has a direct impact on food production. The current emphasis on diets that are low in carbohydrates drives food producers to meet the demand for products high in protein. Research informs us that a balanced diet and exercise will ultimately be the best alternative; diet fads will continue to influence eating habits and thereby influence food production, marketing, and pricing.

Technology changes are both predictable and unpredictable. Advances in technology lead to the growth of entire industries. Technology continue to be growing field. The implications are far reaching, including research and manufacturing areas. Changes in technology can create new products but can also result in other products becoming obsolete.

Consider the phone. The corner phone booth where Clark Kent turned into Superman is almost obsolete. For many households, phones no longer are anchored to walls. The fact is that for American households, the landline phone may become a thing of the past. In the first decade of the twenty-first century,  9 out of every 10 American households had a landline phone. Fast forward to today and it's just every second household. The Center of Disease Control and Prevention who track phone ownership across the nation shared this information in their biannual National Health Interview Survey. [9]

It is hard to predict what new product will sweep the country or even the globe, but it is safe to predict that changes in technology will continue to produce new opportunities.

The very way that consumers purchase products influences labor possibilities. It is hard to remember a time when eBay and Google were not a part of our vocabulary. TV and the Internet have not been the only changes in how consumers purchase products. Fickle consumers no longer purchase a product alone but purchase the experience. In fact, *experience purchasing* is giving rise to a whole industry of boutique products, from specialty coffee shops to clothing retailers. Successful career changers stay flexible and responsive to change.

National security will continue to be a major issue. Overnight an entire industry was created as we responded to an attack on our cities. But attacks and war are not predictable. Countless documents, publications, and Internet articles have been written about life in a post-9/11 era. It is impossible to predict what will happen in the future. Living with this uncertainty is a reality of today's worker. The needs that arise from living in turbulent times in and of themselves create unique opportunities for those seeking to begin or change careers.

Change in the marketplace is inevitable. Today, the global concern with the conservation of environmental resources has given rise to new industries, products, and even attitudes. The savvy career decision maker will take the external market factors into consideration but will not be defined by them. What is a major marketplace factor one day can be old news the next.

For those who fail to take advantage of opportunities for self-development and self-direction, the future may look dismal. Their best hope may be to hit the lottery big or to squeak into a cushy retirement. For those who recognize the available opportunities and are willing to take full advantage of them, the future has never been brighter. It is a perceptual difference! When we view the future through the eyes of fear, we become victims of our feelings. Seeing the promise of the future generates hope, energy, and enthusiasm. It's your choice!

## The Bureau of Labor Statistics

Understanding the current nature of work is important.

Perhaps two of the most misused factors in selecting a career are the concepts of workplace trends and occupational projections.

Ignored, quoted out of context, or taken as indisputable facts, the misuse of these factors have resulted in poor career choices for many people.

It is important to be informed. Armed with reliable information, a person can make a great decision about their future.

Sources of good information come from organizations with little to no agendas such as political leanings, interest in causes, or funding from sources which could benefit from certain findings. Start with the BLS.

The BLS is a traditionally nonpartisan government agency under the DOL. According to http://www.bls.gov/bls/infohome.htm, their mission is as follows: "The Bureau of Labor Statistics of the U.S. Department of Labor is the principal Federal agency responsible for measuring labor market activity, working conditions, and price changes in the economy. Its mission is to collect, analyze, and disseminate essential economic information to support public and private decision-making. As an independent statistical agency, BLS serves its diverse user communities by providing products and services that are objective, timely, accurate, and relevant."

The Bureau of Labor Statistics has provided essential economic information to support public and private decision-making since 1884. Yet, even this organization shares this caveat as part of their projections:

The BLS projections are focused on long-term structural trends of the economy and do not try to anticipate future business cycle activity. To meet this objective, specific assumptions are made about the labor force, macroeconomy, industry employment, and occupational employment. Critical to the production of these projections is the assumption of full employment for the economy in the projected year. Thus, the projections are not intended to be a forecast of what the future will be, but instead are a description of what would be expected to happen under these specific assumptions and circumstances. When these assumptions are not realized, actual values will differ from projections. Users of these data should not assume that the difference between projected changes in the labor force and in employment implies a labor shortage or surplus. The BLS projections assume labor market equilibrium, that is, one in which labor supply meets labor demand except for some level of frictional unemployment. In addition, the employment and labor force measures use different definitional and statistical concepts. For example, employment is a count of jobs, and one person may hold more than one job. Labor force is a count of people, and a person is counted only once regardless of how many jobs he or she holds.[10]

http://www.bls.gov/news.release/pdf/ecopro.pdf

This technical, legal sounding language essentially says: there are factors we simply cannot control.

Predictions based on solid research and data are to be considered as one of many factors. Successful career decision makers do not look once, but maintain an awareness of the future of a chosen industry or occupation. Economists remind us that changesd to industries are the result of many elements, some foreseeable, some suspected, and some which will catch the industry completely unaware. New inventions can revolutionize an industry—-decimating one part and strengthening another, war or civil unrest in a country can impact the availability of materials essential to the industry, social and political interests can impact funding and consumer behavior.

Complete **Your Career/Predictions** in App 1.3

## Attitudes About Work

How do you view the marketplace? How do you view work? For some, the uncertainties of the economy  provoke anxiety. These stress levels may undoubtedly be elevated by decades of conditioning to seek job security and avoid risk. Pursuing a personal passion may well be the best antidote to "new-age" stress.

In this regard, passion is directly related to energy and inversely related to stress. Unremitting stress robs us of energy, enthusiasm, and hope. These, conversely, are just the ingredients that our personal passions generate. Both stress and passion involve the imagination in anticipation of the future. Personal energy becomes directed, concentrated, and action-focused when we visualize ourselves achieving interesting goals. We motivate ourselves from the inside out—a highly self-empowering process. Stress, on the other hand, involves preoccupation with frightening possibilities, draining away energy into deceptive fantasies—a self-victimizing activity.

How do you measure your own attitudes about work? Are you stressed as you consider your skills against the backdrop of the external market factors, or do you view these market factors as being able to provide you with new opportunities (see figure below)?

Decades ago, an author named Studs Terkel wrote a book that told the stories of real people in real jobs. This book, designed to chronicle the lives of everyday Americans, became a snapshot of the culture of the day. In the opening words of his introduction, Turkel writes:

*This book, being about work, is, by its very nature, about violence—to the spirit as well as to the body. It is about ulcers as well as accidents, about shouting matches as well as fistfights, about nervous breakdowns as well as kicking the dog around. It is, above all (or beneath all), about daily humiliations. To survive the day is triumph enough for the walking wounded among the great many of us.*[11]

Wow! Not sure you can get more depressing than this. One might wonder if Mr. Terkel had it rough in the workplace. His bio says he graduated from acclaimed schools and held interesting jobs. He also came of age during very rough points in the American experience. How did this influence his view of career? Or did he simply find out that work was hard from the countless interviews with average citizens?

Terkel writes more in his introduction:

*It is about a search, too, for daily meaning as well as daily bread, for recognition as well as cash, for astonishment rather than torpor; in short, for a sort of life rather than a Monday through Friday sort of dying. Perhaps immortality, too, is part of the quest. To be remembered was the wish, spoken and unspoken, of the heroes and heroines of this book.*[12]

> Up to this point, how do you define work? Is it a job for survival, a paycheck, a means to an end? Or is work something that is fulfilling and enjoyable? Think about how you define paid work and your own perspectives. What did you think about work before? How might your thinking change as you read this book and go through these exercises? Before you go on, write some of your own thoughts here.
>
> **My current thoughts on work:**

## Writing Your Story

Your career is about YOU. Throughout this book, you will have the opportunity to gather information about you and the world of work. You will be taking a few assessments. These assessments are not designed to tell what you should be doing with your life, but to help you develop a language that you can use to explore your opportunities. The assessments should not put you in a box. They are intended to help you think outside of the box and open up your choices. In each chapter in the early part of the book, you will be able to gain an understanding of a different aspect of yourself. It is important that

What gives you meaning? What are you doing when you feel most alive? If you are in the stage of early adulthood, this might be a tough question to answer. Limited life experiences may not have yielded a lot of thought on this subject. Later in this book you will have the chance to do some accomplishment exercises. These exercises will allow you to think through the things, perhaps maybe even small things that will give you clues about the places where you will find energy. Before you go on, write some of your own thoughts to this here. Reflect on something you did recently that really energized you. Write a few sentences about that experience.

My current thoughts on work and an experience that energized me:

you remember that each chapter and the assessments in these chapters will give you information on a specific area and will help you understand how you might fit in with these areas. The assessments included in each chapter will take a measurement of how you respond to a specific set of questions on a specific day. Take this into consideration as you develop your career profile. If the results of one assessment seem out of step with all of the others, you may want to consider how you were feeling on the day you took the assessment. If you were feeling stressed out by the people around you, you may have selected answers that reflected a greater-than-usual desire to work alone. If tasks were stressing you out, this may have had an influence on your responses as well. The assessments are used to begin your self-discovery and not end it.

Many of the activities in the book are designed to get you to think deeper. Use them as a jumping-off point for your career exploration. What you will get out of the self-discovery sections depends on what you put into them. Take these exercises and assessments seriously, but think of them as getting you started in the process of being able to articulate your career dreams and goals.

During your self-exploration, expand your world. If some of the assessments are pointing in a specific direction, try it out. Use the citizen and leisurite roles to do some volunteering or take on a new hobby. You are probably thinking that you'd love to, but you don't have the time. Think of how you can incorporate these activities with things you already do. Get your friends to volunteer with you. Play basketball with the kids at the shelter instead of the guys at the gym. Take an accountant to lunch to learn more about the accounting profession. It is true that there are some skill and interest areas that are easier to try on than others, so you may need to be creative. Bounce ideas off others and get their input on how you can try out some of the ideas that will be presented in this book.

If you do engage in volunteer or other experiences as you are working through this book, by the time you get to the final chapters on job searching, not only will you know what you want to do but you will also have gained tangible experiences that you can write about on your resume and talk to employers about in an interview.

**Beginning the Journey**

If you are reading this book for a class, there is a good chance that you took the course because you were looking for some direction in your career decision. We are sure this book and your class will help. But as you begin, it is important that you relax. Let's get a few things straight before we move any further. Number 1: If Donald Super is correct (and we believe he is), then career is about a lot more than what we do for paid work. If you are looking for that total be-all, life is wonderful, total fulfillment sense from a job, and then perhaps you might want to manage those expectations. Some people have jobs that are pretty good most of the time. They are a good fit. They make sense for them. We hope that this will be you. But if you think that the job is going to be the only thing that will satisfy you—or you feel that you need to find a job that will satisfy 40 hours a week, 52 weeks a year— then perhaps it is time to take the pressure off. Paid work can be wonderful! It creates necessary structure for lives, income, and, in many cases, meaning and purpose as it uses our skills and passions. But, paid work does not do this always or completely. Sometimes, just sometimes, work is hard. Bosses are not encouraging, clients are demanding, the hours are long, and the pay is low.

But a career, when taken to mean the totality of all of the roles that we play, allows us to use many skills, explore many passions, and have multiple experiences that result in meaning and satisfaction. As you are working through the activities in this book that will lead to increased self-discovery and new knowledge about yourself and work, remember that it doesn't need to all happen in the arena of paid work. If you discover that you love being with little kids but don't really want to be a teacher, recognize that you can do some volunteering on the weekends that will enable you to act on this passion. Be creative!

So relax. Take the pressure off. In the coming weeks, you will undertake a journey of self-discovery that will enable you to write your own story, taking into consideration opportunities outside of paid work as well as paid work. You will find that you will see some naturally recurring patterns in your own life that will shape your story. As you enjoy the self-discovery and learning about all of the opportunities available to you, you will begin to see some patterns emerging. Patterns will help you shape and define your story. It may be a bit frustrating at times. It may even be a bit strange to be doing all of this self-focus in the beginning. But it is important. As you take the time to discover your interests, skills, abilities, values, thinking style, and decision-making style, you will uncover career opportunities that are a good fit for you. Enjoy the journey!

Does the idea of "having a career" bring a role model to mind for you? Perhaps your career role model is a parent, a spouse, or someone you greatly admire.

1. What individuals come to mind whose careers might serve as ideal role models for you?

2. In what ways do you identify with the individuals you listed in question 1?

Complete **Your Life and Work** in App 1.3

## Summary

Career is about more than just a job. It is about integrating many roles in a way that brings satisfaction and meaning to an individual. The focus of every chapter is the reader. The activities used throughout this book will impact, inspire, and at the very least inform decisions that need to be made regarding a career direction or a job selection. The readings and activities in the book are designed as a resource to uncover information that is necessary for learning about the world of work and discovering a career direction. Throughout this book, a new language will be learned that will lead to effective self-analysis, career research, and career decision-making. This book will provide the tools that are necessary to define goals and conduct an effective job search.

## Endnotes

**APP 1.2**

1. Jim Valvano. (n.d.). BrainyQuote.com. Retrieved March 10, 2017, from BrainyQuote.com Web site: https://www.brainyquote.com/quotes/quotes/j/jimvalvano358454.html.

2. Donald Super, "A Life-Span, Life-Space Approach to Career Development." In *Career Choice and Development*, D. Brown and L. Brooks, eds. (San Francisco: Jossey-Bass, 1990).

3. Gill Farnham and Ward McLean, *Listening Hearts: Discerning Call in Community* (Harrisburg, PA: Morehouse Publishing, 1991).

4. William Bridges, *Job Shift: How to Prosper in a Workplace Without Jobs* (Reading, MA: Addison-Wesley, 1994).

5. Jeremy Rifkin, *The End of Work* (New York: A Jeremy P. Tarcher, 1995).

6. William Bridges, *You & Co.: Learn to Think Like the CEO of Your Own Career* (Reading, MA: Addison-Wesley, 1997).

7. John C. Crystal and Richard N. Bolles, *Where Do I Go from Here with My Life?* (Berkeley, CA: Ten Speed Press, 1978).

8. Nancy Schlossberg, *Overwhelmed. Coping with Life's Ups and Downs* (Lexington, MA: Lexington Books, 1989).

9. Centers for Disease Control and Prevention, National Center for Health Statistics (December 2014) (n.d.).

10. Bureau of Labor Statistics, *News Release www.bls.gov/news.release/pdf/ecopro.*

11. Studs Terkel, *Working* (New York: Pantheon Books, 1974), p. xi.

12. Ibid, p. xi.

# APP 1.3 APP ACTIONS

## YOUR CAREER/LIFE ROLES

What life roles are you engaging in currently (i.e., child, student, worker, parent, partner, homemaker, citizen, leisurite)?

_____

_____

_____

What do you enjoy about these roles?

_____

_____

_____

How can you use these roles as places to gather information that would be helpful in making a career decision?

_____

_____

_____

Think about the life roles you anticipate playing (child, student, worker, parent, partner, homemaker, citizen, leisurite). How do you think these roles will blend together to help you create a satisfying career/life?

_____

_____

_____

## YOUR CAREER/LIFE DECISIONS OF THE PAST

A career/life decision is one that has had a significant effect on your career and your life. In the spaces provided, list several of the most significant career/life choices you have made so far in your life. Examples include: early childhood memories (changing training wheels on bike, joining a youth choir, etc.), first work experience, summer job, selection of high school courses, decision to attend college, first job, job change, getting married, having children, leaving home, moving, joining the service.

Start by listing the earliest decision you can recall and then record each subsequent major career/life choice in chronological order to the present time. Enter your decisions to the right of the numbers below, leaving the line to the left blank for now.

My Career/Life-Shaping Decisions of the Past and How I Made Them

_____ 1. _____

_____ 2. _____

_____ 3. _____

_____ 4. _____

_____ 5. _____

_____ 6. _____

_____ 7. _____

_____ 8. _____

_____ 9. _____

_____10. _____

Fill in the lines to the left of each decision above with the appropriate letter(s) from the following list:

  A. Took the safest way.

  B. Took the easiest way.

  C. Let someone else decide for me.

  D. Did what I thought others expected me to do.

  E. Did what I had been taught that I should do.

  F. Did the first thing that came to my mind.

  G. Did nothing.

  H. Chose what I felt was intuitively right.

  I. Consciously weighed all of the alternatives available and then chose the best one.

  J. Used some other approach. _____

_____

1. What did you learn about the way you have made your career/life decisions in the past?

_____

_____

_____

2. What effects have your past career/life choices had on your life? How do the outcomes of these decisions affect you now?

_____

_____

_____

3. Based what you learned about your past career/life decision-making style and the effect of these choices on your life, what changes would you like to make?

_____

_____

_____

## CAREER PREDICTIONS

Go to the BLS website (www.bls.gov)

Write three things you can learn about work from their site:

1. _____

2. _____

3. _____

**YOUR LIFE AND WORK**

1. If you were to write a novel of the story of your life to date:

    a.  What titles would you give to your major chapter headings? List several of them:

    _____

    _____

    _____

    b.  What do you see as the primary themes of your life story to date?

    _____

    _____

    _____

    c.  What title would you give to the novel of your life story to date?

    _____

    _____

    _____

    d.  What might the jacket cover of your life story novel look like? What are some of the things that might be on the jacket cover? Draw one; let your imagination run freely!

    _____

    _____

    _____

2. If you were to continue your life story into the future:

    a.  What are some themes you might elect to write into the continuation?

    _____

    _____

    _____

    b.  What are some possible titles you might elect for the next chapter of your life story?

    _____

    _____

    _____

    c.  What are some titles you might consider for Part II of your life story?

    _____

    _____

    _____

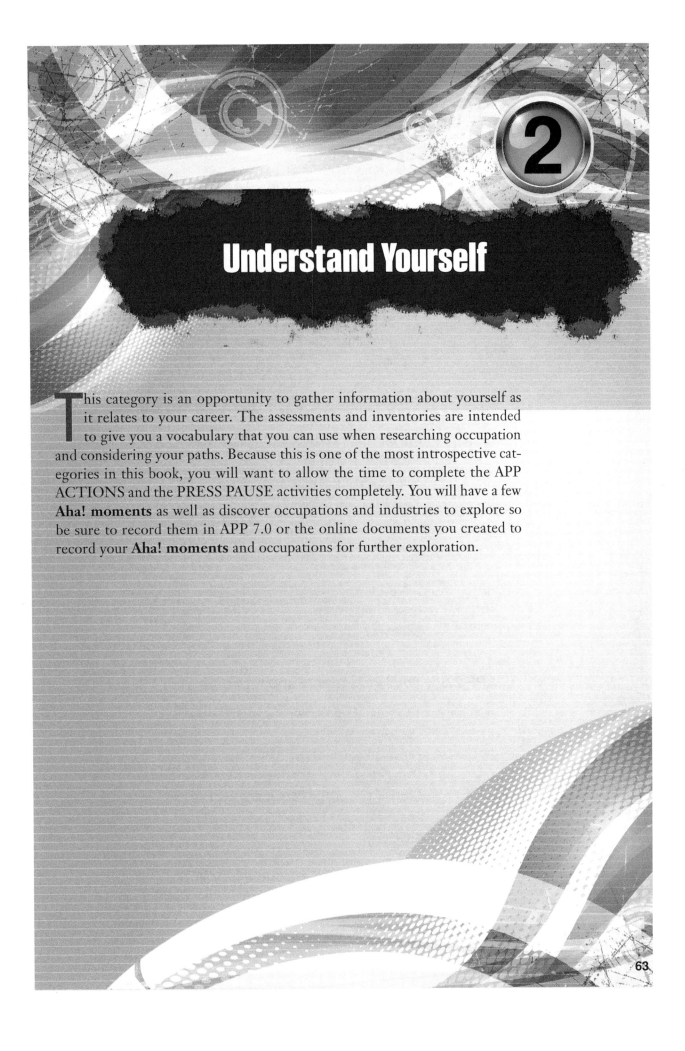

# Understand Yourself

This category is an opportunity to gather information about yourself as it relates to your career. The assessments and inventories are intended to give you a vocabulary that you can use when researching occupation and considering your paths. Because this is one of the most introspective categories in this book, you will want to allow the time to complete the APP ACTIONS and the PRESS PAUSE activities completely. You will have a few **Aha! moments** as well as discover occupations and industries to explore so be sure to record them in APP 7.0 or the online documents you created to record your **Aha! moments** and occupations for further exploration.

**APP 2.1**   **Your Skills Outline**

Abundant Skills
Types of Skills
Functional Skills
Value of Functional Skills
Everyone Has Functional Skills
O*NET
Using Your Skills to Choose a Career
The Relationship of Work To Data, People, and Things
Functional Skills Versus Self-Management Skills
Assessing Your Special Knowledge Skills
Distinguishing the Three Types of Skills
Summary

**APP 2.2**   **Your Thinking Style in Work and Learning**

Traditional Measures of Intelligence
Recent Research on the Brain
Our Two Minds Thinking Styles
Four Ways of Thinking
Whole-Brain Thinking
Your Thinking Style Profile
Case Study—Brad
Case Study—Michelle
Case Study—Joe
Summary

**APP 2.3**   **Your Personality and Interests**

Thinking Style Versus Personality Style
Opposites Attract
Personality and Career Choice
Case Study—Rose and the Scented Markers
Comparison of the Personality Types Chart
The Personality Hexagon
Summary

**APP 2.4**   **Connect Your Personality to Work**

Case Studies
Case Study—Helen
Case Study—Merrill

**APP 2.5     APP ACTIONS**

## APP 2.1 Your Skills in Action

### Do you know people who:

- Believe that they don't have skills?

- Aren't aware of whether they prefer working with data, people, or things?

- Feel that they have skills but don't realize how these can transfer from one job or career to another?

- Are reluctant to change careers because they feel they don't have the right skills for the new career?

- Have highly developed talents but have difficulty finding and keeping jobs?

*"But I don't have many skills . . ."*

*"I've only had unskilled jobs."*

*"I just graduated from high school."*

—anonymous students

If so, then you know people who share common misconceptions about their personal skills. The truth is that all of us have a great many skills, and we are all highly talented in our own ways.

### Abundant Skills

Although almost everyone is uniquely talented, most of us have only a vague awareness of what our skills really are. It's unlikely that we will realize our unique potentials unless we are clear about what skills we possess. Understanding our unique skills can help us choose a career or see how our skills might transfer from one field, occupation, or job to another.

Andison/Shutterstock.com

The word *skills*, as used here, refers to competencies or developed abilities needed to achieve a desired outcome or to make something happen. Skills are the foundation of all human achievement. Your skills continuously come into play in all your activities, from leisure to learning to work-related tasks, from routine actions to complex projects. It takes some blending of skills to do anything, even routine functions like talking, writing, walking the dog, taking out the garbage, or teaching your canary to talk.

As you study this APP and perform the various exercises, we encourage you to keep two important ideas in mind. The first is that you can acquire skills in almost any area you choose. The second is that because each of us possesses unique genetic endowments and life programming, some types of skills will be easier and much more enjoyable to develop than others. Therefore, we encourage you not to underestimate your ability to acquire whatever skills are needed for your career and education. We do recommend, however, that you pay special attention to your natural endowments or your preferred skills. These are the skills that are the most likely to be the keys to your success—the skills that you will be motivated to use and to develop. Take your preferred skills into account as you make your career and life goals. Look for ways to capitalize on them; they are your unique gifts.

## Types of Skills

Three types of *skills* are discussed in this APP: functional, self-management, and special knowledge. Functional skills are abilities or talents that are inherited at birth and developed through experience and learning. They are aptitude related and determine your proficiency with data, people, and things. Self-management skills are the behaviors you have developed in learning to cope with your environment and the people and conditions in it. Special knowledge skills are those having to do with mastering a specific body of information related to a particular type of work, profession, occupation, education, or leisure activity. Special knowledge skills are what you have learned and committed to memory. The table below provides examples of the three different types of skills.

## Functional Skills

Functional skills are natural abilities or talents that are acquired through heredity. Actually, you acquire the potential for certain types of abilities genetically. These potentials are then either developed through your life experiences or remain dormant. If, for example, you inherited an aptitude for analytical problem-solving, writing poetry, or persuading others, you may have developed this functional skill through school coursework and/or practical application. Then again, you may possess a real potential for these skills but just never developed them for one reason or another. Perhaps you neglected to exercise these potentials because your life circumstances hindered their development, or perhaps you accepted a prevailing myth that people like you (of your gender, race, nationality, etc.) aren't good at this kind of thing—for example, women aren't good at solving math problems or men aren't good at nurturing others. There is also the possibility that you may have inherited a limited potential for these specific aptitudes and are unlikely to develop them into highly proficient, functional skills no matter how diligently you apply yourself. The following relationships summarize these principles:

## Three Types of Skills

| Functional | Self-Management | Special Knowledge |
|---|---|---|
| Starting new ventures | Energetic | Financial planning |
| Negotiating contracts | Determined | Real estate brokering |
| Creating new services | Resourceful | Catering |
| Diagnosing interpersonal problems | Insightful | Group dynamics |
| Repairing machines | Dependable | Brake systems (on cars) |
| Calculating taxes | Ethical | Accounting |

| Coaching athletes | Enthusiastic | Basketball strategy |
| --- | --- | --- |
| Making decisions | Responsible | Career planning |
| Analyzing samples | Methodical | Chemical laboratory |
| Advising clients | Tactful | Divorce law |

*Potential plus development = Functional skill*
*Potential plus nondevelopment = Latent functional skill*

*Potential life barrier = Erroneous conclusion that you have no skill in this area*

*Lack of potential plus effort = Frustration (and perhaps a modest skill development)*

Having a functional skill means that you are able to perform some specific type of activity, action, or operation with a good deal of proficiency. Simply put, it means that you can do a specific thing well. To have a functional skill, one must first begin with the potential to develop a certain ability such as selling, shooting baskets, singing, solving complex mathematical problems, or envisioning how an object would look from many different perspectives. This potential must then be developed through experience, education, practice, play, and work.

Incidentally, functional skills are as likely to be developed in everyday activities as they are in the classroom. For example, do you remember the kid on your block who could sell anything, including his rusty old bike, to anyone, or the kid who could make the whole gang laugh anytime she wanted? These are examples of well-developed functional skills in the early formative stages of life. These people today still retain these abilities. The first kid may now be a very successful salesperson and the second a comedian (if they were astute enough to capitalize on their natural endowments). On the other hand, if they didn't, you might find them languishing around in a job and a lifestyle they hate. They may even think that they don't have much to offer and that life's not a whole lot of fun. If you were good at drawing as a child, you undoubtedly retain that potential today regardless of whether you have developed it into a well-used functional skill. If you were the leader of your neighborhood group as an adolescent, you have that same potential to lead today, whether or not you are currently practicing leadership or are even aware of that potential.

## Value of Functional Skills

Your functional skills are perhaps the most valuable assets you have in life. Youthful good looks are great, but they fade with age, while functional skills stay with you over a lifetime. Well-developed functional skills are truly more valuable than money. While money spent unwisely disappears quickly, functional skills actually increase through expenditure. And, even better, your functional skills represent the resources you need to earn money whenever you want. Beyond that, productively using your functional skills feels good. Both financial and psychological rewards are attainable to those who intelligently use their functional skills. One of life's greatest satisfactions comes from fully utilizing your talents toward personally meaningful ends.

And, conversely, one of the greatest causes of dissatisfaction in life is the realization that one's best talents are not being fully used and developed.

In today's world, there is a particularly compelling reason for knowing what our best functional skills are. The world around us is changing at a rapid pace. Most career specialists predict that in our rapidly changing world, younger workers may need or want to change jobs as often as every three to five years and undergo significant career changes every decade or so. In our unstable world, older workers also are not spared from the need to make job and career changes.

Your skills remain with you regardless of the job, occupation, or field in which you might be involved. As long as you know what your functional skills are, rapid change does not have to be a serious threat to you occupationally. If your job is phased out, you have the resources needed to make a successful job or career change because your functional skills are transferable. Your transferable skills allow you to move easily from one job to another where similar aptitudes are required. If you have been feeling trapped in a job that no longer energizes you, it may well be time to transport your transferable skills into a more challenging situation. In fact, when you know exactly what your functional skills are, it is even possible to make changes without extensive retraining.

Skill identification can help you clarify what you have to contribute to a particular type of work and provide clues for suggesting where to go with your career. If, for example, you realize that you are talented at communicating, establishing rapport, and advising others, you may want to explore people-oriented occupations such as teaching, counseling, nursing, or selling. Or let's say you know that you prefer hands-on activities with equipment, tools, or machines: you might consider a job in computer repair, medical technology, auto mechanics, or electrical engineering.

## Everyone Has Functional Skills

Perhaps you've said to yourself, "Well, I don't have many skills." If so, you are not alone in this misconception. People often visit career counselors feeling depressed and lamenting their lack of skills. These blues quickly vanish when they discover how traits or accomplishments they have taken for granted point to valuable skills. Experienced career planning specialists such as Richard Bolles and the late John Crystal, through years of experience, have observed that people completing a thorough skills identification process discover 200–500 or more skills.[1]

The problem is not that you lack skills. Instead, you have so many individual skills that it's probably hard to recognize them. You also might not recognize them because you have used them so long and so well that they have become automatic and unconscious. Or you might discount your skills, erroneously assuming that anyone can perform those things that you can do well. Functional skills are a bit like icebergs in that the greater portion of them lie hidden below the surface of our everyday awareness. Even people who recognize their basic skills are often amazed to discover just how many specific skills the functional skills identification process can reveal.

GIRL/Shutterstock.com

Because people usually enjoy activities that they perform well, your first exercise involves recalling activities that gave you positive feelings. These feelings may come from within and/or may come from other people's favorable responses.

PAUSE

Reflect on the following questions, writing your responses in the spaces provided. Write whatever comes to your mind instead of trying to narrow your responses.

1. What compliments or other positive feedback have you received for particular activities? (Examples: praise for organizing your art club's successful fundraising activity, compliments on the wood cabinet you designed and built.) Positive feedback may be as simple as a smile or as significant as a meritorious pay increase. Write down at least five different compliments, briefly explaining the situation.

2. When have you felt the most alive and energetic? List at least five specific situations. (Examples: jogging two miles daily, planning and preparing food and decorations for a dinner party, building a model airplane, thinking of ways to improve store displays at your first job.)

3. When have you felt the most confident and capable? List at least five situations. (Examples: giving a presentation and getting rave reviews, getting an "A" on a major exam in your toughest subject, having someone ask for your ideas/advice about carpentry work.)

4. What are you discovering about yourself? Are there any similarities in your responses? Make some notes here to help you remember your thoughts.

5. Review your responses to Questions 1 through 4. What skills do you think you used in these various examples? List at least 10 of them in the space provided. You may want to ask a friend or family member to listen as you describe some of the things you have listed and see if they can help you find skills or abilities that you used.

Few people have researched talent development more before than Donald O. Clifton. In his best seller book on strengths he writes, "There is one sure way to identify your greatest potential for strength: Step back and watch yourself for a while. Try an activity and see how quickly you pick it up, how quickly you skip steps in the learning and add twists and kinks you haven't been taught yet. See whether you become absorbed in the activity to such an extent that you lose track of time. If none of these has happened after a couple of months, try another activity and watch—and another. Over time your dominant talents will reveal themselves, and you can start to refine them into a powerful strength." (Donald O. Clifton, Now, Discover Your Strengths)

One of the ways to observe own skills is through the achievement exercise in APP 2.5. Another way is to be aware of the things you are doing through the day. The things you take for granted such as writing or researching or listening to others or tracking your spending are all skills you might want to consider using in your career.

Complete **Achievement Stories** in App 2.5

As you were writing down responses for the Achievement Stories APP ACTION, did you notice that various action words described your skills? If these words reveal your involvement in accomplishing something or making something happen, they are directly describing a functional skill you possess. Maybe you *organized* a team, *composed* correspondence, *operated* equipment, *balanced* a ledger, *prepared* a speech, or *repaired* a radio. These kinds of skills are called functional skills because you can apply them (make them function in) to various situations.

Your paragraphs may also contain words that suggest other types of skills, those that describe your behavioral traits. Descriptive words like *neat, punctual, curious, easygoing, good judgment, honest, resourceful, self-confident, reliable,* and *decisive* reveal your self-management skills.

What functional skills did you use most often?

Do you think this will impact your career choice? Explain.

dizain/Shutterstock.com

**ACTION**

Complete **Identifying Skills from Your Accomplishments** in App 2.5

## O*NET

You may have previously used library references, such as the Guide to Occupational Exploration (GOE) and the Dictionary of Occupational Titles (DOT) to explore careers. Now, however, these references have been replaced by a dynamic and useful online program called O*NET. The O*NET Online can be found at http://www.onetonline.org/. This site will be helpful in exploring career options with regard to the skills, knowledge, and abilities needed in the job, educational requirements, relevant occupations, and tips and links to help you find the right career activities for your interests and skills.

According to the O*NET site, you can use this tool to find occupations by browsing career clusters, industries, job families, and O*Net descriptors. The skills search section will allow you to explore careers based on skill sets similar to yours, and locate occupations by comparing them to other occupational classification systems. As you progress through this course, you will want to return to O*NET often to learn about careers and to identify other options.

## Using Your Skills to Choose a Career

Look at the results from the skills assessment APP ACTION. How does ranking your top skills get you any closer to making a career decision? Knowing your preferred skills gives you a starting point from which to begin identifying career options suited to your unique blend of skills. The task is to learn what kinds of careers and what particular jobs require your combination of preferred skills. It is also useful to be aware of your least preferred skills, or poorest skills, so that you stay away from career options where these types of skills would be used.

Researching also means asking people (e.g., neighbors, relatives, friends, classmates) for their ideas and advice about careers requiring your particular skills. Often a casual conversation can uncover an exciting option that you would not have considered or known about.

## The Relationship of Work to Data, People, and Things

Bell/Shutterstock.com

## Functional Skills Versus Self-Management Skills

Self-management skills are your specific behavior responses or character traits. They describe the way in which you manage yourself and relate to others. Along with functional skills, self-management skills are important components of what people have to contribute in the world of work. Of the two, self-management skills are more widely recognized because they are often easier to observe and identify in work settings. Functional skills, however, are more basic to the actual performance of work tasks.

Knowing your specific functional skills can help you determine how qualified you are to perform the actual tasks of a particular job. Being clear about your self-management skills can suggest how adaptable you would be to the working conditions of a specific job.

### The Importance of Self-Management Skills

According to John Crystal, functional skills are usually the personal attributes that get us hired, and self-management skills are those that get us fired.[3] This

yod67/Shutterstock.com

is true, of course, only when our self-management skills do not fit well with the conditions associated with a particular work setting. For example, the artist's or creative thinker's emotional self-expression and spontaneity might cause conflicts in a business office where working conditions involve highly structured activities, orderly task performance, and an emotional climate of relative calm. It is important, therefore, to really understand your self-management skills and assess how well they might fit with a particular job or work situation that you might be considering.

PAUSE

**Think about the kinds of careers that might be associated with your preferred skills. Make a note of a few careers that immediately come to mind.**

**Consider those careers associated with our least preferred skills. Are there any careers that you think to avoid? List them.**

**What do you think is the major difference between these two lists?**

The importance of self-management skills for job survival can clearly be seen from glancing at any supervisory evaluation form. The majority of evaluation criteria measure self-management skills. Self-management skills that many employers or supervisors particularly value include initiative, resourcefulness, cooperation, dependability, flexibility, and loyalty. A deficiency in one or more of these skill areas will probably cause poor performance evaluations. Consistently low periodic evaluations can lead to a failure to be promoted, a demotion, or even an outright dismissal by an employer.

Self-management skills alone will not qualify you for any positions, except possibly the lower-skill-level jobs. Usually, people qualify for certain jobs or occupations primarily because they possess certain required functional skills, special knowledge, and have relevant work experience. However, in addition to reviewing your written qualifications, a prospective employer or employer's representative will interview you. This interview or series of interviews allows you to display self-management skills to your advantage. Your self-management skills or deficiencies are also important aspects of references from former employers or associates. If the self-management skills you display and your employment references emphasized are particularly or even more qualified candidates. Conversely, just one serious self-management deficiency can knock you out of the running. For example, an employer who is seeking a counselor generally requires the functional skills of listening and speaking effectively, sensitivity to others' emotional needs, and ability to analyze an individual's practical needs and offer appropriate advice. Job applicants who, in addition, display complementary self-management skills such as friendliness, sincerity, warm humor, and cheerfulness will have an edge on their competition, all other qualifications being equal. Notice that in people-oriented occupations, self-management skills are often part of the actual job requirements. In other words, they overlap with functional skills in some careers.

Here's another real-life example to stress just how important it is to match the unique blend of an individual's skills to what's required for a job. To function effectively as a public relations (PR) manager, you would need to possess a number of skills, including the functional skills of creative writing and public speaking and the self-management skills of gregariousness, tact, and flexibility. We know of an individual who was hired as a PR manager at a fairly large organization because of her excellent knowledge of PR work, her impressive functional skills, and the self-management skills she demonstrated competently during the interview process. What the hiring process could not reveal, however, was an inability on her part to work compatibly and cooperatively with her staff and associates. On the job, she turned out to be a disaster. She was constantly squabbling with someone over minor issues that any effective PR manager should have easily been able to handle. After putting up with her poor self-management skills for about a year, the organization was eventually forced to fire this talented and hardworking woman. In retrospect, she should have either recognized this self-management deficiency and corrected it or obtained a job where she could have put her best skills to productive use in a setting where getting along with staff and peers was not a critical requirement of the job.

## Observing Self-Management Skills

Self-management skills are the first skills that an employer can observe when initially meeting job applicants in face-to-face interviews. Imagine, for example, that you are a job seeker and have arranged an interview with a potential employer. Following are some of the opportunities that an employer has to observe your self-management skills.

You have arranged your appointment at 9 A.M., but you arrive at 8:45 A.M. The potential employer already has learned something about your *punctuality*, *dependability*, and, perhaps, *eagerness*.

Upon greeting the interviewer you step forward *confidently* and greet the person *warmly*, at the same time expressing your *enthusiasm* at this opportunity

jesadaphorn/Shutterstock.com

to convince the interviewer of your potential worth to the organization. You have taken care that your *dress* and *grooming* are neat and appropriate for the occasion. In addition, you have taken the *initiative* to research carefully the potential employer's company or organization and have used your *resourcefulness* to identify a special problem within that organization that you feel capable of resolving. All these actions can be planned to convey to the prospective employer your interest in and suitability for the position.

Thus, in the course of perhaps an hour's interview, you have demonstrated to this prospective employer a number of self-management skills. (The *italicized* words in the previous paragraphs are self-management skill words.)

Not all self-management skills are so readily observable in an interview situation. Some, such as *loyalty*, *reliability*, and *resilience*, can be assessed only after a substantial period of time on the job. Because they are so personal, most people have trouble accurately assessing their self-management skills. It is particularly difficult to evaluate self-management deficiencies without being defensive when they are associated with negative or painful experiences. Rely on other people's observations to learn more about your self-management skills, but always look for consistent observations. Get feedback from a variety of people or at least from the types of people likely to be your employers or coworkers.

**ACTION**    Complete **Identifying Your Self-Management Skills** in App 2.5

## Relating Self-Management Skills to Work Settings

Some self-management skills are advantageous in almost any work setting. For instance, cheerfulness, cooperation, enthusiasm, friendliness, good judgment, honesty, kindness, and sincerity are universally appreciated attributes. It is possible, however, for some positive self-management skills to be inappropriate or misunderstood in some kinds of job situations. For example, although cheerful, joking behavior by an employee could be taken as a lack of sensitivity in the office of a funeral director, a very serious and sober demeanor in a counselor might be considered cold and unresponsive in a therapy center. Different work settings require different combinations of self-management skills. For instance, assertiveness, adventurousness, ambition, enthusiasm, and dynamism are important skills for salespeople to possess. Concentration, astuteness, curiosity, deliberateness, and precision are traits more likely to be found in the work setting of engineers or researchers. Knowledge of your unique combination of self-management skills can help you reach an appropriate career decision.

## Assessing Your Special Knowledge Skills

We all have acquired mastery of certain kinds of knowledge over the years. Perhaps you are acquainted with someone who knows a lot about certain kinds of sports such as football or tennis (special knowledge) even though that person may or may not be able to play them well (functional skills). As you begin identifying your list of possible career options, it's a good idea to take stock of your favorite special knowledge to see how important it might be to pursue a career that would enable you to apply a favorite body of knowledge.

One career changer, for example, had developed a great deal of knowledge about art and also about marketing (special knowledge), was good at selling (functional skill), and had a strong love of art (strong personal interest). He realized, however, that he was not an artist himself. After carefully considering his interests and assets, he decided to pursue a career as an art merchandiser. He is now making a very nice living as an art consultant for organizations looking to enhance the aesthetic appeal of their business offices. His role is to help his clients identify what kind of art would enhance a particular work setting and then negotiate with artists to purchase or obtain on consignment the needed artwork. As you can see, this individual was clever at seeing how to capitalize on his assets and interests. You too may be able to discover clever ways of combining your unique assets in a career in which you can earn a good living.

The Discovering Your Special Knowledge APP ACTION will help you identify the special knowledge you have acquired over the years and to determine if there are any particular knowledge areas that you might wish to pursue in your career. If you are just starting out on your career journey, you may find you haven't had the opportunities to acquire substantial bodies of special knowledge. However, we recommend that you give the exercise a try regardless of your career and life stage, for you could discover an important piece of self-knowledge that might suggest a career path for you when considered with the other assessment data you will be acquiring. As you do this exercise, it can be useful to survey the entire spectrum of your life's history in search of special knowledge skills. Perhaps you will find a clue from childhood that will help put you on the road to a new career. We know of one person, for instance, who loved sports as a child. He played football, watched every football game he could find, and was an expert in professional football. Even though he wasn't talented enough to play at college, he still followed the game and continued to learn everything he could. He is now working for a professional football team in their public relations department. He is able to use his special knowledge and is very happy and successful in his job.

Still stumped? If you're struggling to come up with a list of special knowledge skills, try going to one of the major online job banks, and search for job descriptions that may represent work, leisure, intern, volunteer, or other activities in which you have engaged during your life. Next, review the jobs and see if you can cull skills from the job descriptions. As for identifying knowledge gained through learning, try going onto your school's website and searching for descriptions of previous courses you have taken.

## Distinguishing the Three Types of Skills

|  | Functional Skills | Self-Management | Special Knowledge |
|---|---|---|---|
| How they are acquired | As natural talents or aptitudes we possess from birth | As basic abilities we learn by relating to significant people early in our develop-ment; acquired later in life only through great effort | Learning |
| How they develop | Through practice and further refinement at any time in our lives | Through responses we make to the con-ditions imposed on us by significant people (parents, peers, etc.) and social institutions (schools, church, etc.) | Repetition and memory |
| What they are related to | People, data, and things | Life environments (family, school, work) and their conditions that force us to adapt | Specific work situations |

Complete **Discovering Your Special Knowledge** in App 2.5

## Summary

Everyone has unique talents and skills. Our skills can be categorized into three groups—functional, self-management, and special knowledge. Functional skills are aptitude-related and are transferable from one job, career, or profession to another. Your abilities to work with data, people, and things are defined by your functional skills. By identifying your top functional skills and by knowing your preference for working with data, people, and things, you can both discover and then effectively communicate what you have to contribute to a job or a career. Self-management skills relate to how we cope with or relate to people, conditions, and situations in our world, including our work. Our special knowledge skills are what we have learned and what we know.

Knowing what level of skills you possess and prefer is helpful in understanding yourself and identifying suitable career options. The more you know about your skills, the better the decisions you can make in your career, educational, and job choices. In this regard, the more you know about yourself, the better you can capitalize on your unique assets as a person and prevent your shortcomings from becoming major obstacles.

## Endnotes

**APP 2.1**

1. John C. Crystal and Richard N. Bolles, *Where Do I Go from Here with My Life?* (Berkeley, CA: Ten Speed Press, 1978), p. 70.

2. Adapted from Richard N. Bolles, *The Three Boxes of Life and How to Get Out of Them* (Berkeley, CA: Ten Speed Press, 1978), p. 146.

3. John C. Crystal, Career Planning Workshop, Prince George's Community College, Largo, Maryland, Spring, 1979.

1. **Think back to some of the jobs you've had in the past (volunteer or paying jobs) and answer the following questions:**

   a. **What were some conditions of the work environments to which you were required to adapt?**

   b. **Were your self-management skills compatible with the conditions of the work environments?**

   c. **If they were not compatible, did that incompatibility contribute to your quitting or leaving?**

   d. **If they were not compatible but you stayed on the job, what adjustments did you make in order to be more compatible?**

Complete the **Informational Interviewing Action** in App 2.5

## APP 2.2 Your Thinking Style in Work and Learning

### Do you know people who:

*How we think influences how we communicate, solve problems, deal with relationships and make decisions.*

—Ned Herrmann

- Excel at analyzing facts and coming to logical conclusions?
- Think best when thinking aloud while interacting with others?
- Are always coming up with unique ideas and new ways of doing things?
- Are sticklers for the details and are practical problem solvers?

If so, you know people who process information and experience the world in different ways because they have developed different styles of thinking.

### Traditional Measures of Intelligence

What is your IQ? Do you think of yourself as a genius, highly intelligent, about average, or not too smart? Most of us acquire a sense of how bright we are in our early years and then spend the rest of our lives performing up to (or down to) our conceived potentials. Your concept of your abilities probably came from early interactions with significant people like parents, family, teachers, and friends. It's a rare individual indeed who derives a concept of his or her mental prowess on a highly accurate assessment of true potential.

Once acquired, your intellectual concept may change or be reinforced somewhat through various experiences such as accomplishments, feedback from people whose opinion you respect, and perhaps from IQ tests. The problem with IQ and achievement tests, such as the SAT and ACTs, however, is that although they are generally accepted as objective measures of intelligence, the results are unlikely to be true indicators of your real capability. At best, according to Daniel Goldman, author of the best-selling book *Emotional Intelligence*, "IQ contributes about 20% to the factors that determine life success, which leaves 80% to other forces."[1]

IQ scores probably are not the truest measure of human potential. While a high IQ score probably contributes to a positive self-concept and bolsters self-confidence, it is not a guarantee of life success. It's not uncommon to hear of individuals who are considered to possess moderate or even low general intelligence to be gifted in other ways. Clearly, there is far more than an IQ score involved in the quality of life and personal success. In fact, no one really knows what an IQ actually is. Mind power may be a better way of conceptualizing human capability. The key to developing your potential and functioning at your best lies in your self-concept and the ways you learn how to use, develop, and apply your mind power. There is reason to believe that most of us use and develop only a small portion of our mind power capabilities. Unless one's brain is either physically impaired or irreparably damaged psychologically, just about everybody

donskarpo/Shutterstock.com

has the capacity for accomplishment far beyond what any paper-and-pencil assessment could possibly predict. Think of the loss our world would have experienced had SATs existed in Mozart's day and his score had reported he was incapable of achieving much of anything, or if an ACT test had prevented Joan of Arc from entering into a leadership position, as delighted as the Brits might have been about that outcome.

What does any of this have to do with life/work planning? A great deal, we believe. For one thing, the better you come to understand your mental strengths, the more fully you can develop and apply your best personal attributes. Peter Drucker, world-famous organizational development consultant, advises that you are going to be more successful focusing your career development upon your strengths than by working to develop your weaknesses.[2] It is important, of course, to be aware of your personal weaknesses because they can undermine your success if not understood and managed. There is only one way, however, to become and perform at your best, and that is by knowing and growing your strengths. If you want to put your best abilities to use, it's important to determine how your mind performs at its natural best and to choose the kind of work and lifestyle that plays to your smart zone. The content and exercises in this APP are designed to help you do just that.

**Words of Wisdom**

*Effective thinking and intellectual success are held prisoner by negative expectations. Open your mind and let out your full human potential.*

### Influences on Your Thinking

Have you ever wondered where your thoughts, impressions, and ideas come from? Here's a test. Become aware right now of what you are thinking and then see if you can locate the source of that thought. You may conclude that your thinking originates in the brain in a conscious process, described by scientists in terms of neural interactions involving bio-chemically generated activity with synapses and axons. But what is it in your brain that causes you to think the way you do and to have the thoughts you do? Is there a little genie located somewhere amongst the brain cells operating our thinking controls in Wizard-of-Oz-like fashion? Fascinating as that may be, we shall leave the deep exploration of that subject to the realm of philosophers and brain researchers. But for purposes of life and work planning, there are three thought-generating processes with which we are primarily concerned, because they can influence our decision-making positively or negatively. One of these thought-shaping influences comes from our primary needs and strongest values. In this regard, it's worth noting  that the needs and values you hold today are likely to change considerably in the years ahead and that we tend to make decisions based on what's motivating us today. It is important, therefore, to get really clear about your needs and values, but you wouldn't want to make decisions about your future solely on these ephemeral and subjective influences. For this reason we will spend some time with needs and values in APP titled *Discovering What Motivates You*, and on another key source of input in future-impacting decisions, your deep-seated interests, to be considered in the following APPs.

Another powerful influence upon thinking, behavior, and decision-making comes from our attitudes. An attitude is a mind-set that conditions our views of things. We all have attitudes, always have and always will. Some come in the form of temporary mood swings affected by what's happening in our lives here and now, but others are patterned ways of thinking that provide a mental framework through which we see the world. What's your general frame of mind? Are you more of an optimist or a pessimist in your thinking? Or do you get cagey with your response to that question and refer to your way of seeing the world as a cautious optimist, an idealist, a realist, or pragmatist (as if one were actually able to perceive the world totally objectively without the filters of our conditioned values and biases)? Keep in mind that optimism seems to correlate better to success and satisfaction in life and work than do negative attitudes. Negative attitudes make some people passive (those are the ones waiting for the world to come knocking on their door) and cause others to become discouraged and give up their higher aspirations (they become the ones who spend later years in a state of "wishing they had _____"). If you

Marie Maerz/Shutterstock.com

have a choice in the matter, and you probably do, choose optimism as your general state of mind; it just seems to work best in most situations. Of course, if you are a successful pessimist, enjoy being that way, and have some identity based on that stance, then, by all means, carry-on, but do find a niche where hard-edged criticalness serves you and others well. The topic of mind-set will be addressed fully in APP 4.0, *Empowering Yourself to Succeed*.

### Thinking Beyond the Box

Effective thinking, mental development, and personal success can be undermined by negative expectations. You are far more likely to become your unique and successful best when proceeding from positive expectations grounded in a strong self-concept. The world needs you at your best, so unshackle yourself from any negativity that might be standing in the way of fulfilling your personal greatness, no matter if that may be as an astrophysicist, a soccer dad, a ping-pong champion, or whatever.

The third influence on how you perceive, think, feel, learn, and make decisions is the feature subject of this category; we are talking about thinking styles. Simply defined, your thinking style is the general approach you prefer in seeking to understand information or experience. This APP is designed to help you to determine and understand your own primary thinking and learning style. You will want to choose a career direction that capitalizes on your particular style of thinking. Doing that will enable you to perform with greater ease, joy, and proficiency than someone of equal or higher IQ whose thinking style is a mismatch to the job.

## Recent Research on the Brain

Researchers like Roger Sperry, Nobel Prize winner, and his associates studying "the split brain" and Carl Pribram's studies on the holographic brain have produced startling new insights into how the human brain works. Harvard psychologist Howard Gardner's research suggests that human intelligence is far broader than the simple verbal, linear, and sequential activities measured by IQ tests.[3] Another Harvard psychologist, Robert Rosenthal, an expert on empathy, has shown that when people administering IQ tests treat their subjects warmly, the test scores are higher.[4] Educational researchers are applying their research discoveries to enhance learning. Bulgarian psychotherapist, Gregory Lozonov, for example, has demonstrated new learning approaches involving "whole-brain" activities that accelerate learning performance and tap into little-used creative abilities.

Research-based discoveries about the human brain indicate that we all don't use or access our brains in the same way, and therefore we all don't think or learn alike. We all seem to acquire "favorite" ways of thinking. Our individual ways of thinking do, however, seem to be classifiable into a few characteristic styles of thinking. Howard Gardner, for example, has identified seven different styles of thinking. Ned Herrmann's model of thinking styles is particularly useful in predicting what kinds of work activities best fit the various style preferences. The *Herrmann Brain Dominance Survey* assesses an individual's preference for four different styles of thinking. The exercises in this APP are adapted from Herrmann's work.[5]

## Our Two Minds

In a way we seem to have two brains—one that specializes in objective thought and the other in subjective feeling. As a result of the past several decades of brain research, we now know that the two hemispheres of the human brain tend to specialize in different styles of thinking. In general, the left brain specializes in a logical, linear, analytical mode of thinking that is best suited to activities such as fact finding, analyzing data, mathematical computation, and performing technical and procedural tasks. The left brain is often considered to be the seat of objective, dispassionate, and computer-like thought processes.

## Our Two Minds: Thinking Styles

The right brain is the realm of nonlinear, holistic, spontaneous, and emotional thinking. This is the kind of mental process best suited to creative expression and

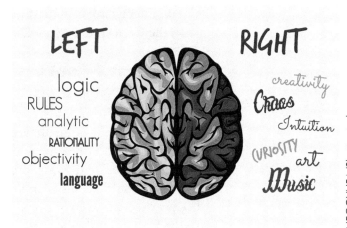

NEGOVURA/Shutterstock.com

in relating to others with empathic warmth and intuitive understanding. The right brain is considered to be the center of feelings, subjective thought, mysticism, and "heartfelt" spirituality. It is the source of intuition, those sudden insights of awareness that seem to come from nowhere, but actually originate from the depths of our unconscious minds.

Our two minds operate together in close harmony, for the most part. The interactions of these two minds, or brain hemispheres, functioning together provide our perceptual understanding of the world and our unique orientation to reality. There are times, of course, when one mind takes management control over our behavior. We commonly think that our logical brain is in management control of our learning and our emotional brain of our affections and loving. Management control can quickly change from one function to the other, as most of us are well aware in recalling those times when our logical mind has suddenly been overwhelmed by emotion when something has "grabbed" our feelings or connected to a deeply ingrained personal bias or value.

For reasons we don't yet understand, most individuals acquire a preference for either left- or right-brain thinking. While there are some individuals who feel equally comfortable with both left- and right-brain thinking, they appear to be the exception. Knowing our thinking preference can be of great value in making life choices. There is rather strong evidence that we do our best work and experience our greatest energy when the activities we are engaged in correspond with our preferred style of thinking. Ned Herrmann refers to this as knowing our "smart" zones and our "dumb" zones.

No one is equally smart across the entire brain spectrum, concludes Herrmann, based on his career-long observations of the styles of people as General Electric's director of corporate management and training.[6] He noticed that left-brain thinkers approached problem solving differently than those favoring right-brain thinking. Left-brain thinkers prefer to solve problems linearly in a fact-based, analytic, and step-by-step manner, favoring words, numbers, and facts. In contrast, right-brainers seek insights and synthesize images, concepts, patterns, sounds, and movements into intuitive generated solutions.

We are moving from an economy and a society built on the logical, linear, computerlike capabilities of the information age to an economy and a society built on the inventive, empathic, big-picture capabilities of what's rising in its place, the Conceptual Age—Daniel H. Pink, *A Whole New Mind*.

## Four Ways of Thinking

Have you noticed how differently various people think and perceive? It's common, for example, for two or more people to observe the same event, such as an accident or an altercation of some kind, and to report seeing very different things. There are many well-known examples of this, such as the shooting of President Kennedy, where some witnesses to this horrific event clearly saw multiple shots and others just as clearly saw only one. You may also have become aware of certain predictable behaviors or responses in your family, friends, and associates. Perhaps you know someone who is totally unpredictable in the way he or she responds to situations, while another's response, in contrast, is so very predictable.

> Complete **The Thinking-Style Assessment Inventory** in App 2.5

After years of research and observation, Ned Herrmann concluded that just four different styles are associated with brain functioning or how people access their brains (see **"The Brain—Four Ways of Thinking"**). Herrmann uses the names of physical regions of the brain to name his thinking styles. These regions are the left and right sides of the outer "cerebral" brain and the inner "limbic" brain. His model is based on research showing that specific areas of the brain are associated with specific kinds of thinking activities. The limbic system appears to specialize in fundamental thinking activities associated with bonding and taking care of ourselves. The cerebral system is associated with higher-level, abstract thinking. The codes being used in this APP are adapted from Herrmann's work.

## Analytical Thinking

*Analytical/Left Cerebral:* This style of thinking is characterized by a careful, logical analysis of all available facts and information to produce answers or insights. This is the kind of thinking that IQ tests like SATs, ACTs, and Graduate Record Examinations (GREs) measure. Those who favor this kind of thinking conclude that logical observation is the only way to determine reality, so truth cannot be determined until the "facts prove it so." People who prefer this mode of thinking tend to rely on a consciously rigorous and critical thought process and they enjoy complexity. A developmental economist describing the lure of problem solving as a strongly analytically inclined thinker put it this way, "While I feel good about my work in poverty alleviation, I have to admit that what energizes me most is the complexity of the issues with which I must deal."

### The Brain—Four Ways of Thinking

| Analytical | Intuitive |
|---|---|
| Left Cerebral | Right Cerebral |
| **Controlling** | **Feeling** |
| Left Limbic | Right Limbic |

### The Left Brain Controller—The BRIGHT and DARK Sides

### The Right-Brain Feelers—The BRIGHT and DARK Sides

At their best, they are warm and caring individuals able to empathize, connect, and communicate with all kinds of people in all kinds of situations.

At their worst, they may become overly emotional and irrationally impulsive or indecisively conflicted.

### The Right-Brain Initiative

At their best they are wonderfully creative and imaginative.

At their worst, they're out of touch with reality and live in a fantasy world.
Analytical thinkers are inclined to question everything until they are convinced of the validity of any premise or assumption through careful examination of the available evidence. The motto of a true analytic might be something like "Don't trust your instincts—to be accurate the facts have to clearly substantiate it." They are not swayed by emotional arguments or unexamined "good" ideas. They want the "cold, hard facts," and they want to know cause and effect. This approach is effective with problems and decision-making situations that can be resolved by finding the "one best answer" and where all the required facts are available for analysis. This kind of thinking involves carefully looking at all possible explanations for something, in order to identify the most plausible explanation. It's this kind of thought process that has freed us from the superstitions of our ancient past and brought us to the age of reason and to modern science. As an example of this thinking style in action, visualize a detective putting all the pieces together to determine "who done it," or a doctor weighing the data to diagnose a medical condition and prognosticate the likely outcome, or a NASA scientist determining the launch specifications required for a venture to land a rover on Mars. Some of the types of careers that favor this style of thinking include scientists, medical researchers, intelligence analysts, detectives, civil engineers, and military strategists.

dizain/Shutterstock.com

## Control Thinking

*Control/Left Limbic:* Those who favor thinking of this style tend to be safe-keepers, in that they seek to manage events, reduce risk, and prevent problems through careful organization and abiding by established policies and procedures. Control thinking emphasizes managing routines and situations through careful attention to detail and solving problems through tried-and-true methods. Individuals with a preference for this left-brained, limbic style of thinking tend to keep their feelings to themselves, remaining cool and unruffled in work situations. They seek to find practical solutions that bring order to chaotic situations.

An example of just how important control-oriented thinkers can be to an organizational setting became clear in the career-counseling center in which one of the authors was working a few years ago. The center, which was staffed entirely by right-brain and feeling-oriented counselors, was a beehive

of activity, with workshops going on, clients working on computers and in the library, counselors in private sessions, telephones ringing, and people seeking information. In those days, confusion and disorder ruled the day, with clients trying to find where the workshops they had registered for were being conducted, other clients trying to get in to see a counselor, counselors trying to find their workshop materials, and so on. But all that changed when Eric, the control-dominant thinker, arrived on the scene. With that blessed event, signs began appearing to show clients where the workshops were being conducted, counselors' workshop materials were prepared and ready for them, instructions on how to access priority information on the computers appeared, library resources became organized and correctly labeled, and a new website was created to make career information readily accessible organization-wide. Quickly and efficiently, and without fanfare, Eric turned a chaotic situation that had been frustrating and irritating to clients and staff alike into a smooth-running and efficient operation.

Control thinkers tend to be conservative in outlook, predictable in behavior, and practical and orderly in their daily activities. They like to have specific tasks to perform and a time frame for completing them. To those of this thinking persuasion, ambiguity and lack of structure is annoying. Because this kind of thinking tends to be task-based, it proceeds in an organized and planned way, time is well managed, and things get done step-by-step and on schedule. A motto for the control thinker might be something like "if it's not broken, don't fix it" or, "there is a reason for procedures, so follow them." To get a better picture of this kind of thinking in action, imagine a person "debugging" a computer program, a highway patrolman determining who was "at fault" in a traffic accident based on the relevant traffic laws, or a manager working out a plan to coordinate employee pay, vacation, and benefit policies.

Like analytical thinkers, controlled thinkers do not see themselves as creative and don't trust emotions or intuition, and the unorthodox in making decisions. Control-dominant thinkers are likely to be conventional in their approach to life and work, risk averse in their decision-making and "down-to-earth," and practical in problem solving. Occupations that rely heavily on this kind of thinking style include event planners, quality control inspectors, police officers, accountants, pharmacists, airline pilots, dispatching agents, and many supervisory and middle-management positions.

## Feeling Thinking

*Feeling/Right Limbic.* This thinking style involves paying attention to emotions, feelings, and the inner self. People preferring this style of thinking

Catle/Shutterstock.com

tend to be empathetic, charitable, personable, and conversational. In problem-solving and decision-making situations, they prefer interacting with others, talking things out, and coming to consensus or agreement. Feelers trust and depend on their emotions for energy, insight, and direction. They also tend to be attuned to, responsive to, and concerned about the feelings of others. These right-brain, limbic thinkers tend to be highly responsive to mood music, lyrical poetry, and the sounds of the human voice. They tend also to be more attuned to their spiritual nature than other styles, as they trust their feelings for guidance and direction. A motto for the feeler might be something like "if it feels right, it is right," or "trust your heart over your head." Feelers are energized in activities that draw on the emotions and are likely to become bored or lose interest if there is nothing happening that touches the heart.

Feelers love to work with, relate with, and help others. Three examples of this "helping" orientation have come to the attention of the authors, the first was Mitzi, the counselor who reported at a team meeting one day, "I just love helping students. Just keep the clients coming to my office all day and throw me in a sandwich now and then." The second example is Randy, a Presbyterian minister who told an associate one day, "I feel like the luckiest person in the world, I get to work with people intimately doing exactly what I love most to do, and they even pay me for this." The third is Lynn, who works with AIDS patients at the Johns Hopkins University Hospital. Lynn is passionate about her work and is known for her nurturing ways with both patients and her colleagues. While she has been in her profession long enough to be eligible for retirement, her husband says, "That won't happen, Lynn is a nurturer and she considers it a great honor to provide care for and be with patients, especially for those who are in the final days of their lives."

Right-brain, limbic dominant feelers tend to excel in thinking that involves emotional awareness, theirs and others, and in exuding a sense of warmth and caring for others. They are responsive to people and to the "inner world" and are excellent at establishing rapport through both verbal and nonverbal communications. For examples of this kind of thinking in action, visualize a therapist assisting clients in problem-solving situations through listening, talking about "it," and being attuned to emotions communicated nonverbally. Or imagine a teacher who is able to influence and motivate students through patient understanding and caring interaction. In addition to the helping professions, feelers are often drawn to the kinds of things that stir the heart and soul. Many well-known folks in the arts and show business have almost certainly been feelers, people like Charlie Chaplin, Picasso, Mozart, The Beatles, Ray Charles, Emily Dickinson, Lucille Ball, Marian Anderson, and so on.

Feeling-dominant thinkers will trust their feelings more than logic or facts and, unlike control-dominant thinkers, are more likely to act on what feels right rather than by the established rules and procedures. For that reason, left-brain thinkers may see feelers as overly "soft," uncritical, unsystematic, and too "touchy-feely." Feelers, on the other hand, are likely to see strong left-brainers as cold, detached, and heartless. Understanding your style and those of others can help you appreciate the gifts that all styles contribute to work and to the human experience and may prevent you from being too judgmental about those who think and see the world differently than you. Occupations in which feeler thinking is an essential ingredient include:

- therapy
- social work
- teaching
- childcare
- nursing
- human resource development
- acting
- music
- ministry

## Intuitive Thinking

***Intuiting/Right Cerebral.*** Have you had intuitive experiences where you suddenly realized a new way of solving a problem, saw a situation differently, or unexpectedly knew something about which you previously had not the foggiest notion? While almost everybody has these kinds of experiences, intuitive-dominant thinkers tend to have them far more frequently and to depend more fully on this kind of mental process.

Possibility thinking, intuition, and creativity characterize the right cerebral style of thinking. Intuition is a flash of insight in which you suddenly understand or know something or realize a solution to something without knowing why you know or the reason for knowing. This kind of thinking was described to one of the authors by an aeronautical engineer, who we'll call Len. Len had been a team leader on the computer system for one of the military's most advanced fighter aircraft. The team had been laboring for weeks over a difficult problem perplexing the system without success. Finally, after weeks of this fruitless effort, Len took a break from the situation and was walking along a moonlit lakeshore one evening when the solution to the computer problem suddenly flashed to mind. The next day he went back and told the team to

Aleksandar Mijatovic/Shutterstock.com

take the computer apart because he knew what was wrong and how to fix it. But the team members were reluctant to do that, wanting first to know the logic for the process before undertaking the painstakingly difficult task being proposed. Len, however, insisted they proceed without further elaboration because, in truth, he had absolutely no clue as to why he had come to know the source of the problem and how to fix it. He was operating totally from intuition rather than from conscious logic.

Len confides that he often receives solutions to difficult problems when, after concentrating on them for a long period, he takes a break to get his mind off the thing. It is often at these times, he says, that solutions seem to reveal themselves to him, seemingly magically to pop into mind. It turns out that in this particular case, Len's intuition was correct, for which he was grateful. He would have been in a highly embarrassing situation if his intuitive-based fix had not worked and the authorities discovered he had no rational basis for his procedure. After all, he was fooling around with a high-visibility, multi-million dollar system.

While nobody really understands the thought process producing intuitive insights, it is well known that we possess an unconscious intelligence capable of producing ideas and insights in flashes of awareness. We also know that such mysterious insights seem to happen most often when seeded consciously by first concentrating on an issue and then taking a break from it by engaging in a diversionary activity such as walking, meditating, or sleeping on it. It seems to be in the mind-shift from concentration to relaxation that we are most likely to be blessed with intuitive insight.

Intuitive thinking tends to be "big-picture" or holistic thinking, where seemingly unrelated issues suddenly come together in mysterious ways. Intuitive thinkers often get their best ideas in unstructured situations and places, such as when reading, dreaming, walking, driving, or listening to music. Writers and composers often rely on this kind of thinking, referring to this inner guidance system as their muse.

Intuitive thinkers often have grand ideas about innovative new ways of doing things or creative redesigns of old methods, products, or services. Intuitives may become visionaries who see creative opportunities in problems, ventures, and the future unimaginable to the masses. To get a picture of right cerebral thinking in action, imagine an artist conceiving an innovative idea and bringing it to completion on canvas, or Beethoven evolving his "Fifth Symphony," a manager coming up with a surprisingly creative new employee development program, or an engineer seeing an ingenious solution to a long-standing problem.

Individuals who are strongly intuitive-oriented thinkers prefer working at their own pace and dislike functioning on regulated schedules. Their approach to problem solving tends to be unstructured, allowing their minds to incubate on a problem and thereafter looking for that sudden flash of insight and the mental spigot to begin flowing with ideas. Intuitives can generate ideas by the barrel-full, and while many of them may not be great, there often is a golden nugget to be found somewhere in the batch. Dominant intuitive thinkers generally are not fond of proving the validity of or analyzing their ideas. Instead, they are usually anxious to experiment with them, to try them out through exploration rather than through a process of in-depth analysis. Right-brain cerebrals tend to do well as:

- creative artists (as opposed to craft or illustrators)
- creative writers
- entrepreneurs
- program developers
- musical composers
- strategic planners
- inventors

A number of studies over the past few years suggest that many of the most successful CEOs have been powerful intuitives, though they are not as likely to acknowledge this preference because of a bias in the business world for left-brain analysis and control.

## Your Thinking-Style Profile

To more fully develop your mind power you will want to capitalize on your best assets and be aware of and learn how to effectively manage your deficits, or what Ned Herrmann refers to as your "dumb zone." You are going to be more successful when you are doing that which uses and develops your top strengths and strongest interests in pursuit of what you truly value. To enjoy your work and perform at your best you want to be engaged as fully as possible in activities that use your preferred style of thinking and that do not make heavy demands of your least preferred style.

matrioshka/Shutterstock.com

Your thinking-style profile most likely consists of some degrees of preference (and avoidance) for all four modes of thinking. There are a total of 71 different four-digit possibilities. Are you uncomfortable labeling yourself by a "four-digit" system? If so, we don't blame you; many people feel that way. And the fact is, we are far too complex to be classified by any four-digit code, or by an IQ score, or even a Myers Briggs type for that matter. But, if you can get beyond the labeling stigma, this assessment, like the Myers Briggs and many other resources, can help you realize, appreciate, and define your unique and most energizing personal strengths. Think of the assessment as an aid for expressing unique aspects of your being. In some ways assessments can help us understand the uniqueness of people in the way that chemical formulas show us the compositional differences of physical elements such as water, iron, and diamond. Understanding the chemical make-up of substances is essential in putting substances together compatibly to create new and highly useful things. Understanding chemical compositions can also help prevent mistakes, such as combining substances that blow up when mixed together. Understanding psychological make-up can help us

1 Review your thinking-style profile and your four-digit code, and then list personal insights acquired. Be as specific as you can about what you prefer and what you should avoid in your work, education, relationships, and life. List a few words that will remind you of the most important aspects of your thinking style.

2 Using the Occupations Grouped by Thinking Style Chart on page 168 in App 2.5 identify those occupations that fall within your preferred mode(s) of thinking. Circle any that are of interest and involve skills you have identified in previous activities. To do that, first, go through the list corresponding to your strongest preference. If your code is 1132, for example, you would look for occupations in the *Analyzing* column. Circle any occupations of interest to you. Then go back to the individual columns corresponding to the next strongest preferences and circle occupations of interest there.

3 After you have circled a number of occupations, narrow that number down to the 10 or 12 that you like best and that probably require some of your best skills. Transfer these to the *occupations of interest* Section in the ABOUT ME worksheet in APP 7.0.

Ned Herrmann concludes that sustained competence in any field of endeavor depends upon performing activities that engage your preferred mode of thinking. By doing that, you are likely to enjoy your work and be productive at it, a good combination for motivation and success. Furthermore, without this compatibility, both employer and employee are likely to suffer. Herrmann's research suggests a major source for discontent and lack of career motivation is in the failure to match personal thinking-style preferences with the activities of work. Think of the challenge, for example, of highly creative people like Stevie Wonder stuck in a job requiring the unique gifts of a control thinker, such as accountant or auto mechanic. On the other hand, isn't the world better off for the fact that Michelangelo realized his passion as an artist rather than pursuing a merchant career as his father insisted?

The Occupations Grouped by Thinking Style Chart on page 168 contains a sample of occupations reflecting the four modes of thinking styles. In using this table, you should be aware that occupations are placed in four different categories based on the style of thinking most prevalent in this type of work. We acknowledge that just about any occupation is likely to involve all four styles of thinking to varying degrees. But, specific occupations are likely to draw most heavily on a particular kind of thinking. An accountant, for example, is much more likely to use left-brained analytic thinking than right-brain intuitive, while a graphic designer is more likely to use intuitive thought processes than control thinking.

find winning combinations for applying our best assets and prevent us from making mistakes that could produce a "blow up" of the human kind.

## Whole-Brain Thinking

While understanding your thinking style is likely to result in your taking fuller advantage of your "smart zones," that awareness can also help you attend to any areas that might fall into your "dumb zone." An ability to resourcefully use the different styles of thinking appropriate to the various kinds of situations you may be faced with a great asset in work, learning, and getting along with others. For example, when a situation calls for creativity and ingenuity you want to be able to access right-brain intuitive skills for generating out-of-the-box ideas. But, when the situation calls for critical thought and analysis, you are best served by left-brain objectivity. When attempting to relate effectively with someone whose perceptual mode is very different from your own, you may need to get in sync by adjusting your behavior to conform to his or her dominant mode of thinking. Let's say, for example, you are a strong intuitive who wants to make a good impression in an interview situation with someone who you know to be a control-dominant thinker. To do that you are going to need to be more direct, practical, organized, to the point, and less abstract, spontaneous, and original than your normal style.

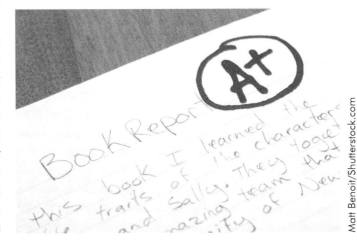

Matt Benoit/Shutterstock.com

This kind of versatility in your ability to use different modes of thinking appropriately to the task at hand is what Ned Herrmann refers to as "whole-brain" thinking. Such versatility is likely to be a positive asset in work situations where you are dealing with a wide variety of relationships, challenges, and problem situations. With the concept of whole-brain thinking in mind, what conclusions can you draw from your own profile regarding the strengths of your thinking style and how to capitalize on those strengths in work, learning, and relating?

Here is an important point to bear in mind as you apply the content of this APP; interest deficits are not the same as "ability" deficits. Because you tend to avoid a certain style of thinking does not mean that you don't have the capacity to be very good at that kind of thinking. Anybody with a fully functioning brain can develop his or her ability in all four styles of thinking. It is difficult, however, to develop a competence in an area where you lack interest. It's a bit like learning how to swim when you dislike or fear the water. Although difficult, it is possible for people who fear the water to overcome their bias and learn how to swim, even well, just as it is for someone to overcome a math or writing bias. Study "Developing and Capitalizing on the Thinking Styles" for ideas on how to capitalize on the strengths of your thinking style. Use this section also for ideas on how you might develop awareness and skill in your "dumb zones."

How do you overcome mental biases? Do you hate mathematics, for instance? Stop saying you can't do it, and consider that you are dealing with a mental preference, which probably has little to do with the functioning capabilities of your brain. Do you believe you are not creative or can't get along with people? Remember, these attitudes are learned, often from isolated experiences that left deep impressions. Learn to manage your attitudes rather than allowing your attitudes to manage you.

### Developing and Capitalizing on the Thinking Styles

### Analyzing

- Be objective—get the facts right
- Use logic to solve problems and make decisions
- Question your assumptions and reexamine your conclusions
- Play devil's advocate
- Be exact and precise in communications
- Treat others with detached fairness and justice

### Controlling

- Plan carefully and keep a schedule calendar
- Solve problems and reach conclusions by staying with the tried and tested
- Prioritize tasks and do the most important first
- Keep a "to do" list and follow it
- Be organized, punctual, and reliable
- Appreciate procedures, rules, and policies

### Intuiting

- Read widely and randomly to expand your perspectives and stimulate ideas
- Look for unique and novel associations in unrelated things
- Trust your instincts and hunches
- Work in bursts of energy—then relax
- Use mental imagery, fantasy, and dreams for ideas and solutions to problems
- Stimulate creativity with play, dance, art, humor, and daydreaming

### Feeling

- Nurture and support yourself and others
- Appreciate your feelings and trust them as a worthy source of input
- Relate with others from your heart rather than your head
- Listen to music for mood enhancement
- Decide with your heart and soul
- Express your feelings and relate to yourself and others with warmth

A good reason to develop skills from your "least preferred" style of thinking is that multidimensional or whole-brain thinking is simply more powerful than one-track thinking. Whole-brain thinkers can do more things well than those who use only a small portion of their brainpower potential. Think, for example, of the analytical thinker trying to solve a problem when only limited facts are available and many solutions are possible, each controversial to some people in the organization. Many problems in business and in life are like that. It's really only in rare situations that all the facts are available and there is only one right answer.

What if you are a great intuitive thinker who is always coming up with terrific ideas but can't get any of them off the drawing board into action? Wouldn't it be nice to be able to access the left limbic controlling portion of your brain for some productive planning, organizing, and structuring? Consult "Developing and Capitalizing on the Thinking Styles" for ideas on how to improve your competency in your least preferred modes of thinking. Sometimes you can change an avoidance area to one of relatively more comfort by experimenting with the activities associated with your nondominant areas. You can develop competency in areas that don't tap your interests; you just don't want to make career choices in areas in which you have good ability but little interest.

## Thinking Styles in Action: Personal Examples

Why bother taking the *Thinking-Style Assessment Inventory* or finding out your brain dominance profile? There are a number of good reasons for doing so, including motivation, self-understanding, self-concept enhancement, and career decision-making. Understanding your thinking style and taking actions to capitalize on your motivated strengths can make you a more successful performer in your career, your education, and your life. Knowing your thinking style can also help you make fewer wrong turns in your career, as the following real-life examples illustrate.

### Case Study   Brad

Several years ago Brad enthusiastically accepted a college position where he assumed he was going to be engaged in his dream job. In many ways that turned out to be so—but there was a big problem. No matter how hard he tried, he seemed unable to connect with his administrative colleagues in a satisfying way. This was extremely frustrating to him because the need for stimulating intellectual collegiality was a primary reason he had chosen this kind of work. He recounted, "It wasn't that I was any more or less intelligent than my colleagues or that we disliked each other. It was that we were different, but how?" He found his answer during an administrative retreat with his colleagues.

The retreat featured the *Herrmann Brain Dominance Survey,* a thinking-style preference instrument. (Similar to the one you take in this section.) From this experience, he discovered that he was a "right-brainer." Not only that, but he was the one and only right-brainer in that whole division of 16 administrators. He and his colleagues were essentially operating on different wavelengths. Their interests were focused primarily on the objective and practical management of the everyday business—a left-brain focus. What grabbed his attention, on the other hand, was the creative possibilities in developing new programs. In very real ways, they were operating in different perceptual worlds.

"We all came away from this retreat with useful and interesting new insights. One was that we now understood why and how we were so different. That experience greatly enhanced our respect for our differences, and we learned how to more effectively relate and work together. After that I no longer went to them expecting to engage in interesting, to me, discussions on the theoretical, the idealistic, or the possible. I did go to them, however, for advice and suggestions on how to make an idea more effective and, more important, how to make it more palatable to the left-brain-oriented executives to whom I needed to sell the 'thing.' They, on the other hand, would often look to me for creative input to problems being confronted," he later shared. As a result of the insights acquired from this retreat, the colleagues were able, in essence, to link the right brain harmoniously to the left, producing a more holistic and effective operation along with a more pleasant working environment.

## Case Study    Michelle

Michelle became a lawyer not because she was particularly interested in the law, but because she was strongly encouraged to do so by her parents and teachers. As an excellent student who had high SAT scores, she opted to take the standard aptitude test required for entry into law schools, the LSATs. She did so well on those that it settled any further career uncertainty—she got a law degree. Michelle then began her career as an attorney with the federal government. She had been advised to go this route because a government position was secure, at least it was thought to be back then, and it came with a good salary and excellent benefits.

She soon discovered, however, that there was more to a career than job security. She found her work to be routine and boring. For a while she thought all work must be that way. Nonetheless, she found herself dreaming about other possibilities. One of her prime interests had always been books. Often she would find herself browsing through bookstores in her leisure, losing herself there for hours on end in reading and exploring. Eventually, she began dreaming about owning a bookstore. The more she thought about it, the more she was captivated by the idea, so much so that she thought she might actually do it. And, while it didn't happen overnight, she eventually decided to make the leap.

Leaving a secure government position for such an uncertain venture shocked her colleagues, who strongly advised her against such a seemingly irrational act. In spite of their dissuasions, however, she went on to develop her passion as a bookstore owner. Exhibiting some marketing savvy, she chose to set up shop in a small, upscale town with a college community and a government training center. Her assumption was that this would be a location where there would be enough book-reading people to make a "go" of it. As it turned out, she was right, although she had to work hard to make her business a success. Today, she is thoroughly enjoying life and her work, even though she clears a bit less money than she would have had she stayed with the government.

As you might have guessed, Michelle is a risk taker, with strong entrepreneurial leanings. She is a right-brainer in her activity preferences, with strongly developed left-brain skills. Had she understood these things about herself earlier in life, she probably would have decided against law and a career based primarily upon security. She might have been better able to visualize a career path more suited to her unique interests and personality. Michelle's story highlights this important point: it is usually better to make your career decision on the basis of deep-seated interests and personality style than strictly upon general intelligence and/or academic achievement.

## Case Study   Joe

Joe is now an artist but he began his career working in a technical job in the U.S. Army, Early in his career, he was offered a technician job with the National Security Administration (NSA) in Tokyo and decided to take it, even though that kind of work never felt right to him when he'd being doing it in the Army.

He took his first art courses just to pass the time until the date he was to report for work in Tokyo. At that time he had no idea that he had a special talent for art, although he had become aware of an art interest. He had been in art school about two months when the call came to report to NSA headquarters for indoctrination. He had 24 hours to make his choice between the NSA job and continuing in art school. In mulling over these two options he realized that something had come alive within himself when he began making art. There was a joy that he had never experienced before. On that basis, he jumped into the life of an artist, knowing only that it seemed "right" for him.

Now, years later, with a master's degree in art from a top art institute and a successful career as a college art professor under his belt, Joe is at the peak of an extremely rewarding career. He says this about the insights he acquired from the *Thinking-Style Assessment:*

When I first saw my assessment results, it was like a new light dawned. Because I had not been so great at math in my early life, I concluded that I must not be very bright—even though I had been successful in college and graduate school. Old self-doubts about my mental ability hung over me like a black cloud. I had to be clever to earn my master's and bachelor's degrees without running into insurmountable problems in left-brain courses. When I saw my assessment results, however, I realized—hey I'm a strong right-brainer, without much going on in the left side! (Joe's thinking style is a 3311.) While I may not be so great at some left-brain activities like math, finances, and schedule books, I'm brilliant at right-brain activities. Seeing those results and understanding what they meant affected my whole self-concept. Ever since understanding this, I have felt great about who I am, rather than depressed about who I'm not. That assessment boosted my self-confidence.

## Summary

Joe's comments contain several valuable insights. First, Joe was indeed lucky to stumble into a profession in which he had great but unrealized talent and passion. How many people have been so fortunate? Undoubtedly there are thousands who have never discovered their career-motivating interests and the special gifts of their thinking style. There are also far too many who have stumbled into the wrong kind of job, educational program, or career path where their interests and talents have not had the opportunity to develop and bloom.

A second point from Joe's story worthy of highlighting is this: when you know and accept yourself, you are on the road to self-confidence and self-esteem. These are not only essential ingredients to feeling good about yourself, but also they are the key in being successful in your career, in your relationships, in your learning, and in your life. It makes no difference if you are more of a right-brainer than a left, a controller rather than a creator, or that your preferences are distributed equally across the thinking-style spectrum. There is no one way to be that is better than any other. The important issue is who you are, what your gifts are, how you capitalize on these, and how you can share them happily in the world. When you can do that, you too can become brilliant—just like Joe.

**Words of Wisdom**

*A brain strained by a new idea never returns to its original shape.*

—Oliver Wendell Holmes

## Endnotes

### APP 2.2

1. Daniel Goleman, *Emotional Intelligence: Why It Can Matter More Than IQ* (New York: Bantam Books, 1994), p. 34.

2. Peter Drucker, "Managing Oneself," *Harvard Business Review* (March–April 1999).

3. Howard Gardner, *Frames of Mind: The Theory of Multiple Intelligences* (New York: Bask Books, 1983).

4. R. K. Cooper and A. Sawaf, *Executive EQ: Emotional Intelligence in Leadership and Organizations* (New York: Grossett/Putnam, 1996), p. xxxiv.

5. Ned Herrmann, *The Creative Brain* (Lake Lure, NC: Brain Books, 1988).

6. Herrmann, *The Creative Brain*, pp. 117–129.

**PAUSE**

### Compare Your Thinking Style to Careers

Read the description of ten occupations that most interest you from your work in this App. The OOH or the O*NET attempt to identify the four-digit thinking-style profile code of these occupations, using the model explained in this APP. Compare your thinking-style profile code with these other codes. How would they appear to fit your thinking-style preferences?

# APP 2.3 Your Personality and Interests

## Do you know people who are:

- Physically active and enjoy engaging in activities requiring manual agility and body conditioning?
- Inquisitive and are energized by solving abstract problems requiring mental concentration and persistence?
- Creative and express themselves with originality and distinctiveness?
- Social and enjoy interacting with, supporting, and encouraging others?
- Gregarious and outgoing and take pleasure in exercising influence and persuasion?
- Organized and like systematic work involving details, data, and numbers?

If so, you know people whose motivational interests reveal six classically different styles of personality.

*. . . people are different from each other, and no amount of getting after them is going to change them. Nor is there any reason to change them, because the differences are probably good.*

—David Keirsey,
Please Understand Me II

## Thinking Style Versus Personality Style

While the last APP focused on your brain, or, more accurately, the way you think and perceive, this APP deals with your personality and what engages your interests. We're not talking about good and bad personalities here, but about personality styles. You are born with certain neurological characteristics that cause you to prefer one type of thinking over others. You can actually change the neurological structuring of your brain through cerebral exercise; we're talking about learning and mental skills development here. Your personality, on the other hand, probably develops through a combination of genetic programming and early life experiences. Research on personality styles informs us that by the age of about 21 your personality has crystallized; we're talking maturation here. Since personality shapes what engages your interests and what doesn't, it is very probable that after the age of 21 your personality-style-based interests will remain fairly constant. For this reason, understanding your personality is a key factor in career and life planning. In this APP, you will have an opportunity to clarify your personality style and discover the kinds of interests associated with your style, along with those of six general styles of personality.

## Opposites Attract

Have you noticed that people tend to associate with those who share similar interests? Do you accept the commonly held belief that opposites attract? If that's what you believe, there is a little test for that assumption. Consider how enjoyable it is for you to interact for any prolonged period of time with people with whom you can find no common interests.

That's a lot of fun, right? Of course, there are some who can seem to communicate effectively with just about anybody, and even enjoy that. But we're talking about genuine sustained interpersonal, interactive, invigorating interest. How long do you really believe that you can actively remain engaged, attentive to, and attracted to others with whom you share no strong mutual interests?

When we have a choice, we either consciously or unconsciously seek out others who share at least some of our interests. In contrast, you may notice that sooner or later you disengage from people who don't respond to your interests. While opposites may attract, at least initially, they are not likely to "click" over the long run.

The belief that opposites attract is true for magnets, but the dynamics are more complex for humans. Our values or needs may motivate initial attraction to our opposites. However, when our interests are truly opposite, we can expect compatibility challenges. This is true in relationships and it is true also in work. For sustained interest in your career, choose work that is compatible with your interests.

## Personality and Career Choice

During our formative years, we develop interests linked to the uniqueness of our environmental experience, our cellular biology, and the times in which we live (people in the Middle Ages didn't get excited about space travel, and today we don't think much about exploring the seven seas in manually rowed galley ships). Your interests crystallize, or become ingrained patterns, with maturity. These distinctive patterns of interests thereafter determine what energizes you and what depletes you. For example, some people love scientific investigation, while others hate it. Some prefer unstructured creativity such as envisioning a fantasy story in their minds, while others are far more attracted to structured activities such as keeping close watch over their finances. Some enjoy social activities, while others prefer solitary endeavors. Some prefer working with their hands, others with their minds, and others with their personalities.

Because the matured personality reflects your crystallized interests, you're likely to feel motivated when engaged in favorite activities and unmotivated

Rawpixel.com/Shutterstock.com

in things alien to your personality. In fact, just discussing your favorite interests with others who share them can arouse your attention and spring those brain cells into stimulating activity. Unfortunately, too many people overlook their personal interests in career planning, focusing exclusively upon their "practical" skills and/or what's popular in today's media. The problem with this is that skills don't necessarily connect directly to your interests or to the careers popularized by the media. We have seen many clients who have been engaged in work nicely matched to their skills, but hate what they are doing. Speaking of motivation, have you ever noticed how hard it is just to get out of bed on those mornings when you have nothing to which you are looking forward? You don't want to spend your entire working life, about 11,880 days of life for a 20-year-old, dreading Mondays. Most of us need things to look forward to for our days to be pleasurable experiences.

Sara, did you ever say to yourself, "Geezie Peezie, sometimes I think maybe I made the wrong career choice."

Knowing your interests and what kinds of activities engage them allows you to develop career plans that are realistic and likely to produce both success and enjoyment. An additional plus of developing a career based on interests is a health benefit. People who enjoy their work tend to be healthier, both physically and emotionally, than those who view work as a "rat race" or just another boring day at the office. We need to add a disclaimer here: what we are advocating is developing your career goals around your deep-seated interests. We are definitely not suggesting that you develop only skills associated with your strongest interests. The world does not, of course, allow us to do only what interests us. We need to develop a broad range of skills, but focus our career direction around our sustainable interests.

## Identifying Your Personality Style

What's unique about you? What are the strengths and shortcomings of your personality? In thinking about your career future, it is important to be able to answer questions such as these. In fact, in most interview situations for professional and managerial positions you will be asked these kinds of questions. So, how do you describe your personality in career-relevant terms? While there are several methods for assessing and clarifying personality styles, we recommend four well-known inventories: the *Myers-Briggs Type Indicator* (MBTI), the *Strong Interest Inventory* (SII), the *Holland Self-Directed Search* (SDS), and the *Campbell Interests and Skills Survey* (CISS). These inventories

Thinglass/Shutterstock.com

are available in most college career-development centers and through most career-counseling practices. If you plan to take these inventories, be sure to review them with a professional counselor who has training and experience with the instruments.

Whether or not you choose to take the SII, SDS, or CISS, the following exercises should be helpful in evaluating your personality-related interests. Complete the Interest and Activity Assessments in the page 167 section before skipping ahead to further reading. Reading ahead may alter the way you respond to the questions and give inaccurate results. In doing these exercises, be as frank and honest with yourself as you possibly can. Respond to each item the way it really is for you rather than the way you would like it to be or the way you think it should be.

## Case Study    Rose

A few years ago, a colleague from another unit sat in the office of one of the authors and declared that a unit in her division was made up of a bunch of scented markers. Rose was frustrated by their energy but seemingly lack of attention to detail. They handled things with broad lines, were creative, and "you experienced them with not only sight but smell," she declared. To Rose, this was frustrating. She saw herself as a colored pencil. More detailed but open to a little creativity. Her significant other had been on a job site a few days before and was frustrated by the single-minded, follow the rules, and stay in the lines thinking of the workers on a particular contract. His boss had redirected his rant and encouraged him to think of them as number 2 lead pencils. With this analogy in place, he was able to understand that they enjoyed having a direct, single dimension role and he was then able to respond in kind. And so the phrase "you are such a smelly marker" was born. Over the years Rose often smiled when thought her highly scented marker colleagues were being just a little too fragrant or someone was being such a stickler for rules and she had to remember that they perhaps enjoyed being a pencil.

Rose, the colored pencil noted that her favorite teammate was a bit of a colored sharpie. This peson was a little more broad than she was, a little harder to erase, but not quite the extreme of a scented marker. Rose noted that they made a good team. She saw the details, and her teammate saw the big picture. She focused on the numbers, the other focused on the people. Her teammate came up with crazy ideas while Rose helped her figure out how to implement them. On her teammate's most creative days, Rose allowed her to be a scented marker but made it clear that she couldn't handle that personality for the long term. Rose shared how she was often relied on for her ability to see the details but she needed her teammate to help her see how they were part of something bigger.

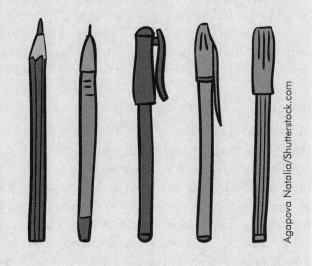

Agapova Natalia/Shutterstock.com

PAUSE

What about you? What functions do you like to play? What types of work do you most enjoy? If your friends and colleagues had to describe you as a writing implement, what would it be? It is a silly question but it is telling. Perhaps you identify with the scented markers, but realize that you need at least one pencil around. Perhaps you even think the ideal teammate is one of those cool pens that has four colors in it because you need someone who is detailed but can change easily. Look at the list below and describe the writing implement. Then, go ask a few friends and colleagues to pick the one that is most like you.

Pencil

Ballpoint pen

Scented marker

Mechanical pencil

Multicolored pen

Designer pen

Sharpie

Dry erase marker

Chalk

Regular marker

Crayon

Highlighter

This exercise was for fun but it was designed to get your brain moving. What did you learn about yourself? What types of personalities do you like to be around? What types of personalities frustrate you? How can you use this analogy to help you better understand others? How can it help you to form teams that are diverse and work best in your current situation? How can it help you be more accepting of others?

## What Your Profile Shows

Developing your Interests Profile provides a graphic picture of your personality-style-related interest patterns. This profile and the proceeding exercises are based upon the work of Dr. John Holland (*Making Vocational Choices: A Theory of Vocational Personalities and Work Environments*). Dr. Holland's work informs us that in our formative years we develop preferences for certain groups of related activities. These preferences develop as a result of environmental influences (family, community, ethnic background, socioeconomic status, religion, and race), the nature of our early life, and our genetic make-up. By the age of 21, these preferences have shaped your personality, and your personality determines your general preferences (likes and dislikes). A mature personality remains fairly stable throughout

Blend Images/Shutterstock.com

the remainder of life, which means that once crystallized, your general interests are very likely to remain fairly constant thereafter. What tends to engage your primary interests in your 20s is likely to be similar in general terms to what engages your interests when you are 40, and even when you are 60. Your preferences guide your behavior, including what you are inclined to do and how you do

To learn more about yourself, complete **South Sea Island Fantasy, My Favorite Kinds of Problems, Interest and Activity Assessment, Identifying Interests from Skills,** and **Compiling My Interests Profile located in APP 2.5.**

it. For these reasons, you can probably see the importance of knowing yourself in terms of personality-style-related preferences for career-planning purposes.

Holland identifies six personality styles, giving them the following labels:

R    Realistic

I    Investigative

A    Artistic

S    Social

E    Enterprising

C    Conventional

Look at the short description of each of the following six personality styles. In the box to the left of the appropriate description, place the number "1" next to the letter with the highest score on your Interests Profile.

Then read that description and evaluate how well it fits you. Place the number "2" in the box corresponding to your second-highest personality-style score. Do this with each of the remaining styles.

❑ **R**    You enjoy physical activity and prefer outdoor work. You like working with your hands using tools, operating mechanical equipment, and seeing the concrete results of your work.

❑ **I**    Intellectual things turn you on. You prefer to analyze situations and solve challenging mental problems. You prefer to work alone and are attracted to scientific pursuits.

❑ **A**    Creative modes of self-expression suit you. You enjoy unstructured and free-flowing environments where you can express your originality and innovative ideas.

❑ **S**    You like to work with people—helping, teaching, or training them. You prefer to resolve problems through discussion.

❑ **E**    You enjoy exercising influence with people and feel comfortable in situations where you are in authority and control. Economic objectives are important to you.

❑ **C**    You like to know exactly what is expected of you and prefer to do well-defined tasks. You are organized, efficient, practical, good with numbers and data, and are precise in doing things accurately and thoroughly.

Did you notice that the description for the letter corresponding to your highest score, your #1 letter, sounds the most like you, and your #2 letter the next most like you? And conversely, did you notice that the description corresponding to your lowest score, your #6 letter, was the least like you?

Study *Comparison of the Personality Types table*, to learn more about the six interest-based personality types.

**PAUSE**

You have just completed a few inventories intended to help you think about your career interests and then develop a visual picture. React to these results in a few sentences.

# Comparison of the Personality Types

| | Realistic | Investigative | Artistic | Social | Enterprising | Conventional |
|---|---|---|---|---|---|---|
| Characteristics | Stable<br>Physical<br>Practical<br>Frank<br>Self-reliant | Analytical<br>Independent<br>Curious<br>Intellectual<br>Precise | Imaginative<br>Idealistic<br>Original<br>Expressive<br>Impulsive | Cooperative<br>Understanding<br>Helpful<br>Tactful<br>Sociable | Persuasive<br>Domineering<br>Energetic<br>Ambitious<br>Flirtatious | Conscientious<br>Orderly<br>Persistent<br>Conforming<br>Efficient |
| Likes | Outdoor work<br>Mechanics<br>Athletics<br>Working with plants, tools, and animals | Abstract problems<br>Science<br>Investigation<br>Unstructured situations<br>Mind work | Ideas<br>Self-expression<br>Creativity<br>Unstructured situations<br>Working alone | People<br>Attention<br>Discussion<br>Helping<br>Socializing | Power<br>People<br>Status<br>Persuading<br>Managing | Order<br>Detail work<br>Organizing<br>Structure<br>Working with data |
| Dislikes | Theory<br>Self-expression<br>Working with people | Repetitive activities<br>Close supervision<br>Working with People | Structure<br>Rules<br>Physical work<br>Details<br>Repetitive activities | Physical work<br>Working with tools<br>Working outdoors<br>Solitary activities | Systematic activities<br>Precise work<br>Concentrated intellectual work | Unsystematized activities<br>Lack of structure<br>Ambiguity |
| Preferred skills | Building<br>Repairing<br>Making and growing things<br>Operating equipment | Problem solving<br>Analytical reasoning<br>Developing models and systems | Creating<br>Visualizing<br>Unstructured tasks<br>Imagining<br>Idea generating | Interpersonal activities<br>Establishing rapport<br>Communicating<br>Helping | Leading<br>Managing<br>Persuading<br>Motivating others | Detailed tasks<br>Following directions precisely<br>Repetitive tasks |

| | Realistic | Investigative | Artistic | Social | Enterprising | Conventional |
|---|---|---|---|---|---|---|
| People who characterize the styles | Thomas Edison | Albert Einstein | Alex Haley | Helen Keller | Henry Ford | E. F. Hutton |
| | The Wright Brothers | Sherlock Holmes | Ludwig von Beethoven | Carl Menninger | Winston Churchill | Dr. Watson (Sherlock Holmes' assistant) |
| | Antonio Stradivari | Marie Curie | Michelangelo | Florence Nightingale | Martin Luther King, Jr. | Noah Webster (dictionary) |
| | Johannes Gutenberg | Sigmund Freud | Luciano Pavarotti | Mother Theresa | Nelson Mandela | Melvil Dewey (Dewey decimal system) |
| | Neil Armstrong | Charles Darwin | William Shakespeare | Mahatma Gandhi | Oprah Winfrey | Carolus Linnaeus (botanist) |
| | Amelia Earhart | Dr. Jonas Salk | Mikhail Baryshnikov | Coretta Scott King | Madeleine Albright | Miss Manners |
| | Arthur Ashe | *Stephen Hawking* | Emily Dickinson | Desmond Tutu | General George Patton | *Charles Schwab* |
| | Michael Jordan | *Mark Zuckerberg* | Frank Lloyd Wright | *Mr. Rogers* | *Walt Disney* | *Marcie* |
| | Phil Mickelson | *Steve Wozniak* | Maya Angelou | *Lucy* | *Steve Jobs* | |
| | Willy Mays | *Linus* | Stevie Wonder | | *Mark Cuban* | |
| | *Pele* | | Elton John | | *Bill Gates* | |
| | *Peppermint Patty* | | Toni Morrison | | *Snoopy* | |
| | | | *Charles Shultz* | | | |
| | | | *J.K. Rowling* | | | |
| | | | *Schroder* | | | |

One way of understanding Holland's categorizations is to apply it to something outside of jobs and academics.

**PAUSE**

Make a list of the things you enjoy doing. Include the obvious such as taking classes, playing sports, hanging out with friends, cooking, and so on. Then go back and try to think about the specific parts of the activity you enjoy such as helping your friends solve personal problems, lifting weights to improve your muscle tone to help you perform better in a sport, and doing experiments in a class with a laboratory.

Connect each activity to up to three Holland themes.

For example, Playing Guitar would be ARTISTIC, Coaching Baseball could be REALISTIC and SOCIAL, and Reading Mysteries could be INVESTIGATIVE.

Which themes occur most frequently?

Write a few sentences about how you can connect this to a career choice.

Are there themes you would like to explore? Talk to other classmates to learn about their activities. Get ideas of other activities to try as you listen to them.

Siberia Video and Photo/Shutterstock.com

**ACTION**

**Complete the Likes and Dislikes as Guides in App 2.5**

Det-anan/Shutterstock.com

The "people who characterize the styles" row on the Comparison of the Personality Types Chart shows our best guess as to the personality styles of a few famous individuals. The Thomas Alva Edison ("RIA") profile, for example, portrays Edison as a hands-on inventor, relentlessly trying out applications ideas until he eventually finds the one that works. The "RIA" code attributed to Edison represents a career pattern dominate in working with one's hands to invent things (an "R" activity). We know that Edison almost lived in his laboratory, where he created hundreds of inventions such as the phonograph and light bulb. But Edison was also an idea person, creating a stream of ideas for new technology ("A" activity). But these ideas had to be analyzed and tested. Edison would not have persisted in developing his ideas beyond the thought stage without a passion for investigative research and rational problem solving ("I" activity).

The Michelangelo ("AIR") profile represents this magnificent artist–scientist as first and foremost a creative genius ("A"). Second, he was an analytical problem solver in many respects, creating abstract ideas in marble and paint, and complex architectural designs (both "A" and "I" activities). Michelangelo is assigned an "R" to reflect the hands-on type of activity that was involved in actually sculpting a statue or painting the Sistine Chapel.

Alexandra Petruk/Shutterstock.com

Some famous people are represented by nearly all the styles because they were such multifaceted personalities. Take Thomas Jefferson, for example. Jefferson is listed as an "EAI" on the assumption of a dominant "E," which he probably would have had to want to be the President of the United States. He was also an architect, talented writer, and music lover ("A" activities), as well as a scientific thinker ("I"), a cataloger of data ("C"), a gardener ("R"), and a humanitarian ("S").

Career/life planning is much easier for those who have only one or two peaks in their interest profile from which to make career decisions. While a profile like Jefferson's represents great natural gifts, the problem multi-interested people find is in narrowing down their choices. If all these interests do not find an outlet, conflict and frustration result.

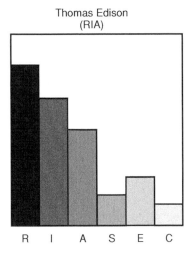

Thomas Edison
(RIA)

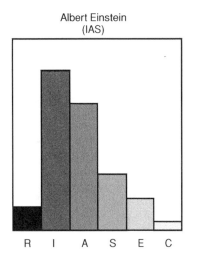

Albert Einstein
(IAS)

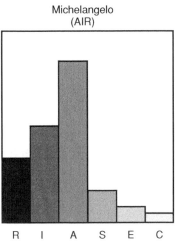

Michelangelo
(AIR)

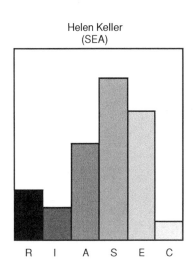

Helen Keller
(SEA)

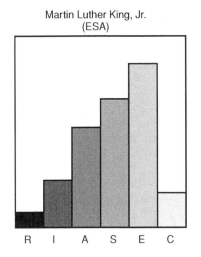

Martin Luther King, Jr.
(ESA)

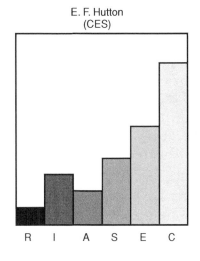

E. F. Hutton
(CES)

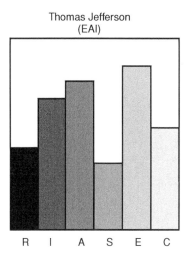

Thomas Jefferson
(EAI)

**Famous Personality Profiles**

Look at the Comparison of the Personality Types chart. Charles Shultz, creator of the Peanuts comic strip, recounted how each of his characters reflected a part of his personality. Linus was the deeper spiritual side, Schroder the artist, and so on. For his profession, you will find Charles Shultz as Artistic. The characters he created have been added for fun.

Add other famous people under each theme as appropriate. Why did you put them in the theme area?

You are learning about yourself and careers through all activities in this book. It may be putting something you already knew into words or it might be a new nugget of knowledge. Write something you learned from this activity.

However, intelligent career/life planning can balance the range of favorite interests in a combination of work, leisure, and learning activities.

## The Personality-Style Hexagon

Holland's six personality styles are geometrically arranged in the shape of a hexagon. The shape of this figure is significant because it shows important relationships among the six different styles, such as:

■ Personality types that are adjacent to each other on the hexagon share some similar characteristics. For example, strong "R," "A," and "I" types generally prefer working alone, while strong "S," "E," and "C" types tend to enjoy close personal interactions with others. The "A" and "I" types prefer unstructured activities that involve working with the mind and ideas. The "S" and "E" types are verbally oriented, gregarious, and personable. The "C" and "R" types prefer structured work settings where expectations are clear and procedures are well established.

■ Personality types that are opposite each other on the hexagon share few characteristics. For example, the "S" and "R" types are opposite: "S" types dislike work that gets their hands dirty, while "R" types don't seem to mind that a bit; "S" types like social situations with groups of people, while "R" types prefer a more solitary, out-of-doors lifestyle.

■ The distance separating types on the hexagon represents the degree of similarity or difference between types. The closer the types are, the more alike they are. The farther apart the types are, the more different they are. For example, since "R" and "I" are next to each other, they are somewhat alike. They share some common characteristics such as a preference for solitary

The Six Personality Types

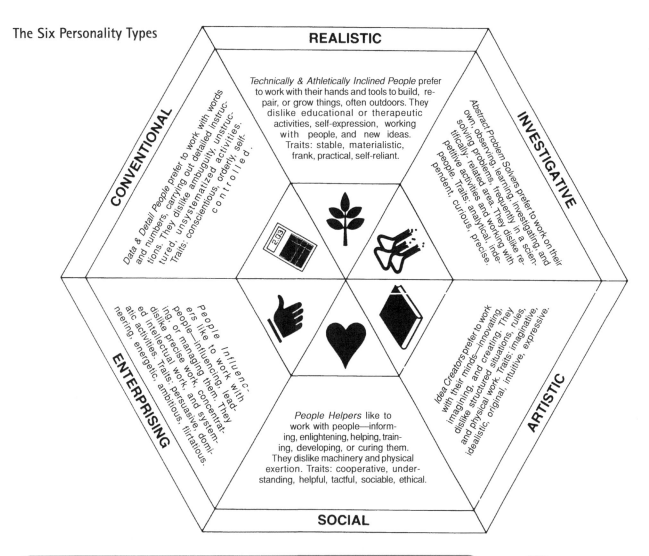

REALISTIC

*Technically & Athletically Inclined People* prefer to work with their hands and tools to build, repair, or grow things, often outdoors. They dislike educational or therapeutic activities, self-expression, working with people, and new ideas. Traits: stable, materialistic, frank, practical, self-reliant.

CONVENTIONAL

*Data & Detail People* prefer to work with words and numbers, carrying out detailed instructions. They dislike ambiguity, unstructured, unsystematized activities. Traits: conscientious, orderly, self-controlled.

INVESTIGATIVE

*Abstract Problem Solvers* prefer to work on their own, observing, learning, investigating, and solving problems, frequently in a scientifically related area. They dislike repetitive activities and working with people. Traits: analytical, independent, curious, precise.

ENTERPRISING

*People Influencers* like to work with others—influencing, leading, or managing them. They dislike precise work, concentrated intellectual work, and systematic activities. Traits: persuasive, domineering, energetic, ambitious, flirtatious.

ARTISTIC

*Idea Creators* prefer to work with their minds—innovating, imagining, and creating. They dislike structured situations, rules, and physical work. Traits: imaginative, idealistic, original, intuitive, expressive.

SOCIAL

*People Helpers* like to work with people—informing, enlightening, helping, training, developing, or curing them. They dislike machinery and physical exertion. Traits: cooperative, understanding, helpful, tactful, sociable, ethical.

PAUSE

**After considering these illustrative examples, see what new insights you have gained from studying your own profile.**

**Answer the following questions regarding your profile.**

1. **Do I have a narrow range of interest areas, or do they spread across several areas?**

2. **Who are some people who have profiles similar to mine? What kinds of activities and/or interests did/do they seem to have? Does this provide clues for new activities and interests to investigate?**

3. **How do I feel about my profile? In what ways does it seem to be an accurate reflection of me? What does it confirm about me and what surprises me?**

**From the list of personality characteristics below, check those that you would prefer in your coworkers.**

| | | |
|---|---|---|
| Intellectual | Creative | Popular |
| Idea oriented | Emotional | Controlled |
| Analytical | Impulsive | Orderly |
| Self-reliant | Imaginative | Data oriented |
| Independent | Impractical | Practical |
| Curious | Nonconforming | Conforming |
| Reserved | Sociable | Serious |
| Adventurous | Understanding | A loner |
| Energetic | Helpful | Frank |
| Aggressive | Idealistic | Involved with things |
| Argumentative | Cheerful | |
| Other _____ | _____ | _____ |
| _____ | _____ | _____ |

3. **What did you learn about yourself? What ideas did you get for career possibilities? Write a few observations in the AHA section of APP 7.0 . Add any new occupation ideas to the Occupations to Consider page.**

activity and a no-nonsense preference for the hard facts. While there are differences between the two types, they are not as great as the differences between "I" and "E," represented by their opposite positions on the hexagon.

## Summary

Personalities and interest patterns can be grouped according to six personality types. While most of us have characteristics from all six types in our personalities, we tend to favor one style over others. We have a primary, a secondary, and a tertiary preference. The strength of the difference from our primary to secondary preference may be great, as it probably was for a Michelangelo, or slight, as it seems to have been for a Thomas Jefferson.

Identifying your own personality style will help you know what kinds of people you are likely to be more energized by, what kinds of activities you most enjoy, and where your strongest career and educational interests lie. With this understanding, you are in a better position to appreciate your style of personality and make intelligent career and educational decisions.

## Endnotes

### APP 2.3

1. Adapted from Richard N. Bolles, *The Party Exercise* (Berkeley, CA: National Career Development Project, n.d.).

2. John L. Holland, *Making Vocational Choices: A Theory of Vocational Personalities and Work Environments*, 2nd ed. (Odessa, FL: Psychological Assessment Resources, Inc., 1992).

# APP 2.4 Connect Your Personality to Work

## Do you know people who:

- See their work as little more than a necessary evil to support weekend escapes into leisure?

- Enjoy their work so much that they look forward with enthusiasm to getting to their jobs on Monday mornings?

- Frequently call in sick to avoid going to work because they find their jobs so draining?

- Find their educational coursework so fascinating that they are inspired to work hard out of pure interest rather than just to obtain good grades?

- Keep changing their academic major, hoping to find one that connects with their interests?

If so, you have become aware of the difference that making a career choice that is compatible versus one that is incompatible with your personality style can make in your overall motivation and success in life and work.

So Miss Anderson, do you feel your personality is suited for a career as a corporate attorney?

*The single most important contribution you can make to a child's development is to help him toward a field where his talents best suit him, where he will be satisfied and competent.*

—Daniel Goleman, Emotional Intelligence

## Case Study — Helen

Helen, a 40-year-old mother, decided her children were old enough that she could begin a new career. She wanted to get into something that was secure, had good employment prospects, and was useful. She was advised that a special education specialty in speech pathology would accomplish her stated objectives, so, on that basis, that's what she decided to do. Helen had some indication that this kind of work might not be a great fit for her when she realized that the coursework was not engaging her interests. But, overlooking this telltale clue of a personality style mismatch, she persevered to become certified and then to get a job as a speech pathologist. Now, one year into her new work, she has come to the sad realization that this profession just is not for her. She simply does not have the right temperament for it. At the time of this writing she is paying for the services of a career counselor for help in getting redirected into something that fits her better. Why, she asks herself, did I not seek this kind of assistance before investing so much time, money, and effort into something that fit me so poorly?

## Case Study — Merrill

For several years Merrill had worked as an economist with the World Bank, engaged in an extremely demanding field of poverty alleviation in the developing world. She loved being in a position of devising economic development projects for helping people move out of poverty. But after a few years of this work a major problem developed: she was working herself into a state of total exhaustion, emotionally and physically. Her health deteriorated to the point that she was forced to take a prolonged disability leave. During her recovery period she came to the realization that she could not continue with her economic development work—she needed to make a career change. For help in finding a career better suited to her unique personality and lifestyle needs she sought the services of a career counselor. Through various types of assessment activity she concluded, among other things, that she was a Holland code SAI and that she wanted to work with people in a much more direct way than she had been doing. She also knew that she needed to do much less traveling, to have more control over her time, and, if at all possible, to work with animals. The desire to be involved with animals resulted from a long-term love of animals and the fact that pets had played a very important role in her own recovery and healing process. In putting all of these pieces together, she eventually decided to obtain a degree in social work. She is currently developing a unique practice as a social worker in creative association with a veterinarian. In her new profession, she has chosen to work with people dealing with serious emotional issues such as anorexia, autism, depression, and drug addiction. Often, in appropriate situations, she will prescribe treatments that bring her clients into association with the healing presence of animals. Through her explorations in seeking a new career direction she discovered that there was a developing body of research indicating that people dealing with emotional issues

such as these seem to recover more quickly and more fully when they are caring for animal pets. Her work now seems to be an excellent way for connecting her personality, values, and talents with work about which she is passionate and that provides her with a strong sense of purpose and meaning.

There are a number of career-relevant lessons to be gained from these case studies. First, and most important, is the need to do what the title of this APP suggests—connect your personality to your work. By personality we mean those interest styles we discussed in the previous APP along with your deep-seated values, needs, and your thinking style. Choosing a career strictly on the basis of good employment prospects, job security, and pay may sound totally practical. It's a poor strategy for choosing or changing your career, however, because it fails to take your deeper personal needs and motivations into consideration. Helen, in the first example, is a vivid illustration. Because she failed to do enough self-assessment and occupational exploration before jumping into a new career, she ended up frustrated in her work and angry with herself. While speech pathology is a great fit for the right personality, it happened to be an exceedingly poor fit for Helen's.

There are a number of career-relevant lessons to be gained from these case studies. First, and most important, is the need to do what the title of this chapter suggests—connect your personality to your work. By personality we mean those interest styles we discussed in the previous chapter along with your deep-seated values, needs, and your thinking style. Choosing a career strictly on the basis of good employment prospects, job security, and pay may sound totally practical. It's a poor strategy for choosing or changing your career, however, because it fails to take your deeper personal needs and motivations into consideration. Helen, in the first example, is a vivid illustration. Because she failed to do enough self-assessment and occupational exploration before jumping into a new career, she ended up frustrated in her

Gajus/Shutterstock.com

Clipart deSIGN/Shutterstock.com

work and angry with herself. While speech pathology is a great fit for the right personality, it happened to be an exceedingly poor fit for Helen's.

Merrill, on the other hand, found a better fit for herself as an economist in poverty development work. What she hadn't realized, however, was that her passion for helping others, especially those living in poverty, would be so all-consuming that it would drive her to the brink of emotional and physical exhaustion. She came to realize, with the aid of counseling, that she was the type of person who needed to manage her obsessive inclination to be of service with awareness and care. Merrill also came to understand a deep-seated desire to combine working with people and therapeutic involvement with animals.

The latter awareness came from her very positive experience with animals while she was recovering her health. During this period she obtained a horse and a cat for companionship and to draw her attention away from her health problems through caring for her pets. Through this experience she came to realize that there is great therapeutic benefit in tending animals. Her love for these animals, and we presume their affection for her, brought her out of her state of emotional exhaustion and helped to restore her in body and mind. Aware of the healing power that she had realized through her relationships with these delightful creatures, she longed to help others similarly afflicted. Her counselor suggested some ideas for how she might do this and encouraged her to look for innovative ways she might combine these interests by talking with people in the fields of human health and animal care. Finding the right connection between personality and work for Merrill took a combination of pain-induced awareness, self-assessment, exploration, and creativity. Her investment has paid dividends, however, in that she has found a productive way to make a good living by doing good work.

## Connecting People and Occupations

Having acquired a better understanding of your personality style in Holland code terms from the previous APP, you will want to select a career direction that fits your unique personality-style-related interests. To do that, you need to have some way of matching personality style with occupations. Holland's system is particularly useful in this regard in that it facilitates relating your unique personality traits with the typical kinds of work activities involved in various occupations (see the figure below).

The Holland model profiles occupations in the same manner as personality styles were profiled in the previous APP. So, for example, occupations primarily *realistic* in nature usually involve hands-on work activities such as building, repairing, operating, maintaining, growing, checking, or producing things. Some typical realistic work tasks are operating a large crane, building a wooden cabinet, piloting an airplane, repairing an antique clock, and doing home repairs. Examples of primarily realistic occupations include: diesel mechanic, computer technician, civil engineer, carpenter, dental technician, National Park service ranger, air-traffic controller, and industrial arts teacher.

Occupations primarily *investigative* in nature involve using mental effort to solve problems, understand cause-and-effect relationships, or make intelligent meaning out of facts and data through research, analysis, and objective reasoning. (Referring back to the brain-dominance APP, we're talking left-brain cerebral here.) Some typical investigative tasks are studying science journals, developing new computer programs, analyzing tissue cultures for laboratory research, engineering new computer systems, and analyzing demographic data from National Census Reports to understand the changing nature of the U.S. population. Examples of primarily investigative occupations include economist, computer scientist, biochemist, mathematician, medical researcher, NSA intelligence analyst, and astrophysicist.

Occupations primarily *artistic* in nature typically involve mental intuition in creating artistic renderings and innovations in the form of ideas, metaphors, images, music, and verbal expressions. (Again referring back to the brain-dominance APP, we're talking right-brain cerebral here.) Some typical artistic tasks are generating cartoons for the *New Yorker* magazine, singing in the choir of a Broadway stage production, scriptwriting for a TV sitcom, developing designs for a toy manufacturer, and creating advertisements for Apple Computers. Examples of some primarily artistic occupations include: literature teacher, children's book writer, landscape architect, organizational creativity consultant, film director, public relations director, art therapist, country music singer, and Web site designer.

Occupations primarily *social* in nature usually involve exercising interpersonal intelligence in relating with people for the purpose of educating, healing, training, and providing general support and nurturance. Some typical social tasks include working as a Red Cross care provider, providing therapy in a health center, teaching first graders to read, mediating grievance disputes as an organizational ombudsmen, showing someone how to express feelings in a more socially acceptable way as an employee assistance specialist, and providing solace to people in the final stages of life as a hospice worker. Examples of some primarily social occupations include: vocational rehabilitation counselor, registered nurse, special education teacher, speech and drama teacher, and school psychologist.

Occupations primarily *enterprising* in nature commonly require a head for business and/or a facility in exercising influence with others, organizational

Clipart deSIGN/Shutterstock.com

decision-making, risk taking, and finding cost-effective and practical solutions to business-related operations. Some distinctive enterprising tasks include chairing an important civic committee, providing consultation services to managers, starting your own business, running for political office, leading a work team, acting as spokesperson for a group, and selling a product or an idea. Examples of some primarily enterprising occupations include National Park superintendent, real estate agent, bank manager, organizational development consultant, travel agency manager, captain of a cruise liner, and sales manager.

Occupations primarily *conventional* in nature commonly involve a facility for working with numbers and data, carrying out or developing detailed plans, managing client accounts, bookkeeping, relating policies to practice, and overseeing detailed operations. Some typical conventional tasks are keeping accurate fiscal records, preparing reports and graphs, analyzing fiscal expenditures, and developing quality-control instructions. Examples of some primarily conventional occupations include proofreader, computer programmer, accountant, finance officer, procurement specialist, NASA space data technician, and credit analyst.

## Personality and Occupational Profiles

As we hope you will see from the previous discussion, personality styles and occupational functions are relatives. For example, those of us who are strong "Is," primarily *investigative* in nature, are drawn to cerebral activities such as observing, scientific investigation, contemplating complex problems, and analyzing and evaluating possible meanings from available data. Isn't it fortunate that investigative occupations involve functions, such as observing, learning, abstract analytical problem solving, and seeking to understand the nature of things like the cosmos, the brain, and bed bugs? Similarly, we *enterprising* types like to work with people, doing things like selling, leading, making business-related decisions, engaging in risk-taking adventures in launching new products or services, and motivating others to achieve goal-oriented results. *Enterprising* occupations fit "E" types nicely because in them we get to do things like make business decisions, persuade, lead, sell, and influence others for gain, fame, fun, and—oh yes—profit.

John Holland assigned three-letter codes (referred to as Holland codes) to both personality styles and occupational types.[1] The nature of work involved in a specific occupation can readily be appreciated and understood by its three-letter code. The below figure shows characteristic profiles for a few selected occupations. In reference to the figure, the functions or activities performed by laboratory testers include using hands-on skills to set up and run testing equipment and instruments ("R" activities), analyzing materials to determine their chemical or physical properties ("I" activities), and performing tests according to prescribed standards ("C" activities). Laboratory testers, therefore, have "RIC" Holland code classifications because the primary functions of this work involve "R" activities, the secondary functions involve "I" activities, and the third-level functions characteristically are "C" activities.

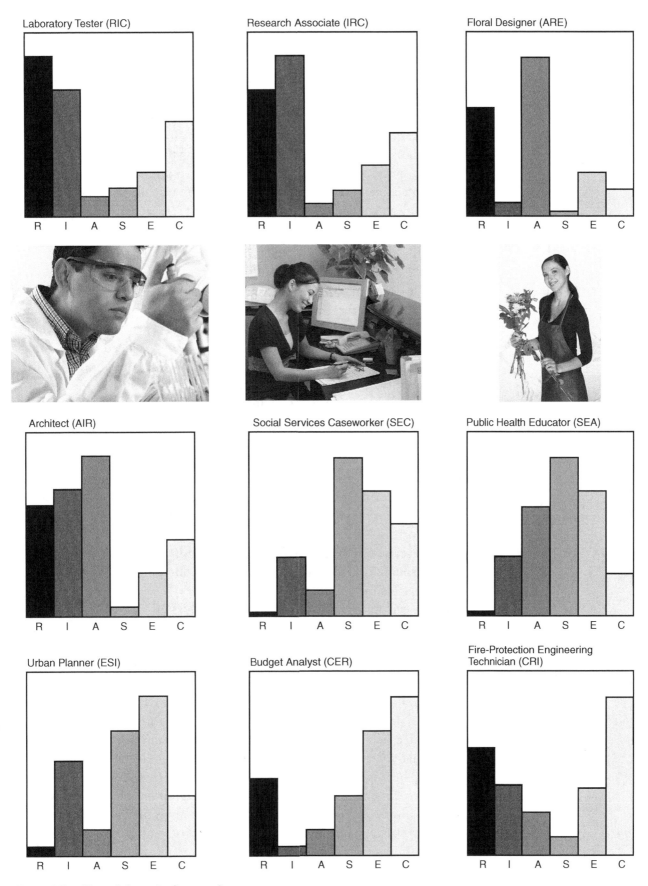

**Typical Profiles of Sample Occupation**

Three-letter Holland codes can be assigned to most occupations. An "SEC" code, for example, is assigned to social service caseworkers, since the chief set of functions of their work is counseling and assisting individuals and families ("S" activities). The secondary function is to influence their clients to utilize appropriate community resources ("E" activities). A third-level function is to complete forms, compile records, and do client follow-up ("C" activities).

A "CRI" code is assigned to the occupation of fire-protection engineering technician because this work first involves ensuring that fire-protection systems conform to specifications and building codes, and drafting detailed drawings for fire-protection systems ("C" activities). Secondary functions include using and operating a variety of fire-fighting equipment ("R" activities). A third-level function is analyzing blueprints prepared by architects ("I" activities).

## Finding a Compatible Occupation

Don't let anyone talk you into pursuing a particular career just because an occupational field offers good job opportunities and/or good pay. We're not suggesting that you forget about employment prospects or career development opportunities, nor even good salary prospects. Instead we encourage you, in addition to these things, to choose an occupation compatible with your personality! You have a far better chance of succeeding (getting promoted, getting salary increases, being self-motivated, having fun, and getting into more interesting challenges) in work compatible with your Holland code. To help you find work that matches your style, Dr. Holland spent years creating an elegant methodology for career choice.

To find occupations that match your personality style, explore those with the same or similar Holland codes in the table, *Personality Types and Occupational Characteristics* (see APP ACTION 2.4 at the end of this APP). Since this is a short list of occupations, selected to provide you with examples of how careers can be coded, see the reference section at the end of the book for additional sources of information. Also, we encourage you to consult with a career counselor for additional assistance.

When developing your list of occupational possibilities, keep in mind that there is a great deal of variety among the different occupations associated with a particular field. Be sure also to consider the long-term promotional opportunities within the fields you are exploring. We know of many professionals who have both enjoyed and been successful in their early work experiences only to become derailed later on by getting promoted into work that is very different from their nature. Promotions are not always good things, especially if they promote you away from the kinds of work that taps your interests. Let's say, for example, that you are particularly interested in the career field of mechanical engineering because, as an "IRA," you find the intellectual, hands-on, and creative work of this field to be particularly interesting. After being in this field for some time, however, you may be looking for a promotion but see that the only way for that to happen is to move into management, which is likely to involve ESC work. If you take that promotion, you just might find that your work is no longer very enjoyable. In fact, this kind of thing happens very frequently. So think about both the short and the long range in making your career decisions.

The range of possibilities within a particular occupational field is illustrated by the options available within the broad field of psychology. If you are highly motivated to help people live more effective and satisfying lives, you would probably want to consider the occupations of counseling psychologist or marriage and family counselor. If, on the other hand, you are interested in assisting people afflicted with severe emotional or thinking disorders, you might choose to become a psychiatrist or a clinical psychologist. Should you have strong research and investigative interests, you might choose to become an experimental or development psychologist. Or, if you are interested in using the study of psychology to assist industry in managing its human resources more effectively, you might decide to become an industrial-organizational psychologist.

## Predicting Outcomes of Occupational and Academic Choices

In thinking through these concepts, you should be better able to predict what is likely to happen if a particular personality type enters a specific occupation or academic program. Artistic personalities, for example, are far more likely to experience satisfaction if they enter occupations that are primarily "A" in nature. Holland's research informs us that people who enter occupations compatible with their personality type are more satisfied in their work and happier in their lives—and don't you really want this for yourself?

What alternatives are available for people with Holland codes that are not adjacent on the hexagonal model? For example, what happens if the essentially artistic person with a primary "A" has a "C" or conventional code as the second or third letter in the personality profile? It is possible, with some creativity, to find occupations with unusual Holland code combinations, as the example of Merrill at the beginning of the APP suggests. Another alternative is to select an appropriate creative occupation, but choose a more conventional, orderly working environment for the specific job. Still another alternative is to choose work compatible with your strongest Holland letter and reserve an enjoyable leisure activity for a lesser code letter. Read the following case study of Gene for an example of how this might be done.

Make some **PREDICTIONS TO SUCCESS** as to the most likely outcomes in each of the following examples. How satisfied and motivated do you think people are likely to be in each example? Why? If you get stumped, check out the insights provided at the end of this APP.

1. How successful and motivated is the "E"-oriented person likely to be who enrolls in a biology curriculum?

2. How successful and motivated is the "I"-oriented person likely to be who becomes a sales representative or a warehouse manager?

3. How motivated is an "A" personality type likely to be who enrolls in an interior design curriculum?

4. How engaged is a "C" type likely to be doing theater set design work? What personality style might be especially energized by this kind of work? Why?

5. How motivated are "S" types likely to be about their work if employed as electricians, surveyors, carpenters, or mechanical engineers? What if they were employed as organizational trainers, social workers, or college professors in the humanities?

## Case Study    Bill

Through his school years, Bill had always been interested in music. He played the piano, guitar, and electronic keyboard. He organized a musical group with some of his friends, and they often played until late into the night in his basement—usually until the neighbors complained.

Bill aspired to a music career, visualizing himself as a concert pianist, playing before appreciative audiences all over the world. He allowed his dream to be squelched, however, by his well-meaning father. His father advised him to be more realistic about his career, warning

Volodymyr Burdiak/Shutterstock.com

echoevg/Shutterstock.com

that pursuing a career in music was impractical because of limited employment opportunities, which would make supporting himself or a family difficult, if not impossible.

Bill did what his father prescribed for him, which was to become an accountant. His father's reasoning for that was that Bill had always been good at math and that the employment outlook for accountants was excellent. After getting an accounting degree, Bill obtained a job with a large firm. He worked hard and was rewarded with promotions and salary increases.

Eventually, Bill married his childhood sweetheart, and they had a child. He seemed to have all the ingredients for the good life—good job, steady income, great wife, family, home. But there was a problem—he felt terrible! He had become anemic, sickly, and had no energy. Eventually his deteriorating health forced him to see a doctor because he thought he must have diabetes or some other major problem. His doctor, unable to find anything physically wrong with him, advised Bill that the cause of his problem was probably mental rather than physical.

Suspecting job-related stress and dissatisfaction, his doctor referred him to the nearby college career-counseling center.

Bill came into the center looking emaciated and tired. He was so thin that his clothes hung on him like the drape on a scarecrow. In discussing his situation with a career counselor, Bill decided to enroll in a career planning class, where he discovered the source of his physical issues. He learned that he was an "ASR" on the Holland test and a primary reason for his unhappiness in his "CIE" accounting job was that the activities of his work in no way connected with any of his personality traits and top interests. Even though he had a good job and appropriate skills for it, this particular kind of work was draining his energy and vitality. He literally had to force himself to work each and every day. His career choice had pleased his father, but the cost to Bill had been severe.

On the basis of this awareness, Bill, with his wife's consent and support, decided he must make a major lifestyle and career change. Bill's wife went to work and he went back to college to pursue his first love—music. For a while, they had to struggle to get by on less than their previous income, but they felt energized and optimistic about their career and life possibilities. Bill began putting on weight, and his health has improved. Today he has a job with a music company where he combines his love of music with his computer skills and musical knowledge. He also has organized a group of talented musicians in a bluegrass group and plays gigs on weekends for fun—occasionally they even generate a little extra spending money.

Bill's story seems to have a happy ending. What do you think would have happened if Bill had enrolled in a career planning course when he was in college initially?

Bill was influenced by his father's input. In what ways are you experiencing the expectations and input of family as you make your career decisions?

What steps can you take to make career decisions now that will make you happy instead of redoing them later?

PAUSE

## Case Study    Gene

Gene, a 50-something engineer ("IRC" code), came to a career-planning center to talk about a career change. There he learned, among many other things, that he was an "ASE." This was a major revelation to Gene, who had concluded, based upon comparing himself to his engineering colleagues, that he must be lazy and not nearly as bright as the other workers.

Actually, Gene was an extremely bright man, but neither his interests nor his thinking style were compatible with the work of an engineer. With such a gap between his personality and the nature of his work, Gene simply had been experiencing a serious and prolonged lack of motivation. Gene's job used some of his skills, but they were not his best talents, and the work certainly did not connect with his interests. There were some rather severe consequences that came with spending so much time in work ill suited to his best talents and interest. It had taken a toll on his self-esteem, his dignity, and his sense of self-worth. That's often what happens when someone stays in work that's a misfit with their personality for too long.

Janos Levente/Shutterstock.com

In Gene's case the remedy he chose was not simply to change careers. He elected not to do this because he had only a few more years remaining to be eligible for a pension. Instead, he decided to stick with his current job but to make some constructive changes in other areas of his life. To find expression for his strongest interests he started acting in amateur theater productions, taking creative writing courses, and very actively participating in social/learning activities with his church. Gene found a piano accompanist and began singing solos in his church, but singing mostly for the sheer fun of it. With a rich tenor voice and a strong Italian lineage, singing was something he had done a lot of in his earlier life but had stopped doing in the course of his career.

Through his new leisure activities, Gene was able to restore his energy and improve his self-confidence and sense of self-worth. By engaging in activities that matched his interest patterns, Gene literally transformed his life and created enough satisfaction through his leisure activities to carry over and energize him in his work. When you are able to energize one part of your life through uplifting activities, there is often a transferal that occurs in other areas of your life, even when those areas may not be very happy situations. That was the case with Gene, whom you can now often find singing his heart out in church and making his church's adult education program a very interesting learning opportunity.

Christine Krahl/Shutterstock.com

Gene decided to hang in there with his career but pursue leisure activities to express his interests and passions.

For all of us, like Gene, work is not completely fulfilling. We need to work to pay the bills. College students often complain about being in jobs that they don't enjoy but have flexible hours to allow them to concentrate on their studies.

Have you ever been in a situation where work was something you did but didn't enjoy? If it occurred before, what could you have done to find satisfaction in other areas? If it is your current reality, what other activities can you be engaging in that are more suited to your interests, skills, passions, and values?

## Summary

The characteristics and activities that typify each of the six personality styles also apply to occupations and academic programs. Once you have identified your personality style, you are in a better position to select occupations and academic programs that are compatible with your personality-related interests. Pursuing an occupation or an academic program of study that is compatible with your personality type is an essential task for personal motivation, for self-concept development, and for career and academic success. It is crucial for life satisfaction as well, since your occupational choice plays a major role in your energy and emotional disposition.

Wiktoria Matynia/Shutterstock.com

### Words of Wisdom

*To experience satisfaction and fulfillment in your work and in your life, choose a career direction that allows you to pursue your top interests, engages your preferred style of thinking, and puts your preferred talents to productive work.*

## Predictions of Success Answers

1. Since biology is primarily an "I" curriculum and is opposite "E" on the Holland hexagon, the "E"-type person is likely to be very dissatisfied. Types that are opposite each other on the hexagon are very dissimilar. The "E" type here would probably drop out, flunk out, or wisely change to an academic program that would be compatible with the primary "E." The "E" type, persisting in the "I" curriculum, would be likely to experience a very low energy level, a tendency to be ill frequently, and a general lack of interest in academics and probably life in general.

2. Here again, the "I" type is going into an occupation that is just the opposite. Both salesperson and warehouse manager are "E" types. The "I" type is likely to be very dissatisfied on the job and search for ways to experience satisfaction outside of work, if not look for a more compatible occupation.

3. An "A" person who enrolls in an "A" curriculum is likely to experience satisfaction. Both personality type and curriculum are compatible. The "A" person is likely to be very energetic and enthusiastic about and attentive to his or her studies.

4. The "C" person is not likely to last very long in an "A" occupation. The "C" and "A" types are opposite on the hexagon. The "A" environment would be too flexible and frustrating for the "C" person, who would want structure and a schedule of activities to follow. The "C" person in this situation would be most likely to channel energy into looking for a new, compatible occupation.

5. The energy level of an "S" person in an "R" job would be very low. The chances for success and stability would be extremely low since these types are opposite and characteristics are very dissimilar. The "S" person might experience a high absentee rate from work due to illness or lack of interest. Here again, any energy might be directed into seeking a compatible occupation.

## Endnotes

### APP 2.4

**1.** John L. Holland, *Making Vocational Choices: A Theory of Vocational Personalities and Work Environments*, 2nd ed. (Odessa, FL: Psychological Assessment Resources, Inc., 1992).

Another source related to this APP:

**2.** Daniel Goleman, *Emotional Intelligence: Why It Can Matter More Than IQ* (New York: Bantam Books, 1994), p. 34.

# APP 2.5 APP ACTIONS

## APP ACTIONS 2.1

### Achievement Stories

Here is another chance to look at skills. This exercise involves describing successful experiences you have had in order to identify the skills you were using in the process. This is one of the best ways to become aware of and clarify your top skills. Once you know what skills you have used successfully in the past, you can make plans to capitalize on these same skills in the future.

Make a list of 15 achievements, large or small, from your past. These should be descriptive phrases of memorable activities or events where *you* contributed to a satisfying, but not necessarily perfect, outcome. The satisfaction may have come from improvement in a particular activity. Try to list particular events rather than general situations. For example, if getting good grades is one of your achievements, list the most satisfying "A" you've ever obtained, or if traveling is one of your achievements, indicate one particularly significant travel experience you had. The following is a list of some sample achievements to help you start thinking about your own achievements.

- Cooking a gourmet meal (e.g., cordon bleu)
- Helping a neighbor cope with her husband's death
- Training a horse
- Figuring out a new approach for an office project
- Playing basketball (learning to play, or a particular game)
- Decorating the community center for Christmas
- Writing song lyrics
- Enforcing regulations in a particular situation
- Structuring a research project
- Creating a report with complex tables
- Analyzing people's needs for improved computer equipment
- Playing a computer game well
- Persuading someone to buy something
- Classifying information for a biology experiment
- Managing people to reach a fundraising goal
- Repairing an auto engine
- Playing guitar for an audience
- Refinishing a valuable old piece of furniture
- Writing a feature story for a community newspaper
- Designing a prize-winning Halloween costume
- Teaching a child to read
- Writing a piece of poetry

Your List of Achievements: (Keep in mind that achievements can be simple everyday things, but the requirement is that you had to put forth effort or work to make them happen.)

_____ 1. _____

_____ 2. _____

_____ 3. _____

_____ 4. _____

_____ 5. _____

_____ 6. _____

_____ 7. _____

_____ 8. _____

_____ 9. _____

_____10. _____

_____11. _____

_____12. _____

_____13. _____

_____14. _____

_____15. _____

From your list of 15, select the 5 achievements that made you feel the happiest, most satisfied, or most energetic. You may want to choose achievements that resulted in positive reactions from someone else, although this is not essential. Copy each of these descriptive phrases at the top of a blank sheet of paper. Next, write a paragraph or two describing each achievement. Start at the beginning and say it simply. Don't worry about grammar, organization, or any fine points of writing. Just tell what happened, describing exactly what you did to contribute to the satisfying outcome. Choose action words to tell what you did and include as much relevant detail as you can recall. The following examples show how a satisfying achievement can be elaborated on in preparation for identifying skills.

### *Example 1: Doing a Bass Fish Mounting*

Because I enjoy fishing a lot, I decided that I wanted to learn how to do fish mounting. The first step I took to achieve my goal was going to the library and checking out books about fish mounting. There I got some pretty good ideas of the types of mounts and procedures involved. Then I got in touch with a taxidermist who agreed to train me. I went to the taxidermist once a week for about three months. I would always bring a fish I had just caught to practice with. He showed me, step-by-step, how to clean and skin the fish and how to dry and preserve it. He also taught me how to put the finishing touches on a fish and then how to mount it in the desired position. I worked with him for about three months until he felt the work I was doing was of professional quality.

Shortly after I finished my training, I caught a large bass and decided to try out my skills. I cleaned the fish carefully, not leaving any meat behind that would spoil. Then I salted the skin and braced the fins in the positions that I wanted them in. Next, I put a filler in the bass to give it its original shape back. I mounted the fish in an open-mouthed position in order to give it a fierce look as if it were feeding. After a few weeks of drying, my bass was ready to paint. I selected colors to bring back the original look and then gave it a coat of shellac to seal the paint and give the fish a wet look and the lifelike appearance. I think my final product is very professional; it's hanging on a wall in my house.

*Example 2: Buying a Townhouse*

I decided that I wanted to buy a nice place to live after my husband and I divorced. I dreamed of a place that would be attractive and located in a pleasant neighborhood where I could go to bed in the evening and hear the sounds of the wind in the trees and awake in the morning to the music of birds singing. I also envisioned a place that would not require much yard work and would be within a half-hour commute to work.

First, I analyzed how much I could afford for a place and what my monthly payments ought to be. In considering the options within my price range, I figured out that a townhouse would be my best buy. Next, I began exploring the area to see what was available. Initially I thought I would like to buy in the Crofton area and found a realtor to work with. I looked at several places there but didn't find exactly what I wanted within my price range. Then I learned that there were some nice townhouses being built along the golf course in Upper Marlboro, so I drove out and took a look. I loved the location and the models.

It didn't require much consideration to decide that this was where I wanted to live. I selected the lot and the model I wanted and signed a contract. I was concerned that my monthly payments would be more than I could afford, but trusted that it would be possible to rent out the spare bedroom for about $400.00 per month.

I am now in my new townhouse and decorating it with a modest budget to make it feel like home. I was able to rent out the space by placing an ad in the *Post*. With this additional income I have been able to make my monthly payments by sticking closely to a budget. While things are currently a bit tight financially, I am confident that I will be able to make it.

## What Types Of Skills Do You Have?

As you were writing down responses, did you notice that various action words described your skills? If these words reveal your involvement in accomplishing something or making something happen, they are directly describing a functional skill you possess. Maybe you *organized* a team, *composed* correspondence, *operated* equipment, *balanced* a ledger, *prepared* a speech, and *repaired* a radio. These kinds of skills are called functional skills because you can apply them (make them function in) to various situations.

Your paragraphs may also contain words that suggest other types of skills, those that describe your behavioral traits. Descriptive words like *neat, punctual, curious, easygoing, good judgment, honest, resourceful, self-confident, reliable, and decisive* reveal your self-management skills.

Reflect on this in here or in the Press Pause connected to this activity.

## SKILL ASSESSMENT SURVEY

This survey is designed to assist you in assessing your functional and self-management skills and deciding what specific skills you prefer to use in your career.

**Directions**

1. Read the paragraphs you wrote describing your achievements.

2. Highlight all of the skill words you used.

3. Make a list of all of these skills in the following chart (ATTACH CHART).

4. On your list, note if these are self-management skills or functional skills.

5. Give your skill a rating based on the extent you used this skill in your achievement.

   To What Extent Did You Use a Skill in This Achievement?

   0 = Did not use this skill at all

   1 = Used this skill minimally

   2 = Used this skill moderately

   3 = Used this skill to a considerable extent

   4 = Used this skill very extensively

6. Now that you are familiar with these words that describe skills, go back to your original achievement descriptions, adding more descriptive sentences including skills you may not have originally considered.

7. Add these skills to the chart.

8. After determining the degree to which you have used these skills in your favorite achievements, determine your level of enjoyment in using these skills. Give the skill a rating in the ENJOYMENT column.

   *0 = Dislike, didn't really enjoy this skill*

   *1 = Indifferent, not really good or bad*

   *2 = Somewhat prefer, it was OK*

   *3 = Really enjoy, enjoyed using this skill*

   *4 = Special favorite, this stood out as something I really liked doing*

9. Consider how important it will be for you to use and develop each skill in your new career. Give the skill a rating in the PREFERENCE column.

   Your Preference for Using This Skill in Your Career

   *0 = Dislike,* don't want to use or develop this skill

   *1 = Indifferent,* don't care if I use or develop this skill

   *2 = Somewhat prefer,* would be OK to use and develop this skill

   *3 = Really enjoy,* want to use and develop this skill

   *4 = Special favorite,* very important to use and develop this skill

10. Review your list of skills. Are there skills that are missing? Perhaps there are skills you have that were not included in your achievement stories. Add these to your list and fill in the functional skills, self-management, enjoyment, and preference columns.

**SKILLS RATINGS**

| Name of Skill | Functional Skill | Self-Management Skill | Extent of Use | Enjoyment | Preference |
|---|---|---|---|---|---|
|  |  |  |  |  |  |
|  |  |  |  |  |  |
|  |  |  |  |  |  |
|  |  |  |  |  |  |
|  |  |  |  |  |  |
|  |  |  |  |  |  |
|  |  |  |  |  |  |
|  |  |  |  |  |  |
|  |  |  |  |  |  |
|  |  |  |  |  |  |
|  |  |  |  |  |  |
|  |  |  |  |  |  |
|  |  |  |  |  |  |
|  |  |  |  |  |  |
|  |  |  |  |  |  |
|  |  |  |  |  |  |
|  |  |  |  |  |  |
|  |  |  |  |  |  |
|  |  |  |  |  |  |
|  |  |  |  |  |  |
|  |  |  |  |  |  |
|  |  |  |  |  |  |
|  |  |  |  |  |  |
|  |  |  |  |  |  |
|  |  |  |  |  |  |
|  |  |  |  |  |  |
|  |  |  |  |  |  |
|  |  |  |  |  |  |
|  |  |  |  |  |  |
|  |  |  |  |  |  |
|  |  |  |  |  |  |
|  |  |  |  |  |  |
|  |  |  |  |  |  |

## Examples of Functional Skills

*A. Manual/Technical*

    Assembling/installing
    Constructing/building
    Fixing/repairing
    Manual dexterity
    Mechanical reasoning
    Working with animals
    Using hand tools
    Operating machinery or equipment
    Driving vehicles—cars, trucks, buses, tractors, etc.
    Moving materials by hand
    Horticulture skills—working with plants
    Landscaping and groundskeeping
    Physical stamina
    Outdoor labor
    Other _____

*B. Analytical/Problem Solving*

    Analyzing/diagnosing
    Researching/investigating
    Interpreting data
    Classifying/organizing/systematizing
    Evaluating/assessing
    Scientific/technical writing
    Logical decision-making/analytical problem-solving
    Financial analysis
    Mathematical/numerical reasoning
    Using facts/evaluating
    Separating important from unimportant facts
    Putting facts, figures, or information into logical order
    Scientific curiosity/thinking
    Using logic or rational reasoning
    Other _____

*C. Innovative/Original*

    Using your imagination to create
    Graphic designing
    Using intuition
    Designing programs, events, activities
    Originating ideas
    Creative showmanship/acting/performing
    Creative writing, self-expression
    Possibility thinking
    Artistic sense/aesthetics
    Drawing/artistic designing
    Creative movement/dancing/miming

Synthesizing—putting facts and ideas together in new, creative ways
Being innovative or inventing something new or different
Composing music, songs, lyrics
Other _____

### D. *Social/Interpersonal*

Listening skillfully/hearing
Developing rapport/ understanding
Counseling/helping/guiding/mentoring
Drawing people out/interviewing
Instructing/training/educating
Social grace/putting others at ease
Group facilitating
Communicating tactfully
Being of service/responding
Providing information/advising
Cooperating with others
Showing warmth and caring
Being supportive or cooperative
Healing/nursing/nurturing/curing
Other _____

### E. *Detail/Data*

Working with numerical data
Proofreading/editing/technical writing
Inspecting/examining/inventorying
Word processing/typing
Following directions/procedures accurately
Being exact and accurate/careful
Doing math quickly and accurately
Scheduling/organizing events or activities
Completing details on schedule
Accounting/keeping track of data or numbers
Categorizing/sorting/placing items in the right places
Remembering numbers or specific facts
Attending to details
Filing, classifying, recording, retrieving
Other _____

### F. *Managing/Influencing*

Administering a program or resources
Directing/supervising others
Making business-related decisions
Negotiating/contracting with others or groups
Selling/persuading/influencing
Convincing others through force of personality

Overseeing programs/projects/activities
Organizational/group goal setting/planning
Undertaking entrepreneurial activities
Organizing and managing an activity, a task, or a project
Exercising leadership in a group
Taking risks in a public setting
Negotiating deals or transactions
Coordinating people and activities to work together
Other _____

## Examples of Self-Management Skills

Assertive
Authentic
Cautious
Cheerful
Conforming
Concentration
Cooperative
Determination/drive
Deliberate/careful
Dynamic (high energy level)
Diligent
Easy-going/calm
Enthusiastic
Ethical
Fast and expedient
Flexible
Friendly
Helpful
Honest
Initiative
Integrity
Kind
Loyal
Optimistic
Orderly
Patient
Persistent
Poised
Polite
Punctual
Reliable, dependable
Self-controlled
Self-confident/self-assured
Sense of humor
Sincere

Strong willed
Spontaneous
Tactful
Thrifty
Tolerant
Trustworthy
Resilient
Versatile
Other _____

## Your Priority Skills

After completing the skill assessment, prioritize your top 10 functional skills and your top 10 self-management skills. Your top 10 should come from those skills that you have used and have enjoyed using, and want to use in your career.

My top 10 (most preferred) skills are:

| **Functional Skills** | **Self-Management Skills** |
|---|---|
| 1. _____ | 1. _____ |
| 2. _____ | 2. _____ |
| 3. _____ | 3. _____ |
| 4. _____ | 4. _____ |
| 5. _____ | 5. _____ |
| 6. _____ | 6. _____ |
| 7. _____ | 7. _____ |
| 8. _____ | 8. _____ |
| 9. _____ | 9. _____ |
| 10. _____ | 10. _____ |

**My least preferred skills (those I don't want to use in my career):**

| **Functional Skills** | **Self-Management Skills** |
|---|---|
| 1. _____ | 1. _____ |
| 2. _____ | 2. _____ |
| 3. _____ | 3. _____ |
| 4. _____ | 4. _____ |
| 5. _____ | 5. _____ |

## My Preferred Family of Skills

| Skill Family | My Rating | My Preference Ranking |
|---|---|---|
| A. Manual/Technical | | |
| B. Analytical/Problem-Solving | | |
| C. Innovative/Original | | |
| D. Customer/Public Service | | |
| E. Detail/Data | | |

## Your Preferred Family of Skills

These exercises above required you to identify your most preferred individual skills. It is also helpful to identify the groupings of functional skills that you most enjoy using. To do that, look at your skills and give these a rating using the following chart:

0 = Did not use this skill family at all

1 = Used this skill family minimally

2 = Used this skill family moderately

3 = Used this skill family to a considerable extent

4 = Used this skill family very extensively

**Go to onetonline.org.**

Enter an occupation in the box next to Occupation Search.

Read about the occupation as you learn to navigate the O*NET site.

As you read, look for information about the occupation you didn't know before such as job outlook, necessary skills, related occupations, or wages. List three things that stood out to you about the occupation from this research.

_____ 1. _____

_____ 2. _____

_____ 3. _____

## IDENTIFYING YOUR SELF-MANAGEMENT SKILLS

1. From the following partial list of self-management skills, circle those that you think of and that others have consistently mentioned as being most characteristic of you. Keep in mind that while a given self-management skill may be characteristic of you; it does not mean necessarily that you are that way in every situation. Add to the end of the list any self-management skills you have that are not included.

| Self-Management Skills | | |
|---|---|---|
| Adventuresome | Easygoing | Poised |
| Alert | Empathetic | Polite |
| Assertive | Enthusiastic | Precise |
| Astute | Energetic | Punctual |
| Attentive | Ethical | Quiet |
| Authentic | Expressive | Reliable |
| Aware | Firm | Resilient |
| Calm | Flexible | Resourceful |
| Candid | Focused | Respectful |
| Cheerful | Friendly | Responsible |
| Collected | Generous | Risk-taking |
| Committed | Helpful | Self-confident |
| Composed | Honest | Self-controlled |
| Concentration | Initiative | Self-reliant |
| Concerned | Insightful | Sensitive |
| Conscientious | Integrity | Sincere |
| Cooperative | Kind | Spontaneous |
| Courageous | Loyal | Steadfast |
| Courteous | Methodical | Sympathetic |
| Curious | Open-minded | Tactful |
| Decisive | Optimistic | Thorough |
| Dependable | Orderly | Thrifty |
| Diplomatic | Outgoing | Tolerant |
| Discerning | Patient | Trustworthy |
| Discreet | Perceptive | Unique |
| Dynamic | Persistent | Versatile |
| Eager | Playful | Vigorous |

2. Prioritize your top 10 self-management skills from those that you have identified as most characteristic of you. Place them here in the order of preference.

My top 10 (most characteristic) self-management skills are:

_____ 1. _____

_____ 2. _____

_____ 3. _____

_____ 4. _____

_____ 5. _____

_____ 6. _____

_____ 7. _____

_____ 8. _____

_____ 9. _____

_____10. _____

## Self-Management Skills and Work Sites

Review your list of self-management skills and make some assessments on how to capitalize on those most characteristic of you and also those least characteristic of you.

1. How might you capitalize on your most preferred self-management skills in the workplace? How could you use them to help yourself and others?

_____

_____

_____

2. Review the list of self-management skills on pages 66–67 and identify the five that are least characteristic of you. List them below.

_____

_____

_____

_____

_____

3. Indicate some things that you might wish to keep in mind about your least preferred self-management skills both in terms of career choice and on-the-job behavior.

_____

_____

_____

## DISCOVERING YOUR SPECIAL KNOWLEDGE

1. Divide a piece of paper into three columns headed *Work, Learning,* and *Leisure.* Then begin listing all of the special knowledge you have acquired over the years in each of these three categories. Be as thorough as you can, keeping in mind that some of your special knowledge skills may not be readily apparent. You may have to do some mental digging to uncover these. You might even need to do a careful memory search to recall that you learned a lot about gas combustion engines while working on your car as a teenager or that you found out how to conduct formal meetings while serving as a class officer in school.

   Other special knowledge skills are less subtle. You might, for example, have learned a lot about computer operations through taking formal courses, or you may have picked up a great deal of knowledge on your own through trial and error in working with your own computer. Special knowledge is often acquired by attending classes or workshops, reading books or manuals, or watching how someone else does something. Remember, you were not born with these kinds of skills: you acquired them through learning.

2. After identifying your own list of special knowledge, go back over your list and circle your favorite knowledge skills. Work with this list until you have narrowed it down to the 10 special knowledge skills that seem most important to you, the ten that you might want to use in the next phase of your career.

3. Prioritize your list of 10, using the prioritizing process that follows. As you go through the prioritization process, ask yourself how much do I value this special knowledge and how important might it be for me to use it in my career?

4. List your top five special knowledge skills below, then list some career options in which you might put your knowledge to use.

| Your Top Special Knowledge Skills | Possible Career Options |
|---|---|
| 1. | |
| 2. | |
| 3. | |
| 4. | |
| 5. | |

**Items** — Numbered lines 1 through 10 (blank for filling in).

**Number of Times Circled** — blank lines for each item.

**Final Prioritized Order** — blank lines for each item.

**Grid / Row**

| Row | Grid pairs |
|-----|-----------|
| A | $\frac{1}{2}$ $\frac{1}{3}$ $\frac{1}{4}$ $\frac{1}{5}$ $\frac{1}{6}$ $\frac{1}{7}$ $\frac{1}{8}$ $\frac{1}{9}$ $\frac{1}{10}$ |
| B | $\frac{2}{3}$ $\frac{2}{4}$ $\frac{2}{5}$ $\frac{2}{6}$ $\frac{2}{7}$ $\frac{2}{8}$ $\frac{2}{9}$ $\frac{2}{10}$ |
| C | $\frac{3}{4}$ $\frac{3}{5}$ $\frac{3}{6}$ $\frac{3}{7}$ $\frac{3}{8}$ $\frac{3}{9}$ $\frac{3}{10}$ |
| D | $\frac{4}{5}$ $\frac{4}{6}$ $\frac{4}{7}$ $\frac{4}{8}$ $\frac{4}{9}$ $\frac{4}{10}$ |
| E | $\frac{5}{6}$ $\frac{5}{7}$ $\frac{5}{8}$ $\frac{5}{9}$ $\frac{5}{10}$ |
| F | $\frac{6}{7}$ $\frac{6}{8}$ $\frac{6}{9}$ $\frac{6}{10}$ |
| G | $\frac{7}{8}$ $\frac{7}{9}$ $\frac{7}{10}$ |
| H | $\frac{8}{9}$ $\frac{8}{10}$ |
| I | $\frac{9}{10}$ |

[3] Adapted from *The Three Boxes of Life and How to Get Out of Them*, by Richard N. Bolles, © copyright 1978, by Richard N. Bolles. Used by special permission. Those desiring a copy of the complete book for further reading may procure it from the publisher, Ten Speed Press, P.O. Box 7123, Berkeley, CA 94707.

## Prioritizing Grid[4]

**Grid** (Row)

| Row | Grid |
|-----|------|
| A | 1/2  1/3  1/4  1/5  1/6  1/7  1/8  1/9  1/10 |
| B | 2/3  2/4  2/5  2/6  2/7  2/8  2/9  2/10 |
| C | 3/4  3/5  3/6  3/7  3/8  3/9  3/10 |
| D | 4/5  4/6  4/7  4/8  4/9  4/10 |
| E | 5/6  5/7  5/8  5/9  5/10 |
| F | 6/7  6/8  6/9  6/10 |
| G | 7/8  7/9  7/10 |
| H | 8/9  8/10 |
| I | 9/10 |

| Items | Number of Times Circled | Final Prioritized Order |
|-------|-------------------------|-------------------------|
| 1. | ___ | ___ |
| 2. | ___ | ___ |
| 3. | ___ | ___ |
| 4. | ___ | ___ |
| 5. | ___ | ___ |
| 6. | ___ | ___ |
| 7. | ___ | ___ |
| 8. | ___ | ___ |
| 9. | ___ | ___ |
| 10. | ___ | ___ |

[4] Adapted from *The Three Boxes of Life and How to Get Out of Them*, by Richard N. Bolles, © copyright 1978, by Richard N. Bolles. Used by special permission. Those desiring a copy of the complete book for further reading may procure it from the publisher, Ten Speed Press, P.O. Box 7123, Berkeley, CA 94707.

**INFORMATIONAL INTERVIEWING**

1. Brainstorm with your family and/or friends to find names of people they know who use preferred skills similar to yours in their work. If they don't know anyone personally, perhaps they might refer you to someone else who does.

2. Select one of these people and conduct an informational interview, focusing on the skills they use as a part of their jobs.

# APP ACTIONS 2.2

## THE THINKING-STYLE ASSESSMENT INVENTORY

In completing the inventory, keep these points in mind:

- Defining your best career-relevant attributes depends on being accurate in your responses.
- There are no "bad" outcomes or "bad" thinking styles that result from this exercise. You are simply discovering your preferred mode of thinking.

## The BRIGHT and DARK Sides of the LEFT and RIGHT BRAINS

### The Left-Brain Analytic—The BRIGHT and DARK Sides

At their best they are logical evaluators of the facts who make their judgment and decisions on the basis of dispassionate reason.

At their worst they may become overly exacting or cynical, and become bogged down in meaningless analysis.

### The Left Brain Controller—The BRIGHT and DARK Sides

At their best they are practical thinkers concerned about observable outcomes and effective task managers.

At their worst, they may micromanage details or become heavy handed about procedures and "going by the book," with little concern for others.

### The Right-Brain Feelers—The BRIGHT and DARK Sides

At their best, they are warm and caring individuals able to empathize, connect, and communicate with all kinds of people in all kinds of situations.

At their worst, they may become overly emotional and  irrationally impulsive or indecisively conflicted.

### The Right-Brain Initiative—The BRIGHT and DARK Sides

At their best they are wonderfully creative and imaginative.

At their worst, they're out of touch with reality and live in a fantasy world.

## Complete the thinking-style assessment inventory

This assessment will help you identify your brain-dominance preference and link your preferred style of thinking with career options that bring out your best. The inventory is based upon the work of Ned Herrmann, who as head of management education at General Electric pioneered the study of applying knowledge acquired from brain research to personal performance and business productivity. Specifically, Herrmann's work focused on how individuals' thinking preferences, or "brain dominance," influence the way they perceive, learn, communicate, and behave.

The assessment consists of four sections:

- *Part 1: Personal Traits Assessment* will identify those traits that best describe the way you perceive and think.

- *Part 2: Rating Your Personality Traits* rank the ordering qualities that best describe you.

- *Part 3: Work Activity Preferences* clarify the work activities that engage your strongest interest.

- *Part 4: Developing Your Thinking-Style Profile* translate the results of the three assessments into a graphic profile depicting your thinking-style preference.

### Part 1. Personal Traits Assessment

Use this scale to rate how well the traits listed below describe you.

| Rating Scale | |
|---|---|
| 4 | Most like me |
| 3 | Next most like me |
| 2 | Somewhat like me |
| 1 | Least like me |

### Directions

*Step 1:* Your task is to decide which word in each row best describes traits of your personality. Using the rating scale, start with row 1 and decide which word from the four available choices best describes you and assign 4 points to that trait (place the number 4 in the box preceding the trait). Next decide which word in that row next best describes a general trait of your personality and assign 3 points to that word, then assign 2 points to the next closest description, and 1 point to the word that is least descriptive of you.

*Example:* For row 1, Ben decides that *Visualizer* best describes him, *Sociable* next most, *Logical* somewhat, and *Deliberate* the least. He assigns scores for row 1 as follows:

| A | B | C | D |
|---|---|---|---|
| 1. [2] Logical | [1] Deliberate | [3] Sociable | [4] Visualizer |

Complete the assessment by ranking your choices one row at a time. When finished with all 10 rows, add up your totals from each of the four columns and record them in the *Totals* boxes at the bottom of the table.

If you are not sure what some of the terms in the table mean, check the *Definition of Terms* section placed after the table.

**Part 1. Summary Table**

| | A | B | C | D |
|---|---|---|---|---|
| 1. | ❑ Logical | ❑ Deliberate | ❑ Socializer | ❑ Visual |
| 2. | ❑ Analytical | ❑ Orderly | ❑ Compassionate | ❑ Intuitive |
| 3. | ❑ Factually accurate | ❑ Detail oriented | ❑ Warm-hearted | ❑ Idea-generator |
| 4. | ❑ Critical thinker | ❑ Systematic thinker | ❑ Emotional thinker | ❑ Expansive thinker |
| 5. | ❑ Quantitative | ❑ Pragmatic | ❑ Authentic | ❑ Original |
| 6. | ❑ Verbally precise | ❑ Straightforward | ❑ Tactfully considerate | ❑ Creatively expressive |
| 7. | ❑ Scientific | ❑ Businesslike | ❑ Relational | ❑ Imaginative |
| 8. | ❑ Meticulous | ❑ Planner | ❑ Spontaneous | ❑ Futuristic |
| 9. | ❑ Objective | ❑ Task oriented | ❑ Sympathetic | ❑ Innovative |
| 10. | ❑ Rational | ❑ Conventional | ❑ Empathetic | ❑ Individualistic |
| **1st Totals** | | | | |
| | ❑ A Total | ❑ B Total | ❑ C Total | ❑ D Total |
| **2nd Totals** | | | | |
| | ❑ A Total | ❑ B Total | ❑ C Total | ❑ D Total |

Your total scores for boxes A + B + C + D should equal 100 for the "1st Totals."

*Step 2:* After completing your ratings, note the items to which you have assigned a score of "4." Do these seem to describe you fairly well? For that group of traits to which you have assigned a "4," do the following:

- Identify the one word that best describes you and change that score from a "4" to "10."

- Decide which of the remaining "4-rated" words next best describes you and change that number from a "4" to an "8."

- Determine which trait is your third best descriptor, and change that number from a "4" to a "6."

*Step 3:* After renumbering your top 4s in step 2, re-total the columns with your revised values. Your new grand total for columns A + B + C + D should equal 112.

## Definition of Terms

**Analytical:** Natural ability to make logical sense of things by carefully examining the facts and data and systematically considering all the implications.

**Authentic:** Committed to being honest with yourself and genuine with others (a genuine person with no false fronts).

**Compassionate:** Genuine concern for others with a desire to be helpful.

**Conventional:** Abiding by the usual, the traditional, or the standard way.

**Creatively** expressive: Ability to communicate with originality and flair.

**Critical** thinker: Discriminating. Good at judging the value of an idea or product. Adept at seeing gaps in the logic of an argument or an idea.

**Businesslike:** Takes a practical approach to things, looks for the most efficient and economical ways of achieving the intended result.

**Deliberate:** A careful, planned way of thinking and making decisions. Going about things sensibly in an orderly way.

**Detail oriented:** Paying attention to the essentials, big and small, of any undertaking to ensure things are complete with nothing overlooked.

**Empathetic:** Ability to appreciate how another sees, understands, and feels about things. Mental ability to nonjudgmentally "walk in the shoes of another."

**Emotional thinker:** In touch with feelings and trusts and relies on them in making decisions.

**Expansive thinker:** Thinking outside the box, seeing the big picture. Conceptual. Seeing how the pieces of something might fit together in new, interesting ways.

**Factually accurate:** Careful and concerned for getting the facts right.

**Futuristic:** Facility in mentally projecting yourself ahead in time to imagine what the future could bring. Ability to envision future possibilities.

**Idea generator:** The ability to come up with novel ideas in most situations.

**Imaginative:** Able to conceive new ideas and visualize what others have not.

**Individualistic:** A unique or unusual way of seeing, thinking, and behaving.

**Innovative:** Conceives novel ideas, methods, actions, or devices for doing things.

**Intuitive:** Knowing something without the conscious use of reasoning. A sudden flash of insight.

**Logical:** Able to think and reason sensibly and come to rational conclusions. Cause-and-effect thinking based on reason rather than emotion.

**Meticulous:** Being exact, precise, accurate, and careful in your thinking and work.

**Objective:** Impartial, taking into account the available information and the implications while consciously separating your biases from your conclusions.

**Orderly:** Proceeding about things in a careful, step-by-step, and efficient manner.

**Original:** A creative thinker. Unique individual in thought and action.

**Planner:** Careful in thinking things through to develop and follow a plan.

**Pragmatic:** Concerned with practical results rather than theory or speculation.

**Quantitative:** Adept at translating concepts, problems, and/or understandings into hard facts and numerical terms.

**Rational:** Ability to think through all sides of an issue and come to thoughtful conclusions by mental concentration.

**Relational:** Person-oriented viewpoint. Having a naturally friendly disposition.

**Scientific:** A seeker, always attempting to understand. Having a great interest in finding out why and how things are as they are.

**Systematic thinker:** Deals with things and ideas carefully in an orderly way.

**Socializer:** Friendly, outgoing personality who enjoys and is most fully energized when interacting with others.

**Spontaneous:** Uninhibited. Acting from natural impulse rather than plans.

**Straightforward:** Mincing few words, comes to the point directly. States opinions bluntly with little concern for tact or cordiality.

**Sympathetic:** Having concern for and interest in the welfare of others.

**Task oriented:** Ability to concentrate with a single-minded focus on the business immediately at hand.

**Tactfully considerate:** Socially gracious, takes feelings of others into account.

**Visualizer:** Ability to see things intuitively (in the mind's eye); can envision options and future possibilities that are out of the ordinary.

**Verbally precise:** Communicates with great care both in content and context.

**Warm-hearted:** Friendly, caring person with a natural ability to put others at ease and make them feel comfortable.

**Part** 2. Rating Your Personality Traits

### Directions

***Step 1:*** Use the following rating scale to assess how like you and unlike you are the traits presented in the following "Prioritizing Your Traits" survey. Assign a number in the "Value Rank" box from "1" to "5" for each of the 20 traits.

| Rating Scale | |
| --- | --- |
| 5 | Completely like me |
| 4 | Considerably like me |
| 3 | Somewhat like me |
| 2 | Mostly unlike me |
| 1 | Completely unlike me |

*Note:* In doing this assessment, *award no more than four of any one value ranking numbers to the listed traits.* That means you should award a total of four "5s," four "4s," four "3s," four "2s," and four "1s."

### Part 2. Prioritizing Your Traits

| | Trait | Value Rank | | Trait | Value Rank |
| --- | --- | --- | --- | --- | --- |
| 1. | Investigative | | 11. | Procedural | |
| 2. | Conceptual | | 12. | Controlling | |
| 3. | Enterprising | | 13. | Dispassionate | |
| 4. | Evaluative | | 14. | Resolute | |
| 5. | Conservative | | 15. | Probing | |
| 6. | Impartial | | 16. | Feeling oriented | |

| 7.  | Organized          |  | 17. | Mentally venturesome |  |
|-----|--------------------|--|-----|----------------------|--|
| 8.  | Harmony seeking    |  | 18. | Ingenious            |  |
| 9.  | Helpful            |  | 19. | Resourceful          |  |
| 10. | Personable         |  | 20. | Nurturing            |  |

*Step 2:* When you have assigned a rating to each item, record your scores in the Summary Table on the following page.

*Step 3:* After recording your scores, add up the totals for each of the four columns.

**Part 2. Your Summary Table**

| Trait | A | B | C | D |
|-------|---|---|---|---|
| 1. Investigative | | | | |
| 2. Conceptual | | | | |
| 3. Enterprising | | | | |
| 4. Evaluative | | | | |
| 5. Conservative | | | | |
| 6. Impartial | | | | |
| 7. Organized | | | | |
| 8. Harmony seeking | | | | |
| 9. Helpful | | | | |
| 10. Personable | | | | |
| 11. Procedural | | | | |
| 12. Controlling | | | | |
| 13. Dispassionate | | | | |
| 14. Resolute | | | | |
| 15. Probing | | | | |
| 16. Feeling oriented | | | | |
| 17. Mentally venturesome | | | | |
| 18. Ingenious | | | | |
| 19. Resourceful | | | | |
| 20. Nurturing | | | | |
| Totals | | | | |

*Note:* Your totals for all four columns (A + B + C + D) should add up to 60.

**Definition of Terms**

**Conceptual:** Able to mentally conceive designs, ideas, plans, and programs. Seeing how things can fit together into a meaningful whole.

**Controlling:** Managing events and situations through efficient plans and by following rules and procedures.

**Conservative:** Being cautious and averse to taking risk or unnecessary chances.

**Dispassionate:** Ability to remain detached from your emotions. Not allowing feelings to override thinking.

**Enterprising:** Having the initiative and willingness to undertake new, often risky projects. A strong desire to see what you can accomplish through wit and effort.

**Evaluative:** Forming and reforming opinions on the basis of observing things in practice.

**Feeling oriented:** Responsive to your own emotions and to those of others.

**Harmony seeking:** A concern for getting along congenially with others. Attempting to avoid conflict and/or smooth over disagreements.

**Impartial:** Favoring no one side, issue, or party over another. Being fair and just.

**Ingenious:** Clever, resourceful, inventive. Creative and original.

**Investigative:** Seeking the facts and examining them in detail in an attempt to fit the pieces of a puzzle together, like a detective determining "who done it."

**Mentally venturesome:** Highly inquisitive, always exploring new territory.

**Personable:** Agreeable, friendly, amiable. Ability to get along well with others.

**Procedural:** Paying attention to the expectations for any ventures you are involved in and being careful to abide by them. Playing it safe and by the rules.

**Probing:** Searching for the truth, delving deeply into things, seeking for answers.

**Resourceful:** Cleverness in coming up with new and original ways of solving problems or ways of doing things.

**Resolute:** Persistent, steady, and purposeful in thinking and behavior.

**Nurturing:** Caring about others. Supporting others in positive ways.

## Part 3. Work Activity Preferences

This process assesses the kinds of work-related activities that are compatible with your thinking-style preference. The assessment requires that you imagine yourself in ten different types of work situations and in each case prioritizing your preference among four options presented.

### Directions

*Step 1:* Use the following scale to rate your personal preference for the four options presented for each of the ten work-related situations. In each of these situations, prioritize your preference for the activities shown by awarding a "4" to the one most interesting, a "3" to the next most interesting, a "1" to the least interesting, and a "2" to the remaining choice. *Be sure to make your choices on your natural tendencies and personal preferences rather than what you think you should do in these situations.*

### Rating Scale

| Rating Scale | |
| --- | --- |
| 4 | Most interesting |
| 3 | Next most interesting |
| 2 | Little interesting |
| 1 | Least interesting |

1. I would prefer working as:
   A. ❑ a financial analyst
   B. ❑ an office administrator
   C. ❑ a teacher or counselor
   D. ❑ a creativity consultant

2. I would prefer a job that involves working primarily with:
   A. ❑ facts and information
   B. ❑ plans and policies
   C. ❑ people's feelings and behavior
   D. ❑ ideas and possibilities

3. If I were to work at a large plant nursery, I would prefer to be:
   A. ❑ business manager/accountant
   B. ❑ plant and garden manager
   C. ❑ customer service assistant
   D. ❑ garden/landscape designer

4. If I were the manager of a company, I would most enjoy:
   A. ❑ making decisions logically based on hard data
   B. ❑ establishing clear and efficient procedures
   C. ❑ seeing that employees were growing on the job and enjoying their work
   D. ❑ devising interesting future possibilities and opportunities for the company

5. In my ideal work setting, I would like to:
   A. ❑ work alone doing research with sophisticated equipment
   B. ❑ plan, organize, and oversee the daily business operations
   C. ❑ lead a team of people, helping them become the best they could be
   D. ❑ work alone in a quiet setting generating ideas for innovative applications

6. In a work situation I would prefer to use the computer for:
   A. ❑ performing complex analytical functions
   B. ❑ increasing office efficiency and productivity
   C. ❑ communicating with others via email
   D. ❑ creating graphic design possibilities or writing up ideas for new programs

7. I would prefer to be:
   A. ❑ a scientist or technical specialist
   B. ❑ a midlevel manager or supervisor
   C. ❑ an educator or talk-show host
   D. ❑ a "think tank" specialist or fiction writer

8. If I were to work in the theater I would prefer to:
   A. ❑ conduct feasibility studies for putting on a particular play
   B. ❑ be the stage and lighting manager
   C. ❑ be an on-stage performer
   D. ❑ be a playwright

9. If I were in the military, I would rather be:
   A. ❑ an intelligence expert or military historian
   B. ❑ a helicopter pilot or tank driver
   C. ❑ a chaplain or medical support professional
   D. ❑ a strategic campaign planner or designer of new weapons systems

10. Were I assigned to a large, inhabited, orbiting space station, I would prefer to be a(n):
    A. ❏ nutrition scientist studying the health benefits of colony-grown foods
    B. ❏ events planner who schedules and coordinates the various activities
    C. ❏ space psychologist helping people adjust to space-colony life
    D. ❏ entrepreneur developing business products to serve community needs

*Step 2:* After completing items numbered 1–10 in the foregoing assessment, tally up all of your scores
on the following *Part 3. Summary Table* and then add up your total scores for all four columns.

**Part 3. Summary Table**

| Question Number | Points Awarded for Item: | | | |
|---|---|---|---|---|
| | **A** | **B** | **C** | **D** |
| 1. | | | | |
| 2. | | | | |
| 3. | | | | |
| 4. | | | | |
| 5. | | | | |
| 6. | | | | |
| 7. | | | | |
| 8. | | | | |
| 9. | | | | |
| 10. | | | | |
| Totals | | | | |

*Note:* Your totals for columns A B C D should equal 100.

## Part 4. Developing Your Thinking-Style Profile

**Directions**

*Step 1:* After completing Parts 1, 2, and 3, summarize your scores using the Combined Scores Table
below. Do that by entering your total scores from each part in the appropriate boxes, then add
up grand totals for each column.

*Example:* Ben's total "A" score from the Part 1 summary table was "20." Accordingly, Ben looks for
the Part 1 row on the combined summary table, and enters "20" in the *Choice A* column.

**Combined Summary Scores for Parts 1, 2, and 3**

| My summary score from | Choice A | Choice B | Choice C | Choice D |
|---|---|---|---|---|
| Part 1 Personal Traits Assessment | | | | |
| Part 2 Rating Your Personality Traits | | | | |
| Part 3 Work Activity Preferences | | | | |
| Grand Total | | | | |

*Note:* Your combined totals from all four columns should add up to 272.

*Step 2:* Use the grand totals for your Choice A, B, C, and D scores to plot your thinking-style profile on page 103. To do that, first mark your combined "A" score on the A diagonal of the profile. Then mark your combined "B," "C," and "D" scores on the corresponding diagonals.

*Step 3:* Draw your profile by connecting your plotted marks on the "A," "B," "C," and "D" diagonals. The resulting profile represents a graphic visualization of your thinking-style profile.

## Your Thinking-Style Profile

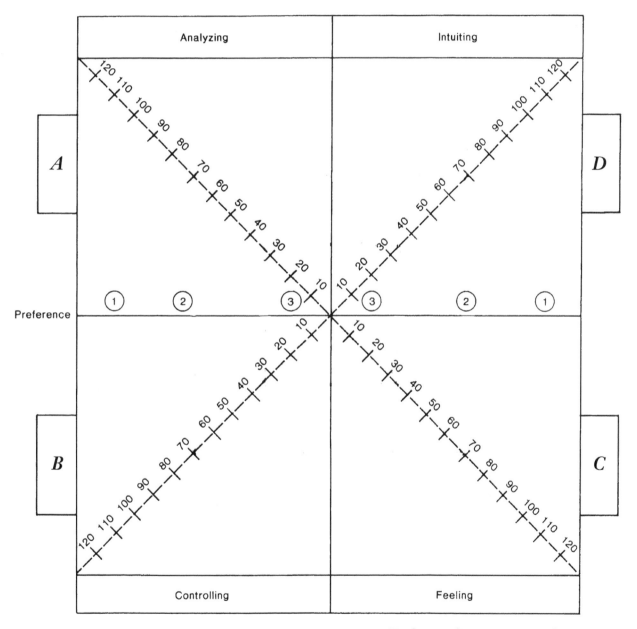

*Note:* This graphic is adapted from Ned Herrmann's Brain Dominance model. For information about the Herrmann Brain Dominance Instrument, visit www.hbdi.com/.

### Understanding Your Mental Powers

| The Three Thinking Predilections | | |
| --- | --- | --- |
| **Number** | **Biases** | **Range of Scores** |
| 1 | Prefer | 70 and over |
| 2 | Use | 35–69 |
| 3 | Avoid | 0–34 |

## Identifying Your Profile

Your thinking-style profile provides interesting clues about your tendencies in thinking, perceiving, and performing (behaving). This information can be extremely useful in identifying the kinds of work activities that capitalize on your natural strengths (talent energized by preference). This kind of understanding can be invaluable in developing your plans for the future. You are far more likely to perform better, be more successful, feel more satisfied, and enjoy your work when you are applying and developing your strongest and most energizing natural assets.

Your profile serves as a visual representation of you, or at least the way you are most inclined to think. You can take this visual representation a step further by assigning a numerical code to your profile based on the strength of your preference. The table below shows how to do that with a four-digit numerical code that provides a kind of rough approximation of your preference for using the four styles of thinking. Look over this table and then determine your four-digit code obtained in the Thinking Style Inventory *What's Your Number?*

## Thinking-Style Degrees of Preference Codes

| Code | Degree of Preference | Description |
|---|---|---|
| 1 | Prefer | Strong preference; a favorite mode of thinking |
| 2 | Use | Comfort zone; you have no problem using this kind of thinking |
| 3 | Avoid | Resistance zone; you are likely to avoid this kind of thinking unless it is absolutely required |

*Note:* This scoring model is developed from Ned Herrmann's Brain Dominance Assessment model.

## Example

A 1232 profile indicates a person who strongly favors logical thinking, plays things safely, avoids feelings, and pays some attention to intuition.

*Question:* What kind of occupations might be appropriate for a person with this kind of profile? What kind of learning activities and/or subject matter would he or she favor? Avoid?

## What's Your Number?

Using the numbering system from the "**Thinking-Style Degrees of Preference Codes**" (above) and the combined scores that you plotted on *Your Thinking-Style Profile*, complete the following table. Note the correct score ranges for degree of preference (prefer, use, avoid) at the bottom of the *Thinking-Style Profile*.

### My Four-Digit Thinking-Style Code

| Thinking Style | A Analyzing | B Controlling | C Feeling | D Intuiting |
|---|---|---|---|---|
| My numerical preference (1, 2, or 3) | | | | |
| General preference (Prefer, Use, or Avoid) | | | | |

## Characteristics of the Four Styles of Thinking

| Quadrant | A<br>Analyzing | B<br>Controlling | C<br>Feeling | D<br>Intuiting |
|---|---|---|---|---|
| Thinking process | Logical analysis of facts and data for understanding | Linear, proceeding step-by-step from A to B to C | Inner awareness Attuned to the emotional state | Intuitive, visualizing the "big picture" |
| Traits most valued | Intelligence | Conventional | Harmony | Ideas and concepts |
| | Logic | Rule adherence | Empathy | Vision |
| | Rationality | Efficiency | Communicating | Originality |
| | Dispassion | Control | Touching | Creativity |
| | Analysis | Loyalty | Relating emotion | Possibilities |
| | Reason | Risk aversion | | Conceptualizing |
| Traits least valued | Feelings | Intuition | Detachment | Conventional |
| | Guesswork | Abstraction | Cold facts | Procedural |
| | Subjectivity | Ambivalence | Impersonal | Sequential |
| Some favorite leisure activities | Chess | Cards | Clubs | Expressive arts |
| | Science | Fishing | Music | Creative writing |
| | History | Bowling | Cooking | Reading fiction |
| | Computer games of | Spectator sports | Dancing | Art museums |
| | Logic | Yard work | Social events | Poetry |
| Some favorite subjects | History | Business | Humanities | Art |
| | Mathematics | Management | Drama | Literature |
| | Economics | Computer | Music | Design |
| | Physics | Programming | Religion | Philosophy |
| | Science | Accounting | Psychology | Metaphysics |
| Skills | Examine data | Budget | Act as liaison | Design |
| | Scrutinize | Coordinate | Counsel | Conceptualize |
| | Observe | Plan | Communicate | Generate ideas |
| | Research | Organize | Entertain | Compose music, poetry, etc. |
| | Read for information | Schedule | Perform | |
| | Evaluate | Maintain records | Interview for | imagine possibilities |
| | Test | Monitor | Information | Integrate |
| | Analyze | Proofread | Host | Prognosticate |

| | | | |
|---|---|---|---|
| Quantify | Implement | Discuss feelings | Initiate |
| Solve complex | Plan | Mediate | Synthesize |
| Problems | Follow through | Motivate | Visualize |
| Estimate | Expedite | Promote | Write |
| Evaluate | Classify | Teach, train | Develop scenarios |
| Assess | Supervise | Negotiate | Solve problems |
| Critique | Coordinate details | Nurture | Intuitively |
| Find flaws in ideas | Troubleshooting | Coach | |

## Occupations Grouped by Thinking Style

| Left-Brain Dominant Occupations | |
|---|---|
| **A Analyzing** | **B Controlling** |
| Accountant | Accounts manager |
| Analyst | Air traffic controller |
| Artificial intelligence engineer | Auto mechanic |
| Biologist | Automobile dealer |
| Chemist | Administrative assistant |
| Computer scientist or engineer | Bookkeeper |
| Computer systems analyst | Bank manager |
| Criminal investigator/detective | Computer technician |
| Dentist | Computer programmer |
| Economist | Credit advisor |
| Engineer (e.g., agricultural, automobile, aeronautical, electronics) | Database manager |
| | Driver (bus, taxi, train) |
| Etymologist | Electronics technician |
| Financial analyst, administrator, or planner | Emergency medical technician |
| Geologist | Factory supervisor |
| Horticulturist | Firefighter |
| Lawyer—corporate or tax attorney | Government bureaucrat |
| Market researcher | Hotel/motel manager |
| Mathematician, math instructor | Health care manager |
| Mechanical diagnostician | Human resources compensation and benefits manager |
| Medical researcher | Insurance agent |
| Meteorologist | Law enforcement officer |
| Military strategist | Librarian—cataloger |
| Neurologist, neurosurgeon | Marketing manager |
| Nutritionist | Manufacturing manager |
| Optometrist | Military line and technical officer |

| | |
|---|---|
| Orthodontist | Medical records technician |
| Orthopedic surgeon | Merchant mariner |
| Osteopath | Office manager |
| Pathologist | Paralegal |
| Physician (medical doctor) | Pharmacist |
| Pharmacologist | Pilot |
| Physicist | Proofreader |
| Printer technician | Purchasing agent |
| Psychologist (research) | Real estate agent |
| Radiologist | Research assistant |
| Researcher (technical) | Restaurant manager |
| Scientist, science teacher | Retail manager |
| Statistician | Robotics technician |
| Stockbroker | School administrator |
| Strategic planner | Technical writer |
| Web master, Web analyst | Travel agency route planner, manager |
| | Tugboat skipper |

## Right-Brain Dominant Occupations

| C Feeling | D Intuiting |
|---|---|
| Actor, performer | Advertising designer |
| Humanities teacher, instructor | Architect |
| Child-care provider | Art administrator |
| Coach (athletic, speech, drama) | Art museum curator |
| Communications specialist | Artist (fine arts) |
| Cosmetologist, hairdresser | Attorney—trial lawyer |
| Counselor (drug, eldercare, education, family, geriatrics, marriage) | Cartoonist |
| | Choreographer |
| Customer service representative | Creativity consultant |
| Dancer | Culinary experimenter (chef) |
| Day-care center associate | Designer (creative, nontechnical) |
| Diversity trainer | Editor (book, journalist, newspaper) |
| Funeral counselor, director | Entrepreneur |
| Health care provider | Exhibit designer |
| Human resource development (HRD) specialist | Fashion designer |
| Humanities professor | Filmmaker, producer |
| Hospice counselor, manager | Floral arranger |
| Massage therapist | Futurist (nontechnical, theoretical) |
| Mediator, arbitrator, conflict resolution specialist | Graphics designer |
| Minister, priest, rabbi | Humorist |

Musician, music teacher

Newscaster

Nun

Nurse

Occupational therapist

Ombudsman

Organizational development consultant

Parole officer

Pediatrician

Physical therapist

Psychologist (counseling, school)

Psychotherapist

Public relations specialist

Recreational therapist

Religious education director

Salesperson (not technical)

Social worker

Sociologist

Special education teacher, consultant

Teacher (elementary, special education)

Therapist (art, music, dance)

Translator/interpreter

Training and development specialist

Vocational rehabilitation specialist

Interior designer

Landscape architect

Literary agent

Manager of creative enterprises

Movie set designer

Mythologist

Musical composer

Playwright

Philosopher (theoretical: abstract as opposed to logical-analytical)

Poet

Psychiatrist

Physicist (theoretical)

Set designer

Strategic designer, theorist

Software developer, concepts innovator

Theorist (creative, nontechnical)

Toy designer

Web site designer

Writer (nontechnical, science-fiction, creative)

*Note:* Individual occupations are placed into categories based on the predominant style of thinking most often required in the workplace. The groupings should be thought of as approximations rather than absolutes because in actual practice: (1) most occupations use all of the thinking styles to varying degrees, and (2) the nature of the work activity can vary a great deal from one work setting to another.

# APP ACTIONS 2.3

## SOUTH SEA ISLAND FANTASY

For this exercise, imagine that you are flying an airplane alone, having taken off for a day's pleasure excursion. After flying for some time, you find yourself approaching six remote islands. Suddenly, your plane develops engine trouble, and you realize that you are going to have to make a forced landing on one of the islands.

Imagine that the figure below is an aerial view of these islands. From the information available, you know that highly civilized and advanced people populate each island. They have moved to these locations to associate with other compatible people and to enjoy the balmy climate.

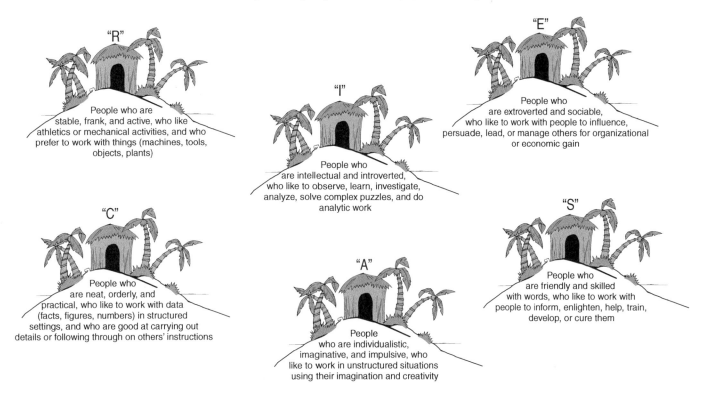

The people on each island have the characteristics described in the diagram. You realize that you will be on the island for a long time since ships make only infrequent visits. You also know that transportation between these six islands is nonexistent. Where you land, therefore, determines what kind of people you will be staying with for a long while. Thus, you will want to choose your landing spot with care.

Which group of people would you prefer as companions for a significant amount of time? Write the letter for that island in the box below marked *first choice*.

Then assume that for some reason you cannot land on your preferred island. Which group of people would be your *second choice* as companions? *Third choice? Fourth choice?* Write the letter of the island for each choice in the boxes below:

☐ First choice     ☐ Third choice
☐ Second choice    ☐ Fourth choice

## MY FAVORITE KINDS OF PROBLEMS

Problem solving can be stimulating, but different people have different preferences in the types of problems with which they like to grapple. The following exercise describes six kinds of problems. Assume that you have a job involving 100 hours of your time. You have the option of spending those 100 hours working with any of the six kinds of problems.

You might, for example, decide that you would prefer to spend 50 hours of time working with the "A" types of problems, 30 hours with the "S" types, and 20 hours with the "I" types. In that case, you would mark 50 in the "A" box, 30 in the "S" box, 20 in the "I" box, and 0 in the "E," "C," and "R" boxes. You are free to choose to spend all of your time working with just one instead of several kinds of problems.

Do not place the same amount of time in more than one box. Take a moment to decide which one you really want to spend at least a little more time doing. Make sure that your combined score for the six boxes adds up to 100.

I prefer to spend my 100 hours of time working with and solving the following kinds of problems:

- [ ] R  Problems that involve using your hands to resolve challenges, such as operating a piece of equipment, putting an addition onto a house, or building a computer from scratch.

- [ ] I  Problems of a scientific or mathematical nature that require mental concentration, fact finding, analysis, and logical thinking.

- [ ] A  Problems that can be solved by combining various concepts or artistic elements to create new approaches, methods, programs, art forms, or literature.

- [ ] S  Problems that involve situations where you are interacting with others for assistance in solving their personal problems, providing difficult feedback to improve their behavior, or helping them improve academically.

- [ ] E  Problems associated with persuading and/or motivating others to accomplish the objectives of an organization or a community-based project.

- [ ] C  Problems that can be solved through organization and orderly use of data (information, words, records, and numbers) or through carefully applying appropriate policies or regulations.

Total score (This total must equal 100.)

## INTEREST AND ACTIVITY ASSESSMENT

This process is designed to help you assess your personality-style-related preferences. Decide whether you like or dislike each of the listed activities. Using the following scale, assign a numerical value to your like or dislike for each activity. The greater your like or dislike is, the higher the number. Be sure to focus on your known or suspected interest rather than whether or not you believe you would be good at it.

| Like | Dislike |
|---|---|
| 1–2 like a little | 1–2 dislike a little |
| 3–6 like considerably | 3–6 dislike considerably |
| 7–10 love it | 7–10 hate it |

*Example*

If your reaction to *home repairs such as carpentry, plumbing, etc.* is that you definitely already enjoy or would likely enjoy the activity, then place a number between 7 and 10 in the *LIKE* box for *Home repairs*, depending upon the intensity of your preference for this particular or similar type activity.

If you know or are fairly certain that you would dislike designing your own Web page, you would place a number between 1 and 6 in the DISLIKE box, depending upon the strength of your dislike or your probable dislike based on experience with similar activities.

LIKE   DISLIKE

| ❏ | ❏ | $R_1$ | Home repairs such as carpentry, plumbing, etc. |
|---|---|---|---|
| ❏ | ❏ | $I_1$ | Designing my own Web page |
| ❏ | ❏ | $A_1$ | Playing a musical instrument |
| ❏ | ❏ | $S_1$ | Going to social functions and actively interacting with other people |
| ❏ | ❏ | $E_1$ | Organizing and leading a club, conference, or business meeting |
| ❏ | ❏ | $C_1$ | Keeping detailed accounts of personal expenses |
| ❏ | ❏ | $R_1$ | Reading magazines like Popular Mechanics, Hot Rod, Aviation Week, and Space Technology |
| ❏ | ❏ | $I_2$ | Studying the stars through a telescope |
| ❏ | ❏ | $A_2$ | Writing a novel or a piece of music |
| ❏ | ❏ | $S_2$ | Working as a hotline counselor at an addiction center |
| ❏ | ❏ | $E_2$ | Persuading others to buy a product, service, or idea you are selling |
| ❏ | ❏ | $C_2$ | Completing business tasks and projects by studying and carefully following procedures and policies |
| ❏ | ❏ | $R_3$ | Performing maintenance work on your car |
| ❏ | ❏ | $I_3$ | Reading science magazines such as American Scientist, OMNI, or Discover |
| ❏ | ❏ | $A_3$ | Acting or singing in a play or musical |
| ❏ | ❏ | $S_3$ | Reading children's stories at a day-care center |
| ❏ | ❏ | $E_3$ | Meeting and getting acquainted with influential people |
| ❏ | ❏ | $C_3$ | Preparing reports and documents using spreadsheet applications such as Microsoft Excel |

| | | | |
|---|---|---|---|
| ❑ | ❑ | $A_4$ | Reading poetry, philosophy, or fiction |
| ❑ | ❑ | $S_4$ | Serving on a social events committee |
| ❑ | ❑ | $E_4$ | Debating an issue or delivering a presentation |
| ❑ | ❑ | $R_4$ | Doing hands-on work in a plant nursery or fish hatchery |
| ❑ | ❑ | $I_4$ | Solving math or logic puzzles |
| ❑ | ❑ | $C_4$ | Taking accounting or business ethics courses |
| ❑ | ❑ | $A_5$ | Expressing an idea with a sketch pad or computer design program |
| ❑ | ❑ | $S_5$ | Teaching games to children |
| ❑ | ❑ | $E_5$ | Following politics and working on a political campaign |
| ❑ | ❑ | $R_5$ | Operating a piece of equipment such as a backhoe, bulldozer, or army tank |
| ❑ | ❑ | $I_5$ | Taking a science course such as geology, astronomy, or biology |
| ❑ | ❑ | $C_5$ | Programming your computer |
| ❑ | ❑ | $A_6$ | Decorating the interior of a house |
| ❑ | ❑ | $S_6$ | Helping others deal with personal problems |
| ❑ | ❑ | $E_6$ | Developing a business plan for a commercial venture you would start and manage |
| ❑ | ❑ | $C_6$ | Analyzing fiscal expenditures and compiling budget reports |
| ❑ | ❑ | $I_6$ | Collecting and examining rocks and minerals |
| ❑ | ❑ | $R_6$ | Working as a deckhand on a large oceangoing sailboat |
| ❑ | ❑ | $A_7$ | Generating innovative ideas for an advertising campaign |
| ❑ | ❑ | $S_7$ | Taking a course in psychology, religion, or sociology |
| ❑ | ❑ | $E_7$ | Leading a work team or managing a group of people |
| ❑ | ❑ | $C_7$ | Sorting and categorizing data, records, or files |
| ❑ | ❑ | $I_7$ | Surfing the Internet for scientific news |
| ❑ | ❑ | $R_7$ | Playing fast-paced computer games that require quick reactions and physical dexterity |
| ❑ | ❑ | $A_8$ | Creating eye-pleasing arrangements with flowers, pictures, furniture, etc. |
| ❑ | ❑ | $S_8$ | Reading self-help or personal-development books |
| ❑ | ❑ | $I_8$ | Doing work with a microscope |
| ❑ | ❑ | $E_8$ | Reading the Wall Street Journal or magazines like Fortune, Money, or Success |
| ❑ | ❑ | $C_8$ | Keeping an accurate appointment calendar for a busy office |
| ❑ | ❑ | $R_8$ | Taking a home maintenance course to learn how to make home repairs and do home improvements |
| ❑ | ❑ | $A_9$ | Painting with watercolors |
| ❑ | ❑ | $S_9$ | Participating as a team member on projects providing a useful social service |
| ❑ | ❑ | $I_9$ | Playing chess and/or doing highly complex crossword puzzles |
| ❑ | ❑ | $E_9$ | Giving a business presentation to a group of important people |
| ❑ | ❑ | $C_9$ | Proofreading documents and putting them in final form |
| ❑ | ❑ | $R_9$ | Working as a technician in a mechanical engineering laboratory |

After you have assigned numbers to each of these items, use the table "Summarizing Your Likes and Dislikes" to record and add up your total LIKE and DISLIKE scores. The code numbers on the left of this table correspond to the numbers found beside each of the six letters in the exercise. For example, if you put a 7 in the *LIKE* box for home repairs ($R_1$), you would put a 7 in the L column directly under R in the row labeled 1.

L = LIKE; D = DISLIKE

## Summarizing Your Likes and Dislikes

| | R | | I | | A | | S | | E | | C | |
|---|---|---|---|---|---|---|---|---|---|---|---|---|
| | L | D | L | D | L | D | L | D | L | D | L | D |
| 1 | | | | | | | | | | | | |
| 2 | | | | | | | | | | | | |
| 3 | | | | | | | | | | | | |
| 4 | | | | | | | | | | | | |
| 5 | | | | | | | | | | | | |
| 6 | | | | | | | | | | | | |
| 7 | | | | | | | | | | | | |
| 8 | | | | | | | | | | | | |
| 9 | | | | | | | | | | | | |
| Total | | | | | | | | | | | | |

## IDENTIFYING INTERESTS FROM SKILLS

This exercise is based on the Skill Assessment Survey you completed in APP 2.1. On the basis of the insights acquired from that process, decide what percentage of time you would like to spend using each of your preferred families of skills in your work. Make sure that your percentages add up to 100.

*My Top Five Skills-Family Percentages*

| | | |
|---|---|---|
| **R** | The percentage of time I prefer to use my manual/technical skills in work. | % |
| **I** | The percentage of time I prefer to use my analytical/problem-solving skills in work. | % |
| **A** | The percentage of time I prefer to use my innovative/creativity skills in work. | % |
| **S** | The percentage of time I prefer to use my social/interpersonal skills in work. | % |
| **E** | The percentage of time I prefer to use my managing/influencing skills in work. | % |
| C | The percentage of time I prefer to use my organizing/data skills in work. | % |

### Compiling My Interests Profile

Having completed four applications to explore your personal preferences, you can now identify your own personality-style profile. This profile will help highlight your unique interest patterns and provide valuable career- and life-planning insights. To develop your profile, complete the following steps.

1. From **South Sea Island Fantasy**, list the letters for your first four choices below.

|  | *Island Letter* | *Points* |
|---|---|---|
| The island of my first choice | _____ | 20 |
| The island of my second choice | _____ | 15 |
| The island of my third choice | _____ | 10 |
| The island of my fourth choice | _____ | 5 |

Notice that each letter you have listed above has a corresponding point value. After you rank the island letters, put the point value for each of the island letters in the designated space on the Combined Scores Table.

### *Example*

1. If the island corresponding to your first choice was "R" and your second, third, and fourth choices were "I," "C," and "E," respectively, write the number "20" in the *R* column of the *Combined Scores Table* on the following page (in the Application 5-A line). Also write "15" under *I*, "10" under *C*, and "5" under *E*. Leave blank spaces on this line for the other two letters you did not select.

2. Transfer the scores you listed in each of the six problem boxes to the *Application 5-B* line of the *Combined Scores Table*. Be sure to place all six scores on the *Application 5-B* line, each in the appropriate column.

3. In Application 5-C you added up the totals for all the scores you listed under the *LIKE* and *DISLIKE* boxes in the table provided. Transfer your LIKE scores for each of the six letters to the Combined Scores Table. Do nothing with your DISLIKE scores for now; we will discuss those later.

4. Record your scores for Application 5-D on the *Combined Scores Table*.

5. After recording all your scores in the *Combined Scores Table*, total each column and record the sums of all in the *Total Score* row.

## COMBINED SCORES TABLE

|  | R | I | A | S | E | C |
|---|---|---|---|---|---|---|
| Island Fantasy Scores |  |  |  |  |  |  |
| Favorite Problem Scores |  |  |  |  |  |  |
| Activity Preference Scores |  |  |  |  |  |  |
| Preferred Skills Scores |  |  |  |  |  |  |
| Total Score |  |  |  |  |  |  |

6. After you have determined your total scores, use them to form a bar graph on the *My Interests Profile* grid. To do that, first find the number corresponding to your total *R* score along the side of the grid. Then form a bar in the R column by filling in with pen or colored marker from the bottom of the grid up to your total "R" score. Do the same for each of the remaining scores.

# MY INTERESTS PROFILE

| | R | I | A | S | E | C | |
|---|---|---|---|---|---|---|---|
| 180 | | | | | | | 180 |
| 170 | | | | | | | 170 |
| 160 | | | | | | | 160 |
| 150 | | | | | | | 150 |
| 140 | | | | | | | 140 |
| 130 | | | | | | | 130 |
| 120 | | | | | | | 120 |
| 110 | | | | | | | 110 |
| 100 | | | | | | | 100 |
| 90 | | | | | | | 90 |
| 80 | | | | | | | 80 |
| 70 | | | | | | | 70 |
| 60 | | | | | | | 60 |
| 50 | | | | | | | 50 |
| 40 | | | | | | | 40 |
| 30 | | | | | | | 30 |
| 20 | | | | | | | 20 |
| 10 | | | | | | | 10 |
| 0 | R | I | A | S | E | C | 0 |

## LIKES AND DISLIKES AS GUIDES

Throughout APP 2.3 you have identified a profile of your likes and dislikes, useful information in career and life planning. You can use your top interests to choose compatible careers, jobs, and goals, just as you can use your dislikes to determine what activities you will want to avoid in your work, leisure, and learning. Review your work in this section and record on the following page your insights from that exercise.

| *My favorite LIKES were:* | *My major DISLIKES were:* |
|---|---|
| 1) _____ | 1) _____ |
| 2) _____ | 2) _____ |
| 3) _____ | 3) _____ |
| 4) _____ | 4) _____ |
| 5) _____ | 5) _____ |

| **I can use that information in planning to:** | **I can use that information to avoid doing:** |
|---|---|
|  |  |
|  |  |
|  |  |
|  |  |
|  |  |
|  |  |
|  |  |
|  |  |
|  |  |
|  |  |

# APP ACTIONS 2.4

## HOLLAND CODE OCCUPATIONAL INTERESTS CHART

Scan down the list of occupations corresponding to the primary letter in your three-letter Holland code and circle those occupations you find interesting. Then go on to the occupation groups corresponding to the second and third letters of your Holland code and circle any of these occupations that interest you. Write the names of occupations you have circled under *Career Possibilities* in the ABOUT ME APP.

_____

_____

_____

_____

_____

**Personality Types and Occupational Characteristics**

*Occupational Groups (Realistic)*

| Occupational Group | Occupation | Holland Code |
|---|---|---|
| **REALISTIC**<br><br><br>"Hands-On" Technically Oriented | Access Coordinator, Cable TV | REI |
| | Airbrush Artist | RCA |
| | Animal Trainer | RES |
| | Architectural Drafter | RCI |
| | Auto Mechanic | RCI |
| | Biomedical Equipment Technician | RIE |
| | Cable TV Line Technician | REC |
| | Commercial Airline Pilot | ERI |
| | Computer Technician | RIC |
| | Dispensing Optician | |
| | Emergency Medical Technician | RSI |
| | Electronic Technician | RIS |
| | Estimator | RCE |
| | Firefighter | RES |
| | Fish and Game Warden | RES |
| | Helicopter Pilot | RIC |
| | Historical Restoration Specialist | RIC |
| | Home Inspector | RCI |

|  | Industrial Arts Teacher | REI |
|---|---|---|
|  | Landscape Gardener | RIS |
|  | Locksmith | REC |
|  | Merchant Mariner | REA |
|  | MRI Technologist | RIC |
|  | National Park Ranger | REI |
|  | Nuclear Medicine Technologist | RIS |
|  | Piano Tuner | RCS |
|  | Prosthetic Technician | RSE |
|  | Quality Control Inspector | RSC |
|  | Radiographer | RIS |
|  | Robotic Machine Operator | RSE |
|  | Ship's Crew | RCI |
|  | Solar-Energy-System Installer | RCI |
|  | Sound Mixer | RCS |
|  | State Highway Police Officer | RSE |
|  | Tool Designer | RIS |
|  | Ultrasound Technologist | RSI |
| **Evolving Careers** | | |
| Bionic limb technician | | |
| Robotic technician | | |
| Mechanics for new engines (solar, hydrogen, ion) | | |
| Space vehicle pilot | | |
| Holographic imagery technician | | |
| Communication satellite television | | |

## Occupational Groups (Investigative)

| Occupational Group | Occupation | Holland Code |
|---|---|---|
| | Actuary | ISE |
| | Aeronautical Engineer | IRS |
| | Anthropologist | IRE |
| | Astronomer | IRA |
| | Astrophysicist | IAR |
| | Biologist | IAR |
| | Biomedical Engineer | IRE |
| **INVESTIGATIVE** | Chemist | IRE |
| | Computer Science Faculty Member | IRC |
| | Criminologist | IRC |
| Abstract Problem Solving | Dentist | ISR |
| | Economist | IAS |
| | Exercise Physiologist | ISR |

| Science Oriented | Geologist | IRE |
| --- | --- | --- |
| | Internal Auditor | ICR |
| | Laser Technician | IRE |
| | Market-Research Analyst | ISC |
| | Mathematician | IER |
| | Mechanical Engineer | IRS |
| | Medical Researcher | IAR |
| | Meteorologist | IRS |
| | Museum Curator | IRS |
| | Optometrist | ISE |
| | Pharmacist | IES |
| | Physician | ISR |
| | Physicist | IAR |
| | Psychiatrist | ISA |
| | Research Dietician | ISR |
| | Research Psychologist | IAE |
| | Science and Technology Writer | IAE |
| | Statistician | IRE |
| | Systems Analyst | IER |
| | Translator | ISC |
| | Veterinarian | IRS |

| **Evolving Careers** |
| --- |
| Global economist |
| Genetic engineer |
| Artificial intelligence engineer |
| Ecology scientist |
| Information architect |
| New product researcher |

## Occupational Groups (Artistic)

| Occupational Group | Occupation | Holland Code |
| --- | --- | --- |
| | Actor/Actress | AES |
| | Advertising Manager | AES |
| | Architect | AIR |
| | Art Teacher | ASE |
| | Book Editor | AES |
| | Cartoonist | AES |
| | Columnist/Commentator | AES |
| | Commercial Designer | AER |
| **ARTISTIC** | Copywriter | AIS |
| | Dancer | AER |
| | Drama Teacher | ASE |

| Idea Creators | English Teacher | ASE |
|---|---|---|
| | Entertainer | AES |
| Artistic and Self-Expressive | Exhibit Designer | ASE |
| | Fashion Artist | AER |
| | Graphic Designer | AER |
| | Illustrator (traditional and digital) | AER |
| | Landscape Architect | AIR |
| | Lawyer—Trial Counsel | AER |
| | Musician, Instrumental | ARC |
| | Music Teacher | AES |
| | Newswriter | AEI |
| | Paintings Restorer | ASR |
| | Pastry Chef | ASE |
| | Photojournalist | AEC |
| | Promotions Manager | AEI |
| | Prose Writer | AIE |
| | Public Relations Manager | ASE |
| | Reporter | ASI |
| | Sculptor | AER |
| | Set Designer | AES |
| | Stage Technician | ARS |
| | Technical Illustrator | ARI |
| | Website Designer | AIC |

| **Evolving Careers** |
|---|
| Creative director |
| Actors, seniors and multilingual |
| Web graphics production artist |
| Presentation graphics consultant |
| Cross-cultural writer |

## Occupational Groups (Social)

| Occupational Group | Occupation | Holland Code |
|---|---|---|
| | Air-Traffic-Control Specialist, Tower | SER |
| | Athletic Trainer | SRE |
| | Athletic Coach | SEI |
| | Clinical Psychologist | SIA |
| | Corrections Officer | SER |
| | Counselor | SAE |
| | Elementary Teacher | SAE |
| **SOCIAL** | Employee Relations Specialist | SEA |
| | Equal Opportunity Officer | SRI |
| | Faculty Member, College/University | SEI |

| People/Plant/ Animal Helpers Nurturing | Health Care Administrator | SER |
|---|---|---|
| | High School Teacher | SAE |
| | Interpreter, Deaf | SCE |
| | Librarian | SAI |
| | Minister, Priest, Rabbi | SEA |
| | Music Therapist | SAE |
| | Nurse | SIA |
| | Occupational Development Consultant | SRE |
| | Occupational Therapist | SEI |
| | Organization Learning Specialist | SEI |
| | Passenger Service Representative | SEI |
| | Park Naturalist | SER |
| | Personal Coach | SEI |
| | Personnel Recruiter | SIA |
| | Physical Education Instructor | SCE |
| | Physical Therapist | SIE |
| | Probation and Parole Officer | SIE |
| | Professional Athlete | |
| | Respiratory Therapist | SRC |
| | School Counselor | SIR |
| | Social Worker, Psychiatric | SEA |
| | Special Agent, Customs | SEC |
| | Speech Pathologist | SRI |
| | Teacher, Learning Disabled | SAI |
| | Vocational Rehabilitation | SER |
| | Counselor | SEC |
| **Evolving Careers** | | |
| Accelerated learning consultant | | |
| Actualization psychologist | | |
| Cultural diversity consultant | | |
| Conflict resolution mediator | | |
| Age 60+ career/relationship counselor/coach | | |
| Corporate ethics consultant | | |

## Occupational Groups (Enterprising)

| Occupational Group | Occupation | Holland Code |
|---|---|---|
| | Airport Manager | ESR |
| | Budget Officer | ESI |
| | Business Manager | ESC |
| | Camp Director | ESA |

| | | |
|---|---|---|
| | Chef | ESR |
| | College Administrator | ESC |
| | Criminal Lawyer | ESA |
| | Day Care Center Director | ESC |
| **ENTERPRISING** | Federal Government Executive | EIC |
| | Flight Attendant | ESA |
| People Influencers Power/Status/ Prestige Oriented | Food Services Director | EIS |
| | Fundraising Director | ESA |
| | Golf Club Manager | ECS |
| | Head Waiter/Waitress | ESA |
| | HMO Manager | ECI |
| | Hospital Administrator | ESC |
| | Hotel/Motel Manager | ESR |
| | Judge | EIA |
| | Lobbyist | ESA |
| | Media Marketing Director | ESR |
| | Merchandise Manager | ESR |
| | Military Officer | ECR |
| | Museum Director | ESR |
| | National Park Manager | ESR |
| | Newscaster | ESI |
| | Organizational Development Consultant | EIA |
| | Research and Development Director | ERI |
| | Real Estate Agent | ESR |
| | Sales Manager | ESA |
| | Salesperson, Clothing | EAS |
| | Sales Representative, Sporting Goods | ESA |
| | School Principal | ESI |
| | Securities Trader | ECS |
| | Tax Attorney | ESI |
| | Travel Agent | ECS |
| | Umpire/Referee | ESR |
| | Urban Planner | ESI |

**Evolving Careers**

High-technology sales
Global trade attorney
Medical research center manager
Multimedia project manager
Coach for entrepreneurs

*Occupational Groups (Conventional)*

| Occupational Group | Occupation | Holland Code |
|---|---|---|
| | Abstractor | CSI |
| | Account Manager | CSI |
| | Accountant | CSI |
| | Budget Analyst | CER |
| | Bursar | CEI |
| | Caseworker | CSE |
| | Central-Office Repairer | CRE |
| **CONVENTIONAL** | Computer Security Specialist | CIS |
| | Computer Programmers | CIA |
| | Congressional-District | CES |
| | Aide | CSE |
| | Court Clerk | CIE |
| | Cost Accountant | CSE |
| | Customer Service Representative | CEI |
| Orderly and Efficient | Customs Inspector | CIA |
| | Editorial Assistant | CIA |
| | Financial Analyst | CES |
| Data and Detail Oriented | Fire Inspector | CSE |
| | Insurance Underwriter | CSE |
| | Legal Secretary | CSE |
| | Library Assistant | CSR |
| | Loan Review Analyst | CIR |
| | Medical Records | CES |
| | Technician | CRS |
| | Medical Secretary | CIS |
| | Mortgage Loan Processor | CRE |
| | Paralegal Assistant | CSI |
| | Payroll Clerk | CES |
| | Proofreader | |
| | Quality Control | CES |
| | Coordinator | CSE |
| | Reservation Agent | CES |
| | Secretary | CSE |
| | Tax Preparer | CSE |
| | Title Examiner | |
| | Tourist Information Assistant | CES |
| | Word Processing Supervisor | |

| Evolving Careers |
| --- |
| Information system security expert |
| Robotic programmer |
| Office information system manager |
| Electronic information specialist |
| Space telemetering analyst |

# Pull It Together

As you enter this new section, you have completed most of the self-exploration work. This section will help you to pull things together, make tentative decisions, and consider the next steps. As you put it together, you will want to revisit the places where you reflected in the Press Pause sections and the results of activities in the APP Actions. These reflections and activities are not the end result but rather starting points, providing you with clues related to your career direction. A good APP requires some information—data points so that the APP can do what it does best. Map APPs want to know your current location and your intended location. Fitness APPs want to know about your body shape so you get on a scale and take your measurements and input those into the APP to get started. As you have progressed through these self-awareness activities, you have developed a sense of you. Like a scale and a measuring tape, you have data about you! Success is not about picking a career and putting the car into drive and following the map APP. It will take more input from you as you continue to gather information about yourself and the world around you. In this APP, you will continue to learn about yourself and explore opportunities. You will take the steps to set goals and make tentative decisions. You may uncover new information about yourself. You may uncover new opportunities. You may even feel a little overwhelmed—all of that is a part of the process that will eventually get you to the next step of your career journey.

That is why wise career counselors treat such tests with caution, using them as only one of many ways of exploring who you are. Human personality does not neatly reduce into 16 or any other definitive number of categories: we are far more complex creatures than psychometric tests can ever reveal. And as we will shortly learn, there is compelling evidence that we are much more likely to find fulfilling work by conducting career experiments in the real world than by filling out any number of questionnaires (—*Roman Krznaric, How to Find Fulfilling Work*).

Assessing Compatibility and Employment Outlook
Conducting Informational Interviews
Brainstorming with Individuals
Decision Check List
Making a Definite Decision
Group Brainstorming

# APP 3.1 Discovering What Motivates You

## Do you know people who:

- See life as a "dog-eat-dog" existence in which it is impossible to get ahead?
- Never feel part of a group because they have difficulty relating to others?
- Drive themselves to be equally successful at everything they attempt?
- Consider their work devoid of meaning and purpose?
- Are unsure about what is important in their lives?

*[A human] is a wanting animal and rarely reaches a state of complete satisfaction except for a short time.*

—Abraham H. Maslow, Motivation and Personality

If so, you know people who have not clarified their needs and values and turned them into constructive influences.

## Needs and Values

Of all the individual preferences explored so far, needs and values are the most deeply personal. When people are asked to talk about their own needs and values, they often give "socially acceptable" answers, rather than speaking frankly. Other people are confused about what needs and values actually are, since these forces have been totally unconscious influences in their lives. This is unfortunate because real needs and values are especially powerful motivators in most people's lives. Ignoring or distorting them in career/life planning can cause painfully wrong decisions and wasted effort. This APP category will help you clarify your own true needs and values and put them in proper perspective. Once this is accomplished, needs and values become an invaluable reference for making better choices in life and career.

## Needs and Motivation

Have you ever seen anyone try to motivate somebody else by offering inducements or threats? The research of Abraham Maslow clearly demonstrates that this approach is useless in the long run. All people can be motivated, but motivation cannot be imposed from the outside. Instead, Maslow's work shows us that all people are motivated by inner drives or impulses called needs.[1] A need is an urgent requirement for something that is essential. Because needs reflect some vital deficiency, a strong sense of inner discomfort motivates people to get their needs met.

Although some basic needs are shared by all, higher-level needs vary from person to person. You might, for example, be strongly motivated by a need to compete with others, while a friend might be highly motivated by the need to help others. Some people have needs for security and others for risk taking. Some require independence, and others need dependency. Some needs may be readily fulfilled, but others remain unsatisfied for the greater part of our lives. Each of us, however, has a few dominant needs in our life at any one time.

## Needs, Behavior, and Satisfaction

Your unsatisfied needs drive you; they provide the energy that directs your actions. Once you satisfy a dominant need, you reduce inner tension and experience fulfillment. You also cease to be motivated by any goals that were connected to this particular need[1]. This dynamic is the reason it is a mistake to set up a career goal based solely on a temporary need. On the other hand, needs cannot be ignored because satisfaction itself is only a temporary experience. You undoubtedly know that it is human nature, once one pressing need has been satisfied, to quickly become aware of a new unsatisfied need. In this manner, the needs satisfaction process is cyclic, and everyone is destined to be motivated throughout life by needs. Perhaps that is fortunate. Wouldn't life be boring if all your needs were fully met, and you possessed no motivation at all?

## Unacknowledged Needs and False Motivations

Your dominant needs motivate you regardless of whether or not you are consciously aware of them. And most people are not consciously aware of their real needs, even though they may be obvious to others through your actions. You may be ineffective at getting your needs met because you have not determined what they are.

Typically, when people lose touch with their real needs, they substitute a false need for a real one. For example, people who hunger for love and affection in their lives may substitute a false hunger for food. While these people appear to be motivated by the need for food, the underlying need is really for intimacy. Another example of "false" motivation is illustrated by people who mask a real need for security with a desire to dominate or to become subservient to others. None of the people represented by these examples are getting closer to meeting their real needs. Instead of fulfilling their deficiency, they are often creating other problems.

## Maslow's Needs Hierarchy

Research psychologist Abraham Maslow found that people have patterns of needs that make behavior predictable.[2] Abraham Maslow classified all needs into five basic categories. Maslow concluded that needs conform to a hierarchy; that is, they are structurally organized from a lower to a higher level of need. The five needs from lowest to highest are physiological, safety, belongingness and love, esteem, and self-actualization.

Maslow's work shows that there is a natural progression and growth associated with the way that people experience their needs. This progression involves a step-like structure as illustrated in the Steps of the Basic Needs System table. The general tendency is for a person to move progressively from the lower to higher steps in the needs hierarchy. The lower steps represent deficiency needs for physiological survival and physical safety and then progress through emotional support to the need for self-esteem and self-fulfillment. People living at the highest need level experience little difference between work and pleasure. See the Basic Needs table for key points about needs.

Maslow does not see these high-level self-actualization needs as deficiency needs. People become motivated by the self-actualization needs only when all of their deficiency needs have been satisfied as a general condition in life. Only then are people free to discover, explore, develop, and unfold their true potential. This upward-moving tendency is what Maslow calls the growth process. Of course, not everyone grows at the same rate and some not at all.

## Key Points about Needs

- An unsatisfied need produces a state of inner tension or discomfort that motivates the individual to satisfy that need.

- Unsatisfied basic needs are the primary sources of motivation in life.

- Basic needs that have been essentially satisfied in life no longer create discomfort and cease to be prime motivators of behavior.

- There are five basic needs systems that operate to influence most of human behavior.

- The five basic needs are arranged in a hierarchy from lower to higher.

- There is a natural tendency to progress from the lower-level to the higher-level need system.

- A person becomes aware of a higher-order need system only when a lower-order need system has been essentially satisfied.

- Should the satisfaction of a basic lower-order need be blocked, a person will not become aware of, or motivated by, a higher-order need system.

- While no need is ever fully satisfied, there is some minimal level of satisfaction at which a particular basic need ceases to be a major discomfort in life. At that point, the lower-level need ceases to motivate behavior, and a new higher-level need begins to capture one's attention and motivate behavior.

- Living at the higher level of needs is healthier and more satisfying than living at the lower levels.

- It is difficult for someone to think about volunteering for a worthy cause if the rent is due and there isn't enough money to meet the bills for the month.

- There are times when we all take "survival jobs" just to get through. These jobs may lack fulfillment and do little for us than give us a paycheck. These jobs should last a season not a lifetime if at all possible.

## Steps of the Basic Needs System[3]

| | | | 4 | 5 |
|---|---|---|---|---|
| | | 3 | € | (A) |
| | 2 | (B) | | |
| 1 | (S) | | | |
| (P) | | | Esteem<br>1) Self-respect<br>2) Esteem of | Self-<br>Actualization |
| Physiological | Safety | Belongingness<br>and Love | Others | |

| Personal Needs | | Social Needs | | Transcendent Needs |
|---|---|---|---|---|
| physical comfort | avoiding risk | friendship | self-respect | self-fulfillment |
| food and water | feeling of being safe | affiliation | desire for acknowledgment | achieving one's full potential |
| shelter warmth | emotional security physical security | feeling part of a group | demonstration of | desire to know and understand |
| sexual gratification | harm avoidance | belonging with someone else | competency and mastery | self-realization |
| other bodily needs | predictability | giving and receiving love | advancement | personal growth |
| | protection | | recognition | meaning in life and |
| | stability | affection relationships with | self-confidence independence and | work satisfaction through doing |
| | dependency freedom from fear | people a place in a group or family intimacy | freedom reputation attention status | making a contribution |
| | need for structure and order, law, limits | | sense of self-worth adequacy being useful and necessary | serving a worthy cause |

It is also possible to move downward on the needs hierarchy because of certain life events. For instance, the sudden, unexpected death of a spouse or loved one could result in belongingness and love reappearing as a strong motive when previously it had been satisfied. Or the devastation resulting from the loss of one's job and the inability to find another could plunge an individual all the way down the hierarchy to a personal need for safety and security.

**Think of your most recent job. Looking at Maslow, what needs did it meet?**

## Basic Needs on the Job

So far we have discussed the basic needs hierarchy in general terms. These needs also operate in the work setting to motivate characteristic types of behavior. Study the table to see if you can identify on-the-job behaviors typical of you and of other people you know.

**The Basic Needs on the Job[4]**

| The Basic Need | Work Motivation/Behavior |
| --- | --- |
| Physiological | Concern for subsistence (making enough money to survive). Concern for adequate time for meals and rest breaks. Concern for the physical working conditions and avoiding bodily discomfort. |
| Safety | Concern for fringe benefits such as retirement/pension plan, hospitalization insurance, safe working conditions, seniority protection, clear and consistent working standards (knowing exactly what is expected of a person). |
| Belongingness and Love | Concern for good relationships, harmonious interactions with peers and superiors, being a member of a working team or group, giving and receiving nurturing. |
| Esteem | Concern for ways of demonstrating skills and proving self to others. Seeking out opportunities for advancement and promotion. Obtaining work assignments to demonstrate special knowledges and skills. Preoccupation with the best work in return for various types of rewards available (titles, salary, praise, promotions, recommendations, status). |
| Self-Actualization | A concern for testing one's self (challenge), proving something to one's self. Preoccupation with personal growth, along with a need to be involved in challenging and interesting work that allows learning, growth, creativity, productivity, and contribution to a worthwhile cause. |

## Case Study   Brad

After 10 years with his company, Brad moved up to a position of considerable respect and responsibility. Then, suddenly, his life was thrown into chaos. Brad received notification that he was being laid off. Upon learning this, he was shocked, hurt, and frightened. How could he support his family? How could he obtain another job that would pay a comparable salary? How could he find work he liked and was interested in? How could he replace his friendships at work? Where could he have a comparable amount of responsibility and respect?

At this point, Brad sought the help of a career counselor to assist him in deciding where to go with his life. Brad's primary concern was finding work that would interest him, best use his talents, and associate him with people he really liked. This latter concern, being with people he liked, was Brad's major preoccupation at this point. Brad decided upon a new career as a career counselor. Once he had chosen his new career, Brad worked hard to implement it, first by getting the necessary education and then by obtaining a career-counseling position.

When Brad acquired his new job, he was excited about it and very much involved. By belonging to an organization of his choice and by associating with clients and coworkers he liked, Brad's needs were being met. Gradually, however, Brad began losing his enthusiasm for counseling. Instead, he noticed that he was skilled at designing counseling materials as well as planning and developing counseling programs. This new love eventually became a problem for Brad. People seeking his counseling services were filling up his time, which he thought could be better spent in program development.

Eventually, Brad applied for and obtained a position where he could spend most of his time and efforts designing, planning, and developing programs. At this point, Brad reexperienced the interest and enthusiasm for his work that he had felt when he first acquired his counseling position.

Brad's primary motivation now is creating and implementing effective counseling programs to serve large numbers of people. His achievements have begun earning him recognition, and he feels very good about that. Recently, however, Brad has experienced a new tension: he feels he is still not using his strongest talents for a cause that is deeply meaningful to him.

Brad's physiological, safety, and belongingness needs had been essentially satisfied in 10 years at his old career. Upon receiving his termination notice, however, Brad was set back both physically and emotionally. His needs for security and belongingness suddenly became unmet needs. On the job, his primary motivation had been satisfying his need for esteem. Now he was plummeted all the way down the needs hierarchy to physiological concerns about how he was going to provide the basic necessities for himself and his family.

In counseling, Brad quickly learned that he possessed many employable skills. Although losing his job was a serious setback, his future was actually still quite secure. He was still young and employable, and he had sufficient savings to survive until he could obtain a new position. In looking at these aspects, Brad felt reassured. In fact, he really wasn't at the physiological or security level of the needs hierarchy. His primary preoccupation was at the belongingness and love level. His personal pride and esteem had suffered a great deal in his setback, but the primary motivation for his present career was with the need for affiliation, the need to feel wanted by and associated with others. Brad had chosen this career far more on the basis of his "hunger" for affiliation than out of consideration for his primary interests, talents, and personality style. And that proved to be a mistake.

Although Brad was an effective counselor, he quickly started losing his interest and enthusiasm for counseling as soon as his belongingness needs were generally satisfied. He then reexperienced the need for esteem. This occurred in the form of motivation to develop his skills and to produce significant achievements through work. In this respect, however, Brad became aware that his skills and interests were more in creative program planning and development than in personal counseling.

At the time he made his selection, Brad was unaware of how one's motivation changes when a need is satisfied. Had he been aware of this important dynamic, he would have developed plans for a career track that led more quickly to his fundamental interests and talents. Fortunately for Brad, his career choice and his organization allowed for a transfer that used his talents and fulfilled his current primary needs for esteem.

The closing statements in the case study suggest that a new shift in Brad's motivation may be occurring. His concern appears to be less in achievement for esteem and more in personal development for a worthy cause. Perhaps Brad's needs for esteem are becoming satisfied, and he is responding to inner needs for self-actualization.

While most of the lessons to be learned from the case study are obvious, a few points warrant further elaboration. We can infer from this case study that while needs must be included in the career-choice process, they should be considered as just one part of the whole picture along with what you have to contribute through preferred talents, interests, values, and life goals. While talents and personality styles change very little after the age of 21, needs change continuously over a lifetime. In career planning, therefore, you must take into account both where you are now regarding personal needs and where you will be in the future.

PAUSE

Carefully review the information on needs, and then answer the following questions.

1. Which of the basic needs in your life appear to be the most fully satisfied? Explain why this is so.

2. Which basic need, because it is not fully satisfied, now appears to be your primary motivator? What would have to happen for this need to be generally satisfied in your life?

3. If your current primary motivating need were generally satisfied, what need would then probably become your primary motivator? Include the possible ways your life could change.

4. How will you use the information obtained from this examination of your needs in planning your career future?

## Needs vs. Values

Clear, consciously held values are another important factor in effective career choices. The relationship between needs and values can be demonstrated by examining how each is acquired and how each influences current and future behavior.

Needs arise out of a perceived deficiency primarily physiological or social in nature. For example, the office manager whose work routine is disorderly and chaotic feels the need for a predictable sequence of work tasks. The perceived deficiency is one of structure, order, and organization. As soon as the office manager gets the safety and security of a structured and ordered work environment, that need disappears.

Unlike needs, values do not arise from perceived deficiency and do not disappear once satisfied. Values are learned and chosen from one's life experiences. For example, children whose strong interest in reading is supported and whose curiosity about natural phenomena is encouraged by understanding parents and teachers will most probably value education. As adults they may later seek out both formal and informal continuing education and encourage their children to do the same.

Both needs and values change over time, although values change to a far lesser extent than needs. Needs change as they are temporarily satisfied, whereas values change due to life adjustments and/or personal growth resulting from changing circumstances. As crises occur and circumstances change over time, needs emerge and reemerge up and down the hierarchy. If what seems to be a need remains consistently strong after being satisfied, it has become a value.

Needs are the key motivators for current behavior, whereas values serve as guides to current and future choices of action. Your immediate behavior is strongly influenced by potent, unmet needs. Clear, consciously held values aid you in making consistent decisions about appropriate courses of action.

The interplay of needs and values can be illustrated by the following example: Your neighborhood experiences a sudden increase in theft, harassment on the streets, and other similar occurrences. The sense of safety and security in your community is threatened. You and your neighbors are motivated to take specific action to return the area to its former state. The neighborhood improvement association calls a meeting of interested parties, and suggestions are elicited from the group.

Proposed actions include initiating a Neighborhood Watch Program, increasing illumination in the neighborhood after dark, maintaining a lookout and reporting system for unfamiliar people and vehicles in the neighborhood, investing in a security system, and purchasing handguns. While you may agree and actively support most of the suggestions, you deem the purchase of handguns unacceptable. Here your values regarding the sanctity of human life guide your decision not to purchase a handgun and to dissuade your neighbors from such a purchase.

The need to restore your community to its previous safe and secure condition motivates several types of behavior. But your clear, strongly held values determine the types of actions you would support and those you would oppose. Your needs motivate the necessity of taking immediate action, but your values guide the choice of actions that you would take or support.

## The Importance of Values in Going for What You Want

There used to be a popular television beverage commercial that implored us to "Go for it with all the gusto you've got." "After all," it continued, "you only go around once in life." For those involved in career decision-making, this is excellent advice, but going for what you want in life is not an easy task. In fact, few people know what they want in life because they have never, at a deep level, taken the time and effort to determine what matters in their lives. To determine what you want, you must first know what is important in your life—the values that give your life meaning and relevance.

Values are not lofty ideals dreamed up by experts in ivory towers and held up as examples by which you ought to live. Instead, people choose, formulate, and reformulate their values as they direct their lives. Values can be seen most clearly in your everyday actions as you make decisions. You are not always consciously aware of your values, however, unless you dig deeply and search widely through your life experiences.

You will discover that values are the principles or standards upon which you make all decisions that shape the course of your life. Life in our culture is enormously complex, and each day we are bombarded by a wide array of lifestyle choices. Some are simple. For example, when you shop for groceries, do you choose nutritious foods such as grains, fresh fruits and vegetables, and low-fat dairy products? Or do you choose prepared foods that save you time? Do you look for money-saving bargains? Or do you prefer to pay more for brand-name items? Even these simple choices reflect your values.

More complex choices in your life require considerable and often difficult deliberation. Young people, for instance, face decisions such as whether to live at home, where their basic needs are met, or to risk moving out and fending for themselves. Young couples are often faced with the dilemma of how to balance the demands of family and career. Men and women of all ages ponder whether to terminate relationships that are not working. Men and women at midlife contemplate significant career and lifestyle changes. Older people often face the difficult choice of living alone in familiar surroundings or moving into living complexes with other senior citizens. People can best make these and other important decisions on the basis of clear, consciously held values.

## Defining and Clarifying Values

Directing your life in a world full of confusion and conflict is like charting a course through unknown and often dangerous waters. Values clarification provides a means of charting a course through the unknown waters of your life. Through values clarification, you can carefully examine your life experiences to discover the content and strength of your own values system. This self-assessment method will help you discover what values you actually live by or act upon rather than what you think your values should be. Values clarification is a positive, forward-looking process that focuses on both your current values and your evolving values.

Before you can clarify your values, however, you need to be clear on what constitutes a value. A value is something we prize, choose, and act upon. *Prizing* emphasizes the emotions or feelings, *choosing* relies on thinking and reasoning, and *acting* implies behavior. Therefore, our values are formed by a combination of our feelings, thoughts, and behavior.

## Criteria for Determining a Value

*Prizing*

1. *Prized and Cherished.* To prize and cherish something is to have an emotional attachment to it. This attachment may be to an intangible concept or to a tangible object. For example, a political activist who has been imprisoned in her own country for opposing a dictatorial regime experiences strong emotional ties to free political expression. To her, the concept of freedom is prized and cherished. Someone else may cherish a family ring or family heirloom not for the object itself but for what it represents: a deceased parent, a loving family, a proud cultural heritage.

2. *Publicly Affirmed.* Public affirmation is simply acknowledging a belief, feeling, or attitude to others. For example, local activists who make their views known to their neighbors through a community newsletter represent a public affirmation. Wearing a uniform (scout, military, religious order) is another more subtle way of publicly affirming certain values.

*Choosing*

3. *Chosen Freely.* Freely chosen values are those you have ultimately chosen yourself as opposed to simply buying into the subtle or overt influence of others. For example, choosing a religious or political affiliation of your own volition rather than merely following what your parents or family believed represents free choice.

4. *Chosen from Alternatives.* Without two or more alternatives, there is no choice and no true value. A true choice involves awareness of the widest variety of possible options or alternatives and committing to what seems inherently important to you.

5. *Chosen after Consideration of Consequences.* Making the choice that is right for you first requires a careful examination of the probable consequences of each of your identified alternatives. For example, when deliberating upon a career change, factors such as job security, salary and benefits, seniority, degree of dissatisfaction, and the possibility of lateral movement should all be weighed and considered carefully before reaching a decision.

*Acting*

6. *Acted Upon.* You affirm your values by acting upon them. Unless you act upon something, it is not a value but only a good idea or belief. For

example, if you value your role as citizen, then you would demonstrate it by voting, supporting candidates, lobbying, or publicizing officials' actions. Failure to act can prevent an idea or belief from becoming a value.

7. *Acted Upon Repeatedly and Consistently to Form a Definite Pattern.* A single act does not constitute a value. Examining your life for patterns of repeated and consistent action will help you identify your values. For example, if you consistently arrange regular physical and dental checkups, exercise three times per week, plan and eat nutritious meals, and sleep six to eight hours per night, then you undoubtedly value healthful living. Your repeated pattern of consistent actions promotes health as one of your values.[5]

ACTION      Complete the **Life Values Assessment** in App 3.3.

### Acquiring and Changing Your Values

The predominant view about how values are acquired has been that they are transmitted from adults to children. Parents or parent substitutes articulate and model the values that they desire their children to acquire. According to this traditional view, children take the values they have been taught and make them their own.

Proponents of values clarification reject the traditional idea that values can be taught or transmitted.[6] Instead, they believe that values are learned directly from an individual's life experiences involving various influences.

As you grow and develop, you change, and so do your values. What is a value to you now may diminish in importance as you gain new information and acquire additional skills, or as your life circumstances change in significant ways. For example, in first grade, children often value their relationship with the teacher above all else, but in the upper elementary grades, children place a higher value on their relationships with peers. In adolescence, relationships with the opposite sex are usually most highly valued. Later, young adults often find that family and career values take precedence. On the other hand, some core values may remain relatively stable throughout your life.

### Discovering your Hidden Values

Often you are not consciously aware of your values. Being asked to express your values directly is like asking you to count all the muscles in your body. Some are obvious and visible to you, but most are hidden from your view.

The way you choose to live your life provides clues to these hidden values. For instance, when you have free time, what do you choose to do with it? Do you read, jog, play the piano, or call a friend? Other than obtaining the necessities of life, how do you choose to spend your money? What kinds of things get you riled up enough to take a stand or to take action? What do you fantasize or daydream about? When do you feel most alive and vibrant in your life? In answering these and other similar questions, you are uncovering your true values.

Clues to our values are constantly around us. Everything you do or say reveals something about what you value. If you find yourself living for those quiet moments when you can be alone, then you probably value self-reflection. If, on the other hand, you live for the moments of raucous, roughhouse play with your children or time with your friends, then you probably value gregarious interaction.

Two good ways of discovering your hidden values are through examining past events or accomplishments in your life and by looking at your future objectives. The events or accomplishments represent choices you have made in the past and reflect what motivated you at that particular time. They tell you much about what you may still consider important in your life. Your future objectives come from the dreams and fantasies you have about the future. They, too, tell you what is important in your life right now.

> Complete the **Uncovering Your Hidden Values assessment** in App 3.3.

## The Importance of Values in Work

For your work to be satisfying, it must be compatible with your values. For some people, money, power, prestige, and status are what it takes for a job to be rewarding. Others may have these external rewards in their work but still find it unsatisfying. Some people must experience meaning or purpose in the work itself for a job to be satisfying.

Years from now when you reflect on your work life, will it be with a sense of satisfaction or a sense of regret? Satisfaction comes from knowing that what you did with your life was important, that your life's work had some significance and benefit for yourself and perhaps for others.

There are some values that will most likely stay consistent throughout your career, while others may change depending upon your situation. Young parents may value stability and flexibility to allow for a steady income but time to care for their children. Recent college graduates often value new experiences and social interaction at work. Many career counselors acknowledge that their clients come to them when moving from one life stage to another. The desire to move from the excitement of a large city to the quietness of the suburbs is heard from those thinking of having children. Finding work that is challenging with potential for high income even if it means working long hours is often heard from those at early or late career stages. Travel is considered a perk in some life stages and a burden by others. As you are completing the exercises, think of your current life stage, where you anticipate being in five years, as well as those values that will most likely remain consistent across your career.

The following exercise contains a listing of values that can be derived from work. These are arranged in four categories: workplace conditions, workplace outcomes, workplace rewards, and family/personal considerations.

Before you take the next APP ACTION, PRESS PAUSE

Think about a recent job or volunteer activity. Why did you work or volunteer in the role you held or for that particular organization?

Complete the **Work Values Assessment** in App 3.3.

1. Reflect on what you choose to do when you have free time. Think of the free time you had last week. What did you choose to do with it? What, if anything, does this tell you about your values?

2. By answering the following questions, what values do you discover?

   a. Other than purchasing necessities, how do you choose to spend your money?

   b. What kinds of things get you riled up enough to take a stand?

   c. What do you daydream about?

> **d.** **What do you find yourself doing when you feel most alive and vibrant in your life?**

## Summary

Your needs are experienced as an inner feeling that something essential for you is missing. This awareness produces a sense of acute personal discomfort or inner tension that motivates you to satisfy this need. For career planning, consider your needs seriously, but do not let them overshadow the importance of other personal attributes and preferences. Choose a career that will meet your currently dominating need and provide upward progression through the other needs. It is important to understand not only your current needs, but also the ways these needs are likely to change in the future.

The process of values clarification is also crucial to career/life decision making. To prove satisfying over the long haul, choices must be based on realizing what is truly important in your life.

People derive certain values from their jobs and careers. For some, work provides external values, such as money or material success. Others require the fulfillment of more internal values, such as helping others or seeking knowledge. Success and fulfillment in life and work is a matter of achieving what you value. To feel successful, know what you value and act on that in life and work.

## Endnotes

### APP 3.1

1. Abraham Maslow, *Motivation and Personality*, 2nd ed. (New York: Harper & Row, 1970).
2. Maslow, p. 44.
3. Maslow, p. 45.
4. Adapted from the Intensive Course in the Crystal Life/Work Planning Process, John C. Crystal Center, Inc., 894 Plandome Rd., Manhasset, NY 11030.

Other sources related to this APP:

6. Hall and Williams, Work Motivation Inventory.
7. Louis E. Raths, Merrill Harmin, and Sidney F. Simon, *Values and Teaching* (Columbus, OH: Charles E. Merrill, 1966) pp. 28–30.
8. This process is adapted from Howard E. Figler's *PATH: A Career Workbook for Liberal Arts Students* (Cranston, Rhode Island: Carroll Press, 1975) pp. 77–79.

# APP 3.2 Alternatives and Decision Making

## Do you know people who:

- Make decisions without knowing what their alternatives are?
- Have no idea how to find information about occupational alternatives?
- Can only seem to identify unsatisfactory choices?
- Seem to ponder their alternatives endlessly without ever deciding?
- Just let others tell them what to do?

*Far too often, people tend to lay out alternatives for you. As a result, you may focus on only those alternatives. But you should always keep in mind that there may be other alternatives that haven't been mentioned by anyone. Also, you are bringing what is uniquely you to the situation, so that an alternative that may be best for most people may not be best for you.*

*—Gordon Porter Miller, Life Choices*

If so, you know people who lack the skills required to assess their available alternatives and make the best career/life decisions.

The world of work is a huge universe consisting of thousands of occupations. Statistically, picking a suitable occupation by chance or luck is inconceivable. You will need effective decision-making skills.

What is your current approach to decision-making? Do you immediately want to know the "right answer?" Most people do. Good chess players, however, realize that there is seldom a single best course of action. Instead, they contemplate their full range of options, each leading to different consequences. They are likely to be asking, "What strategy do I choose to pursue? What are my alternatives right now, and how might they change depending upon the next move?" Only after surveying the whole range of alternatives and their consequences do successful chess players decide what move to make.

Successful chess playing is similar to effective career decision-making. Chess players who cannot see the full range of alternatives available to them are unlikely to be consistent winners. People faced with career/life decisions are also unlikely to make winning decisions unless they too can see their full range of alternatives and evaluate their consequences (see "Sample Occupations for the CIR" Personality Style" for sample occupations).

inspired_by_the_light/Shutterstock.com

At this phase of your decision-making process, try to be thorough, patient, and alert to all of your best possibilities. We have seen many people in the career planning center who, after assessing their talents and goals, became impatient with the task of identifying alternatives. They wanted to pick the first seemingly good choice they found. Some people are afraid that too many choices will just confuse them. It is true that having a lot of possibilities makes choosing more complicated. But why miss your best available option because of impatience? We urge you to take your time with this APP's exercises as an investment in your future.

## Envisioning the Task

To better understand career decision-making, consider the following example. Janet, Rodney, Tim, and Cynthia all have a "CIR" Holland personality code. At this point in their career planning, each has identified the following career alternatives of interest to them:

| Janet | Rodney | Tim | Cynthia |
|---|---|---|---|
| Accountant | Computer | Management Analyst | Medical Records |
| Computer Operator | Programmer | Civil Engineering | Technician |
| | Building Inspector | Technician Computer | Management Analyst |
| | Nurse | Programmer | Accountant Civil |
| | Elementary Teacher | | Engineering |
| | | | Technician |

Which person do you think has identified the best alternatives for a "CIR" personality style? Why?

All together, these four people have identified a total of 10 alternatives. These alternatives vary in suitability for a "CIR" personality style. In the following table, these alternatives have been separated into categories labeled "good" and "poor." These alternatives are ranked on both suitability to the "CIR" personality style and on the job-market outlook.

| The Five Best Alternatives | The Five Poorest Alternatives |
|---|---|
| $B_1$ Medical Records Technician | $P_1$ Elementary Teacher |
| $B_2$ Management Analyst | $P_2$ Physical Education Instructor |
| $B_3$ Computer Programmer | $P_3$ Nurse |
| $B_4$ Civil Engineering Technician | $P_4$ Building Inspector |
| $B_5$ Accountant | $P_5$ Computer Operator |
| **Note:** | |
| $B_1$ = The best alternative | $P_1$ = The poorest alternative |
| $B_2$ = The second best, etc. | $P_2$ = The second poorest, etc. |

## Assessing the Sample Options

Janet has identified only two alternatives, one in the "good" column ("B5—Accountant") and the other "poor" ("P5—Computer Operator"). As a consequence, Janet's "best" choice is only a moderately good ("B5") alternative. Her list does not give her much to choose from.

Rodney's three alternatives can be ranked as follows:

## Sample Occupations for the "CIR" Personality Style

| Rating | Occupation | Holland Code | Comments |
|---|---|---|---|
| $B_1$ | Medical Records Technician | CIR | This is the best alternative. It represents the best Holland code match, and the job-market demand for medical records technicians is excellent. |
| $B_2$ | Management Analyst | ICR | This is the second-best Holland code match, and again, job-market demand is excellent. |
| $B_3$ | Computer Programmer | IRC | This is the third-best Holland code match with a fair employment outlook. |
| $B_4$ | Civil Engineering Technician | RIC | This is a good Holland code match with a fair job market prospect. |
| $B_5$ | Accountant | CSI | While the Holland code does not exactly match the example, with two out of the three letters the same, this would be a fairly good match. The employment outlook for accountants is fair. |
| $P_5$ | Computer Operator | CSR | While the Holland code of this alternative matches fairly well, the employment outlook for computer operators is extremely poor as this occupation is fast becoming obsolete. |
| $P_4$ | Building Inspector | RCE | The Holland code here matches fairly well. The occupational outlook is tied to the highs and lows of the construction industry, which are difficult to predict. |
| $P_3$ | Nurse | SIA | While the job market for nurses is fair, this Holland code is significantly different from the example. |
| $P_2$ | Physical Education Instructor | SER | While this Holland code does share one letter with the example, it is a significantly different code. The employment outlook for this occupation is fair. |
| $P_1$ | Elementary Teacher | SAE | This is rated as the poorest alternative since it has no Holland code letters in common with the example. |

$B_3$ for Computer Programmer
$P_3$ for Nurse
$P_4$ for Building Inspector

As a consequence of his alternative selection, the best pick that Rodney could make would be only slightly better than Janet's choice.

Tim has selected alternatives that can be ranked this way:

$B_2$ for Management Analyst
$B_4$ for Civil Engineering Technician
$P_1$ for Elementary Teacher
$P_2$ for Physical Education Instructor

Tim has more and better options than either Janet or Rodney. On the other hand, his list also contains the two poorest options identified on the overall list. If Tim makes a poor decision, he could end up even more dissatisfied than either Janet or Rodney.

Cynthia, through careful alternative assessment, has identified the five best alternatives on the total list. Accordingly, with a good pick, she could choose the one alternative capable of producing the greatest amount of eventual career satisfaction. Even with a poor selection, she would still be choosing from the "good" list.

## Becoming Aware of your Alternatives

In real life it is difficult, or even impossible, to identify all of the best career alternatives for yourself. However, you will be able to find many alternatives leading to considerable career/life satisfaction by completing the following exercises. They are designed to use both your creative and logical abilities to find a large number of alternatives. The time for narrowing down your options will come later.

For now, concentrate on finding your full range of winning career alternatives.

### Seeking Career Alternatives from Functional Skills

In APP 2.0, you listed your specific functional skills and figured out your top five preferred skills groups based on personal preference and feedback from others. A good way to begin developing your career alternatives is to review your favorite functional skills, brainstorming with others to discover what kinds of careers would welcome these capabilities. Brad, our case study from APP 3.1, used this process to begin developing his list of occupational alternatives.

Brad's top five skills groups were identified as follows:

1. Inventing/Developing New Ideas
2. Communicating/Teaching
3. Planning/Organizing Data
4. Analyzing/Evaluating/Researching
5. Investigating/Observing/Experimenting

Brad gave this list of preferred skills families, along with a copy of his specific skills list, to a small group of people. He asked them to come up with a list of possible occupations where these skills would be used extensively. In just six minutes of brainstorming, the group came up with the following list of occupations:

- Scientist
- Lecturer
- Developer of training aids
- Learning lab director
- Investigative reporter
- Teacher
- Researcher
- Developer of textbooks, educational materials, and programs
- Patent investigator
- Inventor
- Trainer
- Technical writer
- Campaign manager
- Pollster
- Editor
- Speech writer
- Lobbyist

Brad was interested in most of these career ideas. Imagine the list this group might have compiled if they had spent 30 minutes or more on the task instead of just 6.

Go to the end of this APP and spend time processing your results. First, complete **APP ACTION: Envisioning Process.** This process will take time to complete, so be sure you set aside at least an hour for your personal reflection.

## Gaining More Careers To Consider

After you have taken the time to do your own personal reflection, you may want to reach out to others for their input. APP ACTIONS—Brainstorming with Individuals and Group Brainstorming will help you to gain an external perspective. Keep in mind the fact that for many people the concepts of jobs, careers, occupations, and work may be interchangeable. You may offer insights into industries or very specific jobs at one unique place of employment. Use the information offered as a jumping off point in your exploration, being sure not to eliminate ideas you had because it was mentioned in your brainstorming activities.

You have gathered information about yourself. Without referring to your APP ACTION results, list the factors most important relative to your career choice that are most important to you at this moment. Consider a skill you are certain you wish to use, a value that is a must have, or a passion you wish to pursue.

Complete **APP ACTION: Group Brainstorming** in App 3.3.

## Career Research

As previously covered, there are many tools available to assist you with career research. While some websites come and go, sites such as the O*Net and the Occupational Outlook Handbook have become staples for career research. The *Occupational Outlook Handbook* (OOH) at **www.bls.gov/oco/** is a nationally recognized source of career information, designed to provide valuable assistance to individuals making decisions about their future work lives. Revised every two years, the OOH describes what workers do on the job, working conditions, the training and education needed, earnings, and expected job prospects in a wide range of occupations.

Do not rule out the use of reliable print publications, internet sites designed to support various professions such as the medical field at ama-assn .org. Many of these are listed under the "Sources for Additional Information" on the OOH and the O*NET.

## Decision-Making Time

Now that you have identified at least –40 alternatives, it's time to begin narrowing down the list to select your best choice. Your first step is to eliminate all but the best 10 from your list. Then you will research your "top 10" to learn more about these fields to decide which one is your very best choice.

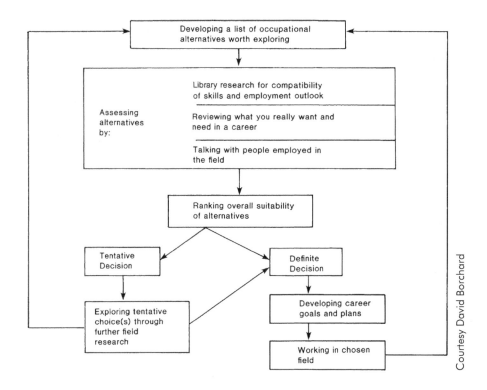

Courtesy David Borchard

The diagram below illustrates the steps in this process. Notice that the process shown here leads either to a tentative or a definite choice. Sometimes it is appropriate to make tentative choices when you have narrowed your list down to two or three choices but need more time to further explore these choices before making a final commitment.

A tentative choice, as we use it here, is different from the avoidance behavior of not deciding. A tentative choice involves allotting yourself time to explore specific options that you have identified. A tentative choice is particularly appropriate for a beginning college student who has the luxury of time to explore before needing to make a final choice.

Career changers rarely have that luxury, however, and will need to use this process to make a definite decision. The good news is that career changers usually have more experience and self-knowledge to draw upon for a definite choice.

Following are two case studies to illustrate definite versus tentative decision-making.

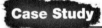 **Chris**

Chris was confronted with a major crisis when he lost the job he had held for over 10 years. With career-counseling assistance, Chris discovered that his personality style was incompatible with his previous job and career. He learned that his preferred families of skills were in the innovating, creative planning, writing, and teaching areas. On the basis of self-assessment, Chris developed a lengthy list of suitable alternatives and then narrowed the list down to the following:

- Psychology
- Counseling
- Public relations/advertising
- Cartooning
- Journalism
- College teaching

These were so appealing that Chris couldn't make any further instinctive decisions. He was advised to learn all he could about these occupations. Primarily, Chris accomplished this task through career research using sites such as the Occupational Outlook Handbook and by identifying and talking with people working in fields he found interesting. He got their names from his networking including friends and acquaintances. Initially, conducting these interviews was hard for Chris. He vividly recalls his tension and sweaty palms as he prepared to go talk with people.

Chris soon found, however, that if he reached out to them in advance, was considerate about people's time, and was straightforward about his purpose, most people really enjoyed talking with him about their work. Eventually, Chris started enjoying these information interviews. Best of all, he began learning what it would really be like to pursue a career in these kinds of occupations. At his counselor's suggestion, Chris carefully wrote down his observations and reactions from each of these information interviews immediately after conducting them. These notes were far more valuable than vague memories when he prepared to make his decision.

In conducting these interviews, Chris found that different people in the same occupation had completely different ideas and perspectives about the field. He realized how important it was to discuss the same occupation with several people. He learned, too, that there are wide ranges of differences within an occupation depending on the work setting. He also acquired a much better appreciation of what work settings were most likely to be hiring in the future, what settings offered the best advancement opportunities, and what settings had the best salary and benefits programs.

After completing these interviews, Chris reviewed what he had learned from his field research about outcomes he could expect if he pursued various careers. He also reaffirmed that what he wanted most in a career was to be associated with people he liked, to continue learning and using his knowledge, and to develop creative methods for helping adults live more satisfying lives. On the basis of what he had learned, Chris chose counseling in a community college as his best career alternative.

Chris recalls both the relief and exhilaration that accompanied this selection. He knew that he still had to establish his specific career goals and develop his implementation plans, but he also realized what a giant step he had taken toward creating a new and satisfying career. Later, when Chris's needs changed again, he became aware of new suitable career alternatives available to him. This placed him in a new decision situation.

His experience in the decision-making process benefited Chris in many ways. First, he learned how to make career-choice decisions more effectively and easily than ever before. Second, he learned to view his career as a lifelong process. As a result, he could recognize new alternatives and opportunities when they arose. He was also far more inclined to act on these opportunities.

## Case Study   Julie

Julie graduated from high school with absolutely no idea of what she wanted to do, other than to go on to college. In high school she had acquired a large group of friends and concentrated on having fun. Julie was intelligent, attractive, and sociable, but she just had never discovered anything in school that really engaged her serious interests.

After graduating from high school, Julie decided to pursue a general studies curriculum at the local community college until she discovered a compelling career interest. After taking general elective requirements during her first year, she enrolled in a career planning course. In that course she discovered that she had skills, interests, and values that she had never really thought about before. She realized, for instance, that she had excellent communication skills, which enabled her to establish rapport, make excellent presentations, sell her ideas, and entertain others. She was also an excellent organizer and planner when it involved some activity that really interested her. She realized that she enjoyed helping others and that she wanted to have a balance between family and career. A job that involved performing a useful service to others, perhaps to children, was appealing.

In the course, she identified about 40 career possibilities, including many she had never considered or heard of before. Eventually, she narrowed this list down to three: teaching, psychology, and communications. She felt unwilling to commit to any one of these at that time. She needed more information and some related experience to eliminate alternatives from this list she felt enthusiastic about. She found out that each of these choices was a broad field in itself. What age groups did she want to work with? What types of organizations were appealing? What particular work settings did she want? If she decided on teaching, for example, what age group did she want to work with? Did she want to go into special education, elementary education, or learn a specific subject matter to teach in a high school, college, or business setting?

With the help of a career counselor, Julie worked out a plan of action that would enable her to explore all three areas and cover her bases until she was ready for a definite career commitment. She selected an arts and science major that enabled her to meet the general education requirements for each of the three fields. She also selected introductory courses in psychology, education, and communications to sample these subject areas and get a clearer idea of how her skills, interests, and energies would be useful.

In addition, Julie decided to participate in extra-curricular activities that allowed her to express her interests and develop the skills she now knew she wanted to use in her career. These activities included being in a college play, working as a technical assistant in the college media department, participating in the readers' theater, taking voice lessons, and trying out for and making the college forensics team. As a team member she won numerous awards and traveled across the country.

Upon obtaining her associate in arts degree from the community college, Julie decided to transfer to the University of Iowa. Based on her previous activities and coursework, Julie decided to major in communications. At Iowa, Julie took advantage of work/learning experiences that included working with a local radio station, where she learned marketing activities and even got to develop and record a short advertisement. During the summer, she obtained an internship with PBS, where she became familiar with the research, marketing, and management areas of a large TV and radio operation. In her senior year in college, Julie is continuing to broaden her experience by working as a production assistant. She is also refining her resume and setting up job interviews through the career services office on her campus.

Julie still wonders sometimes whether she has made the right choice. She occasionally

Kzenon/Shutterstock.com

catches herself thinking, "Maybe I should become a child psychologist or a speech teacher." She is now content to try out her career choice in communications and to gain some experience and wisdom in the "real world." She realizes also that she is young and that she can make a career change in the future. She is not afraid of that prospect because she now knows a useful decision-making process and intends to use this process continually throughout her life. She knows that at some point in the future she will want to go on for a master's degree. For now, she wants to become financially independent and learn about herself and her possibilities on the job.

**PAUSE**

**Considering the case studies of Chris and Julie, list at least two things you can apply to your own career journey.**

**We meet Julie as a college student and Chris at a later point in his career. In what ways does age impact the career process?**

## Narrowing Down

Throughout the course of this book you have identified a number of occupations from the various exercises and recorded these in your Career to Consider list in APP 7.0. Now it is time to narrow that list down to the best ones for you. The goal is to select from this list the 10 best choices for you and your unique interests, skills, and values.

Begin by crossing out those that are not particularly interesting or not practical for your situation. For example, you might aspire to be a jockey but are 6'2" and weigh 240 pounds. Or perhaps you want to become a psychiatrist but are not up to the 10 years of education and training that would entail. Next, eliminate duplicate entries that have been entered with slightly different names.

Once you have cleaned up your list, reduce the number further by assigning Holland codes to the remainder and eliminating any obvious mismatches. This process will enable you to weed out not only the poor choices on your list, but also some seemingly appropriate choices that wouldn't work out in the long run.

arka38/Shutterstock.com

## Holland Coding Your Career Alternatives

As discussed in APPs 2.2 and 2.4, you will recall that people have characteristic personality styles and that occupations can also be classified by three-letter Holland codes. By comparing your own Holland code with the Holland codes of these occupations, you can determine how compatible an occupation is with your particular interests and personality style.

1. Refer now to that portion of Careers to Consider entitled *Career Possibilities*. Under the column heading *Occupations of Interest* you have listed career alternatives based on insights obtained from the assessments you completed in APPs 2.1, 2.2, and 2.3 and exercises included in this APP. Identify the Holland code, as best you can, for each of the occupations on your list and place it in the adjacent column under the heading *Holland Code*. If necessary, review the information in APP 2.2 that relates to the Holland coding of occupations. Six examples are provided on the next page to assist you in your identification. While the Holland Code is not essential, it will help you group your occupations and see patterns.

| Occupations | Holland Code | | |
|---|---|---|---|
| Examples: | | | |
| Newspaper Reporter | A | S | I |
| Medical Laboratory Technician | I | R | E |
| Architectural Drafter | R | C | I |
| Office Manager | E | S | R |
| Accountant | C | S | I |
| Secondary Teacher | S | A | E |

In the first example, newspaper reporter, "A" is listed as the primary letter, since a reporter's primary function involves the process of creative writing. The second letter is "S" because a reporter needs to develop rapport with people in order to obtain essential information from them. Third, a reporter needs to be a problem solver of the "I" kind.

Using the O*NET, look up the occupation. Most occupations listed in the O*NET, list the related Holland Code in the section called "Interests."

2. After coding each of your occupations, decide which are compatible with your personality style.

   My Holland code is _____.

3. If an occupation has none of the three letters that are contained in your Holland code, consider removing this alternative from your list. For example, your Holland code is an ASI, and an occupation on your list has a CER code. That occupation is likely to be a very poor match for you.

   ■ If an occupation has one letter that is the same as a letter in your Holland code, you will need to decide whether to keep that occupation on your list or not. For example, your code is ASI, and an occupation on your list is CSE. If you have no interest in the occupation, you may want to delete it. On the other hand, if you are uncertain about it, retain the alternative for further consideration.

   ■ Be sure to retain for further exploration any occupations that share two or three letters in common with your Holland code. For example, if your code is an ASI, you should retain occupations with codes such as SAI, SIA, IAS, ISA, SEA, ASE, SIR, and IAR.
   If there is no connection to your Holland Code or the occupation is not able to be coded, consider keeping it on your list but be sure to note why. There are many reasons to keep careers but be sure to take the time to note the reason for your future review.

4. After completing your assessment, record the 10 best occupational alternatives that are compatible with your Holland code in the space below.

| Career Alternatives | Holland Code |
|---|---|
| 1. | |
| 2. | |
| 3. | |
| 4. | |
| 5. | |
| 6. | |
| 7. | |
| 8. | |
| 9. | |
| 10. | |

## Exploring Your Top 10

Now that you have identified your 10 best career matches, you will need to apply the information you have already discovered about yourself and to acquire additional information about your 10 selections. The chart in the Developing and Assessing Your Career Alternatives APP ACTION 3.2 has been designed to facilitate this process and contains a numbering system to support your assessments. The following exercises will guide your assessments and information searches to find your best and most compatible alternative. The information search will help you find crucial information about the employment outlooks of your top 10 matches.

The process begins by assessing how each of your "top 10" will enable you to use your "most preferred" transferable skills.

This is one APP ACTION with many steps. Allow time to complete it then return here for next steps. The ⬤ APP ACTION: Developing and Assessing Your Career Alternatives is one large table that will allow you to process the information you have already gathered about yourself and work. The steps involved with completing the table will allow you to process this information and make a career decision.

To get started, go to the Developing and Assessing Your Career Alternatives and write down your top 10 occupations in the first column.

Complete **Developing and Assessing Your Career Alternatives** in App 3.3.

Complete **Making a Definite Decision** in App 3.3.

What rating did you give yourself?

Write a few sentences as you react to this rating.

## Dealing with a Tentative Decision

In some situations, it is very difficult to come to a definite decision. Perhaps you lack the information, experience, and/or time needed to make a realistic decision. In such cases, it might be best to remain temporarily in your present employment situation if you are working, or to pursue a general studies curriculum if you are in college. Meanwhile, acquire further insight and experience with one of your better alternatives. You may want to explore several appealing alternatives, one at a time. Some good ways to explore a tentative decision are discussed in the section *Further Field Research for Tentative Decision Makers.*

### Case Study    Carol

Carol serves as an example of a tentative decision-maker. She completed the decision-making process defined in this text, but felt that she could not make a definite career choice because of financial circumstances. She was interested in several art-related careers, but was unsure of her talent in these areas.

She was reluctant, therefore, to quit her job and go back to school full time to study. Accordingly, she decided to remain in her current full-time job, maintaining her financial security, while exploring the art-related careers. She decided to accomplish this by enrolling in studio art courses at a nearby college. At the same time, she will be interviewing many people in art fields to obtain information about the art careers and about the job market. If Carol discovers that she does have marketable talent and finds the job market promising, she will then definitely choose an art career. In the meantime, she has the security of her present job. She also knows that if her pursuit of an art career does not work out, she still has other interesting alternatives to explore.

**PAUSE**

What can you learn from the previous example of Carol that you can apply to your own decision-making situation?

### Case Study    Timothy

Timothy was frustrated. Laid off from a job he described as "dull, boring, but at least it has a paycheck," Timothy couldn't figure out where to go next. His list of possible careers all involved going back to college: Nursing, Cyber Security, Electrical Engineering, and Teaching. He understood that he failed to take action when he saw the signs indicating his employer was headed under and his industry wasn't growing. Now, three months without a paycheck, he couldn't figure out where to go or what to do. Returning to school seemed to be the only option.

During a meeting with his career counselor, he joked that he should just put all of the career choices in a hat and then pick one.

His career counselor challenged him to rethink his situation and consider using his skill set, education, and knowledge in other ways. While going back to school shouldn't be ruled out, his career counselor encouraged him to think of other ways he could bring value to another employer in another industry. Just like rice is a food, it can also be used to dry out electronics. Same product. Different use.

"So, maybe I am like duct tape," offered Timothy. That weekend, he looked up all of the uses for duct tape. He was shocked! Originally designed for waterproofing ammunition casings during World War II, it is now used for a variety of purposes including repairing many products, mending clothing or even creating clothing! Thinking about being a roll of duct tape, he began to list all of the problems he could solve.

Armed with a list of 34 possibilities, he returned to his career counselor where he began developing strategies to obtain a job. His research yielded a few contacts able to give him an insider view of their companies and their current needs. He learned that if he leveraged his knowledge of one industry along with his analytical and

Anteromite/Shutterstock.com

communication skills, he was actually a needed asset to some companies. By realizing that like duct tape, he had value beyond the obvious, he went down a path he couldn't see initially.

---

"Alternative uses for common things" are popular topics for magazine articles, social media, blogs, and websites. Like rice and duct tape, someone figured out that an item could go beyond its intended function. What about you?

PAUSE

Take a minute and think of all of the problems you could solve. To get started, you may want to think of a single skill then think of the places where this skill is used. If you like to brainstorm with others, find a few classmates and help each other think beyond the obvious.

---

List those career alternatives that appear about equally suitable right now. Divide these into the following categories, according to which alternatives you find most appealing.

| The Alternatives That I Am Most Interested in Right Now | The Options I Am Less Certain About Right Now |
| --- | --- |
|  |  |
|  |  |
|  |  |
|  |  |

Once you have identified the alternatives you want to explore now, decide your best method by answering the following questions:

1. Which alternative am I inclined to investigate first?

_____

_____

_____

2. How much time can I realistically give myself to explore that option?

_____

_____

_____

3. Given the time consideration, what are the best ways I can explore this alternative?

_____

_____

_____

4. What will I need most to learn about myself in this exploration?

_____

_____

_____

5. What will I need most to find out about the job market and the career field in this exploration?

_____

_____

_____

6. Are there any other things I need to do or keep in mind while undertaking this exploration?

_____

_____

_____

7. If my exploration suggests that this alternative would not be a good choice, which alternative should I explore next? Have I meanwhile discovered other interesting alternatives missing from my original list?

_____

_____

_____

## Further Field Research for Tentative Decision Makers

The best way to explore your options further is through firsthand experience. If you must complete your exploration in a brief time, your best bet is simply to talk to as many people as you can who are working in your fields of interest. Follow the guidelines on informational interviewing in APP 7. If, on the other hand, you have enough time to conduct a thorough exploration, consider some or all of the following methods:

1. Interning involves spending time with people working in a field you find appealing to observe directly the nature of their work, their duties, and their responsibilities. This method lets you experience a typical day of a person working in a particular career. As you can imagine, this kind of investigation can be more revealing than just asking people what their work is like. Formal internships include collegiate work/learning experiences.

2. Volunteer work is also an excellent way of both gaining realistic insight and acquiring general work experience. You can obtain valuable job references and sometimes salaried job offers in the process. Many organizations are happy to use the services of a volunteer worker, particularly when the individual has enthusiasm along with some knowledge of the area.

3. Part-time or temporary work is another excellent way to acquire firsthand experience in an occupational field. You probably won't get a paid, part-time, or temporary job in the position you really are interested in. However, you can often acquire a lower-level job in the general field. In addition to getting a job reference, you'll be in a position to find out whether you would enjoy working in that particular field.

Your main goal in any kind of field research is to find out how appropriate an occupation would be for you. It is helpful to answer relevant questions as you explore the alternatives. Among the questions to consider are:

1. What specific kinds of information will I need to learn for this field?
2. Would pursuing a career in this field get me closer to what I really want in my career?
3. What are the least appealing aspects of a career in this field?
4. What are the most appealing aspects of a career in this field?

## Deciding and Taking Responsibility

If you have followed the career/life decision-making model to this point, you have made a decision. Consider for a moment what a decision is and is not.

Your decision is not:

- someone else's responsibility;
- the option you fell into or had to choose because there was nothing else to choose from;
- a perfect choice that will make your life wonderful forever;
- likely to be the last decision you will ever have to make about your career.

Your decision is:

- fully your responsibility and no one else's;
- made from among alternatives that you clearly identified and investigated;
- your best alternative given your self-knowledge and your available options;
- likely to create new decision situations that will enable you to continue freely making choices and taking charge of your career.

Congratulations! Your decision is probably the very best one that you can make at this time. If your needs change later or the outcomes of your decision do not seem to be getting you closer to what you want, remember that you can make a new decision at that time. This is the freedom associated with "taking charge."

PAUSE

**The following situations are provided for you to consider how willing you are to make and implement a career decision in the face of typical pressures people often experience. Answer the following questions candidly, telling how you really believe you would respond in each situation.**

1. You decide on a career that really interests you, but others are discouraging your plans, what would you do or say?

2. After pursuing a career for many years, you decide at age 49 to return to college to prepare for a new career. People around you call your decision a mistake. They say you should stay with what you are doing because of your age, and besides, you're too old to go to college. How would you handle this situation?

3. In completing this workbook, you decide that a career in an enterprising field (E) is exactly what you want, but your parents, spouse, or friends try to pressure you into a career in an investigative (I) area. How would you respond to them?

4. You are a 34-year-old housewife whose children no longer require constant personal care. You decide to return to college to begin preparing for a new career. Your spouse, friends, and/or family strongly discourage you from that, arguing that a mother and wife's role is in the home. How would you answer? What would you do?

5. Although you like your job, you decide to retire early to begin doing some of those things you have always planned but have never accomplished. Friends and associates tell you that you are foolish to quit a job you like and that people generally are not very happy in retirement. What would you do and why?

6. You have gotten into a career you dislike, but it offers good benefits and a high salary. Based on what you learned from career planning, you know you want to make a career change. But the career you want requires further education or training. Your family, friends, and/or acquaintances say you are foolish to give up your job benefits just to pursue something you are interested in. How would you respond? What would you do?

## Summary

To come to a satisfactory decision about your career, you look for a match between self-insights and your identified choices. This process starts with a systematic assessment of your skills and the skills required by your occupational alternatives. Next, clarify your career needs, wants, and values to determine which of your alternatives are most likely to fulfill these. By studying the employment outlook, you can assess which of your alternatives will provide the best employment prospects. Once you have acquired and compiled this information, you are usually ready to make a realistic decision. A realistic decision offers a high probability of obtaining employment, achieving satisfaction, and being productive in your career.

Career/life decision-making is a unique experience for everyone. Because no two people are the same, no two people are likely to come to the same decision after completing the same process. No two people are likely, either, to complete the process in the same amount of time. Some people complete the entire process and reach a definite decision in just a few weeks of concentrated work. Others may need many months to complete the process. It is far more preferable to take the time you need to make a realistic decision than to hurry through the process and make a poor decision.

If you have completed the career/life decision-making model, you can have confidence that you have made a good decision, either tentative or definite. Having learned this process, you can use it whenever you are faced with major career/life decisions. Though the model has been used in this book to make career decisions, it can be used to make other major life decisions as well.

# APP 3.3 APP ACTIONS

## APP ACTIONS 3.1

### LIFE VALUES ASSESSMENT*

*Directions*

1. Place an X on the line next to each of the following values that are truly important in your life right now. For a value to be truly important in your life, it must be reflected in your behavior on a regular basis. For instance, if variety is one of your current values, then you may behave in ways that result in frequent changes in various aspects of your life, such as your job, location, friends, physical appearance, or recreation.

2. Circle the 10 values that are currently most important in your life.

—Achievement (accomplishing something important)

—Adventure (seeking challenging new experiences)

—Aesthetics (appreciating beauty in all its forms)

—Affection (giving and receiving love)

—Authenticity (genuinely being yourself)

—Creativity (freedom to express new ideas/develop new things)

—Cultural Heritage (appreciating your ethnic background)

—Economic Reward (earning a high rate of compensation)

—Emotional Strength (managing your feelings in positive ways)

—Ethical Living (living morally and justly)

—Expertise (being good at something worthwhile)

*This assessment is adopted from a process developed by Fontelle Gilbert. Used by permission.

—Family (having a strong bond through shared heredity and/or experience)

—Friendship (affiliating with others)

—Future Orientation (seeking to learn what the future holds)

—Health/Fitness (actively maintaining vitality)

—Inner Serenity (seeking peace within)

—Personal Safety (being safe from bodily harm)

—Pleasure (enjoying fun activities)

—Recognition (being known by others)

—Risk-Taking (seeking excitement via living on the edge)

—Satisfying Career (having meaningful and challenging work)

—Integrity (maintaining congruence of your words with deeds)

—Security (having a stable future)

—Self-Confidence (feeling positive about yourself)

—Intellect (having a keen and lively mind)

—Service (contributing to the welfare of others)

—Leadership (having influence over others)

—Spirituality (seeking the ultimate meaning in life)

—Orderliness (living an organized life)

—Variety (seeking change in activities and surroundings)

—Personal Development (continuing self-exploration and growth)

—Personal Freedom (making choices independently)

—Wisdom (seeking maturity understanding)

3. After identifying the 10 values, rank them from 1 to 10 based on how essential you consider each value to be.

## UNCOVERING YOUR HIDDEN VALUES

1. This exercise requires you to imagine that you have just been given a gift of one million dollars with only one stipulation: You must use the million only for yourself.

    a. List under Column A some of the possible ways you would like to use your gift. What would you want to do, have, or be? Some examples are provided to help start you thinking about this exercise.

| *Column A* | *Column B* |
|---|---|
| Uses | Possible Values |
| **Examples:** | |
| 1. Invest in stocks and bonds | 1. Financial security, challenge/risk taking |
| 2. Reserve season tickets to symphony, theater, and dance performances | 2. Aesthetics, pleasure |
| 3. Set aside funds for continuing education | 3. Intellect, personal development, job security |
| 4. Start a small business | 4. Independence, risk taking, achievement |
| *Uses* | *Possible Values* |
| Your Selections: | |
| | |
| | |
| | |
| | |
| | |

    b. Having determined how you would use your million dollars, assess what values are represented by your choices. In our first example, for instance, investing in stocks and bonds represents the value of financial security to those who invest in safe, low-yield securities. But to those who prefer more chancy, high-return investments, it represents the value of risk taking. Analyze each of your million-dollar choices for the value(s) they represent to you and list those values in Column B. Refer to the list of Life Values from Application 7-B for possible values words.

2. You are the recipient of yet another million-dollar gift, this time with a different stipulation: This gift is to be used only for the good of others.

    a. Ask yourself what needs doing in your family, neighborhood, country, and the world. How could you best contribute? List the ways you would make a contribution under Column A. Refer to the examples below in Column A to stimulate your thinking.

| Column A | Column B |
|---|---|
| *Uses* | *Possible Values* |
| Examples: | |
| 1. Create an institute for peace studies | 1. Ethical living, freedom, spirituality |
| 2. Reform the educational system | 2. Intellect, personal development, and freedom |
| 3. Establish parenting classes for young parents | 3. Affection, family, and emotional strength |
| 4. Implement a neighborhood watch in my community | 4. Service, personal safety |
| *Uses* | *Possible Values* |
| **Your Selections:** | |
| | |
| | |
| | |
| | |

    b. Again analyze your list of choices in Column A for the value(s) that each represents and place them (the values) in Column B.

## WORK VALUES ASSESSMENT

1. Read the definitions of the work values listed in four categories (a through d) below. Rate each work value according to its degree of importance to you. Use the following scale in assigning your ratings:

1 = unimportant in my choice of career

2 = somewhat important in my choice of career

3 = very important in my choice of career

Place the number corresponding to your rating in the blank to the left of each work value.

a. *Workplace Conditions.* Characteristics of the workplace environment.

_____ *Safety/Security*—a work environment free from physical danger or personal harassment.

_____ *Pleasant Setting*—an aesthetically pleasing and comfortable work setting.

_____ *Caring Coworkers*—working with people who get along and cooperate with one another.

_____ *Respectful Supervision*—having understanding supervisors who respect your wants and needs.

_____ *Competition*—a work setting where outdoing your coworkers or exceeding your own or the company's standards is important.

_____ *Fast-Paced Work*—working rapidly to meet time or performance deadlines.

_____ *Variety/Change*—performing many different work tasks.

_____ *Travel*—work where travel is an integral part of the routine.

_____ *Inside Work*—working inside a building, usually in an office setting.

_____ *Outside Work*—working outdoors exposed to the elements.

_____ *Both Inside and Outside Work*—striking a balance between both inside and outside work.

_____ *Working Alone*—doing assignments by yourself involving minimal contact with coworkers or the public.

_____ *Working on a Team*—carrying out work responsibilities as an integral part of a group of coworkers.

b. *Workplace Outcomes.* The purpose(s) that work serves in your life.

_____ *Being Competent*—striving to excel at the work that you do.

_____ *Using Abilities*—utilizing the competencies you possess to their maximum.

_____ *Making Things*—using your hands to produce or repair concrete, tangible things.

_____ *Problem-Solving*—figuring out how something should be done.

_____ *Developing New Ideas*—improving upon the ways things have been done or coming up with new ways of doing them.

_____ *Precise Work*—performing work that meets exacting standards.

_____ *Mental Challenge*—performing demanding tasks that challenge your intellect.

_____ *Social Contribution*—seeking to improve the human condition.

_____ *Influencing Others*—affecting others in ways designed to change attitudes or opinions or motivating them to take action.

_____ *Supervising/Directing Others*—being in a position to oversee and/or take responsibility for the work of others.

_____ *Aesthetic Contribution*—performing work that contributes to making the world a more beautiful place.

_____ *Spiritual Fulfillment*—doing work that contributes to the religious or spiritual fulfillment of yourself or others.

c. *Workplace Rewards.* The rewards you expect from your work.

_____ *High Salary*—choosing an occupation where the rate of compensation is in the top third (33%) for all occupations.

_____ *Good Benefits*—having healthcare, disability insurance, etc. as part of your compensation package.

_____ *Equitable Pay*—being compensated at a rate that is commensurate with the amount and quality of work you do.

_____ *Opportunity for Advancement*—having a good chance to advance into positions of increasing authority and responsibility.

_____ *Job Availability and Security*—working in an occupational field where you have a good opportunity to obtain and maintain a job.

_____ *Recognition/Prestige*—being perceived by others as doing important work or being an expert in your field of endeavor.

d. *Personal/Family Considerations.* Attempting to balance work and personal life.

_____ *Time Flexibility*—arranging your own work hours or working according to your own schedule.

_____ *Job Sharing*—being able to share the duties and responsibilities of a job with another person or other people.

_____ *Autonomy*—having discretion in how you complete or perform your job tasks.

_____ *Self-Employment*—being employed by and working for yourself.

_____ *Ethical/Moral Standards*—being free to act in accordance with a set of standards regarding what is the right or fair thing to do.

_____ *Regular Hours*—working a regular work schedule that allows you time for yourself and/or your family.

_____ *Easy Commute*—living close to where you work.

_____ *Acceptance*—being accepted for what you can contribute although your lifestyle may differ from those of your coworkers.

2. List below your three or four most important work values in each of the four categories. Add any others that are important but were not covered above.

*Workplace Conditions*

_____

_____

_____

*Workplace Rewards*

_____

_____

_____

_____

_____

_____

*Workplace Outcomes*

_____

_____

_____

*Personal/Family Considerations*

_____

_____

_____

_____

_____

_____

3. Select your 10 most important values from those you have listed in number 2.

_____

_____

_____

_____

_____

_____

_____

_____

_____

_____

_____

## THE CORE OF YOUR VALUES

1. List below your top five to ten values from each of the values from the previous exercises.

| Life Values Assessment | Uncovering Your Hidden Values | | Work Values |
| --- | --- | --- | --- |
| | Million/Self | Million/Others | |
| | | | |
| | | | |
| | | | |
| | | | |
| | | | |
| | | | |
| | | | |
| | | | |
| | | | |
| | | | |

2. Combine the values in the four columns above in order to come up with your top five values. Pay particular attention to those values that appear in more than one column.

3. Place your top five values in the following box.

**My Top Five Prioritized Values**

_____ 1. _____

_____ 2. _____

_____ 3. _____

_____ 4. _____

_____ 5. _____

# APP ACTIONS 2.2

## ENVISIONING PROCESS*

1. To begin this process, review your specific skills from the APP Actions in APP Category 2.0. Rank the top five of these skills based on the skills you enjoy using the most. List the top five below.

   *Note:* Be sure to prioritize your list on the basis of those functional skills you now possess and prefer using. Do not list functional skills you lack or would like to possess.

   **My top five individual functional skills**

   1._____

   2._____

   3._____

   4._____

   5._____

2. Use the envisioning process to begin developing your list of career alternatives. To do this, set aside about one hour of time in which you will be alone and undisturbed. Then do the following:

   a. Review the results from envisioning process

   b. Review your top five skills (APP 2.1), your thinking-style profile (APP 2.2), your personality-style profile (APP 2.3), and your needs and values (APP 3.1).

   c. With these skills, needs, and preferences fresh in your mind, prepare to do the envisioning process by asking yourself: What kinds of careers might enable me to use my preferred skills and have the kind of life I want?

   d. Ask yourself this question several times. Can you picture yourself in the career(s) you are thinking about? Don't worry about whether you come up with anything or not. If the process doesn't work for you, go on to the other exercises.

   e. After you complete the envisioning process, immediately list below any thoughts or images that you had and record any occupations you come up with in your **Aha Moments** and Careers to Consider in APP 7.0.

---

*Notes on the envisioning process:*

_____

_____

_____

_____

_____

_____

_____

_____

## THE ENVISIONING PROCESS

When using the envisioning process, we suggest you follow these steps:

1. Make arrangements to be quiet and completely uninterrupted for 20 minutes to an hour. That may mean turning down your phone, not answering the doorbell, and ensuring that someone does not walk in on you during the process.

2. Verbalize, write, or ponder (left-hemisphere processes) what you would like to accomplish with the right-hemisphere intuitive process.

3. Sit in a straight-back chair or lie on your back on a carpeted floor.

    a. If you sit in a chair, sit erect with your back straight, your feet flat on the floor, head facing straight forward, and shoulders level and relaxed. Sitting this way helps reduce muscle tension and facilitates a general state of relaxation.

    b. If you recline on the floor, lie flat on your back with your feet spread slightly apart and your arms flat on the floor, palms up, about 6 to 12 inches away from your sides.

4. Close your eyes. While remaining awake:

    a. Relax the muscles between your eyes, and experience the flow of energy released from the previously tensed muscles.

    b. Relax the muscles in your jaw and chin while letting your mouth drop slightly open.

    c. Continue relaxing your body, one part at a time, by concentrating on and then loosening your tensed muscles, letting any tension flow out of your body.

    d. Take deep and even breaths, and consciously relax your body, starting with your toes and feet and working progressively upwards to your head.

    *Note*: As you relax, you may notice a flowing sensation throughout your body. That is caused by the energy released from tightly held muscles that are now relaxed.

5. In this relaxed state, just let your mind go. Do not consciously think or try to force your thoughts; just let them come freely and spontaneously.

   a. Do not try to figure out the meaning of anything you may be experiencing while in a relaxed state. To do so may result in switching from right- to left-hemisphere functioning of your brain.

   b. Remain relaxed and detached from your thoughts and mental imagery. Just let happen what will, and be an observer of your mental processes as if you were viewing a movie in your mind.

6. As you are nearing the end of the process, decide how you want to feel when you finish the process, and then allow yourself to feel that way.

7. When you are finished, come out of your relaxed state gradually. It can be a bit of a shock to your system if you bolt out of a relaxed condition (or are jolted out) too quickly. Begin by moving your feet and/or hands about slowly, recalling your external surroundings. When you are ready, open your eyes.

8. Give yourself a few minutes of detached inactivity as you return to fully conscious thoughts. Then, before doing anything else, begin recording any insights that you acquired during the envisioning process. Do this immediately, so that you will not forget and so that you translate your envisioned insights into language.

   a. Write down what happened in the process, even if you are not aware of any significant insights you had during the process. Sometimes, the process of writing is necessary to make you aware of new insights acquired from envisioning.

   b. By writing, you are likely to more fully understand the insights you had. You also will produce a written record to assist you in career decision making and planning for the future.

9. You may find it helpful to repeat the same envisioning process over several days, continually building and expanding on previous insights.

10. You may also want to discuss your insights, acquired from envisioning, with an interested listener to develop your understanding further.

## DEVELOPING AND ASSESSING YOUR CAREER ALTERNATIVES
## CREATE YOUR LIST

1. List your 10 occupations on the chart. These are the occupations connected to your Holland Code you created in APP 3.2.
2. Research the careers you are considering. Write a brief summary of the career alternative on the chart in the second Column. Note the O*NET code if available under the first column.

| Career Alternative | Brief Description | Compatibility Ratings 1–5 scale (low–high) | | | | | | My Evaluation |
|---|---|---|---|---|---|---|---|---|
| | | A | B | C | D | | | |
| O*NET # (if available) | From Internet, Information Interview, O*Net, OOH | Transferable Skills | Personality Style | Needs, Wants, Values | Employment Outlook | Cumulative Score | Overall Suitability | What I like most and least |
| EXAMPLE: Athletic Trainers: 29-9091.00 | Evaluate and advise individuals to assist recovery from or avoid athletic-related injuries or illnesses, or maintain peak physical fitness. May provide first aid or emergency care. | 4 | 3 | 5 | 2 | 14 | #5 | Excellent match for my values and thinking style. Will enable me to use most of my best skills and to stay connected to athletics, which I love. Bright job outlook. Not sure about I want to do that much education. |

| Career Alternative | Brief Description | Compatibility Ratings 1–5 scale (low–high) | | | | | | My Evaluation |
|---|---|---|---|---|---|---|---|---|
| | | A | B | C | D | | | |
| | | Transferable Skills | Personality Style | Needs, Wants, Values | Employment Outlook | Cumulative Score | Overall Suitability | |
| O*NET # (if available) | From Internet, Information Interview, O*Net, OOH | | | | | | | What I like most and least |
| | | | | | | | | |

| Career Alternative | Brief Description | Compatibility Ratings 1–5 scale (low–high) | | | | | | My Evaluation |
|---|---|---|---|---|---|---|---|---|
| | | A | B | C | D | | | |
| O*NET # (if available) | From Internet, Information Interview, O*Net, OOH | Transferable Skills | Personality Style | Needs, Wants, Values | Employment Outlook | Cumulative Score | Overall Suitability | What I like most and least |
| | | | | | | | | |

| Career Alternative | Brief Description | Compatibility Ratings 1–5 scale (low–high) | | | | | | My Evaluation |
|---|---|---|---|---|---|---|---|---|
| | | A | B | C | D | | | |
| O*NET # (if available) | From Internet, Information Interview, O*Net, OOH | Transferable Skills | Personality Style | Needs, Wants, Values | Employment Outlook | Cumulative Score | Overall Suitability | What I like most and least |
| | | | | | | | | |

| Career Alternative | Brief Description | Compatibility Ratings 1–5 scale (low–high) | | | | | | My Evaluation |
|---|---|---|---|---|---|---|---|---|
| | | A | B | C | D | | | |
| | | Transferable Skills | Personality Style | Needs, Wants, Values | Employment Outlook | Cumulative Score | Overall Suitability | |
| O*NET # (if available) | From Internet, Information Interview, O*Net, OOH | | | | | | | What I like most and least |
| | | | | | | | | |

| Career Alternative | Brief Description | Compatibility Ratings 1–5 scale (low–high) | | | | | | My Evaluation |
|---|---|---|---|---|---|---|---|---|
| | | A | B | C | D | | | |
| O*NET # (if available) | From Internet, Information Interview, O*Net, OOH | Transferable Skills | Personality Style | Needs, Wants, Values | Employment Outlook | Cumulative Score | Overall Suitability | What I like most and least |
| | | | | | | | | |

## TRANSFERABLE SKILL ASSESSMENT

Consider your transferable skill. You may find it helpful to review the first part of the Envisioning Process APP ACTION and the lists you created in APP 2.1, deciding which skills are essential for you to use in your work. Rank these skills below, starting with the most important.

### The Individual Transferable Skills My Work Must Have
My most preferred skills are:

1. _____

2. _____

3. _____

4. _____

5. _____

3. After identifying the skills involved in each of your occupational alternatives, compare these with the skills you identified above as being essential in your work. Using the following scale, rate how well the skills involved in each occupation match your preferred functional skills. In the *Transferable Skills*, list from the scale below the rating that most accurately evaluates the compatibility.

### Transferable Skills Evaluation Scale
Rating

5. Would enable me to use all my preferred skills fully.

4. Would enable me to use most of my preferred skills to a considerable degree.

3. Would enable me to use some, but not all, of my preferred skills to some extent.

2. Would not enable me to use my most preferred skills, but would enable me to use my secondary skills to a considerable extent.

1. Would not enable me to use any of my preferred skills to any extent.
   Unsure how well this occupation would enable me to use my preferred skills. I need more information than the DOT provides.

3. In the *My Evaluation* column, record any other information you may wish to remember about these occupations. Record any insights you discover about specific responsibilities and/or duties that are particularly appealing or unappealing to you.

## IDENTIFYING YOUR CAREER-RELATED NEEDS, WANTS, AND VALUES

Your next step in narrowing the options is to review what you really need and value in your career and life. Review your *What Motivates Me* from APP 3.1 to refresh your memory about your primary values. Then consider the following:

1. Do these priorities still seem accurate? If not, what has changed, or what new insights have you acquired?

   _____

   _____

   _____

2. From your review, decide what is the single most important value in your career, and list that below. Then decide what are the second, third, fourth, and fifth most important characteristics you value in your career, and list them below as well.

   The most important thing I need, value, or want in my career is . . .

   _____

   _____

   _____

   The second most important thing . . .

   _____

   _____

   The third most . . .

   _____

   _____

   The fourth most . . .

   _____

   _____

   The fifth most . . .

   _____

   _____

After completing your employment outlook research along with your information interviews, you'll be ready to evaluate how well your occupational alternatives will satisfy these values.

## ASSESSING COMPATIBILITY AND EMPLOYMENT OUTLOOK

In an age of choice, it would certainly be a mistake to select an occupation simply because it offers excellent employment prospects, especially since these can change. It would be equally a mistake, however, to select a suitable occupation without determining whether you have a reasonable chance of finding employment in that field.

To find the employment outlook of any career alternative, you can check occupational literature or obtain firsthand information from people in the field. These methods have some shortcomings, however. The job market changes so rapidly that printed occupational information quickly becomes outdated. People in the field often have more current information, but they may also have a biased view of the employment outlook. For these reasons, we strongly advocate that you use both recent occupational literature and information interviews.

For this exercise, you will obtain information about employment outlook and your personal/ occupational compatibility for each of your alternatives. The OOH and the O*NET will be your primary sources.

1. Study each of the alternatives on your list that you can find in the OOH. You may not always be able to find information about a particular occupation you are exploring in the OOH. In such cases, you may want to go to other sources of occupational information found in most college career centers.

2. Review your **Aha! Moments** you have listed APP 7.0. With this information in mind, read the OOH and the O*NET. Evaluate how well each of the occupational alternatives you are exploring coincides with your own personal attributes. To what extent will each alternative fulfill what you need, want, and value?

3. Review your **Aha! Moments** you have listed APP 7.0. With this information in mind, read the OOH, and the O*NET. Evaluate how well each of the occupational alternatives you are exploring coincides with your own personal attributes. To what extent will each alternative fulfill what you need, want, and value?

4. In the *My Evaluation* section, record what you learned about each occupation, along with your impressions of how appropriate you think it would be for you. Again, be sure to make your comments clear and complete enough to refer to later and know what you meant.

5. Note and record in the *My Evaluation* section the OOH or O*NET employment outlook information for the next 5 years for each of the occupations you are exploring.

## COMPLETING THE CAREER ASSESSMENT TABLE

After having obtained the data you need about occupational compatibility and employment outlook, use your accumulated information to determine your best occupational alternative. To help you make this choice, we have provided an evaluation scale to assign numerical ratings to your alternatives.

1. List the alternatives you selected on the Top 10 Career Alternatives Column.

2. Review the comments you have recorded in the *Brief Description* and *My Evaluation* sections. Then use the following evaluation scale) to find suitable numerical ratings for personality style, occupational compatibility with what you want/need in a career, and employment outlook. Fill in columns B, C, and D.

3. After assigning your numerical ratings, add the scores from columns A, B, C, and D for each of your occupations. Put the resulting score in the *Cumulative Score* column. Having computed this total for each occupational alternative, you will have a handy numerical guide for determining which of your alternatives is best.

4. Look down your *Cumulative Score* column to determine which alternative received the highest rating. Write "#1" in the *Overall Suitability* column for that alternative to indicate that this is probably your best overall choice. Write "#2" in the *Overall Suitability* column for the alternative that received the next highest score. Continue ranking all of your alternatives in this manner.

**Evaluation Scale for Personal/Occupational Compatibility and Employment Outlook**

| Rating Score | The likelihood that your Holland code would be compatible to the Holland code of that occupation | The likelihood of fulfilling your most important wants and needs in that occupation | The likelihood that you will be able to obtain employment in that occupation |
|---|---|---|---|
| | Column B | Column C | Column D |
| 5 | My Holland code is a perfect match since all three letters are similar and in the same order | Better than a 75% probability | Considerably more job openings than qualified applicants in the location you've chosen |
| 4 | My Holland code is a good match since all three letters are similar but not in the same order | Less than a 75% chance, but almost certainly better than a 50% chance | More job openings than qualified applicants in the location you've chosen |
| 3 | My Holland code is a fair match since two out of three letters are similar | About a 50% probability | Number of job openings about the same as number of qualified applicants in the location you've chosen |
| 2 | My Holland code is a poor match since only one letter is similar | Less than a 50% chance | Fewer job openings than qualified applicants/stiff competition for available jobs in the location you've chosen |
| 1 | My Holland code is a very poor match with no letters in common | Highly unlikely to no chance at all | Far fewer job openings than qualified applicants in the location you've chosen and/or occupation becoming obsolete |

## CONDUCTING INFORMATION INTERVIEWS

The best sources of information you are likely to find are people working in the fields that interest you. These people can offer comments on employment outlook in their locality. They can also give you more detailed information about working conditions in their field to help you decide how well that kind of work suits you. A good way of locating these people is to ask your acquaintances if they know anyone involved in these fields. If they do not, perhaps they might know someone who might know and could give you a referral. Another way to find people is through trade and professional associations. Many of these organizations have Web sites or publications that provide an overview of the profession.

1. Use the provided guidelines to conduct your interviews. Be sure to record your impressions and thoughts immediately after conducting the interview, while it is still fresh in your mind. If you wait, you are likely to forget.

2. As you conduct your information-gathering interviews, be sure to talk to more than a single person in a field. You are likely to find that one person's views are too biased to give you an accurate reflection of that occupation. Also, as you seek out information sources, find people who have been in that field long enough to have fully experienced it. That usually takes three years or more. You will also want to ensure that you are not talking only with people who are very unhappy in their work. Remember that an unhappy person may be misplaced in the field or "burned out," having done the same job too long. Even though that person is dissatisfied, the field involved might be perfect for you.

3. After conducting your interviews, record your overall assessment of the occupational alternatives in the *Brief Description* section.

## BRAINSTORMING WITH INDIVIDUALS

Getting input from other people is helpful for developing your career alternatives. A good technique is to record your ranked individual skills on a piece of paper. Then give your list to someone such as a career counselor, or human resources specialist, or anyone with knowledge of several different occupations. Ask them to look these skills over at their convenience and to advise you of any occupations requiring these particular skills. It is not usually a good idea to use close family or friends in this process, since they often have preconceived ideas about what is best for you. If you do use family or friends, a good technique is to state that you are researching careers for a class project. Give them the list, asking that they brainstorm with you careers related to these skills without mentioning that it for a particular person. You could switch lists with a classmate and share the skills of a classmate with your family member as your classmate does the same with your list. This will help maintain objectivity. Record other people's career suggestions on your Career to Consider list in APP 7.0.

## DECISION CHECK LIST

The following check list will assist you in making your decision.

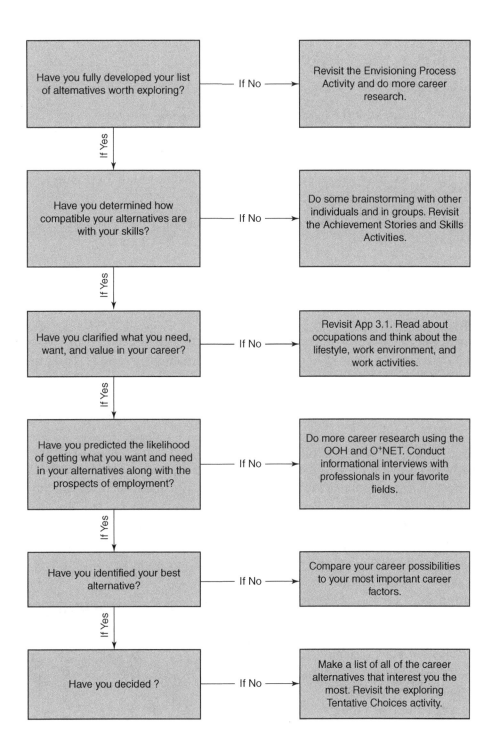

## MAKING A DEFINITE DECISION

Having completed the Decision Check List and the Developing and Assessing Your Career Alternatives APP, you are probably in one of the following circumstances:

1. By clearly identifying your best choice through your assessments, you have chosen a career to pursue. Go on to the section of this APP entitled *Deciding and Taking Responsibility*.

2. Numerically you've identified your best choice, but you don't feel quite ready to decide.

3. You may have one choice with the highest numerical rating, but you're not sure that rating is accurate. Or you may have two or more choices that are so close numerically that you have a difficult time deciding which is the best option.

   *Note:* An alternative is a good choice even if it only provided scores of 3 or better in all four columns (A, B, C, and D).

4. All your assessments have such low cumulative scores that you doubt that any of them are wise choices.

5. You feel frustrated because the alternative you prefer most has poor employment prospects (a low score in Column D).

If you find yourself in situation 2, you are probably close to selecting that alternative as your definite choice. However, it might be helpful to clarify what you would need to do in order to feel comfortable about deciding. What should you do if you find yourself in situation 3, 4, or 5? These are tentative decision situations. For situation 3, you need to consider the time you have available to choose. Depending upon your time, you might want to do limited or considerable field research in the occupation(s) involved to obtain sufficient firsthand information before making a definite decision.

Should you find yourself in situation 4 or 5, ask yourself whether you've missed an alternative or alternatives that would provide a more promising outlook. If so, it would be well worth your while to spend some more time developing additional alternatives. If you are fairly certain, however, that you have already identified the alternatives that interest you most, your task becomes somewhat more difficult. Your best bet is to look for any alternatives that provide a cumulative score of 12 or better. If you have one or more alternatives in this category, decide which consideration—skills compatibility (Column A), compatibility with your personality style (Column B), wants/needs preference (Column C), or employment outlook (Column D)—is most important to you. Then pick the best alternative with this in mind.

If you decide on an alternative with a poor employment outlook, we strongly encourage you to develop your job-hunting skills covered in later APPs. Even in a tough job market, there are almost always jobs available somewhere. However, job openings in crowded fields are unlikely to be listed anywhere. Usually, the person with the best job-hunting skills rather than the best talents gets hired for these jobs.

designer491/Shutterstock.com

## GROUP BRAINSTORMING

Brainstorming in a group is also a very good way to generate a list of career alternatives. Your best bet here is to get a group of 4–8 people together, preferably people familiar with occupations and transferable skills. Then display your top five specific skills and top five skills groups on a large piece of paper or on a chalkboard. Next, have the group brainstorm ideas and record their suggestions on a separate piece of paper. This process will work best if you are not present in the group at the time they are brainstorming with your list. In fact, this exercise works best if the group is unaware of whose skills they are working with. Record the group's suggestions below. Then select those that interest you, and list them in Career to Consider list in APP 7.0.

# Goal Setting and Planning Your Career

This is the last in the series of career planning and decision-making APPs. Additional APPS in this book will focus on the strategies you need to find a job, resources for some specific populations, and career research tools.

For many users, this APP allows them to finally implement their plans but it can be the toughest because it involves facing potential barriers. APP 4.1 will provide strategies for goal setting. APP 4.2 will address a mind-set for success and overcoming any barriers.

Take a minute to picture yourself actually performing in the industry you have selected. On the basis of your research, you should have a sense of your surroundings and the types of tasks you will be performing. Think about the people you will be working with and how you will be interacting with them. Although you may not actually be in this role for months or years, you want to picture yourself in this role. Visualization is a strategy used for effective goal achievement. Weight loss experts for decades have been telling their clients to put pictures of thin people on the refrigerator so the goal can be seen when the temptation to eat poorly arises. The same applies to your career. By creating a mental picture of yourself in your selected career, you will be more likely to be able to overcome obstacles. Write down your goals as well. Armed with a visual and written representation of your goal you are more likely to succeed.

If you have arrived at this APP without being 100% confident of your chosen career, use this time to think about smaller steps you will need to take regardless of your end goal. You may realize that you will need a college degree to achieve your goal, so apply the goal setting strategies to achieving this smaller goal. You may have discovered you need a certain amount of money to start a business. Even if you haven't decided on the exact business, you can set a financial goal related to a few business options and apply your goal setting to meeting your financial saving goal

As you progress through APPS 4.1 and 4.2, take the time to continue to focus on how you define career success. If things change as you are working toward your goal, do not be afraid to revisit earlier decisions. The biology class you have been taking as a part of your goal to be in the medical field may have lead you to realize you like research more than service delivery. Or the part-time job you have in finance may have not only reinforced your love for numbers but also introduced your passion for helping others. Do not be afraid to apply this new knowledge to your previous self-discovery and alter your goals.

Enjoy this time of setting goals and moving forward on realizing your career goals!

## APP 4.1   Setting Goals and Planning Your Career

## APP 4.2   Empowering Yourself to Succeed

## APP 4.3   APP ACTIONS

# APP 4.1 Setting Goals and Planning Your Career

## Do you know people who:

*Control starts with planning. Planning is bringing the future into the present so that we can do something about it now.*

*—Alan Lakein, How to Get Control of Your Time and Your Life*

- Have careers that suffer today because they failed to plan adequately yesterday?
- Are so focused on future goals that they neglect the present?
- Set objectives and then just expect them to happen?
- Have lives that have been made inflexible by overly detailed plans?
- Plan without realistically taking future conditions into consideration?

If so, you know people who do not effectively use goal setting and planning to take charge of their careers and lives.

### The Future in Perspective

Futurists maintain that through collective actions, everyone participates in creating the future.

In his book, **The Innovators: How a Group of Inventors, Hackers, Geniuses, and Geeks Created the Digital Revolution, Walter Isaacson** recounts an interaction between a corporate planning director at Xerox and Alan Kay. Pendery kept asking Kay and others for an assessment of "trends" that foretold what the future might hold for the company. During one maddening session, Kay, whose thoughts often seemed tailored to go directly from his tongue to wiki-quotes, shot back a line that was to become Xerox PARC's creed: "The best way to predict the future is to invent it."[1]

The story of the Digital Revolution as recounted by Isaacson shows how the digital world we take for granted was created by many people, going back not just decades but centuries. "But the main lesson to draw from the birth of computers," recounts Isaacson, is that innovation is usually a group effort, involving collaboration between visionaries and engineers, and that creativity comes from drawing on many sources. Only in storybooks do inventions come like a thunderbolt, or a light bulb popping out of the head of a lone individual in a basement or garage.

Ozerina Anna/Shutterstock.com

## Influencing Your Career Future

Just as collective actions shaped the Digital Revolution, and in many ways the future of work, your individual actions shape your personal destiny. As you will see in APP 4.2, your own mind-set can strongly influence your future through the power of suggestion. The term *self-fulfilling prophecy* describes this phenomenon of individual expectations influencing future results. For example, if you approach a job interview fully prepared and expecting to perform well, you are likely to succeed. In contrast, if you expect to perform poorly ("I never do well in face-to-face contacts" or "I always choke under pressure"), you are likely to fail.

Having chosen a career, you may be tempted to make minimal plans, sit back, and "let it happen." Unfortunately, what usually happens with this approach is failure. Like everyone else, you will probably experience some setbacks as you pursue a career. Lacking shorter-range goals and specific career plans, you may find these setbacks overwhelming and doubt that you can succeed. Feeling out of control, you might then reinforce your pessimism by expecting further setbacks instead of looking for other options and opportunities. Not surprisingly, a cycle of victimization develops, and few career choices are attained.

On the other hand, with comprehensive, short-range goals and plans, it is easy to view setbacks in a large perspective. You can recognize other, often better, alternatives that were not obvious before. Of course, no one can absolutely predict the future. Yet developing and following objectives and plans do give you far more control, direction, and motivation. In this way, your own self-fulfilling prophecy will be success.

## Career Goals/Objectives

Career goals provide you with purpose and direction for your career and life. People without goals experience more conflict and uncertainty because they just react to whatever happens instead of trying to infuse their lives with meaning. These people are likely to have far more days when they have no compelling reason for even getting out of bed. In contrast, people with carefully chosen, clearly defined goals know what they want out of their lives and careers.

Another function of clearly defined goals is that they enable people to channel their energy into meaningful activity and may even create more energy in the pursuit of life goals. The following example illustrates this point.

## Designing and Building Your Future Career and Life

Denise was a conscientious and efficient administrative assistant whose true passion was hiking and backpacking in wilderness areas. Feeling unchallenged and tied down in her office setting, she decided to attend college as a way to initiate a career change. Unmotivated and discouraged by her lack of clear direction, she dropped out her first semester. She was unable to see

Designing Your
Future Life

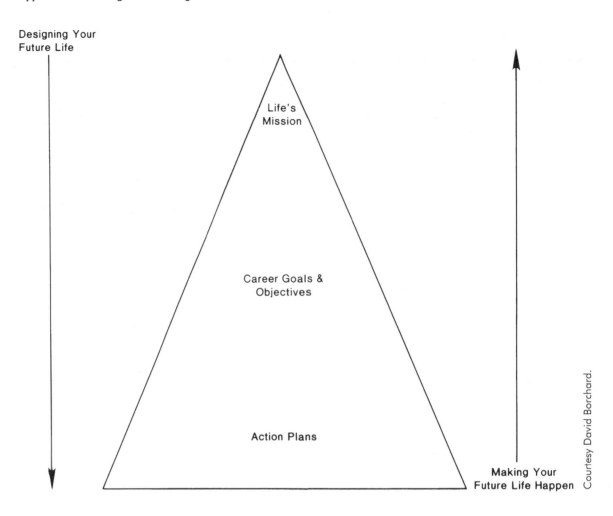

Life's
Mission

Career Goals &
Objectives

Action Plans

Making Your
Future Life Happen

Courtesy David Borchard.

how her love of the outdoors had any relationship to a possible new career direction. Through the assistance of a career counselor, however, she saw that conserving natural resources for the enjoyment of everyone was the motivating force in her life.

With renewed purpose, Denise reentered college, majored in geology, and made the Dean's List in her first semester back. She joined the Appalachian Trail Conservancy in its mission to maintain sections of the

Maridav/Shutterstock.com

Appalachian Trail. Currently, she is collaborating with an architect friend on the development of a design for an energy-efficient home utilizing solar and geothermal power. Having a clearly defined career objective has enabled Denise to channel her energies toward results that amaze even her.

In effect, having clearly defined goals brings the future into the present. Instead of procrastinating, you can take appropriate present action because you are clear about what direction you want to go. Accordingly, you can also see what actions will move you in your chosen direction and what will not.

In this way, goals enable you to take charge of your life. Rather than just sitting back and letting things happen to you, you can use goals as catalysts for action. People who just let things happen to them are actually at the mercy of circumstances. They use up their energy fighting, denying, or rationalizing unpleasant realities.

As you create goals and act upon them, you influence your future. In other words, your mental images and attitudes about the future largely determine the shape of your future. No one can totally control the future because of unknown circumstances over which there is little control. Goal-oriented people, however, tend to be far more successful at getting what they want rather than simply taking what they can get.

## Defining Your Goals/Objectives

Goals and objectives are specific, future-oriented statements of purpose and direction accomplishable within a definite time frame. The time frame can be long, medium, or short range. Although the terms *goal* and *objective* are often used interchangeably, sometimes the term *goal* is used for long-range aims while the word *objective* is used for related short-range intentions. Being well within our grasp, short-range objectives enable us to establish and reach tangible outcomes on the path toward our long-range goals. As we complete our objectives, we are then in a position to set and accomplish new ones.

Trueffelpix/Shutterstock.com

Goals may be stated in a variety of ways corresponding to the strength of your commitment to complete them. The way you state your goals clearly indicates that how determined you are to achieve your desired outcome. According to

Least Powerful

Category 1—Statements of Possibility
"I probably will . . ." or
"I might be able to . . ."

Category 2—Statements of Desire
"I want to . . ." or
"I'd really like to . . ."

Category 3—Statements of Intent
"I'll try to . . ." or
"I'll do the best I can to . . ."

Category 4—Statements of Promise
"I will . . ." or
"I'm committed to . . ."

Most Powerful

Courtesy David Borchard

David Ellis, there is a hierarchy of goal-statement categories, each successively more powerful than the preceding one.[2]

### David Ellis's Hierarchy of Goal-Statement Categories.[3]

Notice that with each higher category, the language gets increasingly stronger and the likelihood that the goal will be completed gets more believable. In people's daily interactions, the strongest language (category 4) is reserved for activities requiring the highest level of commitment, such as marriage vows or promissory notes. In a court of law where the truthfulness of witnesses can mean the difference between life and death of an accused person, the most powerful language is used when swearing in witnesses: "I promise to tell the truth, the whole truth, and nothing but the truth."

Pay attention to the language you use when you state your own goals. If you state a goal in the language of category 2 (desire), "I want to get a better job," examine your willingness to make a stronger commitment to reaching that goal. Then restate your goal in the language of category 3 (intent) or category 4 (promise), "I'll do my best to get a better job" or "I will get a better job."

**Review the Hierarchy of Goal-Statement Categories. Reflect on the words you commonly use and how you state your goals. What category do you use the most?**

**Are there situations where it is okay to represent your goals in category 1 or 2?**

**When it comes to your future, what would it take for you to be able to present your goals using category 4 languages?**

**A goal is a dream taken seriously.**

It has been said before in this book that dreams are good but they need action. Goals are important but can be too short sighted and rigid. Consider this statement by John C. Maxwell, "I've studied successful people for almost forty years. I've known hundreds of high-profile people who achieved big dreams. And I've achieved a few dreams of my own. What I've discovered is that a lot of people have misconceptions about dreams. . . . Here is my definition of a dream that can be put to the test and pass: a dream is an inspiring picture of the future that energizes your mind, will, and emotions, empowering you to do everything you can to achieve it."

John C. Maxwell, Put Your Dream to the Test: 10 Questions to Help You See It and Seize It[4]

Think of the components. First it contains an inspiring picture of the future. It is something that can be visualized. It energizes your mind meaning that it gets the attention of your intellect. You think about it and consider all aspects of the dream. It also energizes your will meaning that it is going to take some effort. You will have positive emotion around it as it energizes your emotions. Finally, it will empower you to action. It is going to be something that you will be willing to take action to achieve.

The dream of being in good physical condition is not going to happen if you sit around eating chips watching movies. You will never realize that your dream of owning a car that really cools if you spend every dime you make on things that catch your attention in the moment instead of saving your money. Without the willingness to do something about it your dream it will just be that—a dream.

Watching a group of college football players get ready for a scrimmage game, a faculty member was impressed with their dedication. It occurred to the faculty member, who himself had endured the rigors of academic preparation, how disciplined these young men were in pursuit of their own dreams. Their daily work outs that often left little free time, their disciplined eating and body training, the memorization of plays, their focus on their own personal performance alongside their ability to integrate those skills with the other players on the field, all impressed their professor. For him, it was a picture of the goal setting principles that he often taught in his classes. Being "all-in" to achieve the end result, these players kept their eye not only on the team goal of winning but also on their own personal long-range career goals, which for many included playing in the NFL.

**Consider your own dreams. Is there anything you want that meets the Maxwell definition of a dream or is seen by others in your disciplined pursuit?**

**If so, explain it here. If not, use the space to consider what that dream could be and elaborate on what it would take to make it happen.**

## Clarifying What You Want in a Career

Knowing what you really want in a career is necessary before you can develop believable career goals. Clarifying your wants, however, may not be so easy. Wants are often confused with "shoulds" that are beliefs about what you ought to do, be, or have. "Shoulds" usually are influenced strongly by the thinking of others. Your parents, social institutions, the media, public opinion, or current popular values try to convince you of what you should do, have, or be. At your place of worship, you may be reminded of your duty to contribute your time and money to the support of the congregation. Marketers bombard you with overt and subtle secular "should" messages: "remove unsightly hair," "think differently," "eat fresh," "just do it." "Should" messages from a variety of sources serve as nagging reminders of what we are "supposed" to do.

"Wants," on the other hand, are expressions of what you really desire to have, do, or be. They reflect those things that attract your interest or enthusiasm, those things that grow from your wishes, dreams, aspirations, and fantasies. They reflect the inner you—the real you.

"Shoulds" can prevent you from being in touch with your true "wants." For this reason, it is important to clearly separate your "shoulds" from your "wants." Career goals created out of "shoulds" do not work because they are too much like New Year's resolutions—full of good intentions, but in the end, usually resisted. Career goals developed out of true "wants," however, enlist our full energy and provide a winning combination. Here is an example of how to transform a "should" into a "want":

- I *should* lose weight.
- I *want* to maintain my weight at a neat and trim 130 pounds.

The exercises in the **GOAL SETTING** APP ACTION are designed to assist you in identifying your "wants" and separating out your "shoulds." Continue reading the material in this APP then use it to complete the Goal Setting APP ACTION.

## Comprehensive Career Goals and Objectives

Establishing reachable long-range career goals is crucial for providing future direction and perspective. But a long-range goal is less useful in clarifying what step you should take next. Long-range goals extend at least 10 years into the future. It would be nearly impossible to sit down today and produce a detailed plan for the next 10 years that would help you attain these goals. Even if you had the patience and perspective to do this, your plan would be foolishly rigid. Your own life will change, and the working world will present new opportunities. Accordingly, your plans and long-range goals will change.

For this reason, the easiest and most productive approach is to devise medium-range and short-range career objectives based on your long-range goals. A medium-range objective generally covers one to five years. As these medium-range objectives are reached, you can devise new ones to direct your progress toward the related long-range goal. Sometimes, you will want to change these medium-range objectives when they no longer are suitable. Short-range objectives cover up to one year. You will frequently revise short-range objectives.

The advantages of medium- and short-range objectives are numerous. First of all, they are totally flexible. As changes and opportunities occur, these short-range objectives can easily be revised. Also, you don't have to wait 10 or more years to attain them. Successfully achieving short-range objectives keeps you motivated. If you feel discouraged because you have not yet found a suitable career choice, setting short-term objectives will provide direction for your continuing exploration. Finally, short-range objectives are specific enough to provide guidelines for making step-by-step plans. Without these plans, your future becomes a question mark—or worse.

## Developing Goals

1. *Long-Range Goals:* These goals establish the general career direction you want to achieve over the long run or at least 10 years into the future. Occasionally, you will find better alternatives and change your long-range goals.
2. *Medium-Range Objectives:* These are the career objectives you want to achieve in the next one to five years, so they are more specific. As these objectives are reached, you will establish others to progress toward related long-range goals. Medium-range objectives are frequently revised and sometimes changed completely as new options appear.
3. *Short-Range Objectives:* These are career objectives you want to achieve in one year or less, so they are very specific. These objectives are frequently revised or changed completely as new options appear.

By beginning with your long-range goals, you can work backwards. You may find that as you progress in your career, your goals will change. If you decided to go on a vacation without a destination, you would be somewhere. But if you decided that you wanted to go on vacation to San Luis Obispo and from there tour the Central Coast of California and you were starting from New York City, you would find a few APPS and chart your course. Deciding to take a plane, train, automobile, or walk would impact your trip. If you decide to drive, you may decide to sightsee along the way. During your sightseeing, you may decide that you want to spend more time in this area and decide not to complete your journey to California. Many careers start off headed in one direction but for some reason wind up at another place. This doesn't mean the initial decision was bad, it simply means that another option was presented along the way that perhaps was not previously considered or was rejected at the time.

Review the goal definitions and examples in the section "Developing Goals." Look these over carefully before devising your own short-range objective statements.

As you move through the Goal Setting APP ACTION, you will want to consider the concept of Life Goals, Action Plans, and Mission Statements.

Mission statements are the ideal outcomes you seek in your life.
Career goals and objectives are the realistic outcomes you seek in your career.
Action plans are the specific actions required to achieve your objectives.

Notice that your mission is your ideal or ultimate outcome, while your objectives and goals define what you can accomplish realistically within a specified time frame. Plans lay out the steps required to get what you want.

| | |
|---|---|
| What do I want ideally? | MISSION |
| What can I accomplish realistically? | GOALS AND OBJECTIVES |
| How can I accomplish it? | PLANS |

## Case Study   William

William was a high school misfit. His parents took him out of public school and placed him in a private school, where William did his best to prove that his parents had made a mistake. The culmination of his efforts came when he failed a class his senior year and was unable to graduate with his class.

After completing summer school to obtain his high school diploma, William jumped from one job to another, either leaving when he got bored or getting fired. He attempted to enlist in the Marine Corps but was unable to pass the physical. Angry and discouraged, William hit bottom when he was apprehended for reckless driving and placed in his parent's custody.

Given an ultimatum by his parents to "shape up" or suffer the consequences, William reluctantly agreed to try the local community college. He took just two classes for his first semester, a career planning class and an art class (art was the only subject William had enjoyed in high school). Finding an environment where his creative interests and talents were recognized and encouraged, William began to believe in himself. Through the career planning process he discovered that what he really wanted to do was express himself creatively, especially through photography.

Prior to the start of his second semester, William changed from an undeclared major to a visual arts major. Filled with enthusiasm and

Tom Tom/Shutterstock.com

having educational and career direction for the first time in his life, William took a full academic load in his second semester, narrowly missing the Dean's List. One of his photographic collages was chosen for the student art show, and he received a second-place ribbon.

This summer, William is working as a photographer's assistant. In his free time, he wanders the countryside taking pictures. He is learning how to obtain the special effects he wants. The best prints will be placed in a portfolio when he transfers to the art institute in one year.

Through realistic goal setting and effective action planning, William has found direction and focus for his career journey.

## Final Notes on Goals, Objectives, and Plans

Setting goals and objectives and devising action plans are skills that can be developed. Both are also ongoing processes. Many people are reluctant to set goals and objectives or make the supporting plans because they fear they will then be committed to them no matter what. Others are afraid of even positive change or afraid of failing to meet the objectives that they have set. All of these emotional reactions are perfectly understandable and normal. However, consider that the only purpose of goals, objectives, and plans is to provide productive direction and motivation, along with the time to accommodate change. Therefore, they should never be turned into nonproductive, rigid commitments, or burdens.

Since people and the working world change, goals, objectives, and plans should change whenever it is in your best interest. You will need to make these minor or major changes as you learn about new options or challenges in your career. In other words, career planning is a lifelong process. The more you practice these skills, the more effective you will become in taking charge of your career and your life.

## Summary

By developing a view of the future, you can build the kind of future you really want to have. No one can predict your fate exactly. However, the taking-charge method of career/life planning does allow you far more control and influence over your prospects. The career/life planning process includes clarifying what you want in your future career and life, setting prioritized goals to get what you want, and translating these into realistic objectives and planned actions.

As your personal needs and aspirations change and the working world changes, you will repeat parts of this process with increasing skill and confidence. Thus, career/life decision-making becomes a life-long process, leading you to as much fulfillment as you seek.

## Endnotes

### APP 4.1

1. Walter Isaacson, *The innovators: how a group of hackers, geniuses, and geeks created the digital revolution* (New York: Simon & Schuster Paperbacks, 2015).

2. David Ellis, *Here & Now Instructor's Newsletter*, November 1986: 1, 4. This newsletter can be obtained by contacting College Survival, Inc., 2650 Jackson Boulevard, Rapid City, South Dakota 57702.

3. Ibid.

4. John C. Maxwell, *Put your dream to the test: 10 questions to help you see it and seize it* (Nashville: Thomas Nelson, Inc., 2011).

Other sources related to this APP:

Edward S. Cornish, *Planting Seeds for the Future* (Stamford, CT: Champion International Corp., 2000). Copies can be obtained by writing to Champion International Corporation, Department 5360, 1 Landmark Square, Stamford, Connecticut 06921.

Intensive Course in the Crystal Life/Work Planning Process, John C. Crystal Center, Inc., 894 Plandome Road, Manhasset, New York 11030.

James D. McHolland, *Human Potential Seminar Basic Guidebook* (Evanston, Illinois: National Center for Human Potential Seminars & Services, 1976). The publisher's address is 2527 Hastings Avenue, Evanston, Illinois 60201

# APP 4.2 Empowering Yourself to Succeed

## Do you know people who:

*Argue for your limitations and sure enough, they're yours.*

—Richard Bach, Illusions

- Feel completely dependent upon others in making decisions?
- Are highly motivated to discover and investigate possible career alternatives?
- Blame others or circumstances for everything that happens in their lives?
- Believe that their career path will be determined entirely by circumstances beyond their control?
- Are optimistic about their ability to create a satisfying career through their own efforts?

If you do, you can observe the differences between self-victimizing and self-empowering people.

## Barriers

At this point, you may know what you want in your career and have some plans for achieving your goals. Unfortunately, many people come this far in the career planning process and then get bogged down. Three types of barriers or obstacles keep people from getting what they want or from even attempting to go after their goals:

- negative attitude pattern or mind-set,
- poor decision-making skills,
- any external circumstance or situation that at least temporarily blocks career progress.

In this APP, you will have an opportunity to identify your own particular barriers and learn how to overcome them.

### Mind-sets

Have you noticed how some people tend to be winners in life and others losers? Ask people who are consistent winners in life what their secret is, and the odds are you will receive an answer like, "I don't know why. I just expect things to go well." Losers are likely to tell you about the same thing in reverse. Patterns of winning, losing, and just getting by often correspond to the distinctive attitudes or expectations that different people have about the course of their lives.

These distinctive viewpoints that most people have about life are called mind-sets. A mind-set is a characteristic pattern of thinking, feeling, and believing. Some people, for example, believe that others have all the luck while they never get any breaks and remain powerless to change their lives. Other individuals expect things to turn out basically well and anticipate success. We refer to these two contrasting orientations as the self-victimizing and the self-empowering mind-sets, respectively. These attitudes become ingrained, characteristically shaping a person's reactions to every situation.

## The Real Victim Versus the Self-Victim

A victim is defined as someone who is injured in some way or suffering from some negative act, condition, or circumstance. Unfortunately, there are many true victims in the world. Some people are impoverished or physically disabled. Other people are imprisoned for crimes they did not commit or are victims of accidents they didn't cause. People like these do live with limitations or restrictions, and they truly lack some of the options that you may take for granted. Yet many of these individuals remain optimistic, gaining strength from dealing constructively with their obstacles to create better lives and careers for themselves. They don't consider their disabilities real barriers and often refer to themselves as simply having "*different* abilities."

In fact, most people who feel like victims are not really victims of external circumstances or fate. These imagined victims are called self-victimizers.

## Barrier 1: The Self-Victimizing Mindset

Self-victimizing people are inclined to be uninvolved, dependent, and inflexible in the career-choice process. They rarely generate much energy or enthusiasm for the process of career choosing or career changing. They may underestimate their potential capability for making good choices. Typically, self-victimizers will rely on others to decide for them or wait for circumstances to determine what happens. Self-victimizers are unlikely to explore the full range of available career alternatives out of the rigid conviction that it doesn't make much difference anyway.

Self-victimizing people often feel harmed by circumstances, agencies, or people whom they perceive as hostile. They may say things like "I just can't get ahead because I am a member of a minority, a member of the majority suffering from reverse discrimination, short, tall, fat, thin, ugly, pretty, too smart, too dumb, too poor, too rich, too unskilled, too skilled, too old, or too young."

The legitimate victim is someone who qualifies for a job but doesn't get it because of race, sex, religion, and so forth. Self-victims are those who do not qualify for a job, but maintain that they were denied because of their age, ethnic background, social class, or whatever. Self-victimizers use circumstances such as these to justify their belief that they are essentially helpless in the career-planning and job-hunting process.

## Case Study    Jack

Jack obtained a job that he wanted very much. Yet he knew that the job didn't pay well and was a temporary position funded by a grant. Nevertheless, he hoped that the position would somehow continue, that his salary would somehow be increased, and that the job would somehow lead to a promotion within that organization.

Since the job had temporary funding, Jack's boss repeatedly advised him to begin searching and preparing for a more secure position. His boss also advised that their organization had no plans to create any new positions or hire additional staff for the foreseeable future. Jack chose not to act on this advice, however, feeling that things would somehow turn out all right.

Three years later, the funding ran out, and Jack's job was terminated. He expressed shock and anger. Jack accused the organization of callous unconcern considering his years of service. Just as he was about to leave, a vacancy did open up. Jack applied for that position but was not hired, losing out to a better-qualified woman employed by the same organization.

Upon learning this, Jack threatened to bring an affirmative action suit against the organization, claiming reverse discrimination. Jack could not admit that this particular woman was better qualified for the position and that the selection had been carefully made by a committee of both men and women. Even if this hadn't been the case, Jack's negative behavior had ruined his reputation at the organization.

Jack clearly exhibits numerous self-victimizing traits. He was unwilling to even consider the future seriously, let alone explore career alternatives. He felt so strongly dependent upon the organization that he expected "them" to take care of him. He was uncompromising in his attitude about considering other options, stating that he was just not interested in working somewhere else and wanted to stay on.

Jack's surprise and anger after his inevitable layoff shows his dependency and lack of responsibility for his career and life progress. When problems arose, Jack blamed others for what happened. Several months after this incident occurred, Jack remained unemployed and was making no progress toward another employment goal. Instead, Jack's energy was tied up in feeling wronged by the organization and complaining about his "unjust" treatment.

PAUSE

**Do you know people like Jack? Perhaps you know students like Jack who fail to meet the requirements of a course but then blame the professor for their poor grades. How do you feel when you are around people that exhibit self-victimizing traits?**

**How do these traits impact the academic or career success of a person?**

## The Self-Empowering Mind-set

*Empowering* means giving someone permission to exercise some type of strength, influence, or power. Self-empowering people give themselves internal permission for exercising power. People with self-empowering mind-sets feel free to engage in activity geared to getting what they want, and they are optimistic about getting it.

Self-empowering people take responsibility for creating the conditions they want in their lives, while self-victimizing people take whatever comes their way. Both groups may begin in exactly the same conditions and circumstances. Because self-victimizing people conclude that they are powerless to change or create, they passively take what they get in life, perhaps hoping for the best. In this sense, they make themselves total victims of chance and circumstance. Self-empowering people, in contrast, will be actively inclined to create and implement desired goals. What happens in the life of the self-empowering person is likely to occur more as a result of self-motivation than external circumstances and conditions.

### Self-Empowerment and Career Choice

Self-empowering people go about choosing and implementing their careers far more actively and effectively than self-victimizers. They are also more involved, independent, and flexible in the career-choice and implementation process than are the self-victimizers. Although the self-empowerers are more likely to achieve satisfying careers, they, too, will end up in some unsuitable situations. However, unlike self-victimizers, they actively initiate career changes that will provide greater satisfaction.

Self-empowerers take the time and effort to learn what they need and want in a career and then go ahead and do whatever is required to achieve it. Once they have established career goals, they are inclined to pursue these optimistically and enthusiastically. But self-empowerers recognize that no career decision is likely to produce perfect results. For this reason, they remain flexible and strive to obtain the best results, given their unique situation.

**Case Study**    **Anne**

At the age of 37, Anne gave up a successful and fulfilling career in teaching to become a "stay at home mom." She put her whole energy, enthusiasm, and creativity into this role, just as she had done with teaching. Years later, after her kids had grown up, Anne decided it was time for her to return to an outside career. As she had been out of the job market for a long time, Anne decided to enhance her credentials by obtaining a master's degree in education.

While working on her M.A., Anne began establishing contacts. Through her networking, Anne obtained a part-time educational research job at a community college. She obtained the job even though other candidates had educational backgrounds far better suited to the position than her own.

Soon this job experience, her new M.A. degree, and her networking efforts paid off, and Anne landed an excellent full-time position as an educational researcher with the American Association of Community Colleges. Through her energy and positive thinking, Anne had created a new career for herself when many were advising her that she was too old to start over again. However, Anne realized that this career was not her final step. Though she got outstanding evaluations, Anne was just not energized by her work.

At this stage most people would probably have said something like, "Oh well, I'm just lucky to have such a good job. At my age, I'd better just keep what I have." But not Anne. Anne had far too much to contribute to simply hang in there and wait it out. She didn't know what kind of work would enable her to use her talents more fully. But Anne knew how to ask questions and then seek answers. Anne attended a workshop where she learned to identify her top skills and interests and came away determined to use her talents as a career/life planning specialist. Once again Anne was faced with a barrier. Her educational background was in high school education and college administration areas. What she wanted to do now involved counseling and teaching in a college setting. The difficulty of making that kind of transition would stop most people. Anne was determined, however. She would

either make it on her own as a consultant in private practice or get a job at a college that was looking for talent above "the right" credentials. Anne did the latter through networking. She identified what colleges within commuting distance had strong career/life planning programs and targeted her first choice.

At the time, however, Anne's potential employer had no immediate or anticipated positions. But the people at that organization were impressed with Anne, and she was a patient and persistent problem solver. As a result, within six months she was teaching a career decision-making course there and working in a part-time career/life planning specialist position. Within one year, she had been hired as a full-time professor of career/life planning. Over the past 10 years, she has helped hundreds of individuals find themselves, clarify their career/life goals, and move into careers that utilize their skills and engage their interests. At this point she has established a reputation for herself within the career/life planning field and is a very popular instructor, guest speaker, and well-paid consultant. Her success has clearly not come through luck. Anne is where she is today because she knew what she wanted, went after it, and didn't let her barriers stop her.

 **PAUSE**

**List some of the characteristics Anne displayed which helped her become successful.**

**Anne's story is told with the benefit of hindsight. As you look back on your own career journey so far, what barriers have you overcome?**

**What steps did you take to overcome them?**

## Traits of the Self-Victimizing and the Self-Empowering Mind-sets

### The Self-Victimizing Mind-set

- sees little or no choice available
- sees problems as hopeless barriers
- believes people who get ahead are just lucky

- is resistant to change and unwilling to seriously consider other options
- feels career is determined by external
- feels unable to influence own career
- is uninvolved in own career development
- gives little consideration to personal desires in career and life
- does not know or investigate the career options available
- allows others and events to make personal decisions
- has either no career objectives or sets unrealistic goals
- avoids future career planning

### The Self-Empowering Mind-set

- sees life as full of choices
- sees problems as challenges to be solved
- feels that people get ahead primarily out of their own efforts and preparation
- is open to change and willing to change for a good reason
- feels career is determined by personal efforts circumstances beyond control
- feels empowered to influence own career
- is totally involved in own career development
- gives serious consideration to personal desires in career and life
- thoroughly investigates the career options available
- actively makes personal decisions
- sets realistic and achievable career objectives
- carefully plans career future

1. **After reviewing the material on the two mind-sets, determine your self-victimizing and self-empowering traits.**

   **I am like self-victimizers in that:**

   **I am like self-victimizers in that:**

2. **Rate yourself on the scale below by placing an "X" at the place that best describes your assessment now. Make this assessment based on your current general attitudes rather than your particular mood at this moment.**

PAUSE

| The Self-Victimizing Versus Self-Empowering Scale | | | | | | | | | | |
|---|---|---|---|---|---|---|---|---|---|---|
| 0 | 1 | 2 | 3 | 4 | 5 | 6 | 7 | 8 | 9 | 10 |
| Totally Self-Victimizing | | Somewhat Self-Victimizing | | A Little of Both | | Somewhat Self-Empowering | | Highly Self-Empowering | | |

3.  a. **What are the main things you learned about yourself in doing this assessment?**

    b. **How do you feel about your assessment?**

4.  **After you have decided where you are currently on the self-victimizing versus the self-empowering scale, decide where you want to be. Go back to the scale now and place a large "G" (for goal) at the point where you really want to be.**

5.  a. **What would you have to change in order to become as self-empowering as you really want to be?**

    b. **Are you willing to make the effort to change?**

## How to Become Self-Empowering

Fortunately, your place on the self-victimizing versus self-empowering scale results far more from the way you perceive the world currently than the way the world actually is. Your attitudes were not acquired at birth. Instead, they were developed over the years through learning a certain style or bias that continues to influence your thinking and behavior today. Just as your attitudes were acquired through learning, they can also be productively changed through learning.

To become more self-empowering, start changing your self-victimizing attitudes now by working on the following steps:

1. Become aware of your actual attitudes and beliefs involving career choice.

2. Don't allow your behavior to be controlled by your ineffective attitudes. You can accomplish this through good decision-making. Make carefully considered decisions. Then carry them out, even though your traditional biases may cause you some initial difficulty.

3. Set productive and accomplishable goals, and complete them. By accumulating minor accomplishments over a period of time, you make a habit of success. In this process, your old self-victimizing attitudes will fade.

4. Acknowledge your successes. Whenever you have a successful experience (big or small), reward yourself. Most people get a perverse kind of payoff in some way from their old self-defeating habits. Acknowledging your successes can help you trade in your negative payoffs for positive ones.

5. Create affirmation statements. Write them out, and place them where you will see them. Repeat them to yourself a number of times. An affirmation statement might be like this: "I am a powerful and effective person. I learn from and am successful in all I do."

## The Five Competencies Involved in Career/Life Decision-Making

How effective you are as a career/life decision-maker is determined both by your mind-set and your competencies. A competency is a special skill, expertise, or facility that you have developed through practice over a period of time. For career planning, you will need to have the following five basic competencies:

1. *Self-Assessment.* This competency is the ability to analyze your career-related attributes, such as your personality style, interest patterns, potentials, needs, and values. It also involves objectively assessing your strengths and weaknesses and being able to see how these influence your career. Knowing yourself is an ongoing life process. The better you come to know yourself, the better able you are to make realistic and satisfying career choices. With poor self-assessment skills, you are unlikely to be able to make realistic career choices.

2. *Identification of Options.* This competency is the ability to identify available career options. It is one of the biggest problem areas in the career decision process because of the large number of available choices and the scattered sources of information. First, you need to become proficient at acquiring information and data about occupations, including knowing what resources are available and what information-gathering methods work best. Then you need to get information about the particular jobs available in your chosen field as well as information about the job market in your chosen work location.

3. *Goal Selecting.* This competency is the ability to select goals or targets that are likely to produce a sense of satisfaction, achievement, and direction. People who have selected meaningful goals experience a sense of purpose, and their goals provide guidance for their careers. If you lack meaningful goals, you are likely to experience frustration and indecision in your life.

4. *Planning.* Planning involves the ability to translate goals into action plans. Meaningful goals have little value unless you set up realistic action plans to accomplish these ideals. Poor planners avoid planning because it is easier to just dream about reaching certain goals. Good planners envision their desired career goals and devise specific steps to accomplish them.

5. *Problem Solving.* Problem solving is the capability of handling obstacles that arise in any phase of your career. While you might hope to avoid career problems, this is unrealistic. Incompetent problem solvers will be stopped whenever problems arise. They may give up in such circumstances, look to others to solve the problems, or just wait for things to work out on their own accord. In contrast, competent problem solvers expect such obstacles and develop a facility for approaching problems as challenges and opportunities to use their skills and to learn.

## Becoming a Star Through Career/Life Decision Making

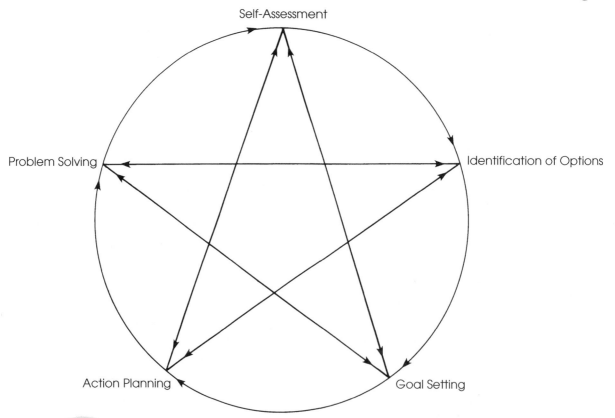

Be as honest as possible as you complete the competencies **Assessing Your Career Choice Competencies** in APP 4.3.

## Common Situational Barriers

For most people the process of selecting and reaching a career goal seems as overwhelming as the huge challenge of "eating an elephant." Having set your own general career goal, you should now approach the goal one step (or bite, using the elephant analogy) at a time. You can no more get a new career going in "one bite" than you can gulp down an elephant in a single mouthful.

By now, you have already taken several big bites out of your career-development elephant. You have selected the kind of occupation you want and developed goals to give definition and direction to your career and your life. That is impressive progress. There are still a number of big bites remaining to make that choice a reality. You have problems to solve, barriers to get over, and actions to take.

By clearly identifying these barriers, you can devise a series of appropriate steps to navigate over, under, or around them. Without this kind of awareness, however, your barriers may remain insurmountable roadblocks, leaving your career/life goals in the realm of dreams rather than reality. The previous sections of this APP have discussed overcoming barriers involving negative mind-sets and faulty decision-making skills. This section will focus on overcoming career barriers common to situations faced by college students without significant job experience and by career changers.

### Common Barriers to Getting Started in a New Career

| College Student Preparing for a Career | Career Changer |
|---|---|
| 1. Fear of beginning a career | 1. Fear of change |
| 2. Procrastination | 2. Procrastination |
| 3. Undefined career identity | 3. Lack of support |
| 4. Lack of experience | 4. Feeling boxed in by current job stereotypes |
| 5. Establishing competencies for initial job in a chosen career field | 5. Establishing credibility and competencies for a job change within a new career field |
| 6. Not knowing what entry-level jobs are available | 6. Not knowing what is available |
| 7. Shyness about networking with contacts in the field | 7. Shyness about networking with contacts in the field |
| 8. Lack of trust in own ability to make and follow through on personal decisions | 8. Relationship conflict about change |
| 9. Inability to visualize job specifics within new field | 9. Inability to visualize self-working in a new career |
| 10. Lack of job hunting know-how, experience, and tools | 10. Lack of an ongoing plan and time frame for making change |

Bruce Rolff/Shutterstock.com

| College Student Preparing for a Career | Career Changer |
|---|---|
| 11. Lack of self-confidence | 11. Poor self-concept or lack of self-confidence |
| 12. Unassertiveness | 12. Unassertiveness |

## Barriers Facing College Students

The barriers facing college students are often related to a lack of working experience. As a member of this group, you may be feeling some fear and concern about getting that first, entry-level job within your career field. Welcome to the club. This is a common "anxiety" with most college students.

A common response to fear is procrastination, putting off those things you need to do to find out what jobs are available within your new field and then making yourself "marketable." Procrastination has left many students with a college diploma but without the foggiest notion of what to do about an entry-level job. Many students decide to go on to graduate school, not with any clear career goal, but mostly to avoid entering that big, strange world of work. But what do you do after getting a master's degree with no specific career goal? Get a doctorate?

Lack of job and career experience can be a real barrier. A crucial part of career implementation is being able to visualize or mentally picture yourself doing what you want in a work setting suited to your tastes. That can be hard to do if you lack work experience. Yet a clear career image of yourself gives you the kind of self-confidence needed to take the next step and to sell yourself effectively to prospective employers. Lack of a clearly defined career identity, however, can fill you with uncertainty and render you unassertive. The "taking charge process" advocated in this book is incompatible with unassertive behavior.

How do college students demonstrate that they have the capabilities needed to perform effectively in an entry-level career position? Employers have businesses and organizations to run, and they need to hire people whom they can trust to get the job done. That means you are going to have to demonstrate clearly your superior strengths and capabilities for doing the job. If you can't, you are not going to get hired. That may sound harsh—but competition and no-nonsense qualifications are a reality. How to establish your credibility is a problem you must solve if you really want to obtain gainful employment in your field.

If you are a young college student, you should start implementing your own life and career plans now, step by step, to gain more confidence and competence. Unless you are a very unusual student, you have probably been depending upon the help and support of parents or other adults in making your decisions. It's a new ball game now. On the one hand, you can no longer rely on others to make and follow through on your most personal career/life decisions. On the other hand, as an inexperienced career and life decision maker, you may be afraid to trust your own guidance.

You might be inclined either to avoid decision-making or to be reluctant to move ahead with your decision until after graduation. The problem is that unless you start taking effective action on your decision now, it will remain a fantasy.

Another major hurdle to overcome is finding out what kind of entry-level jobs are available and how to prepare yourself for getting hired. This requires research and getting out to talk with people in the field. Finding the necessary time can be difficult when you're struggling to find time to prepare your college assignments, write papers, prepare for exams, and have a social life. In addition, talking with people in your potential or chosen career field can be scary. It's all too easy, therefore, to put off these activities until tomorrow and tomorrow and tomorrow. The problem with tomorrow is that one of those tomorrows will be graduation. At that point, suddenly getting a decent job and implementing a career will seem like eating that elephant in one gulp.

If this section seems depressing, we're sorry. We wouldn't be doing you a favor, however, by avoiding those "hard realities." The good news is that you can hurdle these barriers if you confront them head on with a realistic plan of action. That will leave you with far more confidence and competence than many other people in your same situation. Remember, everyone who has ever been employed had to start somewhere. The point is that you want to target your entry-level position, not be grateful for anything you can get.

**Think about the common barriers students face, including those referenced in this APP as well as others that come to mind Note barriers that you believe are particularly pertinent to you. Then list the five barriers that you are most concerned about:**

PAUSE

1 _____

2 _____

3 _____

4 _____

5 _____

## Strategies for College Students

Now that you have considered the bad news, the good news is that most barriers can be overcome. In fact, almost every barrier you will ever face is not so much a "bad condition" that exists in the world as it is a "mental state" that exists in your head. The way to overcome barriers is with positive thinking from which you develop a unique, workable plan of action. The following ideas and suggestions are offered to help you get started.

1. Go to the Visualization Activity in APP 4.3. This activity will help you bring the future into the present as you create a clear picture of your future self. Gain more confidence about your decision-making capabilities. Start

practicing decision-making by looking for all the opportunities available to make decisions and evaluate your performance. When you're in a decision-making situation, follow the steps in a conscious way, making sure that you both gather and analyze the available facts and draw upon your intuitive powers. Keep in mind that only you have the inner knowledge necessary for making effective decisions. Call on other people for information, ideas, and reactions, but don't let anyone else make your decisions for you.

2. Complete your short-term plan from APP 4.1 to achieve your visualized job. Your plan will probably include information research. Your plan might include visits to the college career center. It might also include activities such as networking (conducting information interviews) with people working in your field of interest to learn what those jobs are really like, to see what differences exist in jobs within different settings, to become familiar with businesses and organizations hiring people in that field, and to get tips on getting hired. Your plan could also call for summer work associated with your field, internships, volunteer work, related club and organization activities, and class projects or assignments that help you learn more about your field.

Setting goals, developing a plan, and following that plan is a strategy for career success. Find pictures that represent the outcomes of your goals and post them where you see them daily. Write out your plan and Post it in a place where you will see it daily. Make notes on your plan, indicating what you did and when you did it as a record of your progress. Discuss your plan and your progress with counselors, faculty, friends, and network contacts. Ask them for ideas and suggestions on steps for achieving your goal, and revise your plan whenever necessary. Your plan will be both your tool for success and anti-fear and anti-procrastination assurance.

Here are some ideas for clarifying your career goals while in college and gaining job-related experience and skills:

1. Use class projects to focus on personal career issues. Papers can be an excellent way to research subject areas related to your chosen career field and to establish your writing, thinking, and communicating competencies. Consult with your professors about ideas for such projects. A useful research project would involve visiting and communicating with companies and organizations that you want to learn more about and talking with people who are performing work of interest to you. Keep some of your best papers as examples of some work-related skills that can be applied on the job.

2. Visit the college career center to investigate summer jobs, volunteer work, internships, and cooperative education experiences. Summer jobs are excellent opportunities to gain work-related experience in your field and to establish your competencies. Don't take summer jobs just to earn money. Be creative and look for ways to gain experience, self-information, job possibilities, and job recommendations.

Cooperative educational experience and internships are wonderful opportunities to acquire job-related experiences and to develop your own career identity further. Volunteer work with businesses and organizations related to your field can also be an excellent source of exposure. Perhaps you can include a volunteer work experience as part of a class project or a special study project. You might develop a volunteer project on a career-related activity with a favorite professor. Be sure to ask any employers you have worked for and professors in your field for letters of recommendation. Add these to your job credential file.

3.  Take advantage of the numerous clubs, organizations, student government, and work activities available on almost every college campus. If you are thinking about a career in writing, look into opportunities with the college paper. Interested in communications? Check into possibilities with college radio and cable TV stations. Want to become a manager? Investigate possibilities with the college governance board or involvement in a leadership activity with a campus organization. Considering psychology, philosophy, or anthropology? Become active in the clubs associated with these disciplines.

4.  Develop your job-hunting skills and your awareness of what's available in the job market by reading APP 5.0 carefully. Don't wait until graduation to begin the job-hunting process. If you are visionary and creative, you can move through entry-level job preparation in an organized way and even have fun with it. Since the job market is vast, there are always openings available. Start with the career planning and placement office to find out what is available.

Networking is often the most valuable source of job information. How does the shy or nonaggressive personality handle networking? Remember that assertiveness can be learned. To become a more confident speaker, take speech classes, practice speaking in class, and join activities that involve improving your skills. Drama classes and psychology workshops teach assertiveness skills and help you improve your self-confidence. Remember also that you can "feel" unassertive but act in an assertive way.

## Case Study    Reid

Reid is a big, likable guy with a ready grin and a "laidback" appearance. You soon learn from talking with Reid that he loves to discuss ideas and is a diversified reader, particularly in science-related areas.

Reid comes from a family of professionals. His father is a biologist with a Ph.D., and his mother is a chemist. Reid is the youngest child, with a brother and sister who have also gone on to become practicing scientists. In comparing himself to his family, Reid always felt intellectually inferior. He was pretty much a "C" student in high school and a bit of a loner. He tried college for a while after high school, but dropped out before finishing his freshman year. He just hadn't discovered anything of interest and he failed math, furthering that he wasn't much of a student.

Reid bummed around for a couple of years trying odd jobs here and there, but generally was just drifting along with his life. Eventually, he learned about a career planning class being offered at the local community college and decided to give it a try. In the course, Reid decided that he wanted to be a science writer. He was still concerned, however, about his ability to do college-level work. Reid's ccunselor helped him see that his barrier wasn't lack of intelligence, but lack of self-confidence. Fortunately, finding a career goal had already given him a big boost over that barrier. This really was the first time Reid had ever felt energized about any kind of goal in his life.

Reid started back to college and was amazed at how well he was doing now that he was motivated by his career goal. He worked diligently, and his efforts paid off. He even found that he could "get" math. He obtained a tutor and worked hard. To his amazement, he now got straight A's, even in math.

Reid still had some questions about his ability to be a successful student and a science writer. He knew that he had enjoyed creative writing in high school and that he loved reading science fiction. He had some doubts, however, about whether his family would accept him as a "writer," since he assumed they wanted him to follow the family tradition of becoming a scientist.

Reid began talking with his professor about his science writing goal and obtained names of local science writers to contact for information interviews. Reid set up some interesting research papers to do, including one that involved spending a weekend with a yogi who claimed that he could levitate. Reid's eyes really gleam when he talks about this project and what he learned from the yogi, though he didn't actually observe

him levitate. Reid's instructor regarded his paper highly and suggested he share it with others. Reid did, and received validating feedback on his developing skills. Reid also arranged to take an anthropology course and write a paper on an archeological dig taking place at the site of an old home in the southern part of the county.

Reid has now completed his A.A. degree at the community college and enrolled in the journalism program at the state university. After his first semester there, he arranged to be a summer research assistant with a university biologist conducting research on bats in southern rural Ohio. Reid was optimistic that the results of this project might produce a significant breakthrough in improving intelligence in human beings. Reid maintained a journal for this project to use either in a course project or a feature story in the college paper or alumni journal.

Reid is now serving as a writer on one of the university's numerous publications. He also plans to continue conducting information interviews with science writers and to develop his job-hunting network during his last year in college. Through his networking so far, he has learned that his chances of getting an initial job with a major paper like the *Washington Post* right out of college are slim, but he has several ideas about getting an entry-level position with a smaller paper. Reid continues to check in with the folks in the career office on a regular basis. He is in the process now of adding to his credentials file, refining his resume, and feeling good about himself as a learner, a writer, and a person.

**PAUSE**

**Reid started his career slowly. He dropped out of college and had a hard time finding something he enjoyed. Perhaps you can relate to Reid. What did Reid do to get on a career path?**

**What can you learn from Reid's path?**

Using the ideas and suggestions discussed in this chapter, develop a plan for how you intend to overcome the specific hurdles you identified earlier. Be as specific as you can. Identify real activities that you can and will do to move yourself through your barriers and onto the road to a satisfying entry-level job in your chosen career field.

I plan to take the following actions to hurdle the five barriers I have identified:

| Barrier | Action |
|---------|--------|
| 1. | |
| 2. | |
| 3. | |
| 4. | |
| 5. | |

## Barriers Facing Career Changers

Have you noticed how many people talk about career change but never do it? By career change, we mean a shift to a different kind of work, often in a totally different field. We know people who are desperately unhappy or bored with their jobs or even on the verge of losing their jobs and yet make no move to improve their situation. Why? Fear of change seems to be the biggest culprit. You may not like the situation you're in, but at least you know what you've got. This fear of change is often disguised with concerns like: "I'm too old to change" or "I've got my family, kids, parents, dog to support" or "I've been a widget technician, lion tamer, tank driver all my life. Who would want to hire one of those?" Procrastination usually goes hand in hand with fear. It's hard to get started on a task you fear. It's much easier to complain about the current situation or to engage in "if only I had done it differently" daydreams.

What is frightening about career change? If you have been at a job for a while, you are probably making a stable salary, with some benefits. Even a bad job provides some structure for your life. Changing careers certainly can involve a significant reduction in income and lost benefits. A career change situation also usually involves uncertainty about one's marketable skills and what they may be worth. People under stress tend to discount their worth and ability to make productive changes. It's unusual for people to be positive, realistic, and optimistic about themselves under such circumstances.

Career changers often find it difficult to obtain much support for making big changes in their life from mates, family, friends, and colleagues. That's particularly true the longer you have been in a career, the older you are, and the bigger your salary and/or benefits. It's often difficult to support yourself without the nurturing support of at least one other significant and trusted person. Career change talk has been known to produce serious conflict in relationships.

Another common barrier faced by the person in a career transition is feeling so boxed in by current work that it is difficult to visualize doing something very different. A person's current job title also makes it difficult for others, particularly prospective employers, to see an employee performing in a very different role. How do you develop a belief that you can do something very different from your current work? How do you establish your credibility and competence for doing a different kind of work?

Next, how do you find out what positions are available, where your prospects are best, and how to make the change? Most people have fallen into their careers as a result of circumstances. Few people really know how to make a career switch and job hunt effectively.

With all of these barriers to career change, it's no wonder that most people feel trapped in their current situation. But does it have to be that way? We think not. Are you feeling so unhappy with your current career that it is hurting your emotional and physical health or your personal development? Unless your distress is connected only with your current job, it's worth making a career change or undertaking career redirection. Career redirection involves remaining in your line of work but negotiating some satisfying changes in your job, such as moving out of supervision and into technical applications, for example. To begin resolving your barriers, however, you first need to know what they are so you can take appropriate action. Take a few minutes now to clarify your specific barriers to career change by completing APP Actions at the end of this section. Next, read further for suggestions and ideas to overcome these obstacles.

PAUSE

**Think about the common barriers career changers face, including those referenced in this APP as well as others that come to mind. Note barriers that you believe are particularly pertinent to you. Then list the five barriers that you are the most concerned about:**

1 _____

2 _____

3 _____

4 _____

5 _____

## Strategies for Career Changers

Here are some ways to overcome negative mind-sets and other psychological or emotional barriers:

1. Go to the Visualization Activity in APP 4.3. This activity will help you bring the future into the present as you create a clear picture of your future self. Overcome the barriers of fear and procrastination by making your vision of what you want more vivid than your vision of what you fear. It is impossible to achieve what you really want without knowing clearly what that is. We are not advocating here that you develop some utopian vision, but a realistic picture of where you could use your actual talents more happily. The clearer you can make that picture, the more likely you are to actually achieve it. You will be shifting your energy from fear and avoidance of an unknown future into enthusiasm for where you are going.

2. Conquer the lack-of-support barrier by establishing a support group to help motivate you. Look for people who can really support you, listen to you, and provide suggestions, ideas, and feedback. You want the kind of support that will be both honest and constructive. Avoid both pure critics and well-intentioned but inexperienced supporters who might lead you down a blind alley with naive ideas. Check in with people in your support structure on a regular basis. We highly recommend that you seek out the assistance of a professional career counselor to include in your support structure.

3. Prepare in advance for the possibility of conflicts with your spouse, partner, or family over career change. Communication is the key here. Share your vision with your mate and include him or her in the planning as much as possible. Remember also that you have more to bring to a relationship when you are fulfilled in your work than you do when you're unhappy, bored, depressed, or feeling blocked, trapped, and helpless.

4. Make an action plan that becomes your "antiprocrastination" program of specific steps required to transform your vision into reality. See the previous section for college students to get more details on sources of information for this plan. As you clarify your visualized future, make any necessary changes. Post your plan in a spot you will look at often. A prominent spot over your desk is a good place.

To find out about specific job alternatives and market yourself effectively, read App 5.0. Then consider the following suggestions:

1. Clarify what you really can do in a new career by giving up your current job labels and focusing on your transferable skills along with a vision of what you want. Your goal is to identify specific accomplishments you have achieved in your paid or voluntary jobs that are related to your new career goals.

2.  Develop tools such as a resume and Linkedin Profile focused on the value you bring. This will help you build your credibility and your competency for your career change both on paper and in your mind. You must do that for yourself before you can ever hope to convince prospective employers of your suitability for a job within a new career field.

3.  Networking and job-hunting effectiveness are vital skills and activities in a career change. Networking is how you find out what's actually available, where you want to work, and how to get hired there.

## Case Study   Nels

After a dozen years as a professional hockey player, age caught up with Nels. It was time to look for a different kind of work, but what does an ex-jock do? Nels hadn't been a superstar, so he considered that his days in the limelight were over for good. He had no career preparation, and, as far as he knew, no skills or personal contacts that would qualify him for anything more than a physical labor job. Based on that assumption, Nels felt fortunate to obtain a job as a forklift operator in a food chain warehouse.

After a couple of years of hoisting boxes, Nels decided there had to be more to life than this. The switch from the roar of the crowd to the endless boxes of the warehouse was too great a change for him. But the dilemma remained: what could he do? After an acquaintance told him about a career planning course available at a nearby college, Nels enrolled.

In the course, Nels discovered that he in fact had a number of valuable skills and that his strongest interests were in science and technology. He thought it would be wonderful to be a geologist or a petroleum engineer. At first Nels rejected the idea flat out. He just couldn't picture an "ex-jock" who had never taken a college course doing that. How could he do all that math? Little by little, however, the idea began to shape into a clear vision in his mind. After numerous sessions with his career counselor and considerable self-assessment, Nels reluctantly did a couple of information interviews with a geologist and an engineer. After these interviews Nels was hooked. He knew he wanted to be an engineer.

While he wasn't sure if he could do the college work, he decided to "give it a whack."

A year after taking the course, Nels stopped in to visit his career counselor to ask if there was a follow-up course he could take to verify his career decision. The counselor learned that Nels was getting As in his college coursework but doubted his ability to make it through college. His counselor was able to reassure him and assist him in finding a way to get the support he needed from his friends.

Nels's career counselor saw him again a year later, when he stopped by the office to share a "breakthrough" success he had achieved. From the contacts established over the past two years, Nels had landed a job as an engineering technician. He would be working with and assisting a team of geologists and engineers in the kind of work he had dreamed about. Nels confided that it was only because of his interests, his good grades, and most of all the contacts he had established that he had obtained the job. In fact, he really didn't have the A.A. degree yet that was listed as a job requirement.

Best of all, the company would pay Nels's way to a bachelor's degree in engineering after he had been with the firm for one year. Nels was elated. He realized that if he hadn't been willing to visualize himself in this role and then check out the realistic possibilities, he would still be hoisting boxes in the warehouse. True, he would never be in the "limelight" again, but for him, this would be just as good. Nels would be doing interesting work and developing himself in a direction that appeared right for his skills and interests.

**PAUSE**

Nels held stereo-types about himself. What stereo-types might you have that hold you back from your dreams?

## Case Study   Maria

Maria came to the "Career Direction" workshop looking for promising alternatives to her career as a nurse. It was not so much that Maria disliked nursing, but rather that she was just "burned out" after ten years in the profession. She was tired of waiting on patients and taking orders from doctors. Maria just didn't want to do that anymore.

In reviewing the data from her career surveys, the career counselor saw that the problem was more than just a career burnout situation. Maria's thinking-style profile showed her to be a left-brain oriented, logical, and controlling thinker. While Maria could be empathetic and feeling, that was just not her strongest suit. She liked technical activities and was good at planning and organizing. Maria was introverted and liked to think things through on her own more than to interact with people. She particularly resented following the directives of doctors rather than deciding on her own.

Maria discussed alternatives with her career counselor. The problem was that Maria had some rigid requirements. She had to maintain her current income level, did not want to lose her benefits, and definitely did not want to go back to college for years as part of a career change program. Based on her situation and the information available, the counselor suggested that Maria consider redirecting her career within the health field rather than starting a totally new career.

The health field has enough variety and occupational possibilities to enable one to move away from the service-delivery side of nursing and into a more technical specialty. As a technical specialist, Maria would be able to utilize her fully and would not have to carry out doctors' directives. There were a number of possibilities in the area: computer diagnostics, medical technology, and technical consultant. By selecting a career track that would count much of her previous job experience and by taking selected courses, Maria could probably maintain her current income while making the switch.

Maria was not in a career change situation, but rather a career redirection. The career center could only provide limited information on what kinds of jobs within the health area would best utilize her skills, where these jobs were, and how to get them. Maria needed to learn specifics and get more strategic advice by conducting information interviews and establishing a network of contacts. She was excited about the redirection possibilities, but discouraged about the need for establishing personal contacts with other health professionals, since she tended to be a loner.

But Maria went ahead anyway by talking to some of the nursing instructors at the college and a nurse who had held a variety of interesting jobs in the field. Maria began to engage herself more fully in the networking task and developed her career redirection plan. She realized that she could not make an immediate change, but at least now she had a goal to follow and was identifying what steps to take to get there. As a side benefit, Maria's new goal gave her hope and energy. She was no longer "burned out" as she took charge of developing her career in a more self-fulfilling direction.

**Maria wasn't able to make the change immediately but reported hope and energy? Why do you think this occurred?**

**How does having a goal, even if it is long-term, help you change your thinking and outlook?**

PAUSE

Using the foregoing ideas and suggestions, develop your plan to overcome the specific hurdles you identified. Identify specific activities that you can take to move yourself through your barriers. Whenever you can, specify dates for when you intend to accomplish a specific activity.

I plan to take the following actions to hurdle my five major barriers to career change

| Barrier | Action |
|---|---|
| 1. | |
| 2. | |
| 3. | |
| 4. | |
| 5. | |

## Summary

Successful career/life decision-making requires effective attitudes and decision-making skills along with methods to overcome situational barriers. Your attitudes largely determine how effective you can and will be in implementing your career choices. People develop characteristic outlooks, some inclining to pessimism and others to optimism. Self-victimizing people are characteristically uninvolved, dependent, and inflexible in the career-choice process.

In contrast, a self-empowering mind-set gives you permission to think, feel, and know that what you do makes a difference in the outcomes of your life. Self-empowerers tend to be involved in the career-choice process, independent in decision-making, and open to compromise in order to achieve the best outcome possible in a particular situation. While it is no simple task to transform a self-victimizing mind-set to a more self-empowering inclination, the time and energy involved in making this shift are well worth it.

Career competencies are skills that can be enhanced through learning and practice. Five specific competencies are involved in career/life decision-making: self-assessment, identification of options, goal selection, planning, and problem solving.

To overcome situational barriers, such as being a college student with no professional work experience or being an older career changer, you will need current information sources, realistic self-assessments, support groups, action plans, and personal contacts.

## Endnotes

### APP 4.2

1. Bach, R. (1997). *Illusions*. London: Mandarin

2. Bach, R. (1977). *The Illusions of a Reluctant Messiah*. New York: Random House

# APP 4.3 APP ACTIONS

# APP ACTIONS 4.1

## GOAL SETTING

### STEP 1
### Identifying What You Want in Your Career

1. Before identifying what you do want in your career, it is important to know what you don't want or want to avoid. List below those things you have currently in your life, career, and/or job that you do not want.

_____

_____

_____

2. Some elements of your current life, career, and/or job give you energy and pleasure. List below these current elements in your life, career, and/or job that you do want to retain.

_____

_____

_____

3. Now that you have more clarity about your skills, interests, and values and have made a tentative or definite career choice, what else is important for you to have in your career? List below the things you truly want in your future career and/or job that you don't have now.

_____

_____

_____

4. From numbers 2 and 3 above, develop a list of your top 10 career wants. Eliminate those that are really "shoulds" from your list or restate them as "wants." Now prioritize your list of 10, assigning "1" to the most important and "10" to the least important.

### My Top Ten Wants

1. _____

2. _____

3. _____

4. _____

5. _____

6. _____

7. _____

8. _____

9. _____

10. _____

5. Take the top five career wants from your prioritized list of 10, and restate each one as a specific career goal or objective.

Examples:

a.   I want to work with people who are highly committed to the customers/clients they serve.

b.   I want to obtain recognition from others for the work that I do.

c.   I want to make enough money to maintain the lifestyle I currently enjoy.

d.   I want a job that is within walking distance of my residence.

e.   I want a career that will enable me to use and develop my foreign language skills.

**Five Career Goals**

1. _____

2. _____

3. _____

4. _____

5. _____

## STEP 2

**Follow the Guidelines for Expressing Statements of Career Goals and Objectives as noted in APP 4.1.** Remember, career goal and objective statements follow certain guidelines to define effectively the direction you want your future to take. True career goals and objectives are:

1. *Achievable.* Achievable outcomes can be completed given the physical and mental limitations of the people setting the objectives.

2. *Believable.* People need to feel confident that they can complete the goal or objective—that it is within the realm of possibility for them.

3. *Specifically Stated.* True objectives are stated in concrete terms.

4. *Presented Without Alternative.* True objectives are clearly stated without any either/or clauses.

5. *Compatible with Your Values.* True statements of goals reflect the values that you profess.

## Review Definitions and Examples

Review the goal definitions and examples in APP 4.1. Look these over carefully before devising your own short-range objective statements. Remember these important points:

1. *Long-Range Goals*: These goals establish the general career direction you want to achieve over the long run or at least 10 years into the future.

2. *Medium-Range Objectives*: These are the career objectives you want to achieve in the next one to five years, so they are more specific.

3. *Short-Range Objectives*: These are career objectives you want to achieve in one year or less, so they are very specific.

### Long-Range Goals

| Vague | More Effective |
| --- | --- |
| I want to work with people I like. | I will work with people who are caring, creative, and intelligent. |

### Medium-Range Objectives

| Vague | More Precise |
| --- | --- |
| I want to get a good education. | Within five years, I will have obtained a B.A. degree in psychology. |

### Short-Range Objectives

| Vague Precise | |
| --- | --- |
| I will finish my A.A. degree. | Within one year, I will have completed my A.A. degree in respiratory therapy. |

## STEP 3
### Revise Your Statements of Career Objectives

Check over your top five career objectives to see if they correspond to the guidelines just listed, then make any revisions that you feel are necessary. Perhaps your goal statements need to be more concrete, more clearly stated, or have a timeline added.

1. Career Objective: _____

_____

Revision: _____

_____

2. Career Objective: _____

_____

Revision: _____

_____

3. Career Objective: _____

_____

Revision: _____

_____

4. Career Objective: _____

_____

Revision: _____

_____

5. Career Objective: _____

Revision: _____

_____

## STEP 4
### Develop Comprehensive Statements of Career Goals

For this exercise, you will further revise your long-range statements of career goals. Using these long-range career goals as references, you will then establish related medium-range and short-range objectives. To illustrate, we will follow the example of Marlene. Initially, Marlene completed the following prioritized list of career-related life objectives:

1.  I will be doing worthwhile, important work related to my math skills.
2.  I will obtain professional recognition.
3.  I will have opportunity for self-improvement.
4.  I will have financial security.
5.  I will be contributing to the solution of our inflation problems.

After Marlene's preliminary research with her work options, she decided to become an accountant. At that point, she was able to develop and refine her long-range career goals. Her revised goals are as follows:

1.  I will work in a large public-service accounting firm, serving in a leadership position.
2.  Within 10 years, I will receive recognition for my excellent work as a C.P.A.
3.  I will work for an organization that encourages personal and professional growth by sponsoring workshops and funding continued education.
4.  Within 12 years, I will be earning a salary equivalent to $60,000 in today's money.
5.  I will be helping to solve our economic problems by teaching sound financial management and fiscal responsibility to my clients.

Marlene then developed the following medium-range and short-range objectives related to her top long-range career goals:

### Long-Range Goal #1
I will work in a large public-service accounting firm, serving in a leadership position.

### Medium-Range Objectives
1. Within one year, I will obtain my A.A. degree in accounting.
2. I will graduate with a B+ average.
3. While in college, I will research fully the types of accounting businesses I consider to be potential employers.

### Short-Range Objectives
1. In one-and-a-half years, I will obtain an entry-level accounting position in a firm of my choice.
2. Within two years, I will have received my first salary raise.
3. Within three years, I will earn a major promotion.
4. Within five years, I will have earned my M.B.A. in accounting through part-time study.

### Revise Your Goals
Revise your top five long-range career objectives so they are stated as precisely as possible at this point in your life. If you made a tentative career choice, your long-range career goals will be more vague. However, state them as precisely as you can, and concentrate on constructive short-range objectives to aid your career exploration. Fill in your top two long-range goals in the appropriate spaces.

After writing your long-range goals, write your related medium-range and short-range career objectives. Use Marlene's example as a guide.

### Goal Planning:

| Long-Range Goal #1 |
| --- |
| Medium-Range Objectives |
| Short-Range Objectives |

| Long-Range Goal #2 |
| --- |
| Medium-Range Objectives |
| Short-Range Objectives |

## STEP 5
### Action Planning:
Review the differences among mission, goals, and plans.

| | |
| --- | --- |
| What do I want ideally? | MISSION |
| What can I accomplish realistically? | GOALS AND OBJECTIVES |
| How can I accomplish it? | PLANS |

**Mission statements** are the ideal outcomes you seek in your life.
**Career goals and objectives** are the realistic outcomes you seek in your career.
**Action plans** are the specific actions required to achieve your objectives.

Start the exercise by identifying your first significant step toward achieving your short-range objective and determining when you can complete that step. Use the following example as a guide as you develop your own action plans.

**Example:**

For long-range goal #1, Marlene's short-range objectives were as follows:

1. Within one year, I will obtain an A.A. degree in accounting.

2. I will graduate with a B+ average.

3. While in college, I will research fully the types of accounting businesses I consider potential employers.

From these objectives, Marlene developed the following action plans:

| Steps to Take | Complete by |
|---|---|
| 1. I will change my major from general studies to accounting. | May 15, 2018 |
| 2. I will talk with my academic advisor to see what courses I need to take. | June 1, 2018 |
| 3. I will investigate financial aid possibilities at the financial aid office, so I can afford to take four courses a semester. | June 1, 2018 |
| 4. I will enroll in two summer school courses. | June 15, 2018 |
| 5. I will increase my study time to 30 hours a week to improve my current grades. | July 1, 2018 to May 20, 2018 |
| 6. I will research public-service accounting firms in the area, looking at government directories, and consulting Dun and Bradstreet directories. | May 20, 2018 |
| 7. wThrough the college, I will arrange for an accounting internship with one of the firms I've identified in step 6. | Jan. 1, 2019 |

**Directions:**

1. Using Marlene's example as a guide, develop a list of action steps for the short-range objectives associated with your top two long-range goals.

2. As you review your cluster of short-range objectives for each long-range goal, think through all the related steps required to complete those objectives. List your steps on the following pages in logical sequence.

3. Indicate the approximate deadline for completing each of the steps you identify.

| Action Steps for My First Short-Range Objective | Desired Completion Date |
|---|---|
|  |  |
|  |  |
|  |  |
|  |  |
|  |  |
|  |  |
|  |  |
|  |  |
|  |  |
|  |  |

| Action Steps for My Second Short-Range Objective | Desired Completion Date |
|---|---|
| | |
| | |
| | |
| | |
| | |
| | |
| | |
| | |
| | |
| | |

# APP ACTIONS 4.2

## ASSESSING YOUR CAREER-CHOICE COMPETENCIES

Use the following graphs to assess your current effectiveness in these five career-planning competencies. Base your assessment on where you actually see yourself at this point in life, rather than where you would like to be or think you should be.

1.  Rate your decision-making effectiveness by placing an "X" at the point on each of the following five scales that most accurately describes your current level of effectiveness. Use the "clues for assessment" to help you decide.

    *a. Self-Assessment (Knowing Yourself)*

    Clues for Assessment:

    • How effectively can you describe your best and most enjoyed talents?

    • How effective are you in describing your career-related interests and values?

    • How effective are you in pinpointing what you really want in a job and in a career?

    • How effective are you in describing the working conditions that most appeal to you?

| 0 | 1 | 2 | 3 | 4 | 5 | 6 | 7 | 8 | 9 | 10 |
|---|---|---|---|---|---|---|---|---|---|---|
| Very Ineffective | | Somewhat Ineffective | | A Little of Both | | Somewhat Effective | | Very Effective | | |

    *b. Identification of Options*

    Clues for Assessment:

    • How effectively can you identify kinds of occupations that best match your interest and ability patterns?

    • How effective are you in finding occupational information and using it in your career decision making?

    • How capable are you of developing possible options from your imagination?

    • How familiar are you with current job-market conditions in your field of interest?

    • How effectively can you analyze occupational outlooks for the future?

| 0 | 1 | 2 | 3 | 4 | 5 | 6 | 7 | 8 | 9 | 10 |
|---|---|---|---|---|---|---|---|---|---|----|
| Very Ineffective | | Somewhat Ineffective | | A Little of Both | | Somewhat Effective | | Very Effective | | |

### c. *Goal Selecting (Knowing What You Want for the Future)*

Clues for Assessment:

- How effectively can you define what you want in a career in the form of specific goal statements?

- How effectively can you define what you want to accomplish in your life?

- How effectively can you use self-knowledge and knowledge of the world of work to develop meaningful goals for yourself?

| 0 | 1 | 2 | 3 | 4 | 5 | 6 | 7 | 8 | 9 | 10 |
|---|---|---|---|---|---|---|---|---|---|----|
| Very Ineffective | | Somewhat Ineffective | | A Little of Both | | Somewhat Effective | | Very Effective | | |

### d. *Planning (Knowing How to Get What You Want)*

Clues for Assessment:

- How effectively can you identify specific actions or steps that need to be accomplished to achieve your ideal goals?

- How effectively can you predict possible outcomes of specific actions over a long period of time?

- How effectively do you manage your resources (money, time, energy)?

- How effective are you at regularly getting the things done that you really need to accomplish?

| 0 | 1 | 2 | 3 | 4 | 5 | 6 | 7 | 8 | 9 | 10 |
|---|---|---|---|---|---|---|---|---|---|----|
| Very Ineffective | | Somewhat Ineffective | | A Little of Both | | Somewhat Effective | | Very Effective | | |

### e. *Problem Solving (Creating Alternatives as Possible Solutions)*

Clues for Assessment:

- How effectively can you identify the problems that could keep you from accomplishing your objectives or goals?

- How effective are you at foreseeing possible alternatives when obstacles keep you from achieving what you want?

- How effectively can you select those alternatives that make the best sense for you?

- How effective are you at seeing problems as challenges to be solved?

| 0 | 1 | 2 | 3 | 4 | 5 | 6 | 7 | 8 | 9 | 10 |
|---|---|---|---|---|---|---|---|---|---|---|
| Very Ineffective | | Somewhat Ineffective | | A Little of Both | | Somewhat Effective | | Very Effective | | |

2.  After you have decided where you are currently on the five competencies, decide where you want to be. Go back to each of the five scales and place a large "G" (for goal) at the point where you want to be.

3.  a.  From completing the preceding scales, what did you learn about your current effectiveness level in making career/life decisions?

    b.  What do you see as your main strengths as a career/life decision maker?

    c.  What do you see as primary problem areas in your current ability to make effective career/life decisions?

## VISUALIZATION ACTIVITY*

This activity will help you bring the future into the present as you create a clear picture of your future self. You used this activity in APP 3.2. It is time to use it again for a new purpose. This time, you will want to visualize the kind of entry-level job that you want to have (or your next job if you have experience) and mentally rehearse being in that role. Use the visualization technique described below. Give yourself about 20 minutes of quiet relaxed time for this process. Return to this often—a few times in a month can help you clarify your vision of the future. This visualization technique is a way to bring the future into the present and reduce fear of the unknown. You can then create a clear picture of what you want so that you know what you are going after. This will decrease your fear and procrastination while increasing your confidence.

### Changing Your Thinking

1. Interview three or four people, such as your parents, friends, significant other, acquaintances, colleagues, or others in your network, to find out such things as: what kind of work they do, what they like and dislike about their work, how they got into that type of work, whether they would advise anyone else to get into their line of work, and so forth. As you interview these people, attempt to discover whether they tend to be more self-victimizing or self-empowering about their work. Note: If they are self-victimizing, don't volunteer this opinion. Remember that change has to be initiated by each individual.

2. Think about the following questions:

   a. In what ways might a person with a self-victimizing mind-set go about the career-choice process differently from a person with a self-empowering mind-set?

   _____

   _____

   _____

   b. In choosing a career, is it more effective to be uncompromising or willing to compromise? Why?

   _____

   _____

   _____

   c. Is it preferable to make your own career-related decisions or to have an expert or knowledgeable person decide for you?

   _____

   _____

   _____

---

*From *The Three Boxes of Life and How to Get Out of Them*, by Richard N. Bolles, © copyright 1978 by Richard N. Bolles. Used by special permission. Those desiring a copy of the complete book for further reading may procure it from the publisher, Ten Speed Press, P.O. Box 7123, Berkeley, CA 94707.

d. Why might some people prefer to be uninvolved in the selection and implementation of their careers?

_____

_____

_____

e. In what ways is a person with a self-empowering mind-set more likely to have a more satisfactory career than a person with a self-victimizing mind-set?

_____

_____

_____

# Job and Internship Search

Congratulations! You've done a lot of work identifying your skills, interests, and motivators. You've researched careers, identified your barriers and made some decisions about the direction you want to take your career. Now it's time to take action on your goals and begin moving your career in a direction that is meaningful to you.

APP 5 will help you through the stages of the job or internship search. It will introduce you to the critical stages, tools, and steps that you will take to achieve your job or internship goals. This APP assumes that you have developed a clear career goal; obtained the education or training you need, and are now ready to find and obtain a great job or internship. Incidentally, we define a great job as one that lets you fully use your top interests and skills to perform a valuable service and rewards you with both personal satisfaction and a good income.

Keep in mind that you are likely to be changing jobs and careers many times in your lifetime. By carefully working through this APP and doing the work involved, you will become effective and confident with your search for a job or internship.

Although we will refer to your search as a "job" search, this chapter is relevant to you if you are seeking an internship as well.

## Getting Ready to Launch Your Search

Many people find the job search challenging and sometimes frustrating. Often, this is because they don't know how to effectively and strategically work through the stages. APP 5 is designed to take you step-by-step with explanation, guidance, tips, strategies, and examples. You've already completed the hardest part in the previous APPs. Now, let's take things to the next level so you can begin to realize your career goals.

To prepare for your search, be sure to have all of the information you have collected and developed in the previous APPs. You will need this information as you conduct your research, develop your resume and correspondence, develop your marketing tools, prepare for networking, plan for the interview, and maximize the resources available to you.

### Strategic Planning and the Job Search Market*

Developing and writing out a thoughtful strategy will help you achieve your job search objectives more quickly. Below are 10 tips for planning strategically. Most will be covered throughout APP 5.0.

1. ***Establish a consistent two-hour weekly meeting with yourself.*** Find a day and time that you can commit to every week to focus solely on your job search. Whether it's Monday evening or Saturday morning, you need dedicated time to review your plans, update your resume, and research additional options. Of course, you may very well need to find other times during the week to follow up on job leads, network and manage other job search tasks, but your two-hour meeting should always be on your schedule so you have time to reflect, plan, and take further action.

2. ***Write out a clear career objective.*** Review your work from previous chapters and think about how you envision your career to unfold within the next one to five years. Be clear about the type of employers that interest you, your preferred work environment, the skills you want to use, and other details that are important to you.

3. ***Create a timeline for your job search objectives and tasks.*** Be sure to include dates for completing your first resume draft, timeframe for researching and practicing interview skills, times available to schedule informational interviews or networking meetings and other steps in the job search. Ensure you set realistic timeframes and goals.

4. ***Analyze your career choice in terms of your skills, interests, and values.*** Think about if they align and if your career choice fits with these other factors. For example, if your interest is to quickly climb the corporate ladder into management and earn a high salary, then be sure your career choice is not one that is in a low-paying industry.

---

*From *The Three Boxes of Life and How to Get Out of Them*, by Richard N. Bolles, © copyright 1978 by Richard N. Bolles. Used by special permission. Those desiring a copy of the complete book for further reading may procure it from the publisher, Ten Speed Press, P.O. Box 7123, Berkeley, CA 94707.

5. ***Develop your assertiveness skills and be proactive.*** Your job search is your responsibility. You will set yourself up for failure if you wait for others to reply to your emails, or return calls with job leads or don't take action because you are waiting for someone to share their contacts. Keep moving forward to research employers and opportunities, uncover your own contacts, and discover new job leads.

6. ***Identify and research a minimum of 10 employer targets keeping in mind your geographic preferences.*** Research the employers thoroughly to identify the types of jobs, roles, tasks, etc. that might be available to you at some point. Once you determine that one or more employers do not fit with your interests, be sure to replace that employer with another target. Your goal is to maintain at least 10 employer targets at all times to broaden your opportunities, but having 20 targets or more can also be of value.

7. ***Learn more about your employer targets through informational interviews and research.*** Identify the organizational culture, company values, employee satisfaction as well as the organization's match to your interests and values.

8. ***Meet with your career advisor, if one is available to you through your institution.*** Your career advisor can provide expert guidance and feedback on your job search tasks, give insight into your career choices and how they fit with your assessments, interests, skills, and abilities, and uncover areas and resources that you may not have considered during the job search process.

9. ***Expand your network.*** Set a goal for a certain number of networking activities each week, such as informational interviews, networking meetings, or professional activities. Do not just hide behind the computer. Be sure you get out and make contact!

10. ***Review your career objective, timeline, tasks and goals, career choice, target employer list, and networking contacts at least once a month.*** Analyze to see what has changed and what needs additional attention. Ensure you set goals to move forward and/or redirect your attention to key activities that you may not be giving enough attention, such as networking.

## APP 5.1  Researching and Gathering Information

Although you may know what kind of job you want, you may not know some key information that will lead you to the right job. To reach your career objective, you need to know more about what opportunities are available to you. To do this, there are several steps and strategies that will help you research and gather the appropriate information to make good decisions that will lead you to your career goals.

Some of the research you need to do will help you understand which employers to target, the level of jobs for which you are qualified, and salaries appropriate for your level.

Use the questions on the following worksheet to guide your research. As you gather information, use this worksheet or recreate it in an online document to fill the information you have gathered.

| Research Questions | My Research Findings |
|---|---|
| What markets (employers) have the greatest need for your services? | |
| What unique value can you bring to each type of employer? What past accomplishments make you more valuable than others who may be seeking similar jobs? | |
| What is the salary range for people with your education and experience level? | |
| All employers, including the government, are in business to sell or provide a service to certain kinds of people. Identifying the people you are most interested in serving and best prepared to serve could help you target those employers who cater to these populations. What kinds of people would benefit the most from your service (young or old, uneducated or well educated, male or female, majority or minority)? | |
| What kinds of employers (companies and organizations) would find your education and experience most valuable? (If, for example, you are a gifted idea person, then companies who need bright, innovative people could best use your skills—advertising agencies, political campaign offices, sales and marketing departments, or fundraising organizations.) | |

| Research Questions | My Research Findings |
|---|---|
| How would you summarize your idealistic interests related to your career? Do you have a strong desire to improve the efficiency of the transportation system, clean up the environment, conserve energy, improve people's health and longevity, or create more beautiful cities? What kinds of organizations address these interests in some way? If, for example, your interest is to improve people's health, you might consider the opportunities available with health food stores, hospitals, wellness centers, government and world health organizations, athletic coaching staffs, or sports programs. | |
| Where do you want to work with regard to city, region, state, or country? What area might have the greatest demand for your services? | |
| What size of business or organization do you want to work for? What size of organization is most likely to need your services? Do you want to work with a business with interests and concerns that are local, national, or international? Do you have foreign language skills that might be of service in an international firm, or computer competencies to bring to an employer in need of enhancing their capabilities? Examples: A young college graduate sold his computing knowledge to a printing company in the process of transitioning from a manual to an automated operation. A midlife career changer sold his computing expertise to a travel agency in need of enhancing its data accessing and reporting capabilities. | |
| What kinds of products or services do you want your employer to be associated with (potato chips, computers, plumbing repair, counseling, electronic equipment, bakery goods, day-care centers, toys, family therapy, or financial information)? Suggestion: Review the index or table of contents to the Yellow Pages of a city telephone directory for product and service ideas. | |
| Do you have a preference for working with a profit or nonprofit business or organization? Would you get a greater sense of satisfaction working for an organization or business that was committed to maximizing profits or one devoted to providing valuable service to people or the environment? | |

| Research Questions | My Research Findings |
|---|---|
| What kinds of activities do you want your work associates to be doing? What people would find your skills and interests most useful? What kinds of businesses or organizations would employ those people? For example, a high Holland code "C" person with wonderful organizing skills who enjoys being around creative people might be able to create order out of chaos for a growing electronics firm, a group of architects, or artists. | |

After considering the above questions, make two lists to help you assess where your job-related skills and attributes can best be marketed. Entitle the first list *Types of Organizations* and the second, *Characteristics of My Ideal Organization*.

Under the first heading, develop a list of at least 10 (preferably 20 or more) types of organizations that you would both enjoy working for and where your abilities could be in demand. Be sure to make the categories as specific as possible. Entries such as sales companies or educational institutions are too general to be useful.

Under *Characteristics of My Ideal Organization*, list those things that are important to you in an ideal job setting. List 10 or more items under this heading.

Sample entries might look like the following:

| My Ideal Employment Situation: Research Outcomes ||
|---|---|
| **Types of Organizations** | **Characteristics of My Ideal Organization** |
| Accounting firm | Medium-sized city in USA on west coast |
| Online start-up company | Company size of 500–1000 employees |
| Advertising company | Community-involved company |
| Global consulting firm | Company with ties to Asia |
| Elementary school | Team-oriented projects |
| Arts center | Located within 30-minute commute |
| Engineering firm | Opportunities to move up the ladder |
| Biomedical science research company | Nonprofit organization |
| International development agency | Global involvement |
| Government agency | Opportunities to transfer to other locations |

Next, identify your top three employer types. That narrows down the employers you're targeting to a manageable few categories.

Rank your *Characteristics of My Ideal Organization* list, identifying the top five preferred traits. These specific characteristics will also help you find appropriate employment targets.

| My Ideal Employment Situation: Priorities | |
|---|---|
| **Types of Organizations** | **Characteristics of My Ideal Organization** |
| 1. | 1. |
| 2. | 2. |
| 3. | 3. |
| 4. | 4. |
| 5. | 5. |

## Informational Interviews

Informational interviews help you to make connections with professional individuals and groups of people who can help you build relationships that can lead to jobs and/or career success. This is a research technique to gather information about the job market, industry, and organizational culture. However, if used strategically, can also help to expand a network and uncover job leads.

Your focus should be to meet with professionals working in the type of work you want and professionals working in organizations or industries where you would like to work.

### How to request an informational interview

1. Share your name.

2. Explain how you got their name (if you were referred, give the name of the person who referred you to them) and compliment them, if possible, on their status, accomplishments, LinkedIn profile, etc.

3. Briefly state your situation.

4. Tell them you are not contacting them for a job.

5. Explain to them what you are asking for (advice on . . .)

6. Give them a time frame for the meeting (20–30 minutes).

7. Thank them, reconfirm date/time, and get directions.

| Sample Informational Interview Request Statement |
|---|
| Hello, I'm Sophie Anderson and I was given your name by Fred Jali. Fred said that you are an expert in the accounting field for NGOs. I am currently a business student at [your institution's name] and would appreciate meeting with you to learn more about what you do and what you think of the job market for accountants in the DC-area. I'd be happy to buy you a cup of coffee or tea if you would be willing to meet with me for 20–30 minutes sometime in the next week. |

### At the informational interview meeting

Bring your resume to the meeting and offer it as "background/reference information" about you. Give your 30-second verbal resume. Mention your professional accomplishments and your career goals. Stay focused and don't "chat" too much at the beginning. Have a list of questions ready, but be prepared to get answers to only a few questions. Ask your list of questions (see suggestions below).

During the last three to five minutes, remind them that you are aware that you only asked for (#) of minutes and want to stick to that, so you want to wrap up with these two questions:

1. *Do you know other individuals in this career field (or organization) with whom you think I should speak? Can you provide their names, titles, and contact information?*

2. *May I stay in touch with you and let you know how my job search is going?*

Ask for their business card. If they don't have one, then ask for the correct spelling of their name, title, and full mailing address.

| Sample Questions for an Informational Interview | |
| --- | --- |
| • Would you please describe a typical day? | • What is a typical career path? |
| • Is there a slow/busy season? | • If you had it all to do again, what would you do differently? |
| • How many hours per day do you work? | • Given my background, what additional advice can you offer me as I pursue a career in this field? |
| • What did you do before this job? | |
| • What do you like/dislike about your job? | • Do you see any major weaknesses in my background? |
| • How did you find out about this job? | |
| • What skills are necessary in your job? | • If so, do you have any suggestions for overcoming them? |
| • What skill sets lead to success in this environment? | |
| • Do employees in your area function as a team? | • What would you do if you were in my situation? |
| • Is the management structure formal or informal? | • Would you be willing to refer me to others in this field/organization who might have additional advice or ideas? |
| • What would you change about this organization if you could? | |

### After the meeting

Within 24 hours, send a "thank-you" card or a letter to the individual. Include at least one thing they said that was especially interesting or of help to you.

| Strategies to Maximize the Benefits of your Informational Interview |
| --- |
| • Offer to meet at their place of employment. |
| • Try to obtain 2–3 referrals from each contact with whom you meet. |
| • Stick to the time frame you agree to!!! |
| • *Never* ask for a job. |
| • Follow-up is critical. When you are given a referral, be sure you follow up within two days. |
| • After meeting with a referral, send a thank you letter. |
| • If you have received some good tips on changing your resume, mention in your letter that you will incorporate some of their suggestions into the resume and forward it to them. |

| Strategies to Maximize the Benefits of your Informational Interview |
|---|
| • If they are interested in what you did before, or if you come across another mutual interest, offer to send them information that you may have about the subject (i.e., if they are interested in your home country, offer to send a travel brochure or some websites of the country). |
| • Let all of your contacts know when you are employed and thank them again. |
| • Stay focused and don't "chat" too much. Have a list of questions ready to ask and take notes. |
| • Send a "thank-you" note within 24 hours (email is okay). |

# APP 5.2  Creating Your Branding and Marketing Tools

## Creating Powerful Resumes

You will need a resume for several stages of your job or internship search. Resumes are used for networking and applying for jobs. They also create the foundation for your LinkedIn profile and other social media profiles intended for career or business purposes. This section will help you understand the components necessary for a powerful resume.

It is important to note that in the United States, a document used to provide your professional experience and attract an employer is commonly referred to as a resume. However, if an employer is asking for a CV or curriculum vitae then they are requesting specific information. CVs are typically requested for academic positions or jobs in international development. This section will not cover the CV, but will focus on the shorter resume, which is more commonly used for networking and job applications.

A resume is typically a one- or two-page marketing document that cites your experience in terms of accomplishments and results. It usually contains the following sections:

1. **Contact information**

2. **Qualifications or career summary**

3. **Experience**

4. **Education and training**

If you are soon to graduate or are a recent college graduate, then you may also add a career objective.

Keep in mind that the average U.S. employer spends approximately 10 seconds reviewing an individual's resume. This is not much time to make a strong impression and convince the employer that they should contact you for an interview. Therefore, your resume needs to be carefully crafted to draw the eye of the employer to key information. Thus, the content needs to be powerful and the design crisp and clean. Let's take a look at the components.

It is also important to note that many employers require candidates to submit resumes online. Many times, a search engine filters the resumes for key words before the resume ever reaches a human being. Key words are usually the nouns and phrases most closely related to the positions' duties and qualifications. As you review job descriptions, take note of the keywords used in the description as frequently these words are used in the keyword search. Be sure to include relevant keywords to your resume. Many resume books and websites provide lists of keywords related to different career fields. You can find many words by reviewing the occupational descriptions in the Occupation Outlook Handbook.

## Contact information

Your contact information should be listed at the top of the resume. Note that the resume does not include the title "resume" as a header. The contact information should include the following information listed in this format:

NAME (First, Last or LAST, First)
Street Address
City, State/Region, (Zip) Code, Country
(Country Code) (Local Area Code) Cell Phone
Business/Professional Email
Link to LinkedIn or other online profile and/or portfolio

Bold your name →  **MARK CHAN**   Place a comma only between the city and state

21 G Street, NW, #123

Shorten your LinkedIn URL by going to the "Settings" on LinkedIn and changing the tag after ".com/"

Washington, DC  20009  USA

+1 (202) 999-6655

Always include the area code.   mrc@gmail.com

LinkedIn Profile: www.linkedin.com/myprofilename

Note that your resume should list your first name followed by your last name. Your street address should be a U.S. address. Your telephone number should be a number where an employer can reach you at during the day, preferably a cell phone. Your email address should be an address that has formal information and not a "cute" or "silly" name, such as snowlover@gmail.com. Preferably, your email address has some form of your name in it.

Take note as to what information is NOT included on a resume:

- Age
- Birth date
- Driver's license, social security number, passport or other identification number
- Gender
- Marital status
- Nationality
- Number of children
- Photo
- Place of birth

It is critical that you not include this information as employers are extremely uncomfortable seeing this information, as it is considered information that could be used for discriminatory purposes.

### Qualifications summary

Your qualifications summary is a brief paragraph, often with several bullets that highlight your skills, expertise, and qualifications for the position. You should plan to rewrite the qualifications summary for each individual job to which you apply. Think of the qualifications summary as the most important section of information on your resume. Most employers may never read your entire resume, but they will probably read your qualifications summary. Therefore, include the information that best represents your qualifications specific to the job. In other words, if the employer were to only read the qualifications summary, they should know exactly why they should bring you in for an interview for the position they are offering.

Here is a model to follow when writing your qualifications summary:

---

### Experience Summary Template

**Use/modify this template as needed**

**#** years of international experience and degree in ___ with expertise in **A, B,** and **C**. Background also includes X, Y, and Z. Skills include: 1, 2, 3. Languages: **English, other, other**. Work experience and education in **country, country** and **country**.

*Adapted from © 2017 Passport Career, LLC, www.passportcareer.com*

---

### Experience Summary Analysis

**#** years of international experience and degree in ___ with expertise in A, B, and C. Background also includes , , and . Skills include: , , . Languages: Country's national language, other, other. Work experience and education in **country, country** and **country**.

**A, B, and C** = Top 3 needs of employer

**X, Y, and Z** = Additional expertise/experience you have that complements employer's needs.

**1, 2, 3** = Top skills needed by employer (you can expand this list into columns).

**Languages** = Employer language first. Do NOT qualify your fluency level.

*Adapted from © 2017 Passport Career, LLC, www.passportcareer.com*

## Experience Summary Sample

# years of international experience and degree in ___ with expertise in A, B, and C. Background also includes , , and . Skills include: , , . Languages: Country's national language, other, other. Work experience and education in **country, country** and **country.**

Two years of international experience and degree in business with experience in processing remittances, researching and responding to complex inquiries, and preparing and creating reports. Background also includes managing complex data , developing high level accurate reports, and communicating with all levels within a large corporate environment. Skills include: accurate data reporting, reconciling accounts, and timely deliverables. Languages: English, French, German. Work experience and education in USA, UK and Germany.

*Adapted from © 2017 Passport Career, LLC, www.passportcareer.com*

### Accomplishments and results

Your resume should focus on relevant skills and experience. It does not need to document your entire work history, especially that which is not relevant to the job at hand (or to your interests, if you are writing a networking resume). You should list your experience in reverse chronological order and list your experience headings as the following:

1. **Title, Office Name, Company Name**

2. **City/Country, Year Started—Year Ended**

3. **Bulleted accomplishment and results statements**

You do not need to include salary, names of supervisors, or address of company. You also do not need to include duties and responsibilities, as these would be considered obvious information that does not tell the employer what you did on the job but only what you were supposed to do. Therefore, you need to focus on accomplishments: What did you do that was significant on the job, the result of your direct involvement on the job.

If you are having a difficult time developing your accomplishment statements, think about what your previous employers would say about you. What would they say were your greatest accomplishments?

## Experience Descriptions (accomplishment-focused)

**TITLE, Office Name, Organization**
**Location, Year Started – Year Ended**
- Relevant accomplishment & results statements, using strong action words
- Quantify with $, #s, time saved phrases

Do NOT Include:
Duties, responsibilities, salary, names of supervisor, address unless required.

**FINANCIAL SPECIALIST, Client Services, Finance Corporation**
**China, 2006-2009**
- In a 6 month period, drastically reduced inventory by 25%.
- Hired and trained 3 systems analysts who, in less than 4 months, successfully reduced a major program development backing.
- Negotiated national account agreement with major office supply distributor which resulted in cost savings of $36,000.
- Trained 5 new recruits within 9 months. Ensured new staff had appropriate training and knowledge to work effectively and efficiently in their jobs.

*Adapted from © 2017 Passport Career, LLC, www.passportcareer.com*

### Education and Training

Your education and training information is the final component on your resume, unless you just graduated and have no professional experience. List your education information as the following:

Degree, Name of Institution, Country, Year Completed

You should list your highest degree first, followed by other degrees. You should only list any post-secondary education and not high school/secondary school information.

Following your education information, include relevant training. This information often impresses an employer as many employers want to know that you are keeping your skills current. List it as the following:

- **Name of Training, Institution, Country, Year Completed**

- **Brief Summary of Training Content**

Note that at the end of the U.S.-style resume, do not include hobbies or the wording "References available upon request." Employers will expect you to have references and will ask for them if you are considered a serious or final candidate for the position.

## Education & Training

- Degree, Name of Institution, Country, Year Completed (most recent degree listed 1st)
- Name of Training, Institution, Country, Year Completed (most recent training last)
- Brief summary of content

**Master's in Business Administration,** Georgetown University, 2017.

**Bachelor of Arts in English Literature,** Kirori Mal College, Delhi University, 2015
- University ranked #1 in India
- Graduated with honors.

**Project Management Skills,** KPMG, South Africa, 2007.
- Two week training covering team work, project design and planning, time management, and project management.

*Adapted from © 2017 Passport Career, LLC, www.passportcareer.com*

### Tips for a Powerful Resume:

Be sure to use strong, active verbs. There is a list of recommended verbs in the article that discusses accomplishment and results statements. Also, be sure that your resume has no typos. A typo on your resume often indicates to the employer that you are not thorough with your work or that you have poor writing skills. However, with regard to grammar, you can suspend some grammatical rules. You can list bulleted accomplishment statements that are phrases rather than complete sentences.

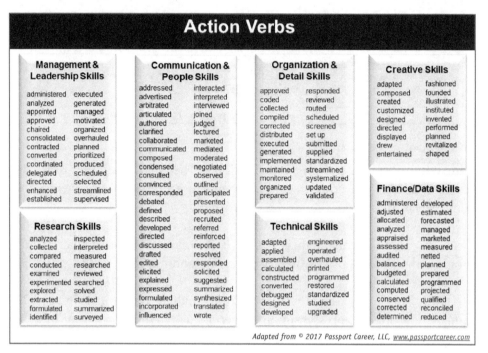

## Action Verbs

### Management & Leadership Skills

| | |
|---|---|
| administered | executed |
| analyzed | generated |
| appointed | managed |
| approved | motivated |
| chaired | organized |
| consolidated | overhauled |
| contracted | planned |
| converted | prioritized |
| coordinated | produced |
| delegated | scheduled |
| directed | selected |
| enhanced | streamlined |
| established | supervised |

### Research Skills

| | |
|---|---|
| analyzed | inspected |
| collected | interpreted |
| compared | measured |
| conducted | researched |
| examined | reviewed |
| experimented | searched |
| explored | solved |
| extracted | studied |
| formulated | summarized |
| identified | surveyed |

### Communication & People Skills

| | |
|---|---|
| addressed | interacted |
| advertised | interpreted |
| arbitrated | interviewed |
| articulated | joined |
| authored | judged |
| clarified | lectured |
| collaborated | marketed |
| communicated | mediated |
| composed | moderated |
| condensed | negotiated |
| consulted | observed |
| convinced | outlined |
| corresponded | participated |
| debated | presented |
| defined | proposed |
| described | recruited |
| developed | referred |
| directed | reinforced |
| discussed | reported |
| drafted | resolved |
| edited | responded |
| elicited | solicited |
| explained | suggested |
| expressed | summarized |
| formulated | synthesized |
| incorporated | translated |
| influenced | wrote |

### Organization & Detail Skills

| | |
|---|---|
| approved | responded |
| coded | reviewed |
| collected | routed |
| compiled | scheduled |
| corrected | screened |
| distributed | set up |
| executed | submitted |
| generated | supplied |
| implemented | standardized |
| maintained | streamlined |
| monitored | systematized |
| organized | updated |
| prepared | validated |

### Technical Skills

| | |
|---|---|
| adapted | engineered |
| applied | operated |
| assembled | overhauled |
| calculated | printed |
| constructed | programmed |
| converted | restored |
| debugged | standardized |
| designed | studied |
| developed | upgraded |

### Creative Skills

| | |
|---|---|
| adapted | fashioned |
| composed | founded |
| created | illustrated |
| customized | instituted |
| designed | invented |
| directed | performed |
| displayed | planned |
| drew | revitalized |
| entertained | shaped |

### Finance/Data Skills

| | |
|---|---|
| administered | developed |
| adjusted | estimated |
| allocated | forecasted |
| analyzed | managed |
| appraised | marketed |
| assessed | measured |
| audited | netted |
| balanced | planned |
| budgeted | prepared |
| calculated | programmed |
| computed | projected |
| conserved | qualified |
| corrected | reconciled |
| determined | reduced |

*Adapted from © 2017 Passport Career, LLC, www.passportcareer.com*

You can make a strong impression by including the language of the employer within the content of your resume. In other words, if an employer uses the word "teach" in a job description then you should use the word "teach." However, if the employer uses the word "educate" then you should also use the word "educate." An employer knows what they want and when they are reading your resume, they are looking for certain words that mean something to them. Often these are the words used in a job description.

Regarding design, use 10–12 point Arial or Helvetica font. If you are sending a hard copy to an employer, then print your resume on white paper, preferably paper that is heavier than normal so the resume has the feel of a presentation document. Be sure to use plenty of white space on your resume so it doesn't appear to be too dense with words. Avoid using underlines or all capital letters as these make a resume difficult to read. Also, it is helpful to use bullets to list your accomplishment and results statements so the reader is drawn to the next bullet if they decide not to finish reading the previous one.

Since most resumes are emailed to employers, it is helpful to convert your resume to a PDF format. By doing so, you can control the design so the resume looks as good as the information it contains.

Be sure to have at least one other person who is good with English to review the resume and critique it for you. A resume should be the best representation of you and your relevant experience. Good luck with your job search!

**SAMPLE RESUME**
Chronological resume for career change
U.S. Naval officer seeking an educational administrative and/or counseling position

## JAMES SMITH
1234 Main Ave | Annapolis, MD 21403 | (410) 749-0220 | jsmith@gmail.com |
www.linkedin.com/jamessmith

### CAREER SUMMARY

Ten years of experience as a seasoned counselor/educator working with diversified populations in a variety of work places and academic settings. Skills include human resource development management, educational development, creative problem solving, and personal motivation counseling. Support skills include writing, conceptualizing, and academic research. A personable and resourceful team player with vision and facility for inspiring individuals and groups to achieve best performance.

### RELEVANT EXPERIENCE

**Political Science Instructor, U.S. Naval Academy, Annapolis, MD**                    2015–present

*Teach courses in U.S. government, foreign affairs, history and international relations. Serve as academic advisor for midshipmen.*

- As a history and government professor at the U.S. Naval Academy, researched and developed course materials, and delivered four different courses for junior- and senior-year students during a two-year period. Received strong student evaluations in all classes, totaling over 500 individuals, in spite of teaching new offerings each semester.
- Developed reading projects and course assignments that resulted in a "love-of-sea" feeling in junior college students enrolled in a naval operations course that had been considered to be a "dreaded requirement."

**U.S. Naval Shipboard Division Officer**                    2012–2015

*Managed a 65-person division onboard a U.S. Naval aircraft carrier. Responsibilities included training, evaluating, and directing all activities of a complex and rapidly changing operation.*

- Continuously solved complex problems involving the maneuvering of aircraft and equipment on the hangar deck, managing five crews of men, to support flight operations by supplying the aircraft needed, at the time and place needed, and garaging aircraft being removed from the flight deck.
- Safely completed all scheduled operations under duress of intensive operating conditions, while maintaining high crew morale through ongoing personalized attention to the personal and professional development needs of individuals.

**Naval ROTC Instructor, University of Minnesota**                    2005–2012

*Taught semester-long, college-credit courses in navigation and naval operations. Served as the academic and military advisor to 60 junior-class NROTC students.*

- Located and discovered how to use complex training aids and visual graphics to motivate students enrolled in a college navigation course. Result was that while previous classes disliked celestial navigation and acquired techniques through rote memorization of formulas, these students became intrigued with content they could visualize and mastered techniques through real understanding.
- Counseled over 100 college students, assisting them with academic decision making within the context of long-term career perspectives.

### EDUCATION

**B.S. in Geology,** Colorado State University, Fort Collins, CO, 2000
**M.A. in Education,** University of Minnesota, Minneapolis, MN, 2005

**SAMPLE RESUME**
Chronological resume for IT field

## MARY ATKINS
354 West 154th Ave
San Francisco, CA 94110
(918) 234-5678
matkins@gmail.com
LinkedIn: www.linkedin.com/maryatkins

### CAREER SUMMARY

Six years of experience designing web pages and developing code for websites. Skills include:

- Programming/Scripting Languages: C++, HTML, Perl, JAVA, and UNIX
- Systems: MacOS, Win95, Solaris
- Software: Aldus Pagemaker, Adobe Photoshop, Corel PHOTO-PAINT, Microsoft Excel, Microsoft Word, QuarkXPress

### RELEVANT EXPERIENCE

**HTML Programmer at Beyer & Associates, 2015–present**

- HTML code for all Web pages designed by Conor Associates public relations firm.
- Developed client Web sites including flow charts, Perl scripts, and web-to-database applications.

**Graphic Designer at Beyer & Associates, 2014–2015**

- Created multimedia presentations, four-color brochures, and magazine ads.
- Product manager for client creative projects.
- Network integration assistant for the art department.

**Assistant Graphic Designer at San Francisco Community College, 2011–2014**

- Assisted in development of advertising/promotional materials for director's presentations.
- Designed posters and flyers for promotional events.
- Assisted in producing mechanicals.

**Assistant Computer Operator at the Quatro Corporation, 2010–2011**

- Entered client data into financial database.
- Managed client files.
- Generated financial reports in response to account inquiries.

### EDUCATION

**BA in Communications,** University of Maryland; College Park, MD, 2010, GPA: 3.55

## SAMPLE RESUME
Chronological resume for career changer
Teacher wanting to move to public relations or marketing field.

### SHAWNA MURRAY
9875 North Springfield Lane | Chicago, IL 60654
(555)654-1234 | smurray@gmail.com | LinkedIn: www.linkedin.com/shawnamurray

### SUMMARY
An experienced "up-front" communicator with experience in education and public relations that includes working with students grades K–12; teachers; and media personalities, such as journalists, disk jockeys, and television broadcasters. Top skills include public speaking, creative writing, innovative presenting, and acting as a media liaison. A dynamic, creative, well-rounded individual who delights in entertaining and influencing. Worked with various forms of media, including radio, television, and print journalism. Track record of success in proposing stories, conducting interviews, and providing public information. Often acknowledged for being "cool under pressure" and diplomatic in handling stressful "on the spot" situations.

### RELEVANT ACCOMPLISHMENTS

**Director, Humane Education and Public Relations, County Humane Society, 2017–present**

- Official spokesperson, participate in weekly television interviews and have a permanent time slot on Channel 23 news.
- Engage in weekly radio interviews to promote animal shelter and animal care.
- Speak to students, youth groups, and civic organizations on requested topics.
- Frequently affirmed by broadcasters and television producers to be "a natural" in conducting broadcast interviews.
- Created and developed Humane Education program for the County Humane Society.
- Taught students grade K–12 and their teachers about proper animal care, wildlife rehabilitation, and animal-related medicine and legislation.
- Prepare all correspondence—letters to students, Congressional representatives, sponsors, and celebrities; editor of a biweekly column for the *Journal*.
- Prepare all media public service announcements.

**Montessori Teacher, 6th Grade, Lincoln School, San Francisco, CA 2012–2017**

- Developed innovative teaching materials and programs, including subjects like Greek and Roman mythology, Arthurian legend, and basic Latin, which had never been taught in the school before.
- Used creativity, teaching skills, and love of interacting with youth to successfully prepare sixth graders for junior high.
- Gained valuable writing experience in college as an English major and taught English.
- Used writing skills to publish school newsletters and write proposals.

**Program Director, Summer Work Program, Day Camp, San Francisco, 2009–2013**

- Served as chief writer/editor and wrote newsletter ANIMAIL.
  Technical Publications Intern, IBM Inc., San Francisco, CA, 2008–2011
- Served as chief writer/editor.

### EDUCATION
**B.A. English**, University of Maryland, 2008

## Developing a Social Media Presence

You are, most likely, adept at navigating the internet and finding information online. However, are you aware of your online "brand" that has developed through social networks?

> Google your name and variations of your name, such as with or without your middle initial or middle name. What do you notice on the first page of search results? How about pages two and three? Are you pleased with what potential employers will learn about you if they Google your name and see the same results?

It is critical these days for you to take control of your social media presence and help develop your online brand, which is how others perceive you through what is shared about you or by you online. You can impact this significantly by taking a few simple steps to create a positive message about you as a professional.

The benefits of engaging with social networks to develop your professional brand will not only support your job search, but can really catapult your career over time.

Later, the three main social networks, LinkedIn, Facebook, and Twitter, will be discussed in more depth.

## Business Cards

In an initial meeting, business cards are exchanged either at the beginning of a conversation or at the end. Even though you may not have a current job, business cards for students are becoming more the norm. It is important to represent yourself as a professional and have your contact information immediately at hand for networking situations.

It is important to keep the card clean with no creases. It's best in a business card holder.

Typically, include your name, your title, your company's name, your company address, telephone number, email address, and any additional text. See the sample below.

Your University Name

**Mary Robinson**

Student Ambassador & Communications Intern
Major: Business; Minor: Journalism
Candidate for internship in:
Finance | Marketing | Analysis

1122 University Lane
University Town, NY USA
mrobinson@gmail.com
(555) 234-5678
LinkedIn.com/in/maryrobinson

University Logo

Leave blank the back of the business card so any additional, relevant information that arises in your conversation can be written here. Business cards are usually given at the end of a business meeting, as a way of politely concluding the conversation as well as confirming that you would like to be in touch with that person again. If you do not have any cards with you, contact the other person via email, text, or phone soon after the meeting, to give your contact details.

If the other person does not have a business card but you very much want their details, offer to write their details on the back of one of your cards.

## APP 5.3   Marketing yourself through effective communication

### Developing Your 30-second Elevator Pitch

You never get a second chance to make a first impression.

If you've ever searched for a job, you have probably been asked the question "Tell me about yourself." Most people fumble around with their reply and often begin sharing inappropriate personal or irrelevant information.

> Think about how you have in the past answered this question, write a few reflections statements below.

This is often the first question asked when conducting information interviews or networking. Your answer to this question is key to making a solid first impression and engaging the other person in a professional dialogue about who you are as a professional.

| Situations That Lead to Someone Saying "Tell me about yourself" |
| --- |
| • Conference networking with other participants |
| • Informational interview with working professionals |
| • Formal interview with potential employer |
| • Email communication with employers, recruiters, networking contacts, etc. |
| • Casual meeting, lunch, or other information situation with someone new |

Your answer can both engage the other in further dialogue to gain their interest in learning more about you, and lead to a more strategic conversation that can catapult you forward in your job search.

This is commonly referred to as an "Elevator Pitch" or a 30-second verbal resume. Why? The length of your reply should be no longer than the time it takes when you meet a person in the elevator and the elevator arrives at their floor. That's not a lot of time to make an impression! Typically, this is 15–30 seconds. That is why we refer to it as your 30-second pitch or 30-second verbal resume. However, many people are able to share powerful pitches in 15 seconds or less. Regardless, you don't want to exceed 30 seconds as going beyond that time frame, you would most likely lose the other person's attention.

Depending on your situation, your reply will vary, but the elements of your response will be similar in most situations. In order to develop an engaging and powerful reply, you need to understand the situation you are in and why the other person is asking the question in the first place.

Your goal with your reply is to create opportunity by setting the tone, engaging the other person in a dialogue, and sometimes moving the situation to action or next steps.

| Tips for Your Elevator Pitch |
|---|
| 1. Use only your first name and pronounce it slowly. Most people will not remember last names. |
| 2. Shake their hand firmly when introducing yourself and look them in the eye. |
| 3. Practice. Practice. Practice. You must know all of the elements so you can comfortably adapt them to your situation. |
| 4. Practice asking thoughtful questions to continue the dialogue. |

## What to include

- Your name.

- General information about where you are coming from.

- Your career focus and years of experience.

- Type of employment you are seeking.

- What you have done in your career.

- What you would like to ask this person.

### . . . all to be communicated in 30 seconds!

| Sample Pitch |
|---|
| Hello. I am Amy. I recently relocated to DC (or am an engineering student at *name of university or college*) and am seeking information about the DC job market. I have several months of experience through an intense internship with a local engineering firm. I am interested in civil engineering employment, but I don't know the local market. Do you know anyone who is a civil engineer or do you know someone who works with such professionals? |

| Good questions | Do NOT say: |
|---|---|
| • Do you know any economists or people who work with economists? <br>• Would you be willing to meet with me for a half-hour sometime next week? <br>• Do you know anybody who knows something about my career field? <br>• Do you know anyone in my career field? <br>• Do you know anybody at the university? | • Can you help me? <br>• Can you find me a job? <br>• Do you know where I can access information about this company? <br>• Do you know of any jobs in this field? <br>• Do you know of any positions at the university? <br>• Where can I find jobs in this field? |
| **Do** | **Don't** |
| • Be specific <br>• Use your first name only and say your name S-L-O-W-L-Y <br>• Use a company name for a previous employer if it is well-known in the United States | • Give general information <br>• Make a statement at the end—always keep the dialogue open—usually with a question <br>• Ask for a job, position, or employment opportunity!!! |

### Develop Your Technique

Write out your own 30-second branding statement:

## Writing Emails and Cover Letters

The quality of your cover letter or email can determine whether or not your resume is reviewed. A strong email or letter is more likely to engage the reader to look at your resume and hopefully be placed in the "read again" pile, while a weak letter could mean that both the resume and cover letter end up in the wastepaper basket or trash folder. Many applicants tend to lavish attention on the resume, while treating cover letters as a nuisance to be scribbled off quickly. We advise that you treat both your resume and your communication letters with the same attention to detail and thoughtfulness.

According to executive recruiting firms, few job hunters know how to write good cover letters. Here are some of the more common mistakes they find in letters:

### Appropriate salutations

The best method is to address the letter to an individual, ideally by finding the person with hiring responsibilities and addressing the letter to him or her. However, there are times when this is not possible and so it becomes necessary to use a generic salutation. In this situation, using "Gentlemen" or "Dear Sirs" could alienate the person receiving it if she is a woman. A more appropriate greeting would be "Dear Sir or Madam," or "To Whom It May Concern:".

### Typos and other mistakes

Errors of any type can send your cover letter and resume into oblivion. Find a friend with a keen eye who will proofread your cover letter and catch mistakes before you send it and the accompanying resume to a potential employer.

## Length

A long cover letter can be as much of an impediment to the job seeker as a brief, minimalistic one-paragraph document. A long letter requires readers to spend more than the usual 30 seconds reviewing it, and if they have a multitude of resumes with cover letters, it is not worth the investment of time. On the other hand, executive recruiters report that they are not impressed by a short letter that simply states that an application is being sent for consideration for an open position and to view the attached resume for more information. From their viewpoint, this is an incomplete application. The consensus is that a three-paragraph letter on one page is appropriate.

## Stating salary expectations

Even when a job description requests salary requirements, "negotiable" is usually a better response. Sometimes, the initial screening is based on salary expectations, and you do not want to be eliminated from the group to be interviewed because your salary expectations are either too high or too low. Salary expectations that are too high can price you out of contention, and if too low, may make you seem less qualified than other candidates.

## Components of the cover letter or email

Frequently, we are asked for a good cover letter sample that can be copied or used for a template to "fill in the blanks." We discourage both, as there is not a single cover letter that applies to all situations. For every application, a new letter should be drafted. You can use samples or templates as guides, but they should not be copied verbatim. Never use a form letter.

Now that the caveats have been covered, the question is what information should the letter include? Generally, a few paragraphs are sufficient. If you are able to personalize the email and send it to an individual, make sure the name and title of the person who is to review your materials are correct.

The opening paragraph should accomplish two things. First, it should announce the purpose of the letter. Second, it should give the reader a compelling reason to read on.

The next part represents the body of the letter. This section can be one to two paragraphs and should focus on how your unique mix of skills and experiences can contribute to the organization and/or how your unique mix of skills and experience fit the job profile for which you are applying. This is the part of the cover letter that can become too long. It should not be a restatement of your resume.

The closing paragraph will depend upon the situation. If you are responding to an announcement without a phone number or one stating "no phone calls," don't end your letter with the obligatory, "I will contact you the week of (date) to arrange a meeting to discuss my qualifications for the position." The closing should indicate the next desired action; if that is receiving a call to schedule an interview, then a simple statement, "I look forward to hearing from you," is appropriate.

## Components of a Cover Letter

Dear _____:

**Opening paragraph.** Grab their interest. Explain why you are writing; name the position or type of work for which you are applying. If writing in response to an advertised vacancy, mention how you learned of this opening. If you were referred by someone, mention his or her name.

**Middle paragraph(s).** Create interest in your background and market yourself. Explain why you are interested in working for this employer and specify your qualifications for this type of work. Highlight your particular achievements or other experiences in this field, and particularly those that address the job requirements. Refer to your enclosed resume, highlighting key points that illustrate how your skills, abilities and experience match the selection criteria.

**Closing paragraph.** Prompt action. Encourage follow-up by requesting an appointment or interview. Offer to call, specifying a time (e.g. "next week") or some similar suggestion to facilitate an immediate and favorable reply. State your interest or enthusiasm for meeting with an individual.

**End your letter with a simple salutation:**
Sincerely,
Your name
Email address
Phone number

**SAMPLE THANK YOU EMAIL/COVER LETTER**
Interview Follow-up

---

**TO:** Ian Russell <ianrussell@stealthfinancials.com>
**FROM:** William Mayer <wmayer@gmail.com>
**DATE:** May 8, 2017
**SUBJECT:** Thank you for meeting with me today

Dear Mr. Russell,

Thank you very much for taking time to meet with me today.

Our meeting confirmed my strong interest in the position of Financial Analyst as described by both you and Ms. Watkins. It would be a perfect match with my experience and skills.

I believe that the skills I developed through my experience in business and manufacturing can be effectively transferred, resulting in an effective and efficient approach to the operational and project needs of your company. Furthermore, I trust that my work experience in private industry, would allow me to make a valuable contribution to your department. I am a fast learner and intellectually curious with strong analytical skills and the ability to synthesize data and information.

Thank you for your consideration. I look forward to be working with you.

Best regards,

William Mayer
wmayer@gmail.com
(234)567-9876
www.linkedin.com/williammayer2

## SAMPLE THANK YOU EMAIL/COVER LETTER
Informational Interview

---

**TO:** Marissa Watkins, Director <Marissa.watkins@idia.org>
**FROM:** Kaitlyn Manning <kmanning@gmail.com>
**DATE:** November 9, 2017
**SUBJECT:** Thank you for meeting with me today

Dear Marissa,

Thank you for taking so much time to share with me the extensive and impressive educational exchange programs sponsored by the International Development Institute of America. I was both surprised and impressed by how much IDIA's office has grown over the last two years. I was also fascinated to hear the details about your career path. It confirms many of my own career interests and plans moving forward.

Also, thank you for sharing with me the names of other professionals in your career field and similar organizations. I have already reached out to Jeff Banner, and will let you know how that meeting goes.

Again, I'm grateful for your time and generosity. I look forward to staying connected and will send you a LinkedIn invitation to connect later today.

All the best,

Kaitlyn Manning
kmanning@gmail.com
234.543.1234
www.linkedin.com/kaitlynmanning

## SAMPLE THANK YOU EMAIL/COVER LETTER
Job application

**TO:** Human Resources <hr@germanicl.org >
**FROM:** John Bagalina <jbagalina@gmail.com>
**DATE:** March 15, 2017
**SUBJECT:** Enclosed resume for German Language Instructor

Dear Sir/Madam,

I am happy to enclose my resume to apply for the position of German Language Instructor at the German Institute of Culture and Language.

I offer over four years of language teaching experience with students at all levels and ages, and I am fluent in three languages: German, French, and English. I am a licensed middle- and high-school level language teacher in the State of New York. In addition, my studies in behavioral development and world cultures have added both dimension and practicality to my teaching experience.

As a life-long student of languages, I recognize the challenges that students can encounter when trying to develop a second or third language. To mitigate this, I encourage and facilitate the students' ownership of the language learning process and help them reach a measurable level of academic achievement as quickly as possible. Given my global academic studies and world travel, I also help students to develop a knowledge and appreciation for the culture behind the language. You can see examples of my teaching assignments and methodology on my LinkedIn profile.

I would greatly appreciate the opportunity to share my skills, knowledge, and love of teaching with your students.

I very much look forward to hearing from you.

Sincerely,

John Bagalina
jbagalina@gmail.com
345-567-7890
www.linkedin.com/johnbagalina

## Mastering Business Protocol/Culture and Etiquette

*Business culture section adapted from © 2017 Passport Career, LLC, www.Passport Career.com.*

Almost everything you do in your job search will have some aspect of culture tied to it. Whether it is the way you greet somebody in a meeting or how you write your resume. Culture, protocol, and etiquette are intrinsically linked to the job search. Your ability to master the nuances of the business culture will serve you well in your job search and throughout your career.

Learning and applying the business culture is critical to making a strong first impression as well as demonstrating professional behavior to your peers and potential employers.

Let's take a look at some of the U.S.-specific business etiquette that you will need to know.

### Greetings and introductions

Protocol for introductions is important. Such issues you should take note or include exchange of business cards, handshakes, gestures, hierarchy of introductions, and monikers including "Dr.," "Professor," or "Ms.," along with many other introductory nuances. Small talk is common and often important to develop business relationships. However, you often avoid small talk related to family, health, and other personal matters as well as politics and religion.

You will find that many people will introduce themselves by first name, and if they do so, then you may call them by their first name. University settings often have a more formal protocol, however, and frequently professors prefer to be addressed by their title of "Dr." or "Professor." You will need to carefully observe your situation to see how people present themselves and then follow suit.

You should feel comfortable presenting yourself by your first name. Keep in mind that people may have a difficult time pronouncing your name (both first and last) if it is not a common name in the United States. If this is the case, then be sure to help them learn your first name by creating a way to help them learn your name.

### Time

It is extremely important to be on time for interviews, networking events, and other job search activities. People are very time-conscious and being late may create a poor professional image. On the same note, you don't want to arrive too early and appear too enthusiastic or anxious. The rule of thumb is to arrive about 5–10 minutes before the beginning of a meeting.

### Communication style

**Nonverbal communication** is powerful. Master the nuances of eye contact, good posture, appropriate gestures and head nods, personal space, facial expressions, touching others on the arms, demonstration of listening, and use and placement of arms, hands, and body.

In the United States, it is important to learn appropriate eye contact. You should always look the person in the eye for a few seconds, then it is okay to look away before looking at them in the eye again. Do not "stare a person down" by continually looking at them without looking away. You look for a few seconds, then look away, then look at them in the eye again, then look away. If you don't look the person in the eye, then they may think you have something to hide, or that you are insecure, or that you are not to be trusted. If you are uncomfortable looking at others in the eye, then practice at home in a mirror or practice with friends, as this is important in the U.S. culture.

Your posture should be straight with no hunched-over shoulders. Stand up or sit up straight with shoulders back. Women should cross their legs at the ankle when sitting, and not at the knee. Men should sit with both feet on the floor, legs closer together.

Handshakes are very important as well. Handshakes should involve a firm grip from both men and women. It is important to practice your handshake with friends and get feedback from them as to whether your grip is too strong or too weak or limp. Make sure it is a confident handshake that is firm—not too hard or too soft—with both men and women.

As for personal space, most people are comfortable with a distance of about an arm's length between you and them.

Avoid putting your hands on your hips when talking or crossing your arms. Leave your arms comfortably at your side, or resting on a table, or hands-only crossed in front of you.

**Verbal communication, assertiveness, and self-reliance** include language/dialects, "small talk," greetings, asking questions, self-promotion, directness, and speaking one's mind. It also includes an accurate representation of skill level, how to present yourself in interviews, and how to appropriately network with both nationals and expats. In addition, verbal communication can help you to take responsibility for planning your job search and making career decisions by asking for help when needed.

Americans are direct with their communication, for the most part. If you ask a question, such as directions to an organization, you will get a direct answer, such as how to get there or they will let you know that they don't know how to get there. However, sometimes there are subtle differences in the culture with regard to direct communication. Americans will not always tell you that they don't like something, such as your resume or your communication style. Americans consider this to be disrespectful, and instead will be complimentary even if they don't like something.

In interviews, you will be asked direct questions, such as questions about your strengths and weaknesses, and are expected to provide an honest reply. These types of questions need to be carefully considered as you want to respond, but don't want to be so honest that you are presenting yourself in a negative way. See the section on interviews for further guidance in this area.

## Workplace norms and time

Workplace norms in the United States include equality among women and men. Although this is the spoken and written practice, there are many "unwritten" rules in many organizations where women face challenges in competing with men for senior-level positions. That said, in most cases, women find there are many opportunities that they may not find available to them in other countries.

Age issues can become apparent in many areas across the country. There is a lot of age discrimination against people who are older. However, there are certain markets where age can be a benefit—especially for consulting positions, where experience is highly regarded. Washington, DC is an example of an area where age can sometimes work in your favor.

The work situation is often informal, with staff addressing management by their first names. This is not always the case, and you should observe the situation to see how others address others.

Opportunities for promotion are available and in many cases offered to those who prove their value to the organization.

Salaries are often negotiated, even when an employer says that they don't have any room in the budget to negotiate it. Many times you can negotiate aspects of the compensation package, such as time off, work hours, flexible work arrangements, and other aspects of the job.

### Gender and Age in Business

Gender and age relate to and affect the following: applying for jobs, getting hired, networking, interviewing, and the ability to be effective in a job. Keep in mind that age and gender play key roles in many societies and cannot be dismissed regardless of your opinion about the subject. Now is not the time to push your own agenda on this topic. This does not mean, however, that you need to succumb to harassment if you are female. It does mean, though, that you need to be aware of the issues and respectfully address them, as needed.

| Business Culture, Behavior, Protocol, and Etiquette<br>Reproduced with permission. Copyright 2017 by Passport Career, LLC. All rights reserved.<br>www.PassportCareer.com | | |
|---|---|---|
| Greetings and introductions | How do you greet others appropriately? How do you introduce yourself and introduce others—or how can you expect to be introduced? | |
| Appropriate dress | What should you wear? What should you not wear? What is acceptable for women and men in the workplace? | |
| Communication: Verbal and nonverbal | What do your body language and gestures say about you? Do they say you are a respectful professional? | |

| Time | What can you expect with regard to starting and ending appointments on time? How can you plan appropriately for these time expectations? | |
|---|---|---|
| Gender and age issues in the workplace and other workplace norms | How are women viewed and treated in the workplace or with a specific employer of interest? How does an employer of interest view young workers versus older workers? What other expectations can you have for the work environment? | |

## APP 5.4  Networking Effectively

### Networking through Informational Interviews

Networking is an effective job search strategy of making connections with individuals and groups of people who can help you to build relationships that can lead to job offers or help you with your career success. Research indicates that more than 80% of all job seekers find their jobs through some kind of networking strategy.

Informational interviews are excellent ways to develop your network and leverage professionals to support your job search.

Networking contacts should include people you know professionally, socially, and personally.

| Potential Networking Contacts | | |
|---|---|---|
| **Professional contacts** | **Social contacts** | **Personal contacts** |
| • Members of professional organizations and associations<br>• Contacts from informational meetings, conferences, trade shows, etc.<br>• Coworkers and former coworkers<br>• Former employers<br>• Chamber of Commerce | • Current/former classmates<br>• Alumni<br>• Acquaintances (sports, clubs, social activities, etc.)<br>• Business people (bank manager, insurance agent, etc.)<br>• Professionals (doctor, lawyer, dentist, etc.)<br>• Religious groups (clergy, members)<br>• Sports clubs | • Friends<br>• Relatives<br>• Neighbors (current and past) |

### How to Leverage your Network to Support your Job Search

Inform them of your job search and ask if they can suggest others who might be of assistance. Keep in mind that upon accepting a job offer, contact those in your network who assisted you and/or are referring you to others. Be sure to thank them and offer to help them in the future.

| 20 Strategies to Grow and Maximize Your Network | |
|---|---|
| 1. Use every opportunity to make contacts. Sometimes contacts come from the most unlikely places or people.<br><br>2. Choose members based on information not position. Most networking is for information and referrals so consider what your information needs are, not the position of the individual.<br><br>3. Be specific about what you want from the people you contact and make reasonable and appropriate requests. | 8. Protect those in your network. Don't refer people who may reflect poorly on you.<br><br>9. Don't be afraid to ask for information. Ask for what you need. Most people want to help others and it makes them feel good about themselves.<br><br>10. Say thank you. Show appreciation to those who help you.<br><br>11. Volunteer to assist in organizing special events and meetings for a group at your academic institution. |

| 20 Strategies to Grow and Maximize Your Network | |
|---|---|
| 4. Follow up when you receive information, advice, or a referral. Let the person know the result of the contact you made or advice you received from them. They will be more likely to help you in the future. | 12. Attend welcoming programs for groups of interest. |
| | 13. Offer to lead a job support program for other students in your career field. |
| | 14. Join LinkedIn and invite participants in this program. |
| 5. Help others. Networking is a two-way street. Others will be more likely to assist you and more individuals will seek you out when you have a reputation for providing information and advice willingly. | 15. Identify and connect with participants of local affiliate groups. |
| 6. Get to know the right people. Our brand/reputation is influenced as much by who we know as by our past work. Get to know the key people in your field or the influential people in your organization. | 16. Attend career service presentations on topics related to your career. |
| | 17. Contact alumni in your area (or U.S. at large) who work in your career field. |
| 7. Identify your social strengths and weaknesses and develop strategies for improving your effectiveness. If you are better in "one-on-one" situations take advantage of them. If you have difficulty in formal situations, such as conferences or meetings, find ways to improve your skills in these settings. | 18. If you are an international student or student with international interests, ask an embassy for a listing of local organizations (for-profit and nonprofit) that are involved with your country of interest or home country, then research and contact them for meetings. |
| | 19. Set up one information meeting each week. |
| | 20. Search LinkedIn to find 10–20 people who currently work in your field and then "cold-call" them for a meeting. |

## Tips to Make a Good First Impression with a New Networking Contact

- Talk about your talent, not your title

- Listen, then share

- Speak slowly and clearly—in an assertive voice

- Be specific, reasonable, appropriate with requests

- Follow up and send a "thank-you" note/email within 24 hours

## Networking through LinkedIn, Facebook, and Twitter

Chances are you are already using social media for personal and, possibly, professional reasons. You may have a Facebook page or Twitter account. You may even have a LinkedIn profile. As you think about these three social media giants, consider the networking power available to you. Learning a few strategies and techniques can move a stalled search into a powerful one. Below are some tips to help you build, nurture and grow your networking power through these three social media.

### LinkedIn

If you haven't already set up a profile on LinkedIn, now is the time to take that step. You will find a plethora of resources and tools available to you to network effectively with professionals in your career field and organizations of interest.

Take time to explore the many Discussion Groups available to you. Try to avoid joining groups that only focus on job postings, and instead focus on groups that actively discuss topics in your career field. As you develop a comfort level with the conversations, be sure to comment on others' posts, contribute resources/links to articles, or pose questions to the group.

You will also want to identify thought leaders in your career field. "Follow" them, try to connect formally as LinkedIn connections, and contribute to conversations they are involved in.

Find companies and organizations that are of interest to you. Recent research shows that more than 90% of employers have an active presence and recruit on LinkedIn. Most of these organizations have a company page where you can learn about what they do and what topics are most relevant to their needs.

Search for alumni in your career field or organizations of interest by visiting the university or college page (search using the institution's name) and click on "Alumni."

Be sure to contribute content with your Groups, on your status page, and with your interactions with organizations. By contributing to professional conversations, you are developing your brand as a leading edge professional.

---

**Tips for Your LinkedIn Profile**

- Develop a profile using key words, skills, and achievements that shares more than what you would on your resume. Take a half hour every month to update your profile and keep it fresh.
- Upload samples of projects or links to blogs/articles/research relevant to your career interests.
- Add skills to the Skills section.
- Add a clear photo/headshot that has you looking into the camera and smiling.
- Ask professors, mentors, current/former employers and colleagues for recommendations. Try to have one to two recommendations for each position included on your profile.
- Remember to include school activities and volunteer work.

---

### Facebook

Although you may already use Facebook for social reasons, there are many professional reasons to be involved with Facebook. If you choose to only use Facebook for personal reasons, be sure to visit the Facebook settings to ensure maximum privacy.

Should you choose to use Facebook for your job search and professional networking, you may need to overhaul your Facebook profile or set up a separate one altogether.

You can build your Facebook network by finding company pages, organizations of interest, alumni groups and other professional groups. Be sure to "like" their page and request to join their group. Once you are accepted in the group, engage in professional discussions with other members.

## Twitter

Twitter is an excellent way to learn about industries, identify and follow thought-leaders, stay in-the-know with organizations, and build your professional brand. You will need to create your Twitter "handle" or username, which you should try to keep professionally using your own name or relevant career key words. Add your photo (can be the same headshot you use for LinkedIn).

You will want to add a professional profile that explains your career background, skills, major achievements, and a brief notation that you are seeking career opportunities. Cross-link your profile by adding a link to your LinkedIn profile.

Be sure to follow thought-leaders, companies, recruiters and others of professional interest, with the hope that they will also follow you. Send out tweets daily or twice a day with career-related information to share. You can use Hootsuite to organize and schedule tweets so you can plan this activity weekly or monthly without having to remember to get on Twitter every day.

## APP 5.5 Finding Jobs and Internships

### How People Really Get a Job!

Most job seekers immediately jump online and search through the plethora of job sites or search on Google for job openings. This seems to make sense. After all, you are looking for a job. However, by doing this, you fall into a common trap among job seekers. Yes, there are millions of jobs posted online, and you will want to stay on top of those opportunities. However, current research shows that most successful job seekers find their opportunities through effective and strategic networking or through targeted job opportunities, such as those found through career fairs at your institution or your institution's online postings by employers who are connected with your career services office.

While you shouldn't completely ignore the numerous websites dedicated to posting jobs, we advise you to spend most of your time focusing on the strategic networking and targeted opportunities.

### Where to Find Relevant Opportunities

If you're looking for job vacancies and internship opportunities, you can find thousands of job websites posting them for every career field and at every level. However, as previously discussed, most people find their job through some form of networking. Try not to be fooled by websites promising exclusive access to opportunities. The jobs that are posted online have millions of other job seekers accessing them and applying.

However, research indicates that many employers that hire through job vacancies tend to have more success with hires who apply for jobs on their corporate or organizational website. Therefore, you may want to identify the employers of interest before hopping online and randomly seeking job postings.

Another strategy for finding jobs is through internal referrals. Many large employers have referral programs in place that reward current employees who refer external job candidates to open vacancies. If the referred job seeker is hired, the employee receives some kind of compensation or bonus.

LinkedIn posts millions of jobs by employers who actively seek out candidates through LinkedIn.

Your university or college career services office also posts job vacancies by employers that have established relationships with the institution. These job leads can be much better than others found through random web searches.

The bottom line is that there is no magic bullet for finding a job vacancy that has high potential without putting in the work that it takes to secure that job. In other words, you need to network, network, network.

Internships, on the other hand, can be a more formal process. To secure an internship, you often need to apply through the formal, online channels shared by employers. Occasionally, networking can help secure an internship, but be aware that the process is often more formal and you will most likely have to apply along with everyone else interested in the internships.

## Participating in Career Fairs

Career fairs are frequently coordinated by the career services office at your institution as well as by professional associations and special interest groups. Career fairs are excellent ways to meet with employers, ask questions about their hiring process and job opportunities, and make contacts with whom you can contact for future opportunities.

Be sure to follow the guidance of the office or institution sponsoring the career fair as many require registration, copies of your resume and sometimes appointments to meet with employers.

## APP 5.6 Acing the Interview

You need to develop interviewing skills well before you reach the job interview stage. If you are not experienced with interviews, seek the help of a career advisor as you must be prepared for the kinds of questions that you are likely to be asked.

Your goal in each job interview is to discover whether you really want the job and, if so, to lead your interviewer(s) to making an attractive offer. To do that, you need to come to each interview prepared to help direct the outcome. That doesn't mean that you aggressively take over the interview. It does mean, however, that you come prepared with information, the right attitude, and a clear goal. A successful interview usually follows these five steps:

1. Personal introductions and small talk.
2. Short introduction of yourself and your interest in the job with that organization.
3. Questions and answers to establish your qualifications and interest in the job and to assess how well you would fit in with that organization.
4. Your own questions to obtain additional information about the organization, the job, and the career possibilities.
5. Closure involving either a job offer and salary negotiation or clarification of the steps remaining to a job offer.

### Preparing for Interviews

Learn as much as possible about the organization for which you are interviewing. You can usually get information online. Be prepared to ask questions as well as to answer them. Remember, interviews are a two-way proposition: You'll be deciding whether a company is the right place for you, just as they assess whether you are the right person for them. Employers are rarely impressed by job candidates who are so passive that they have no questions to ask. On the other hand, don't try to take over the interview.

Prepare for each interview by answering questions like these:

1. What business is the employer in?
   - What products/services does it sell and to whom?
   - What is its history?
   - Where is it heading in the future?
   - What thing is the organization noted for and proudest of?
2. What are the three major challenges this organization now confronts or will confront?
3. What specific value can you be to the company in solving these problems?
4. Which of your top skills would be most valuable to this company?
5. How do your past achievements and current goals relate to the goals and mission of this company?

6. If you were the interviewer, why would you hire you for the job you want? List ten reasons, but use only the top three or so. Blasting the employer with too many reasons on the spot may make you look over- or under-confident.

7. What is the salary range the company pays for a job like this? (Find this out through information interviews.)

8. What is the minimum salary you will accept and your realistic ideal salary?

Envision your interviewers moving from asking you questions to convincing you of the benefits of working at that organization. Picture the interview coming to a close with the interviewers offering you the job at a fair salary and your thanking them and asking for a couple of days to think it over. This envisioning process will help you prepare for the interview and generate the personal confidence you'll need to do a terrific job.

Following are some examples. Practice answering these until you have concise, confident, enthusiastic responses that are always well-targeted to the job you seek:

1. Tell us something about yourself.

2. What are you looking for in a job?

3. Why do you want to leave your current job?

4. Why are you interested in working with this organization?

5. What background and experience do you have to bring?

6. What are your top strengths?

7. What are your weaknesses? (Answer by explaining how you are transforming a former minor weakness into a strength. Don't say that your only weakness is that you work too hard. Employers don't like to hear this.)

8. What are your future goals and plans?

9. What salary are you asking for? What did you earn in your last job?

10. What would you like to know about us? What questions do you have for us?

(Be prepared to ask at least three questions that show you know something about the organization and want to know where it's heading.)

## During the Interview

Be honest, assured, prepared, and energetic during the interview, but most of all, be your best self. During the interview, you will want to stress how your skills/experience relate to the job. Express enthusiasm for the opportunity to provide a valuable service for the organization. Of course, you don't want to be overbearing about your knowledge and skills. Don't pretend to have all of the answers to the organization's needs. That could be a real turnoff to an interviewer. Instead, let your personal confidence in your abilities and your enthusiasm for the job shine through. Be prepared to answer questions honestly, and don't pretend to know something you don't. Be goal oriented during the interview so you and the interviewer stay on track. Remember, you want to get a positive job offer and not just have a nice conversation.

At appropriate times during the interview, be prepared to ask questions like these:

1. What kind of person would you consider an ideal candidate for this job?
2. What kind of challenges does this job offer?
3. What are the organization's primary goals and plans for the future?
4. What achievements in your division make you the proudest?
5. What kinds of people would I be working with here?
6. How would you describe the management style here?
7. What kind of advancement would be possible for anyone performing this job well?
8. What traits do you appreciate most in an employee?
9. What are the major strengths of the organization?

If you are seriously interested in the position, begin moving the interview toward a job offer. Think of yourself as a salesperson closing the deal. Don't leave the interview without offering your interviewer(s) ample opportunity to purchase your services. Ask questions like: "What do you think? Do we have a possible match here between your requirements and my qualifications?" If your interviewers show some reluctance, try to discover their real objections. If they have some reservations about a particular aspect of your experience or skill, respond with positive facts and examples to resolve any false concerns. If their objections are legitimate, reconsider whether the position is suitable for you.

If you are asked salary-related questions early in the interview, answer generally. Just say that your salary requirements are negotiable and depend upon the job requirements. Once there is strong mutual interest, go ahead and discuss salary. Ask the interviewer what salary range is available for the position. If the range is acceptable, decide what your worth is and why you think so. Base that on your experience and skills and not the fact that you need the money. However, if the top of their salary range is below the going rate for this position and below your minimum requirements, express some concern. If your qualifications and experience are limited, it may be fair. But if you are well qualified, don't sell yourself short. You may want to stress again the value you bring to the organization. Ask about additional bonuses, special benefits, or significant salary increases after a three- to six-month trial. When you have a firm offer, express your serious interest. Ask the interviewer to put the offer, including any special agreements, in writing. Finally, inquire when the organization would like your answer.

## After the Interview

Immediately after each interview (within 24 hours), send an email thanking the interviewer for meeting with you. Use the email to indicate any additional points to support your value to the organization. If you are seriously interested in the position, say so and express your hope for a favorable agreement. Include your telephone number so they can reach you for further information or discussion.

If you haven't heard anything from the employer within a reasonable amount of time (two weeks), pursue the matter by telephone.

Also, when you have another job offer, call another company that also interests you. This confirmation that you are valuable to another employer often results in action. Be sure to express the confidence that you could make a valuable contribution to the company. If you have acquired any new information, skills, or insights related to the position, mention them. Close by asking whether you are still a candidate. If so, ask whether they have any questions that you could answer or if there is anything else that you might do to support your candidacy. This kind of follow-up can considerably increase your chances of success.

## Evaluating and Negotiating Job Offers

At some point, after conducting a number of interviews, your efforts will begin paying off in the form of job offers. The ideal situation, of course, is to have several job offers. If you have done a thorough and assertive job search campaign, that is very likely to happen.

As you reach this final stage of the job search, there are a few important things to consider. The first issue is what to do after you get a job offer. Do you take it? Do you try for others? What if it's close to what you want but not exactly? These, of course, are questions that only you will be able to answer, and they warrant discussion with your support group. Consider the advancement opportunities, management style, work environment, and your gut feelings. If you have a tentative offer or are being seriously considered for a job you really want, resist the temptation to halt your job campaign. Tentative job offers often do not pan out. Continue your interviewing process until you get a firm, written job offer that really appeals to you.

| Interview DOs | Interview DON'Ts |
|---|---|
| • Prepare for the interview | • Arrive late. |
| • Know the organization's purpose, strengths, and problems. | • Forget your interviewer's name(s). |
| • Know how you can be of value. | • Ask what the company does. |
| • Dress appropriately (the way people dress at that organization). | • Bring and read notes. |
| • Bring samples of your work. | • Get lost in your own thoughts. |
| • Know what points you want to make. | • Focus on your need for the job. |
| • Be prepared to ask insightful questions. | • Pretend to know things you don't. |
| • Sell your skills, interest, energy, and achievements. | • Indicate that you have all the organization's answers. |
| • Relate your career goals, skills, and achievements to the mission of the organization. | • Just sit and wait for the interviewer(s) to ask questions. |
| | • Answer a question not asked. |
| | • Give long, meandering responses. |

| Interview DOs | Interview DON'Ts |
|---|---|
| • Listen closely to questions, and respond only to what is asked. <br> • Know your field's salary ranges (the "going rate") for the type of position you want and the minimum salary you're willing to accept. <br> • Answer the real question—Why should they hire you? | • Indicate that your main interests are in salary and benefits. <br> • Monopolize the conversation. <br> • Be overly concerned about time off. <br> • Be defensive. <br> • Be dogmatic. <br> • Avoid eye contact. |

# APP 5.7 Tips For Success

## Maximize Your Resources with Career Services

The career services office at your university or college is often one of the most valuable student services available to you. Most offices are staffed with highly skilled career advisors who can help you with your resume, elevator pitch, career plan, interview preparation, and strategy to find employment.

We strongly encourage you to avail yourself of this invaluable resource and service. Schedule an appointment with a career advisor and ask them to review your career plan, action items, and strategy. They can work closely with you to ensure you've got all bases covered and are moving forward.

Keep in mind, however, that they can NOT find you a job. That is your job. However, like any professional sports team, they can coach you on strategy and help you see the bigger picture while you're buried in the minutiae of the job search game.

## Succeeding at Your New Job or Internship

A great job or internship offers three major benefits: opportunities for contribution, professional, and personal growth, and income. Research studies consistently show that the main benefit people want from a job is the opportunity to make a worthwhile contribution. We're unlikely to experience a sense of meaning or purpose in life unless we know that our skills and energies are being used productively.

The second most important benefit your job can offer is the chance to grow. Growing means using and developing your skills along with learning and applying new knowledge. Growing means being stimulated to do and be your best. That is far more important than having a comfortable job. You're likely to become bored and unmotivated in a comfortable job.

The third benefit, usually overemphasized, is income. A good salary is important for a sustainable lifestyle, healthy self-concept, and as compensation for worthwhile service performed. Being paid a good salary alone, however, is insufficient to provide job satisfaction. It takes all three benefits for that. Surprisingly, your income is likely to be the least important benefit unless it is considerably lower than average. That observation comes as a result of our work with numerous career changers who were earning a good salary but hated their jobs because they lacked the first two greater benefits.

We encourage you to keep your career and life goals in mind. Remember that career development is a lifelong process. Your job is the vehicle that enables you to carry out your worthy life goals. Your job, however, is not the end of the line: it's only the beginning. If you have a job where you're performing useful service and growing, you're sure to reach a point where you'll be ready to make a bigger contribution. Then, it will be time for you to revise your career goals and get ready to play a bigger game in your life. And as you do, your valuable service will command a greater income. So let's move forward with your job or internship search, give it all you've got, and exercise your self-empowering skills to the fullest.

One of the major considerations once you get into a job is how to make the most of it and succeed in your job. The following is a list of ideas to help you think of ways to succeed and develop your career.

# APP 5.8 Developing Career Experience Now!

We strongly encourage you to take advantage of the many opportunities available to you to gain professional experience. By doing so, you will add quality content to your resume and make yourself more marketable.

In addition, you will gain invaluable insight into different employers, job environments, and business culture. All of this experience will help you with career decision-making, refining your career objective, and defining your ideal employment environment. Further, you will expand your network and gain confidence with your skills and knowledge.

Below are five ways to develop your career experience.

## Job Shadowing

Identify people working in your career field at various levels (entry, mid-career, managerial, executive) and request the opportunity to observe them for a day, a few days, or even a week or more. Your goal is to see what a typical day is and observe behaviors that help the individual accomplish their job.

## Study Abroad

Most institutions have a Study Abroad office. We encourage you to visit the office and their website to learn about opportunities available to you. Study Abroad opportunities allow you to travel abroad for a week, a month, a semester or longer while gaining college credit and invaluable global experience.

## Internships

Unless you already have work experience, it will be challenging to find a job these days without at least having an internship on your resume. Internships have become an expectation by employers interviewing job candidates who are new to the job world. Internships provide a formal opportunity to gain real-world experience in your career field. Many are paid opportunities and some are not. They range from one month to one year with the average being a semester long. You can add this experience to your resume and social media profiles, thereby having real-world experience to discuss at networking meetings and job interviews. Be sure to connect with your career services office to discuss with a career advisor your internship options.

## Volunteer Work

Volunteering at a charity, religious institution, campus office, or a multinational employer can expose you to the professional world if you take part in designing the volunteer experience and ensure you will be applying your academic knowledge to the situation. For example, if you are studying accounting, you could volunteer to do the accounting for a church group or for a campus organization. Keep in mind that more than half of today's employers consider volunteer work to be equivalent to paid employment.

## Campus Organizations

Participating in campus activities through formal organizations can offer you the opportunity to practice networking skills, participate in professional activities and volunteer for positions that allow you to apply your academic knowledge to gain experience.

| Career Success Tips | | |
|---|---|---|
| • Involve yourself in new tasks.<br>• Take accountability for beginning to end of projects.<br>• Assume increased decision making related to your tasks.<br>• Team yourself with experts from whom you can learn.<br>• Look for challenging situations that require problem-solving or innovation.<br>• Make presentations. | • Join a new project committee.<br>• Join a project with another function.<br>• Create opportunities for exposure to higher levels of management.<br>• Find areas of growth or trouble and create the opportunity to take charge of the situation.<br>• Assume opportunities to influence others including peers, internal and external clients or higher-level managers. | • Conduct an analysis and summarize causes of a failed project.<br>• Study client needs.<br>• Involve yourself in a new technical area or with new procedures.<br>• Involve yourself in an outside, professional organization.<br>• Identify a need and develop a new service.<br>• Study some area, new to you, in which you need to be more effective. |

## Summary

To launch a successful job search, you will need to develop the tools and strategies that will help you network effectively and strategically. It is important that you understand that the majority of jobs are never posted online or in the newspaper. This is what we call the "hidden" job market, which is the opposite of the traditional or visible job market.

Once you're ready to launch your job search, you'll need to assess what you have to offer to different employers before you target them for employment opportunities. Researching employers is also critical in the game—you want to find employers that match your interests, values, skills, and abilities. Next, you'll need to develop a results-oriented resume so you can begin talking with others about potential employers.

Once you get interviews, you need to prepare well for the questions you'll be asked, but, also for the questions you'll want to ask. You'll need to assess job offers and, if all goes well, land a great job in a reasonable period of time. The key to all of these stages is preparation. Preparation can make the difference between finding meaningful work versus finding just another job. Good luck with your job search!

# Special Groups

Congratulations. If you are reading this section, you have probably completed the majority of activities in this book. You have an increased knowledge of the workplace including career options and job description. You have a vocabulary that describes your skills, interests, abilities, skills, passions, and values. You have hopefully set a plan and are ready to take action.

This last section applies to a few populations with specific needs related to career development and plan implementation. While there are many unique categories, for the purposes of this text we have selected the three that are the most general and typical of the students in career classes. This is not meant to minimize the unique situations that are relevant to other groups. If you are in a unique situation, the resources contained in this APP might be of assistance. It is also important to note that this section was written from the perspective of someone doing career exploration and job seeking while based in the United States.

maxsattana/Shutterstock.com

### APP 6.1     International Students

Adjusting to Life in the United States
English language
Social support
Self-reliance
Geography and Career Planning
Resilience

### APP 6.2     Veterans

Just Tell Me What to Do
Identity
Reframe Your Thinking
Your Transferable Skills

### APP 6.3     Adults

Geographic Limitations
Experience
Managing Multiple Roles
Opportunity Cost
Bad Breaks

### APP 6.4     APP ACTIONS

Preparing to Work in Your Home Country
Preparing to Work in a Third Country
Career Planning for Your Home or Another Country
Ten Specific Cultural Barriers and Strategies

# APP 6.1 Career Considerations for International Students

## Do you know people who:

- Are from other countries, recently arrived in the United States to study, and have many U.S. American friends? (Heretofore referred to as "Americans.")
- Have a balance of American friends and friends from their home country?
- Feel confident with their English, even though they are not fluent?
- Ask a lot of questions, but are from a country where this is not common practice?

maximl/Shutterstock.com

If so, you know international students or U.S. immigrants who are acculturating to the United States and are developing a strong balance between their home culture and the U.S. culture.

*The best way to predict the future is to create it.*

—Peter Drucker

Hundreds of thousands of individuals from around the world arrive in the United States each year to study at one of the many institutions of higher education—mostly community colleges and universities. If you are one of these individuals, you already have experienced a significant life transition that rivals that of your impending career transition from college to work. The cultural transition to life and academia in the United States is one that presents both challenges and opportunities, and for many it presents new career possibilities that may or may not have been explored prior to arrival in the United States.

Career planning and related decision-making, goal setting, and action is often rooted in the culture where one plans to work. This book is reflective of a Western model of career planning and a U.S.-style job search. Opportunities are vast, and choices are diverse. This is not true for all countries.

There are many cultural aspects to the career-planning process. As you begin to understand your own cultural orientation and the cultural differences in the country where you are studying, as well as how your background influences this process, you can begin to use your cultural knowledge as a strength and an asset in planning your career.

In this App, you will explore the impact of culture on the career-planning process and identify potential barriers that may impede this process. In addition, you will identify strategies for addressing these cultural differences so that you will be able to recognize what areas you may need to work on and therefore effectively acculturate to the country where you will be living and working.

## Adjusting to Life in the United States

Nearly every country and culture is represented somewhere and in some way in the United States. Why, then, do newcomers struggle to understand the complexity of the culture that seemingly must be mastered in order to effectively acculturate to this country?

If you arrived in the United States to study and it's your first time living in the country, you have probably experienced a fair amount of culture shock. The office that supports international students has hopefully been helpful in guiding you through some of the phases of culture shock. If not, be sure to stop by and ask for resources and support. Doing this will be a significant step toward U.S. acculturation. In other words, by asking for what will help make life easier for you, you are demonstrating a cultural behavior of Americans. Acculturation, then, involves change—both external and internal behaviors—in individuals as they directly experience a new culture.[1]

Research indicates that although many cultural themes impact one's acculturation, there appear to be three consistent themes across the literature that warrant closer examination:[2]

1. Confidence in English abilities and fluency in the language;

2. Social interactions and support of Americans in the new culture and others from home culture; and

3. Individualism versus collectivism.

Let's look at each of these.

focal point/Shutterstock.com

## English Language

Language and culture are inextricably intertwined. Command of the language means understanding colloquial expressions, the business language, pronunciation, intonation, and other subtleties that influence how people react to and interact with you.

If your plans involve working in the United States and English is not your native language, you will need to continually work on improving your English. English continues to be the dominant language in the workplace, and there are few signs that this will change in the foreseeable future. You will need to develop your business English, improve pronunciation, understand humor, and learn the endless colloquial expressions that are often confusing when interpreted literally or out of context.

It is interesting to note, however, that some research indicates that your confidence regarding your English abilities will play a significant role in your acculturation to the country. In fact, some research indicates that confidence in your language skills is more important to your acculturation than fluency in the language.[3]

Self-confidence is a strong American value, which may contribute to the issue of acculturation in the United States. Not only demonstrating self-confidence, but also internalizing it will be empowering to you as you plan your career.

How has your command of the English language impacted your acculturation?

PAUSE

## Social Support

Adjusting to another culture is often made easier when you develop strong support systems. We recommend that you develop a support network of other international students or others from your country or culture, and another support network of Americans—be they students or others living near you.

Rawpixel.com/Shutterstock.com

If you do not feel comfortable interacting with U.S. citizens, you will struggle to adjust to a U.S. work environment that will demand that you do so. You will also miss out on the opportunity to develop your self-confidence in interacting with Americans—thus impacting your language confidence as well.

However, we also recognize that it is critical to be able to connect with others who understand what you are going through with regard to cultural adjustment. Therefore, we encourage you to balance your life with people who will meet your personal, social, and professional needs. This will serve multiple purposes as you plan for your career, including developing a career network, gathering balanced information, and helping you to adapt to a foreign culture without relinquishing the culture that makes you who you are.

Define your current social network. In what ways could it be improved to assist with the career planning and job search process?

PAUSE

## Self-Reliance

In some countries, the culture dictates a stronger familial and community connection than in the United States. Although many Americans have strong connections with their families, there exists the American value of taking individual responsibility to tackle the daily challenges of academic, social, and career situations.

Mastering this independence is a daily struggle for many international students who may be accustomed to having family or community input into daily decisions and making decisions based on how they will impact the family and the community. The implications for independence can be intimidating for one who is not accustomed to "holding the reigns" or acting independently of other's thoughts and decisions.

To act independently regarding career planning, you need to develop a culturally appropriate style of assertiveness. Assertiveness will allow you to ask the right questions to get to the right answers while maintaining your dignity and not risking the embarrassment of others, which many non-Americans fear they may do if they ask too many questions. Assertiveness, on the contrary, is an American value that allows you to ask questions respectfully and be respected in return for doing so appropriately.

**PAUSE**

Define a culturally appropriate style of assertiveness. Think of examples where you have observed inappropriate assertiveness—too strong, too weak, too confrontational, and so on. How will you apply this to your job search?

allstars/Shutterstock.com

## Geography and Career Planning

Many international students hope to begin working in the United States to either gain some U.S. work experience before returning to their home or third country, or in hopes of permanently immigrating to the United States. Other students plan to return to their home country—be it Ghana, India, or Argentina. Others seek employment in a third country—many opting for Western European countries or large, cosmopolitan cities, such as Paris, London, or Hong Kong. Your decision on where you will live in many ways impacts the way you plan for your career. Let's illuminate this by looking at these options.

## The United States

Although it may seem to make sense that a career in the United States should be an easy transition from your studies, this is usually not true for international students. Current politics dictate visa requirements and length of stay in the United States, and many employers are hesitant to engage in the lengthy process and complex procedures required to hire nonnationals.

At the same time, international students have much to offer a U.S. employer when it comes to diversity, global perspectives, other languages, and international experience.

Nonetheless, planning a career in the United States is fraught with challenges—both legal and cultural. The legal challenges are best addressed by your international student office or through the U.S. government's immigration website.

## Your Home Country

For many years, international students were sent to the United States because they were from affluent families who could afford to send them abroad for an education, or they were sent by their governments who paid for their education in exchange for the student returning to the home country to work for the government or corporate sponsor. During these times, career planning was not necessary for most, since they returned to their home countries to take on prestigious jobs and generous salaries that were offered to them because of their U.S. education.

This is rare today, and the need for career planning is increasingly important for students planning to return to their home country, where jobs are more competitive, home-country nationals are increasingly more educated, and career and job security is increasingly less common.

In addition to the infrastructure changes that previously placed international students into jobs in their home countries, the employers in the home country often operate within the cultural context of the country. Many international students who have obtained a Western education are now facing employment in an organization that may not subscribe to the Western values and approaches taught in the U.S. classroom. This could be anything from marketing techniques to management practices.

> If you are planning to return to your home country, use the APP ACTION titled **Preparing to Return to Work in Your Home Country** in APP 6.4 to help you prepare for your reentry.

## A Third Country

Globalization has an impact on many students' decisions to select a third country for career opportunities. This third country may be a country neighboring their home or another that is more open to employment visas.

Success with such opportunities, however, involves significant research, resources, and cultural knowledge of the country of destination. Many of the exercises and applications in this book will help you define a career, and now you need to ensure that such a career is an option in the country where you plan to live.

If this is the plan you are considering, the APP ACTION: **Preparing to Work in a Third Country** in APP 6.4 will be a useful to tool.

## Career Planning for Your Home or Another Country

It is important to place into context the career planning concepts discussed in this book. If you don't plan to stay in this country, you need to be able to translate the skills gained through this book and you need to ensure they are relevant to the country where you plan to live and work. You can start this process by competing the APP ACTION: Career Planning for Your Home or Another Country at the end of APP 6.0. As you review each concept, think about how each fits in with the career opportunities and overall culture of the country where you plan to work—whether it's your home country or another country.

## Ten Career-Specific Cultural Barriers and Strategies

There are many issues that impact your job search. Consider topics such as how to make introductions, verbal and nonverbal communications, and workplace culture. To help you document your awareness of these topics, use the chart in the related APP ACTION at the end of this section. In the APP ACTION, you will find 10 areas that are challenges for international students. Review each concept and write your responses in the appropriate space.

### Resilience

If one word were to summarize what it takes to plan a career in the midst of cultural twists and turns, the word would be *resilience*. According to www.resiliencycenter.com, *resilience* means "able to recover quickly from misfortune; able to return to original form after being bent, compressed, or stretched out of shape. A human ability to recover quickly from disruptive change, illness, or misfortune without being overwhelmed or acting in dysfunctional ways."

As an international student, you already have demonstrated a degree of resilience in planning your career when you tackled the many visa and immigration hurdles in order to study in the United States. The degree of resilience you demonstrated offers some personal insight into your ability to handle career planning in both ambiguous and continually changing times. If you struggle with the ongoing challenges of being an international student, we strongly encourage you to seek the expert assistance offered to you through your institution's international student office and your student career and counseling offices. These resources exist to help you succeed in your academic and personal endeavors.

If you are confident with your resilience, we still encourage you to access the career support available to you at your institution of higher education and to be direct in requesting assistance in understanding potential cultural issues related to your career transition.

Keep in mind that your background and culture are assets in your career. By researching and analyzing your career plans from a cultural perspective, you will see more clearly that cultural differences are neither right nor wrong—they are just different and can be effectively addressed. The better you understand the world through your own cultural lens, then the easier it will be to acculturate and maximize your ability to be effective in a different culture without giving up your own culture.

## Summary

Adjusting to life in the United States can be a challenge if you are from another country. Culture shock often happens within a few weeks and life can become a struggle. However, there are strategies that you can use to help you with the transition to living in the United States. Three areas can help significantly in acculturating: developing strong English proficiency, making friends with both Americans and others from your home culture, and becoming self-reliant.

Planning your career may involve some unique approaches and considerations. You will need to consider where you want to live and whether or not that is a viable option. Once you determine this, you can identify resources and cultural issues related to your career destination. More important, you can develop strategies to ensure that you have optimal opportunity to find meaningful employment.

## APP 6.2 Veterans

We define veterans as those who have served in the military in one form or another.[1]

https://www.opm.gov/policy-data-oversight/veterans-services/vet-guide-for-hr-professionals/

Sergey Kamshylin/Shutterstock.com

Joseph Sohm/Shutterstock.com

By statute, a "veteran" is defined as a "person who served in the active military, naval, or air service, and who was discharged or released under conditions other than dishonorable."[2]

*Title 38 of the Code of Federal Regulations defines a veteran as "a person who served in the active military, naval, or air service and who was discharged or released under conditions other than dishonorable." This definition explains that any individual that completed a service for any branch of armed forces classifies as a veteran as long as they were not dishonorably discharged.*

While it is a technicality, in an amendment to the title 38 of the United States Code pertaining to Veterans' benefits, Veteran also now refers to retired National Guardsmen and Reservists.

If you have honorably separated from any part of the military without retiring or have retired, this section pertains to you! Military veterans are a very diverse group of people with very diverse career needs. There are pages upon pages of laws and policies regarding the qualifications for specific military benefits. You should become very familiar with the benefits that apply to you based on your dates of service, length of service, and branch of service. However, there are considerations for finding employment and mapping a career path that pertain to all of those who served in the U.S. Military.

### Just Tell Me What to Do!

It is common for many people to want someone to tell them what to do and to show them the next steps. But veterans seem to seek this more than other groups. If you are transitioning from the military, you are leaving a space where there was order and rules, you are probably now realizing that finding a job is far from being orderly with specific rules. You are used to following orders. For many, leaving the military and the adjustment to not having orders to follow seems harder than their adjustment to military life experienced when they first joined. It is a psychological change. Taking control of your next steps in a highly uncertain work force is both freeing and paralyzing. Recent college graduates face the same adjustment on a slightly different level. They are going from a mapped out plan to obtain a degree to the freedom to make many more choices.

It is important for those transitioning from the military to grasp this new reality. If you are having trouble doing this, begin with making simple decisions and progress to more complicated ones. If you find that you are having difficulty in this area, seek guidance and support. It is a very natural adjustment and will usually regulate fairly quickly depending upon your personality, the length of time in the military and the type of work you preformed.

Many of those leaving the military find it helpful to create their own structure. This can be accomplished in a variety of ways such as:

- set very specific action steps for each week;
- create a calendar of appointments;
- meet with a trusted mentor to check in on progress;
- develop worksheets for accountability and tracking of progress.

How can you create structure regarding your job search?

PAUSE

## Identity

Another aspect to consider is that you are going from being a part of a team to being an individual. "Being part of a team is integral to military culture, and each member of the team matters."[3] There are two key points to take into consideration. One is that you served as a part of a team. This is a significant selling point for those seeking civilian employment. Individual contribution to a team is as important as the ability to build trust and work as a part of a team. The second part of this that is important, is that you were essential to the team and you mattered. Just try not showing up for duty, roll call, or even breakfast in the military. Regardless of what you did, you had a role to fill and you learned to fill it with pride. An expert in adult career development, Nancy Schlossberg, wrote that mattering includes a number of factors such as "having attention paid to you, having a sense of importance, being appreciated, having people who depend on you, and having pride in what you do" (quoted in Anderson and Goodman).[4]

Militarist/Shutterstock.com

Being a part of a team and mattering is something to deal with while you are transitioning, but it is also something to consider as you are making a career decision. How important is it to do a job that matters? How important is it be proud of the work you do or the organization where you work?

This section so far has covered a few points including the familiarity of being a part of a team and the concept of mattering. How does this relate to your current situation? How does this impact your job search? How does this impact the work you will do?

## Reframe Your Thinking

The Department of Labor provides many resources to assist veterans with their career needs. A recent publication[5] on this topic suggests that you approach the job search like any other military operation:

1. Determine mission and objective(s)

2. Gather intelligence

3. Determine logistics and resource requirements

4. Identify resources and/or training shortfalls

5. Develop primary, alternate, and tertiary plans

6. Integrate assets and resources

7. Establish timelines

8. Conduct rehearsals

Throughout these APPs, you have participated in activities and actions to assist you with all of the steps outlined above. Take a few minutes to think through the vocabulary of a military operation compared to the civilian language used throughout this book.

How does reframing it in a military context help you with this transition?

You may find it helpful to create a worksheet using the military operation steps. List the steps, related information, and document your progress. Define your mission in the most concrete terms possible such as "Obtain a job using mechanical and leadership skills working as a civilian employee with a military contractor" or "Use technological skills for a start-up company."

Taking the time to do this for all of the steps will help you rethink your approach to the job search.

## Your Transferable Skills

Think about the skills you developed from serving in the military. If you have completed the skills assessments, these should have already been identified. But don't forget the skills you developed being a part of the military culture. We have already mentioned teamwork and following orders. Think of the other skills, knowledge or behaviors you have acquired. Think about things such as global outlook, cultural sensitivity, a commitment to excellence, ability to work under pressure, and systematic planning and organization.

David Lee/Shutterstock.com

> List the skills, knowledge, and/or behaviors you have acquired while being a part of the military that you may have overlooked or want to emphasize in your job search.

**PAUSE**

One of the challenges of moving from military to civilian life is knowing how to compare jobs from one classification to another. If you have taken the time to do all of the previous activities in this book, you should have a list of your transferable skills and an understanding of the work you enjoy doing. There are many resources that can help you compare the skills you gained in the military to those in the civilian workforce. One that we highly recommend is the CAREERONESTOP. Found at www.Careeronestop.org, it is sponsored by the U.S. Department of Labor. You may have come across this in earlier sections of this book. In addition to the general resource, the site contains a specific section for veterans. The Veterans Job Finder allows users to match military jobs to civilian careers that use similar skills.

At the time of publication of this book, this book can be found at: https://www.careeronestop.org/Toolkit/Jobs/find-veteran-jobs.aspx

A recent search of Military Job Title "Track Vehicle Mechanic—Army—Enlisted 63Y" yielded civilian occupations including Mobile Heavy Equipment Mechanics, Outdoor Power Equipment Mechanics, and Repairers for Commercial and Industrial Equipment.

Flight attendant manager—air force enlisted 1A600 yielded First-Line Supervisors, Spa Managers, and Protective Services Workers.

Obviously, these are only suggested careers but they provide an awareness of the ways skills can be translated from the military to the civilian workforce. The suggested fields are not an exhaustive list nor do they guarantee a hire by an employer. The other factors discussed in the sections related to job search remind you that skills and knowledge are part of the equation but there are other factors that relate to the hiring decision. Personality, fit, soft-skills, and personal interests and values are all contributing factors to a successful hire and an ultimate fit between you and the employer.

Nice Kim/Shutterstock.com

## Summary

As you have probably discovered, many of the tools taught to civilians seeking civilian work are also applicable to those with a military background. There are many resources for those with military experience to supplement traditional job search methods. Begin with an Internet keyword search of Veterans Services or "Department of Labor Military" and you should find some resources to support the information listed here.

## Endnotes

**APP 6.2**

1. Retrieved March 7, 2017, from https://www.opm.gov/policy-data-oversight/veterans-services/vet-guide-for-hr-professionals/

2. What Is a Veteran? The Legal Definition. Retrieved March 07, 2017, from http://va.org/what-is-a-veteran-the-legal-definition/

3. Mary Anderson and Jane Goodman, "FROM MILITARY to CIVILIAN LIFE: Applications of Schlossberg's Model for Veterans in Transition," *Career Planning and Adult Development Journal* 30 no. 3 (2014): pp. 40–51.

4. ibid.

5. Retrieved March 7, 2017, from https://www.dol.gov/vets/programs/tap/DOLEW-Participant-Guide-2017.pdf.

# APP 6.3 Adults in Transition

The group we refer to as "adults in transition" can refer to people with any number of qualifiers:

- Parents who have taken time to be home with children or their own aging parents and are now returning to work.
- Adults who have been in the workforce but have had a change in employment status due to their voluntary choice to leave their jobs or because of market changes such as downsizing or corporate restructuring.
- Under-employed workers who may have had a job that "paid the bills" but are now ready for something different.

> If you have defined yourself as an "Adult in Transition," describe your situation.

If you have found yourself reading this section as a result of navigating the rest of this book, you have already developed a set of skills and deeper self-awareness that will assist you in taking the next steps. If you haven't taken the time to go through the earlier section of the course, you will find it very helpful.

For the purposes of this section, adults are classified as those older than the traditional aged college student. For general purposes, this could be 25 or older. Our experience says that there are some college students who are younger than 25 and due to life experiences can easily connect with the issues facing "adult" learners and job seekers.

The following section will look at some of the career issues that are connected to adults. You may be able to relate to some. Take the time to "Press Pause" when appropriate.

**Geographic Limitations** Going beyond the preference to not relocate, this limitation prevents the person from moving due to the job of a significant other, family responsibilities, or specific financial concerns.

This is one of the area that impacts many adults. Some people do not want to commute more than 30 minutes while others are willing to travel every day of the week by plane, train, or automobile. Some do not want to move to a city more than 100 miles from family while some are willing to increase their geographic preference circle

Kirill Savenko/Shutterstock.com

by 200, 500, or 1000 miles. Some prefer to at least stay "on the East Coast," "in the Mid-West," or are only willing to relocate to a smaller or bigger city, warmer climate or a city with a better school system.

PAUSE

Take a minute to think about your non-negotiables regarding a move. What would it take to have you move to another location?

one photo/Shutterstock.com

**Experience** The perception of being "over-qualified in some fields and under-qualified in others" creates an imbalance. Once a career path has been selected, getting the job can be difficult based on the difficulty of obtaining an entry-level job or transferring skills from one field to another.

This is the point where many adults think there is age-discrimination. You might be in your late 20s or early 30s looking for your first "real" job after completing your degree yet find yourself being passed over for entry-level jobs. You may be in the last chapter of your working years and find yourself being passed over for jobs that clearly meet your skill sets.

Age discrimination is illegal, yet it can be proven that certain qualified people do not get the job. Conversations with recruiters indicate that age is rarely the factor. The ability to do the job and organizational "fit" are more important. Age discrimination could be personal perception or reality. Regardless, not getting the job is difficult.

hafakot/Shutterstock.com

There are ways to overcome the issues of experience and age. Many of these have been covered in previous sections. It is important to stay on top of the latest technology used in your field, to be sure that knowledge and skills are relevant and current, and to understand the work environment. Your personal network can help you as you seek to understand organizational "fit" by providing you with insights to the company culture or unit style. Be sure to use your network to gain advice on how to best align yourself with the requirements of the job and related culture.

How do you relate to this topic? What ways can you overcome the "over-qualified/under-qualified dilemma"?

**Managing Multiple Roles** Revisit the section on roles. As a refresher, as an adult you play many roles including homemaker, parent, worker, volunteer, and even child. If you are reading this book, you have mostly likely also added student to your list. Think about the places where you spend your time: home, community, school, and workplace. While it is difficult to juggle these roles (there are only 24 hours in a day and only a certain amount of energy to expend in fulfilling these roles), these roles and the environments where they are executed can offer opportunities to grow needed skills or provide examples of using the skills you possess.

Think about your community for instance. Are you already volunteering? How can you demonstrate use of a skill through work you do in this role? You can demonstrate writing through volunteering to write the newsletter or blog for your organization. You can demonstrate technical skills through managing the website. Working with others can be demonstrated in many ways such as managing other volunteers or leading a team. Think creatively about how you have effectively demonstrated the use of skills in this environment.

If you are not currently volunteering, consider places that will allow you to improve and show acquisition of specific skills needed for your dream job or the one on the next step in your career journey. For many adults, volunteering is rewarding on a personal level. Not only are they developing skills, it also provides new relationships and a broader network, as well as a sense of well-being as they share their talents with others.

dizain/Shutterstock.com

Describe ways you can document or improve at least two skills through roles other than that of paid-worker.

**Opportunity Cost** The term opportunity cost is an economic concept referring to the fact that a business has a limited number of resources and must make a choice regarding how those resources are allocated. An organization may not effectively manufacture both shoes and butter. These products require different talent, equipment, and processing resources. The opportunity cost is the decision to select one over the other. A company may decide to manufacture butter. The opportunity cost is shoes.

As an adult, you are keenly aware that you have limited resources. Your time and financial resources have limits. It is often difficult to make a decision of one direction over another, or one job over another. It is difficult to predict the global marketplace of the future to fully understand what jobs will be needed in the next few years. Reframing your decision so that you own the direction rather than seeing it as a default choice may help you take control.

Describe a time when you had to make one significant decision that resulted in closing the door to another option. What did you learn from that experience that can be applied to your current career situation?

**Bad breaks** We all have had them. The last one hired is the first one laid off. The economy had a downturn just as you graduated. The company had a merger and your position was eliminated. The outside forces that seem to control our careers can give us a lot of reasons to be angry. It is critical that these bad breaks (or whatever you want to call them) do not define you. True, you may have had the worse boss in history but that doesn't give you permission to feel sorry for yourself, bad mouth your former company, or abandon your dreams.

Attitude will come across in many ways. It can be so subtle, you may not see it. But an employer will. Hiring managers and search committees look for any clue that you will not be a good fit. If they sense a bad attitude (justified or not), then you may get passed over for the job.

Worse than not getting the job is allowing a bad attitude to derail your own dreams. If external forces are defining you, then you may have lost some of your control over your career. Bad breaks can define us in positive and negative ways. Life isn't always fair but how you overcome the difficulties will set the stage for your long term success and happiness.

Describe your current state of mind regarding your career. If it is at all negative, what can you do to reframe your thinking?

## Summary

In closing, being an adult making a career choice can be very complicated. There are many factors to consider from income needs to lifestyle desires. With age brings wisdom (or so it is said), but it also brings an entirely new set of opportunities and challenges. The options are greater than they have ever been. Many adults in their senior years are getting college or advanced degrees and finding fulfilling careers. Many turn hobbies into profitable businesses. Adults have the benefit of greater self-awareness. They also have large networks that can provide insights and access. A self-confident adult embarking on a new career journey is a person who has set realistic goals and has a plan to excellence.

Rawpixel.com/Shutterstock.com

What makes YOU an asset to a prospective employer?

# APP 6.4 APP ACTIONS

## PREPARING TO RETURN TO WORK IN YOUR HOME COUNTRY

If you're planning to return to your home country following your U.S. studies, you may want to work through the following questions to prepare yourself for the inevitable reentry challenges that lie ahead:

1. How are the exercises/applications in earlier APPs of this book relevant or not relevant to the cultural norms of my home country?

   _____

   _____

   _____

2. What do I need to do to adapt these exercises/applications to better reflect the situation in my home country?

   _____

   _____

   _____

## PREPARING TO WORK IN A THIRD COUNTRY

If you are considering a career in a country other than your home country and not in the United States, consider the following questions:

1. What country or countries are you considering?

    _____

    _____

    _____

2. What major universities are in the country you plan to move to?

    _____

    _____

    _____

3. Do these universities have websites and career information for students? List the websites below and indicate what type of career information is available online.

    _____

    _____

    _____

4. What other career information can you find out regarding the country? How is this information different from what you've learned in this book or this course?

    _____

    _____

    _____

## CAREER PLANNING FOR YOUR HOME OR ANOTHER COUNTRY PART I

1. What cultural influences from your home country and from your U.S. academic experience will impact your career/life decision-making for a career in the country where you plan to live and work?

_____

_____

_____

2. What essential skills do you prefer to use in your future work? How are these skills valued in the country where you plan to work?

_____

_____

_____

3. How are self-management skills, special knowledge skills, and functional skills valued in the country where you will live? What are some self-management skills that may create conflict in the culture of the country where you will live? How can you overcome this potential conflict?

_____

_____

_____

4. Who can you ask for ideas and advice about what career options in this country would be appropriate for your specific skills? What other resources are available to learn more about skills valued in this country in general?

_____

_____

_____

5. How is/isn't your thinking style in work and learning valued in the country where you will live and work? What are some areas for potential conflict regarding the outward expression of your thinking style in this culture?

_____

_____

_____

6. What additional cultural information will you need to research in order to identify what personality traits may be potential areas for conflict given the culture of the country? What other resources can you consult to learn more about the acceptance of behaviors of different personality types and areas of interest in the country where you will live?

_____

_____

_____

7. Given the six personality types in Holland's RIASEC model how are these personality types expressed differently in the country where you will live and work?

_____

_____

_____

8. How do people usually determine their occupation in the country where you plan to live and work?

_____

_____

_____

9. How can you learn more about the work environment for this country that is relevant to your interests?

_____

_____

_____

10. What motivated you to study in the United States (or other country if you are not using this book in the United States)? How are needs expressed differently in your home country?

_____

_____

_____

11. What motivates you to select the country where you plan to live and work? What motivates people to work in this country? How are needs expressed differently in the country where you plan to live and work?

_____

_____

_____

12. How will your values be accepted in the country where you will work? How will you ensure your personal needs are being met while respecting the culture of the country?

_____

_____

_____

13. What career alternatives might you consider when thinking about career options for this country? How are these careers different from your preferred career?

_____

_____

_____

14. On the basis of your knowledge of the country, is the Holland code relevant to careers you would find in this country? If not, why not? What occupational literature is available to determine career options and alternatives for this country? If no literature exists, whom could you contact to get additional insight and information on this?

_____

_____

_____

15. Are your professional needs, wants, and values able to be met in the country where you will live? If not, then how will you address these issues so you feel satisfied in the work you will do?

_____

_____

_____

16. How will you realize your career goals and objectives given the culture and opportunities of the country where you will live?

_____

_____

_____

17. How much control will you have in the country where you will live regarding your short-range, medium-range, and long-range career objectives? How might you need to modify them to realistically fit in with the employment culture of the country?

_____

_____

_____

18. How can the self-empowering mind-set discussed in APP 4.2 benefit you as you plan your career for this country?

_____

_____

_____

19. In addition to the barriers listed previously, what additional barriers would you add given what you know or don't know about the country where you plan to live and work?

_____

_____

_____

20. What culturally appropriate action can you take to address these barriers in the cultural context of the country where you will live?

_____

_____

_____

## CAREER PLANNING FOR YOUR HOME OR ANOTHER COUNTRY PART 2

**Identifying Resources and Cultural Issues Related to Planning a Career in Another Country**

Now, take the information in the previous exercise and plot it on the following chart to help you with the next steps in planning your career in your home country or another country. If you are considering more than one country, copy this page to create a country resource page for all countries you are considering.

**COUNTRY:**

**Resources to explore specific information regarding this topic Known or potential cultural differences to be aware of regarding this concept in this country**

1. Career/life decision-making and cultural influences

2. Preferred skills to use in future work

3. Skills: self-management, special knowledge, and functional

4. Appropriate career options for my skills

5. Your thinking style in work and learning

6. Potential conflict with personality types

7. Expression of personality traits in the workplace

8. Selecting occupations that match interests

9. Work environments relevant to interests

10. Expression of needs

11. Motivation and need to work

12. Your values and needs being addressed in context of the culture

13. Career alternatives

14. Career classification and occupational literature

15. Satisfaction with career decisions

16. Your career goals and objectives

17. Controlling your short-, medium-, and long-range objectives

18. Your self-empowered mind-set

19. Culture or country-specific barriers to getting started in your career

20. Cultural context of the country

## TEN CAREER-SPECIFIC CULTURAL BARRIERS AND STRATEGIES

In this APP ACTION you will find 10 areas related that are challenges for international students. Review each concept and write your responses in the appropriate space. Below are 10 areas related to career planning and job searching that represent challenges for many international students due to the cultural concepts. Review each concept and write your responses to the column headings in the appropriate space. If you plan to work in a country other than your home country or the United States, copy this page and go through the exercise a second time, replacing "U.S." with the name of the country where you plan to work, to compare and contrast your responses.

| | General U.S. culture: list your observations regarding U.S. culture. Ask others, including U.S. friends, other students, and career counselors at your university | Describe how your culture is different from the U.S. culture as it relates to this concept | What you need to do to acculturate |
|---|---|---|---|
| 1. **Protocol for introductions,** such as business cards, handshakes, gestures, hierarchy of introductions, monikers including "Dr." or "Ms." | | | |
| 2. **Time,** such as starting meetings, interviews, information interviews, and other appointments | | | |
| 3. **Nonverbal communication,** such as eye contact, posture, gestures, head nods, personal space, facial expressions, touching | | | |
| 4. **Verbal communication and assertiveness,** such as "small talk," greetings, asking questions, self-promotion, directness, speaking one's mind, accurate representation of skill level, presenting self in interviews, and networking | | | |

| | | | |
|---|---|---|---|
| 5. **Workplace norms,** such as age, gender, rewards system, promotion, rules and procedures, and superior/subordinate relationship | | | |
| 6. **Self-reliance,** such as taking responsibility for planning your career, decision-making, asking for help when needed, and managing your career | | | |
| 7. **Networking and professional relationships,** including initiating contact, following up, and developing a mutually beneficial relationship | | | |
| 8. **Effectively dealing with rejection,** including interviews, networking situations, asking for assistance, and applying for jobs | | | |
| 9. **Job search tools and strategies,** such as resumes, job applications, writing letters, researching, and interviewing | | | |
| 10. **Leading from your strengths,** such as language abilities, and international experience | | | |

*Source:* Adapted from "Job Search Strategies and Cultural Barriers" by Susan Musich, 2017.

# Career Research and Self Reflection Notes

You will be using this APP to supplement and compliment your work in the other APPs. There are many ways to research careers. Two main ones are talking and reading. In this APP, you will find an overview of informational interviewing. Think of this as the process of interviewing a professional to gain information related to careers and education. By speaking with people, you will gain real world insights that are current and personalized. Reading about careers is also important. Pay attention to the source of information so you can assess the reliability and relevance of the content. Section 7.2 includes information on a few recommended resources. Be sure to ask anyone you meet for an informational interview for recommendations of other sources for related information.

You will not find any APP ACTIONS or PRESS PAUSES in this section because the content is tied to other activities and Apps. Instead, the second part of this section is the place for you to record the ideas you have had about yourself and career choices.

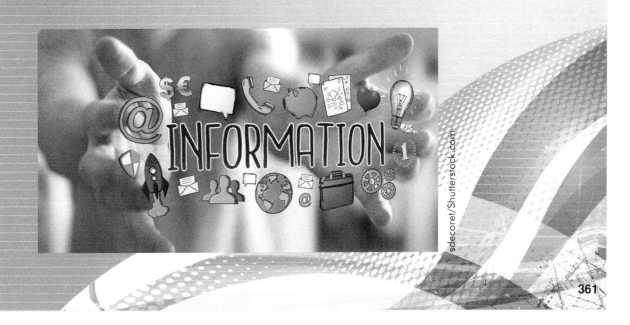

sdecoret/Shutterstock.com

# APP 7.1 Informational Interviewing Overview

## Conducting Career Informational Interviews

Talking to people about their work is an effective way to gather information in your occupational exploration. Initially, to get comfortable with the idea of interviewing people, talk to family, friends, or anybody you know well. This should help minimize your anxiety about interviewing.

Conduct information-gathering interviews to find answers to the following questions:

1. How did the person get started in that kind of work?

2. What does the person enjoy about his or her work?

3. What does the person dislike about his or her work?

4. Who else does the person know who does similar kinds of work or uses similar skills?

5. What can the person tell you about the employment outlook in his or her occupational field with a particular firm, in a particular locality, or in the nation generally?

In making your initial contact with people, be sure to clarify that you are not interviewing for a job. Instead, you are considering that line of work and simply trying to learn more about it. At the completion of your interview, ask the person for the names of other people who are doing a similar kind of work or using similar skills. Make every effort to get a specific person's name, so that you have someone definite to contact for an additional information interview. Also, ask the person you are interviewing if you may use his or her name in contacting this other individual.

LDprod/Shutterstock.com

Conduct additional career information interviews, using the process outlined here. Be sure to send a thank-you letter to the person you have seen within one to three days after the interview. For possible future reference, keep a list of all the people you have interviewed or plan to interview. You may even want to keep a special notebook or cards with interview notes on the five questions covered. Include the main things that you learned from each interview. This file will be a rich source of information as you conduct your occupational exploration.

## A Time Line For an Informational Interview

### Initiating the Meeting

Asking for a time to meet someone for an informational interview can be a little intimidating. Take the time to think about what you are going to say before you initiate a contact.

Any contact should include your name, how you know the person or how you were referred, the reason you are reaching out, a suggested way to connect, and your contact information.

You may want to consider creating a script using the following examples:

*Hello. My name is Cody and I am currently in my second semester at Regional State College. The staff at the Career Center suggested that you would be a good resource for me as I am trying to decide between two career options. My options are currently accounting or marketing. As an accountant, I would appreciate any insights you can provide about your field. Would you be available any evening next week for a fifteen to twenty minute phone call? Please contact me at Cody0348@regionalstate.edu. Thank you for considering my request.*

*Mrs. Alan,*

*You may remember me from a few years ago when I was a student at Peachy High School. I initially began studying to become a teacher. As I approach my senior year, I am having second thoughts. I am taking a career planning course this semester and I have an assignment to do an informational interview with someone on my list of career options. One of the directions I am considering is to go to graduate school and eventually become a guidance counselor. I have read a lot about this career path and think it might be a good direction for me. I have some questions I would like to ask you about your role as a guidance counselor. Could we meet after school on a day in the next few weeks? You can reach me at 555.555.5555.*

*Thank you for any help you can offer. It will great to see you again.*

*Sincerely,*

*Erin Chawla*

### Day of Meeting

Be sure to show up or call at set time. Respect the person and the time they have set aside. Come prepared with your questions. If you see that you are running out of time, be respectful. Ask for a few more minutes or permission to find another time to meet again. You may suggest that you send your questions by email for them to answer but do not send more than a few questions. Be selective.

### After the Meeting

Show your appreciation for the time that was invested in helping you with your career. Send an electronic or print thank-you note. If your connection gave you additional people to contact, then be sure to keep your connection in the loop. As you move forward with your career choice, send updates. You never know how this person could have an impact on your career in the future or where your paths will cross.

TETIANA SUKHORUKOVA/Shutterstock.com

## APP 7.2 Web And Print Resources

There are many print and online resources to assist with your career research. Each one will serve one or many purposes. This section lists a few suggested resources but there are many excellent resources available to you for free through your campus or public library.

### Occupational Outlook Handbook (OOH)

This site is accessed at https://www.bls.gov/ooh/

The OOH will allow you to conduct general research on careers from a few different perspectives. It is updated approximately every two years by the Bureau of Labor Statistics. The "Search Handbook" box allows users to input an occupation then view the profile. The profile typically includes information on the types of things a worker in this occupation will do, the work environment, required education or training, pay, job outlook, and suggested similar occupations. State and area data is provided for further exploration.

### Occupation Groups

The Occupation Groups section will allow for exploration of a variety of occupations based on industry categorization. Each group provides a quick snap shot of occupations including a brief job summary, required education for entry-level employment, and median pay. It also includes a link to more in-depth information on the occupation if it is covered by the OOH.

### Criteria

This section allows for a search based on median pay, entry-level education, types of on-the-job training, projected number of new jobs and projected growth rate. In 2017, this search reviewed 575 jobs. While there are many more job titles, this general research allows for information gathering that can be applied to other occupations. For example, predicted growth in many areas of the medical field may indicate similar growth for other related medical occupations. If you are looking for a high paying job with a higher than average projected growth rate, this is a good place to start your search.

### Featured Occupations

The OOH periodically selects occupations to profile. These are not necessarily high growth jobs, high paying jobs, or even in high demand. The featured occupation may suggest something you have not considered. If you are interested, take the time to do a deeper dive into the information by clicking on the "view profile" link.

### Other Areas for Research

It will also allow you to browse occupations by highest paying, fastest growing, and most new jobs. It is important to note that all of these are general factors and may not allow for differences in geographic area, type of industry, or even required skills.

Fastest growing is based on the current number of people in the field and projected growth. An industry such as Wind Turbine Technician with only 4400 jobs in 2014 will see a 108% growth in the next 10 years. However, this will only amount to an additional 4800 new jobs for a total of 9200 jobs.

Compare this to Personal Care Aids. The growth rate is only 26% but this occupation is expected to go from 1,768,400 jobs in 2014 to 2,226,600 jobs in 2024. This is an addition of 458,000 jobs.

Factors such as new technology, changing market conditions, or governmental policy can all alter job growth. Because of this, it is important to consider many factors when considering a career.

one photo/Shutterstock.com

## O*NET

The site typically used for career research is https://www.onetonline.org/.

This tool is sponsored by the U.S. Department of Labor, Employment and Training Administration. It is a recent addition to career research tools and replaces the Dictionary of Occupational Titles. Information on occupations is updated on an ongoing basis.

The O*NET allows for the search of a specific occupation or allows the user to browse for occupations based on skills and related occupations.

Once you view the occupation, you will find information on how this occupation meets 35 skills. These skills are basic skills such as reading, writing, math, and so on. They are also cross-functional skills such "quality control analysis" that exist in other occupations.

Forty-one Generalized Work Activities are provided including functions such as "interacting with computers" and "organizing."

The interests are grouped according to occupational types. These are based on the work of John Holland and connect to the interest groups you used in APP 3.2.

The work styles over 16 style characteristics that connect to values. These are similar to the values you identified during your self-discovery in APPs 2 and 3.

Work context is covered by 57 physical and social factors.

The final section is "Job Zones" that indicate the required levels of training and education.

Ikeskinen/Shutterstock.com

## Professional Associations

You will find that both the Occupational Outlook Handbook and the O*NET reference professional associations. Professional associations exist to support the careers of those related to a specific industry and advance the overall profession.

Many associations include educational resources and discounts for students. These associations are not only excellent tools for the purposes of information gathering but also for establishing relationships with professionals in a field as a part of your networking efforts.

To find a professional association related to your field, you may perform a basic internet search. In addition, there are many sites offering lists of associations. The careeronestop is a website sponsored by the U.S. Department of Labor. As of the printing of this book, the site could be found at https://www.careeronestop.org/.

To help you find a specific organization, there is a page in their Business Center dedicated to finding professional associations. It can be found at https://www.careeronestop.org/businesscenter/professionalassociations/find-professional-associations.aspx.

## Social Media and the Internet

Most companies will use a branded website as the main page for all related information. This is the place to start when researching companies for internship or job application, prior to interviews, or to stay current on industry-related initiatives. For example, selecting a dozen or so tech companies to follow will provide you with hiring patterns, job growth, product changes, and new developments.

Many companies use various forms of social media as a part of their marketing strategies. Because social media is rapidly changing, you will want to use the ones that are currently popular with a mainstream audience. Twitter, Facebook, and LinkedIn are currently the sites most companies will use to share information.

Digital media such as newspapers and magazines offer insights into companies. Use respected sources to read about the latest executive level hiring, layoffs and expansions, and other "newsworthy" information.

pramot/Shutterstock.com

## Other Areas

Do not neglect good old fashioned library research. Your local librarian can offer you a variety of resources to help you learn about careers, industries, and companies. While libraries may have less print resources on their shelves, most subscribe to online tools that will provide the insights you need to make a good career decision.

Be sure to also take the time to visit a career center on your college campus or a special section of the library for additional resources related to your career interests.

In this day of seemingly unlimited access to information, job seekers are expected to have substantial knowledge of an employer prior to the interview. Career seekers have access to insights and information that will help them make educated decisions. Those considering more education can be informed consumers of training and higher education programs.

Take the time to do your research as you determine your best choices for today and the future.

Maksim Kabakou/Shutterstock.com

## APP 7.3 About Me

Use this space to record your personal
insights from APPs 1 to 4.

arfa adam/Shutterstock.com

**Self-Profile**

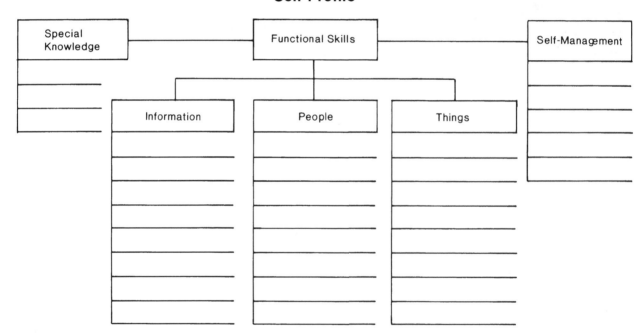

Holland Code

Thinking Style

Cerebral

| Analyzing | Intuiting |
|---|---|
| A ——— | ——— D |
| Left | Right |
| B ——— | ——— C |
| Controlling | Feeling |

Limbic

Values:

Life Goal / Mission:

## My Aha! Moments

scorponce/Shutterstock.com

Use this space to record your **AHA moments** from APPS 1 to 4.

_____

_____

_____

_____

_____

_____

_____

_____

_____

_____

_____

_____

_____

# APP 7.4 Career Research Notes

Use this space to record your research on your careers. This is a page you will return to often and expand upon as you progress through the book. Make additional copies of the page as needed.

## Occupation Research

| Occupational Title | | Alternate Titles or Related Occupations | |
|---|---|---|---|
| Brief Description | | Five things a person in this occupation does | 1<br><br>2<br><br>3<br><br>4<br><br>5 |
| Required Skills and Abilities | | Personality traits and Characteristics | |
| Education (Minimum required, desired certifications) | | Places where training is provided and length of training | |
| Compensation (Salary, hourly pay, benefits) | | Average hours per day spent working and additional work requirements (overtime, travel, schedule) | |
| Job Outlook | | Typical Employers | |

| | | | |
|---|---|---|---|
| Things I LIKE About This Job | | Things I DISLIKE About This Job | |

| | | | |
|---|---|---|---|
| Occupational Title | | Alternate Titles or Related Occupations | |
| Brief Description | | Five things a person in this occupation does | 1<br><br>2<br><br>3<br><br>4<br><br>5 |
| Required Skills and Abilities | | Personality traits and Characteristics | |
| Education (Minimum required, desired certifications) | | Places where training is provided and length of training | |
| Compensation (Salary, hourly pay, benefits) | | Average hours per day spent working and additional work requirements (overtime, travel, schedule) | |

| Job Outlook | | Typical Employers | |
|---|---|---|---|
| Things I LIKE About This Job | | Things I DISLIKE About This Job | |

## Careers To Consider

Use this space or the chart on the following page to record the careers you are considering and to chart your research. This is a page you will return to often and expand upon as you progress through the book. Make additional copies of the page as needed.

| Title | Meets My Interests | Meets My Skills or Potential | Meets My Values | Insights Gained from Career Research | Insights Gained from Informational Interviews | Personal Notes and Next Steps | Current Rating | Final Rating |
|---|---|---|---|---|---|---|---|---|
| **Pet Food Taster** | VERY HIGH: Passionate about food and healthy animals. | MODERATE: Very detailed, note taking, high sensory ability | HIGH: Competitive field, money is fair but not great. Need to move for promotions | Not a lot of information available | Hard to find someone but did talk to a wine taster. Another career to consider | Call a Pet Food manufacturer to learn more, do a larger search. | As of 10/4 I am still considering this as a choice. 4 on a scale of 1 to 5. | |
| | | | | | | | | |
| | | | | | | | | |

| Title | Meets My Interests | Meets My Skills or Potential | Meets My Values | Insights Gained from Career Research | Insights Gained from Infor-mational Interviews | Personal Notes and Next Steps | Current Rating | Final Rating |
|---|---|---|---|---|---|---|---|---|
| | | | | | | | | |
| | | | | | | | | |
| | | | | | | | | |
| | | | | | | | | |
| | | | | | | | | |

## My Contacts

Use this space or the chart on the following page to record information about the people you are contacting for career information and networking. Make additional copies of the page as needed.

| Name | Career Title | Organization or Current Employer | Email Address | Phone Number | How Connected | Date of First Contact | Thank You Note Sent | Notes |
|---|---|---|---|---|---|---|---|---|
| Joe Baggadonuts | Pet Food Taster | Amazing Petfoods in Michigan | Jb123@apf .net | (555) 123–4567 | Friend of my science professor | Sent email of intro on 9/27, First meeting on 9/30 | Sent T U by email on 9/30 Sent TU to science prof on 9/30 | Great meeting. He gave me lots of ideas and career insights |
| | | | | | | | | |
| | | | | | | | | |
| | | | | | | | | |
| | | | | | | | | |

| Name | Career Title | Organization or Current Employer | Email Address | Phone Number | How Connected | Date of First Contact | Thank You Note Sent | Notes |
|------|------|------|------|------|------|------|------|------|
|      |      |      |      |      |      |      |      |      |
|      |      |      |      |      |      |      |      |      |
|      |      |      |      |      |      |      |      |      |
|      |      |      |      |      |      |      |      |      |

# APP 7.5 Supplemental Activities

## Prioritizing Process

In many situations, you need to choose your top preference or preferences from among numerous options. While it's easy to choose with just two options, that task becomes much more difficult as the number of options increases. A quick and easy process to find your top preference and rank the remaining choices is the prioritizing process.[1] In this process, you will be choosing between just two items at a time. This greatly facilitates the process of determining overall preferences from a list of items.

To demonstrate how to use this prioritizing process, consider the following list of sample activities for a Saturday night. We have arbitrarily numbered this list without considering preference at this point.

1. roller skating            6. popular music concert

2. movies                    7. ballet

3. supper club               8. bowling

4. Irish pub                 9. symphony concert

5. sports event             10. dancing

To determine the two most preferred activities you would like to do on Saturday night, you will prioritize the entire list. We have copied each activity from the list to the *Items* blanks down the left-hand side of the sample prioritizing grid on page •••. Once again, we've recorded them in the random order of the original list.

Each number on the right-hand side of the grid corresponds to the same numbered activity. For example, 1 refers to roller skating, 2 to movies, etc. Starting with items 1 and 2 on the list, ask yourself which of the two—roller skating or attending a movie— you would enjoy doing more this Saturday night. Let's assume you say going to the movies. You would then circle item 2 in the pair ½ on the prioritizing grid (see the sample grid). In this way, you have indicated your preference for item 2 when given a choice between 1 and 2. Continue along the top row of the grid, row A, pairing item 1 in turn with items 3, 4, 5, 6, 7, 8, 9, and 10, circling your preference in each pair. For example, when pairing item 1 with item 5, let's assume you would prefer attending a sports event to roller skating, so you would circle item 5 in the pair ⅕. Continue this forced choice process in rows B through I. If you have done the process correctly, only one choice will be circled in each pair of items (i.e., ⅘). Make sure you don't end up with two circled items (i.e., ⅘).

---

[1] From *The Three Boxes of Life and How to Get Out of Them*, by Richard N. Bolles, © copyright 1978, by Richard N. Bolles. Used by special permission. Those desiring a copy of the complete book for further reading may procure it from the publisher, Ten Speed Press, P.O. Box 7123, Berkeley, CA 94707.

Once you have completed circling the items on the grid, record in the second column the number of times each item has been circled anywhere on the grid. You will use this total to determine final priority ranking. For example, item 2, circled seven times, will rank ahead of item 3, which was circled only six times. In the event of ties, check the grid to see which item is circled when the two are paired against each other. For instance, items 1 and 6 are tied, both having been circled three times. To determine your preference ranking, you merely need to look at the grid to see which item you preferred in your initial assessment. If you look at row A on the sample grid, you can see that item 1 was chosen over item 6. Therefore, item 1, roller skating, wins out over item 6, attending a popular music concert. Similarly, the tie between item 4 and item 7 is resolved in favor of item 4. When you have finished counting the circled numbers, you can see from the sample grid that the first choice for Saturday night is to go to a symphony concert and second choice is to go to a sports event. The final prioritized list then looks like this:

| | |
|---|---|
| First choice: | symphony concert |
| Second choice: | sports event |
| Third choice: | movies |
| Fourth choice: | supper club |
| Fifth choice: | Irish pub |
| Sixth choice: | ballet |
| Seventh choice: | roller skating |
| Eighth choice: | popular music concert |
| Ninth choice: | bowling |
| Tenth choice: | dancing |

This prioritizing process will be used many times throughout the book. You will be using it to prioritize your preferred transferable skills, achievements, self-management skills, values, and people preferences.

This process is an extremely helpful decision-making tool in any situation where you have to make difficult choices from among competing alternatives.

## Prioritizing Grid² —Sample

The grid (Row A through I) with circled comparisons:

| Row | Grid |
|---|---|
| A | ①  ①  ①  ①  ①  ①  ①  1  1  1 / 10 9 8 7 6 5 4 ③ ② (with ③ ② circled) |
| B | ②  ②  ②  ②  ②  ②  ②  2 2 / 10 ⑨ 8 7 6 5 4 3 |
| C | ③  ③  ③  ③  ③  ③  3 3 / 10 ⑨ 8 7 6 5 4 |
| D | ④  ④  ④  4 4 4 / 10 ⑨ 8 7 ⑥ ⑤ |
| E | ⑤  ⑤  ⑤  ⑤  5 / 10 ⑨ 8 7 6 |
| F | ⑥  ⑥  6 6 / 10 ⑨ 8 ⑦ |
| G | ⑦  7 7 / 10 ⑨ 8 |
| H | ⑧  8 / 10 ⑨ |
| I | ⑨ / 10 |

| | Items | Number of Times Circled | Final Prioritized Order |
|---|---|---|---|
| 1. | roller skating | ||| | 7 |
| 2. | movie | ||||| || | 3 |
| 3. | supper club | ||||| | | 4 |
| 4. | Irish pub | |||| | 5 |
| 5. | sports event | ||||| ||| | 2 |
| 6. | popular music concert | ||| | 8 |
| 7. | ballet | |||| | 6 |
| 8. | bowling | | | 9 |
| 9. | symphony | ||||| |||| | 1 |
| 10. | dancing | 0 | 10 |

²Adapted from *The Three Boxes of Life and How to Get Out of Them*, by Richard N. Bolles, © copyright 1978, by Richard N. Bolles. Used by special permission. Those desiring a copy of the complete book for further reading may procure it from the publisher, Ten Speed Press, P.O. Box 7123, Berkeley, CA 94707.

## Prioritizing Grid[3]

| Row | Grid | | | | | | | | |
|---|---|---|---|---|---|---|---|---|---|
| A | $\frac{1}{2}$ | $\frac{1}{3}$ | $\frac{1}{4}$ | $\frac{1}{5}$ | $\frac{1}{6}$ | $\frac{1}{7}$ | $\frac{1}{8}$ | $\frac{1}{9}$ | $\frac{1}{10}$ |
| B | $\frac{2}{3}$ | $\frac{2}{4}$ | $\frac{2}{5}$ | $\frac{2}{6}$ | $\frac{2}{7}$ | $\frac{2}{8}$ | $\frac{2}{9}$ | $\frac{2}{10}$ | |
| C | $\frac{3}{4}$ | $\frac{3}{5}$ | $\frac{3}{6}$ | $\frac{3}{7}$ | $\frac{3}{8}$ | $\frac{3}{9}$ | $\frac{3}{10}$ | | |
| D | $\frac{4}{5}$ | $\frac{4}{6}$ | $\frac{4}{7}$ | $\frac{4}{8}$ | $\frac{4}{9}$ | $\frac{4}{10}$ | | | |
| E | $\frac{5}{6}$ | $\frac{5}{7}$ | $\frac{5}{8}$ | $\frac{5}{9}$ | $\frac{5}{10}$ | | | | |
| F | $\frac{6}{7}$ | $\frac{6}{8}$ | $\frac{6}{9}$ | $\frac{6}{10}$ | | | | | |
| G | $\frac{7}{8}$ | $\frac{7}{9}$ | $\frac{7}{10}$ | | | | | | |
| H | $\frac{8}{9}$ | $\frac{8}{10}$ | | | | | | | |
| I | $\frac{9}{10}$ | | | | | | | | |

Final Prioritized Order

Number of Times Circled

Items

1. _____

2. _____

3. _____

4. _____

5. _____

6. _____

7. _____

8. _____

9. _____

10. _____

[3]Adapted from *The Three Boxes of Life and How to Get Out of Them*, by Richard N. Bolles. © copyright 1978, by Richard N. Bolles. Used by special permission. Those desiring a copy of the complete book for further reading may procure it from the publisher, Ten Speed Press, P.O. Box 7123, Berkeley, CA 94707.

## Prioritizing Grid[4]

| Row | Grid | | | | | | | | |
|-----|---|---|---|---|---|---|---|---|---|
| A | 1/2 | 1/3 | 1/4 | 1/5 | 1/6 | 1/7 | 1/8 | 1/9 | 1/10 |
| B | | 2/3 | 2/4 | 2/5 | 2/6 | 2/7 | 2/8 | 2/9 | 2/10 |
| C | | | 3/4 | 3/5 | 3/6 | 3/7 | 3/8 | 3/9 | 3/10 |
| D | | | | 4/5 | 4/6 | 4/7 | 4/8 | 4/9 | 4/10 |
| E | | | | | 5/6 | 5/7 | 5/8 | 5/9 | 5/10 |
| F | | | | | | 6/7 | 6/8 | 6/9 | 6/10 |
| G | | | | | | | 7/8 | 7/9 | 7/10 |
| H | | | | | | | | 8/9 | 8/10 |
| I | | | | | | | | | 9/10 |

| Items | Number of Times Circled | Final Prioritized Order |
|-------|-------------------------|-------------------------|
| 1. | | |
| 2. | | |
| 3. | | |
| 4. | | |
| 5. | | |
| 6. | | |
| 7. | | |
| 8. | | |
| 9. | | |
| 10. | | |

[4] Adapted from *The Three Boxes of Life and How to Get Out of Them*, by Richard N. Bolles, © copyright 1978, by Richard N. Bolles. Used by special permission. Those desiring a copy of the complete book for further reading may procure it from the publisher, Ten Speed Press, P.O. Box 7123, Berkeley, CA 94707.

## Trios—Small Group Discussions

By sharing your individual achievements with two other people, your functional-skills identification can progress far more quickly. Why is this? Most people tend to be too critical about themselves, so they ignore certain talents their achievements reveal. Consequently, it can be very difficult for individuals to identify their own skills completely. However, the process of identifying skills that someone else has used is relatively easy.

Start this process by rounding up two volunteers. Ask friends, classmates, or relatives, making sure that they do not have false preconceived ideas about what your talents are or should be. Your two volunteers might even decide to participate in this process themselves. Once you have selected your group members, decide who will be person A, B, and C. Then follow the remaining steps as outlined.

Murry couldn't decide which discussion group he wanted to attend.

Step 1:  Person A reads a story about one of his or her top satisfying achievements while persons B and C listen closely, noting on paper any functional (transferable) skills that they think were used. If the story is not clear, B and C should interrupt by asking the question, *"What did it take for you to do that?"* The purpose for asking this question is to encourage the storyteller to describe the particular situation more completely. It is important for the listeners (now B and C) to keep asking this question until they fully understand the situation and are able to identify the functional skills involved.

Step 2:  Person A next says what functional skills he or she used to make the achievement happen. Person A names and records these skills *before* hearing what B and C have to add.

Step 3:  Now persons B and C respond to person A's story reading. Person B identifies functional skills that he or she heard in the story. When person B is finished, person C repeats the process. Person A, meanwhile, is writing down all the skills that B and C have mentioned.

Step 4: If desired, repeat this entire process, now giving person B the opportunity to read a story while persons A and C listen. Continue as previously noted.

# INDEX